# THE REAL LINCOLN

ABRAHAM LINCOLN
Photograph by Alexander Hesler, June, 1860

# THE REAL LINCOLN

*A Portrait*

Jesse W. Weik

Edited by Michael Burlingame

University of Nebraska Press
Lincoln and London

Editor's introduction, appendixes, and notes © 2002 by the University of Nebraska Press
Manufactured in the United States of America

⊗

Library of Congress Cataloging-in-Publication Data
Weik, Jesse William, 1857–1930.
The real Lincoln : a portrait / by Jesse Weik ; edited by Michael Burlingame.
p. cm.
Originally published: Boston : Houghton Mifflin, 1922.
Includes bibliographical references and index.
ISBN 0-8032-9822-6 (pbk. : alk. paper)
1. Lincoln, Abraham, 1809–1865.   2. Presidents—United States—Biography.
I. Burlingame, Michael, 1941– .   II. Title.
E457.W4 2002
973.7'092–dc21
[B]    2002018083

*By Jesse W. Weik–*
*to my wife*

*By Michael Burlingame–*
*For John Sellers,*
*scholar and friend*

# Contents

List of Illustrations                                                    xv

Editor's Acknowledgments                                                xvii

Editor's Introduction                                                    xix

Foreword                                                                xxix

Chapter I                                                                  1
Preliminary words—Beginning investigations at Springfield—Estimates of
Horace White and Henry C. Whitney—Comparison of Lincoln and Hern-
don—Visiting places where Lincoln labored—Conference with Hern-
don—Preparing "The True Story of a Great Life"—Description of the
Lincoln and Herndon library—Dismantling the law office.

Chapter II                                                                13
Lincoln's birth in Kentucky—Visiting his birthplace—Some of his early
playmates—Interviewing Austin Gollaher and others at Hodgenville and
Elizabethtown—Dr. Rodman's visit to Washington—Recollections of the
artist Rowbotham—The removal to Indiana—Lincoln's schooling there—
Incidents of his boyhood—Association with Dennis Hanks—Cutting
wood at Posey's Landing—Letters of Dennis Hanks to Herndon.

Chapter III                                                               28
The question of Lincoln's birth and descent—The various books on the
subject—Investigations by Herndon and the author in Kentucky and elsewhere—The Enloe tradition—The Lincoln family Bible record—Sarah
Lincoln—The John L. Scripps incident—Herndon's story of his ride with
Lincoln to Petersburg—Dennis and John Hanks, who they were and
whence they sprang—Their letters to Herndon regarding the Lincoln
family tree.

Chapter IV                                                                47
Removal of the Lincolns from Indiana to Illinois in 1830—Thomas Lincoln

sells the land to Charles Grigsby—Leaving Gentryville—Names of the emigrants and description of the journey—Reaching Macon County, Illinois—Abe leaves the family near Decatur and pushes out for himself—Thomas Lincoln and the Hankses—Story of Thomas Johnston jailed for stealing a watch and how Lincoln saved him—Recollections of Harriet Chapman, who lived at the Lincoln home in Springfield.

Chapter V                                                                           56
Lincoln's several proposals of marriage—Story of his failure to join Mary Todd at the Edwards home, January, 1841—His letter to John T. Stuart—Invitation to John Hanks—Preparations for the marriage to Mary Todd—The story of the wedding—Judge Browne's amusing interruption—Conflicting views of Springfield people—Writer's visit to and interview with Ninian W. Edwards and wife—Refusal of Mrs. Simeon Francis to tell her story.

Chapter VI                                                                          65
Lincoln's attitude toward the ladies—His attentions to Sarah Rickard—What Mary Owens said about him—His conduct in the parlor—The stag literary society—How he, with the aid of Evan Butler and James Matheney, punished the drunken shoemaker—His bashfulness—Whitney's account of his embarrassment before the ladies at Urbana—The evening at Norman B. Judd's residence—What Mrs. Judd recollected—Lincoln's break at the concert—His attentions to the lady performer—What Davis and Swett said to him about it—His reply.

Chapter VII                                                                         81
Lincoln's passion for women—How he dealt with them—Herndon's testimony—Interviewing one of Lincoln's female clients—Her story of his conduct—Lincoln on the circuit—Avoiding social functions—Fondness for concerts and like entertainments at the town hall—Accompanying Henry C. Whitney to the negro minstrel show in Chicago—Efforts of author to determine if Lincoln attended lecture by Thackeray in St. Louis—Lincoln's status as a married man—His wife's temperament and its effect on him—Her traits of character—Her management of the household—Her experience with Springfield tradesmen.

Chapter VIII                                                                        96
Further accounts of Mrs. Lincoln—Herndon's account of the dance with her—The serenade—Riding with the Bradfords—Her difficulties with the servants—Her husband's ingenious scheme to retain them—The government of the children—Lincoln taking them to the office on Sunday—His control over them—Playing chess with Judge Treat—An interesting glimpse by a law student—Description of the office—How Lincoln dressed—How he spent the day—His habits of study—Escorting Mrs.

Lincoln to a ball—Her husband's consideration for her—His action when a storm threatened.

Chapter IX                                                                  109
A Springfield lawyer's opinion of Lincoln's mental equipment—Outline of his physical organization—His appetite—How he ate an apple—His predisposition to melancholy—Description of his figure—His head, arms, and legs—His countenance, his walk, and other physical attributes— His mental processes—His perception, judgment, and conscience—His indifference as to forms or methods—A profound reasoner—Remorseless in analysis—A giant intellect and in full comprehension of his own ability.

Chapter X                                                                   119
Behind the door of Lincoln's home—What the neighbors saw and heard— The testimony of James Gourley—Lincoln's garden and dooryard—The ups and downs of life at the Eighth Street home—How Lincoln and his wife agreed—What Josiah P. Kent saw and remembered—Mrs. Lincoln and the iceman—The family carriage—Buying a ticket to the circus—Juvenile pranks at Lincoln's expense—Mrs. Lincoln's peculiarities of temperament.

Chapter XI                                                                  127
Lincoln as a lawyer—Estimates of David Davis and others—First leaning toward the law manifested in Indiana—Borrowing books of Judge Pitcher, of Rockport—Attending squire's court at Gentryville—Studying law books after reaching New Salem—Admission to the bar at Springfield—His opinion of examinations—Story of an applicant he himself examined— The note to Judge Logan—Hawthorne *vs.* Woolridge, his first case: its history and termination—Scammon *vs.* Cline, his first case in the Supreme Court—His last appearance in court—His three partnerships—His wonderful ability as a reasoner—The scope and extent of his practice—Range and size of his fees—His skill and care in the preparation of papers—The trial of Bailey *vs.* Cromwell proving that a negro girl was not a slave—Also Carman *vs.* Glasscock involving the navigability of the Sangamon River.

Chapter XII                                                                 148
Green *vs.* Green, Lincoln's first divorce case—His dislike for divorce suits— His magnanimity in the trial of Samuel Rogers *vs.* Polly Rogers—His comment on the Miller *vs.* Miller petition—A pitiful story of marital discord— A slow collector—Rarely enforced collection of fees by suit—When in partnership with Logan brought one suit for fee—Retained by Illinois Central Railroad to enjoin McLean County from assessing road for taxation— Lincoln's letter to Brayman—Gains case in Supreme Court—Lincoln sues railroad company for his fee—History of transaction—Dividing fee with Herndon—One of Lincoln's first suits for personal injury—The Horological Cradle case—The slander suit of McKibben *vs.* Hart—Turning the fee

over to his father—The Spink *vs.* Chiniquiy case settled by Lincoln—The Dungey *vs.* Spencer case as recalled by Lawrence Weldon—Fixing Lincoln's fee—Linder *vs.* Fleenor—How Lincoln proved the marriage—Dorman *vs.* Lane—Proposal by Lincoln to his associates that they join him and donate fees as a wedding present.

Chapter XIII                                                                                    169
Lincoln seldom wrote briefs or legal arguments—Scarcely ever made notes—Of the few briefs he reduced to writing Herndon preserved but a portion—One was a petition for rehearing in Patterson *vs.* Edwards, tried in the Supreme Court in 1845—Slander suit between two women—Notable specimen of Lincoln's reasoning—Smith *vs.* Smith, suit on election bet—Vigorous denunciation of those who bet on elections—Hurd *vs.* Rock Island Bridge Company tried by Lincoln in United States Circuit Court in Chicago—Record of Lincoln's argument before the jury as delivered, preserved, and reproduced by Robert R. Hitt, the shorthand reporter—How Lincoln talked when he faced a jury—What he thought of Judge McLean.

Chapter XIV                                                                                     188
Life on the circuit—The Eighth Circuit described—Lincoln only lawyer who traveled over all of it—His horse and buggy—The landlord's welcome—Life at the tavern—Lincoln's dress—Leonard Swett's introduction to Lincoln and Davis—Lincoln's methods described by Henry C. Whitney—Joins Leonard Swett in defense of a murderer—His record in fugitive slave cases—Explanation by John W. Bunn of his few appearances in court in behalf of runaway slaves—Account by J. Birch of Lincoln lounging in the county clerk's office—Also his physical appearance and habits in political campaigns—The Wright case—Befriending the Matheney heirs—Forcing the foreign impostor to disgorge his gains—fee paid by Jacob Bunn and how Lincoln applied it.

Chapter XV                                                                                      206
How Lincoln whiled away his spare moments in Springfield—Places he was in the habit of frequenting—An evening in the office of Colonel W. B. Warren, Clerk of the Supreme Court—Incidents of Lincoln's stay at Urbana in the spring of 1856—Stealing the hotel gong—Apprised of his vote for Vice-President at the Republican National Convention in Philadelphia—Leaving Urbana for Springfield—Riding in the omnibus—Whitney's recollection of Lincoln's modest fees—His financial accumulations—The bank account of Lincoln & Herndon.

Chapter XVI                                                                                     215
Instances of Lincoln's weakness—His unwonted faith in certain friends—His blindness to their faults—His failure to redeem Herndon—Joining

the charmed circle at the tavern—His bland and inexplicable confidence in the ability and moral influence of Ward Lamon—Appoints him United States Marshal of the District of Columbia—Lamon's attempt to influence General Frémont—Scheme to transport troops to West Virginia—The pretended Lamon's Brigade—Investigation by Congressional committee which denounces Lamon in scathing report—Notwithstanding opposition of fifteen Senators Lincoln adheres to him—Mark W. Delahay another instance of Lincoln's misplaced confidence—Surprise of John J. Ingalls—Lincoln finally appoints him United States Judge for the District of Kansas—Congressional committee visits Kansas to investigate Delahay's moral and official conduct—Delahay resigns to avoid impeachment—Lincoln's appointment of Simon Cameron and the trouble it gave him—Herndon's letter to Henry Wilson—Lincoln's real estimate of Douglas—What he told C. H. Moore about Douglas—Incidents of the joint debate—The recollections of Horace White.

Chapter XVII                                                                237
Lincoln as a student—The effect of a college education—Comparison of John Fiske's and Lincoln's conception of social evolution—Lincoln takes up Euclid—Reading "The Annual of Science"—Studying higher mathematics—His attempt to square the circle—His self-confidence and secretiveness—His mechanical bent—Securing a patent—Working on the model of his invention at Walter Davis's shop—Explaining it to his partner and callers at his office—Preparing his lecture on "Discoveries and Inventions"—Delivers it at Jacksonville and Springfield—What some of his colleagues thought about it—Several paragraphs of the lecture—Account by S. H. Melvin of what Lincoln did with the manuscript—Herndon also enters the lecture field—Delivers his effort entitled "The Sweep of Commerce" before an audience in Cook's Hall in Springfield—What the "Journal" said about it.

Chapter XVIII                                                               251
An epoch in Lincoln's life—His political baptism—Signs the call for the Bloomington Convention—Herndon's account of the incident—How Stuart tried to retard him—Lincoln announces himself—His speech at the Bloomington Convention—The prediction of Jesse K. Dubois described by Whitney—Lincoln invited to speak in New York—Effect on his neighbors in Springfield—What John T. Stuart said—The Cooper Institute address—His speeches in New England—How he impressed the Eastern people—Mentioned for President by the press—County convention in Springfield endorses him for President—He attends the Decatur meeting where John Hanks brings in the famous rails—Crowds of Lincoln's friends head for Chicago, leaving him at Springfield—The Chicago Convention—What Lincoln was doing at home—The nomination on Friday—How

Lincoln received the news—The account by Clinton L. Conkling—The
effect at Springfield—Marching to Lincoln's house—His speech—Arrival
of notification committee from Chicago—Incidents of their visit—The
notification ceremony in the parlor of Lincoln's home—Incidents of the
campaign—All paths lead to Springfield—The great rally in August—
Letter of John Hanks supporting the claims of his cousin Abe Lincoln—
Some local campaigners—Herndon's speech at Petersburg—Comments of
the local papers.

Chapter XIX                                                          282
Lincoln the candidate for President—Meeting the expenses of the campaign—Judge Logan's plan—The ten friends of Lincoln who contributed—John W. Bunn's story of the fund—John G. Nicolay selected as Lincoln's secretary—Lincoln's attention to the details of the campaign—Meets
with local committee—Recommends John Hay as assistant secretary—
Interesting reminiscence of John W. Bunn—How Lincoln bore himself
throughout the campaign—The election—Lincoln going to the polls—
Assigned quarters for his office in the State House—His habits as President elect—Goes to Chicago to meet Hannibal Hamlin—Returns to
Springfield—Visitors at his office and incidents of his stay there—Journeys
to Charleston to see his stepmother—Account of his visit and interesting
reminiscence by James A. Connolly—Returns to Springfield and begins
preparations for the journey to Washington—Last visit to his law office—
Final interview with Herndon.

Chapter XX                                                           303
Last social function at Lincoln's home—He receives threatening letters—
Sends a friend to Washington to sound General Scott—General Thomas S.
Mather returns with his report—Plans for Lincoln's journey to Washington
as outlined in the local papers—Personnel of the party selected to accom-
pany him—Leaving the Chenery House—His trunks—Departure from
the railway station—Lincoln's farewell speech—Story of the two versions—
His emotion when the train moved off.

Appendix 1: Weik's Informants
    Ida M. Andrews                                                   317
    George Washington Brackenridge                                  318
    John W. Bunn                                                     318
    Mrs. Arthur H. Carter                                           326
    Augustus H. Chapman and Harriet Chapman                         327
    Harriet Chapman                                                 328
    Robert N. Chapman                                               329
    William Dodd Chenery                                            329
    John Coburn                                                     330
    Jonathan N. Colby                                               333

Clinton L. Conkling 333
James A. Connolly 347
George Perrin Davis 350
Isaac R. Diller 351
William D. Donnelly 353
Dennis Hanks Dowling 353
Elizabeth Edwards 355
Annie M. Fleury 355
Frederick Dent Grant 356
Charles H. Gray 356
B. A. Harvey 356
Robert Roberts Hitt 357
Clara Davis Hoyt 357
Ephraim Fletcher Ingals 357
William Jayne 359
Edward S. Johnson 361
Josiah P. Kent 362
George C. Latham 364
John M. Lockwood 365
W. E. Loomis 367
Hugh McLellan 368
Henry A. Melvin 369
John G. Nicolay 370
S. G. Paddock 370
George Pasfield 371
Edward Lillie Pierce 371
Hiram Rutherford 372
Rev. Mr. W. F. F. Smith 373
Judge Anthony Thornton 374
Lyman Beecher Todd 375
Gilbert A. Tracy 375
Lyman Trumbull 378
Horace White 378
James H. Wilson 386
Louis H. Zumbrook 387

Appendix 2: "A Hard-hearted Conscious Liar and an Oily Hypocrite":
Henry B. Rankin's Reliability as a Lincoln Informant 389

Notes 399

Index 443

# Illustrations

Abraham Lincoln                                    *Frontispiece*
    Photograph taken by Alexander Hesler at Lincoln's home in Springfield a
    few days after his nomination for President. Pronounced by Mr. Herndon
    to be the best and most lifelike portrait of Lincoln in existence. Reproduced
    by permission of Mr. George B. Ayres.

William Henry Herndon                                          2

Lincoln's Pocket Scrapbook carried during the Campaign of 1858 against
Douglas                                                       10

Page from Lincoln's Hand-made Arithmetic, used by him while a Schoolboy
in Gentryville, Indiana                                        22

The Family Record in Thomas Lincoln's Bible, chiefly in Abraham Lincoln's
Hand                                                           32

House near Farmington, Illinois, in which Thomas Lincoln lived, and where
he died in 1851                                                50

Joshua F. Speed and his Wife                                   62
    From a painting owned by the family.

Sarah Rickard                                                  68
    From a woodcut after a photograph by R. T. Jones

Mary S. Owens                                                  68
    From a photograph.

Mary Todd Lincoln                                              96
    From a photograph.

Certificate of Survey written by Lincoln when he was Deputy Surveyor
under John Calhoun in 1834                                     110

Judge John Pitcher                                             130

Page of the Records of the Circuit Court of Sangamon County, Illinois,
for March 24, 1836, showing the Court Order certifying to Lincoln's Good
Moral Character on his Admission to the Bar                                    134

Papers in Lincoln's First Case, Hawthorn *vs.* Wooldridge                      138

Items from Stuart and Lincoln's Fee Book                                       142

Lincoln's Brief in a Case involving the Navigability of the Sangamon River     146

Lincoln's Bill against the Illinois Central Railroad Company, with Copy of
Opinion signed by Fellow Lawyers                                               154

Leonard Swett                                                                  192

Henry C. Whitney                                                               192

Part of a Letter of Lincoln's to a Client (Rowland Smith & Co., April 24,
1844), showing Errors in his Usually Correct Spelling                          238

Page of Lincoln's Manuscript of his Lecture "Discoveries and Inventions"       246

Call for a County Convention to appoint Delegates to the Republican
State Convention at Bloomington, 1856                                          254

Stephen T. Logan                                                               282
    From a painting by G. P. A. Healy.

John T. Stuart                                                                 282
    From a photograph of one of the earliest daguerreotypes made in this
    country, believed to have been taken by S. F. B. Morse, inventor of the
    telegraph.

# Editor's Acknowledgments

I am deeply indebted to The Lehrman Institute of New York for generously supporting research on this and other Lincoln volumes.

To Professor James A. Rawley of the University of Nebraska, who encouraged me to undertake this project and helped expedite its publication, I owe a debt of gratitude.

At the Library of Congress I have received the most cordial and helpful assistance of John Sellers of the Manuscript Division, to whom this volume is dedicated. Others from that same division who have over the years been generous and helpful include Fred Bauman, Jeff Flanagan, and Mary Wolfskill.

In the Rare Book Division of the Library of Congress I have received much-appreciated assistance from Clark Evans.

Douglas L. Wilson and Rodney O. Davis, co-directors of the Lincoln Studies Center at Knox College, have generously shared with me their vast knowledge of Weik, Herndon, and Lincoln.

At Brown University's John Hay Library I have been the fortunate beneficiary of many kindnesses from Jennifer Lee, Samuel Streit, Jean Rainwater, Mary Jo Kline, Andrew Moel, Pat Soris, and their colleagues. To all I extend heartfelt thanks.

To their counterparts at the Illinois State Historical Library, Allegheny College, the Chicago Historical Society, the Lincoln Museum of Fort Wayne, the J. Pierpont Morgan Library, the Henry E. Huntington Library, the Lincoln Museum at Lincoln Memorial University, Connecticut College, the University of Chicago, and the New York Public Library I am indebted for their kind assistance.

Dr. C. A. Tripp of Nyack NY, has been enormously helpful in all my Lincoln researches.

Wayne C. Temple, deputy chief director of the Illinois State Archives, and Thomas F. Schwartz, the Illinois State Historian, have given me the benefit of their legendary expertise on matters relating to Lincoln and his times.

As an undergraduate at Princeton University and as a graduate student at Johns Hopkins University I was fortunate to have the guidance and support of David Herbert Donald.

To John Y. Simon, dean of documentary editing in the field of American history, I am indebted for his encouragement as this volume and others have slowly gestated over the years.

My sister and brother-in-law, Edwin R. and Sue B. Coover, have been hospitable far above and beyond the call of family duty in hosting me for long stretches while I conducted research in Washington DC. Others, including Thomas and Cathy Schwartz, Sarah Thomas, James and Mary Patton, and Robert Bray have been generous in putting me up when I indulge in research binges in Illinois.

The lovely and long-suffering Lois McDonald has uncomplainingly provided indispensable support and encouragement as I have pursued the historical Lincoln.

The R. Francis Johnson Faculty Development Fund at Connecticut College has helped defray the costs of research and travel involved in editing this volume.

# Editor's Introduction

When published in 1922, Jesse W. Weik's *The Real Lincoln* impressed one reviewer as "a singularly rounded, yet unstudied, unretouched portrait of Lincoln as a private man, not that vague abstraction, a public character." Weik's pages, she added, convey "the profound vitality of the man himself" and are "of far more absorbing interest than the smooth surfaces of such a book as Charnwood's *Lincoln*." Readers of Weik's study of Lincoln seem to "just glimpse him disappearing around the corner of yesterday, to catch an echo of his grave, jesting tones," to feel "the pressure of the atmosphere which enveloped him, the deprivations which left their marks upon him." *The Real Lincoln*, she said, should be regarded as "a complement or appendix" to William H. Herndon's 1889 biography of Lincoln, which Weik co-authored.[1]

William H. Townsend, a lawyer-historian in Kentucky who published several books on Lincoln, also found that the sixteenth president came alive in Weik's rendering. He told the author, "When I closed the book a moment ago, it seemed as though the Volk Life Mask of Lincoln on my library mantle piece ought to smile and say 'Goodnight' and that Volk's Cast of the hands, beside the Mask, would grip mine in a warm, living grasp at the close of an evening's confidential chat." *The Real Lincoln*, Townsend predicted, will "rank foremost among all the books ever written on the subject." Many biographers "have written *about* Lincoln, but your book *is* Lincoln himself."[2]

Other readers were similarly enthusiastic. The Indiana senator and Lincoln biographer Albert J. Beveridge found Weik's book "most engaging from the first page to the last." Apropos of the treatment of Lincoln's married life, Beveridge observed: "The best account that has yet appeared of Lincoln's marriage is the narrative of that event in this entertaining volume." The author, Beveridge noted, "gives specific instances of Lincoln's marital difficulties, and the authority for each of them. Indeed, he quotes the exact statements that witnesses made to him personally. It is this care in giving the source of his information that makes this unhappy narrative so impressive. One finds it hard to doubt such clear-cut and positive statements of observers who had no motive for misrepresentation, no axe of any kind to grind." On the discussion of Lincoln as lawyer, Beveridge remarked: "Weik's narrative contains intimate and personal facts about Lincoln as a practitioner not to be found elsewhere; and these are indispensable to an understanding of Lincoln." Thus the book is "invaluable to those who wish to know the man as he appeared to his associates at the bar—how he acted, how he talked, what clothes he wore, what food he ate, his manners, amusements, habits and the like." Beveridge vouched for the author's credibility: "I have known Mr. Weik since my college days in Greencastle, Indiana. Nobody ever questioned his veracity, and his lifelong adoration of Lincoln has in it something of fanaticism; yet the truthfulness of the man would not permit the perversion or suppression of any fact in what he writes about his idol." In sum, Beveridge concluded, "it is facts that Mr. Weik gives us, albeit many of those facts are not attractive to those who demand the impossible and unveracious. In short, here is a source-book on Lincoln, and, as such, a book to be welcomed."[3] Privately Beveridge told Weik that it was "the best source book in all Lincolniana."[4]

Echoing Beveridge's sentiments, a reviewer in the *New York Times* deemed *The Real Lincoln* "an important source book concerning Lincoln's life, his environment at its several stages and his work and development. The author reveals many new facts and incidents and throws fresh light upon almost every phase of Lincoln's life previous to 1860."[5] David E. Lilienthal, who later achieved fame as the director of the Tennessee Valley Authority, lauded the book as "a valuable and intensely interesting contribution."[6] In the *New York Call*, David Karsner praised Weik's "vivid pages" for offering "one of the most exhaustive studies of Lincoln," and commended the author for sparing "neither time nor pains to make his book authentic."[7] A critic in the *New York World* said the "book is profound in its minute and painstaking correctness," predicted that it would "greatly interest lovers of Lincoln," and praised it for seeking "neither to exalt nor tear down" and "making its subject all the greater by showing how poor was the foundation from which he rose to immortality."[8]

In the *Boston Transcript* Sherwin Lawrence Cook described *The Real Lincoln* as "an altogether interesting volume." He acknowledged that many readers "will wish the book had been freer from describing some of the commonplace aspects of his hero, that certain characteristics which seem faults might be minimized." But, he added, no "true lover of Lincoln" should "count himself among these critics. Lincoln's greatness does not need to stand on a plausible picture of perfection. The fibre of Mr. Weik's book is admirable."[9] Another Massachusetts paper termed Weik's volume "an impressive portrayal that throbs with realism."[10] The down-to-earth quality of Weik's portrait won the admiration of *The Bookman*, which described it as an "interesting study of a more human being than the category of virtues which makes up the Lincoln of school-book tradition," depicting "a brilliant intellect and a humanly faulty, as well as divinely virtuous, character."[11]

Weik's preservation of the reminiscences of people who knew Lincoln won accolades in the *Review of Reviews*. *The Real Lincoln*, its unsigned notice said, "contains a great amount of new material" that was "no doubt so familiar to Lincoln's contemporaries that it did not occur to them to pass it on to posterity in the form of written or printed statements. For the later generations, however, a narration of these matters is indispensable to the complete story of Lincoln's life as he actually lived it."[12]

Because Weik interviewed and corresponded with people who knew Lincoln personally, his book is still valuable as an important original source. Some of the material he used was published earlier in *Herndon's Lincoln*, and many of the original reports he received from his Lincoln informants appear in *Herndon's Informants: Letters, Interviews, and Statements about Abraham Lincoln*, the monumental edition of the Herndon-Weik archive edited by Douglas L. Wilson and Rodney O. Davis in 1998. Yet those peerless editors omitted the material Weik gathered after 1891. In the following three decades Weik continued to accumulate more firsthand information about Lincoln. The present volume reproduces in an appendix these letters and interviews dating from 1892 to 1922, thus making it a modest supplement to Wilson and Davis's indispensable volume.[13]

In addition to its value as a primary source book, *The Real Lincoln* offers compelling interpretations of its subject's life, especially his relations with women (including his marriage), his law career, his ancestry, and his Illinois years in general. Also noteworthy is the author's willingness to acknowledge flaws in his hero. The chapter on Lincoln's questionable taste in friends— including Mark Delahay, Ward Hill Lamon, and Simon Cameron—shows Weik to be no worshipful filiopietist. Lincoln's fondness for some rascals is a peculiar aspect of the sixteenth president's character that has been little explored by either Lincoln hagiographers or detractors.

Not all of Weik's interpretations have withstood the test of time. For example, most scholars agree that Lincoln did not leave Mary Todd stranded at the altar in 1841, as Weik suggests.[14] Additionally, abundant evidence demonstrates that Weik was mistaken in believing that Lincoln before 1854 gave the antislavery movement little more "than passing notice."[15]

Evidently motivated by the desire to make his text as readable as possible, Weik frequently rewrote the testimony he collected. Readers should be aware that the exact language of his Lincoln sources can be found in *Herndon's Informants* and in the appendix to this volume.[16] The text of the legal documents cited can be checked against *The Law Practice of Abraham Lincoln: Complete Documentary Edition*, published in 2000.[17]

Weik also makes occasional factual errors, such as his assertion that Herndon visited Kentucky to conduct interviews, that Herndon regularly accompanied Lincoln on his trips around the circuit, and that Henry C. Whitney spent nearly as much time with Lincoln on the circuit as did David Davis.[18] Sometimes Weik credits suspect testimony, like that of John B. Helm of Kentucky. Now and then he misidentifies the source of a quotation, as he did when attributing to David Davis the assessment of Lincoln offered by Leonard Swett.[19]

Though Weik's treatment of Lincoln's Indiana years is rather meager, he nevertheless illuminated the sixteenth president's Illinois years with an incandescent light. The perceptive Lincoln scholar Paul M. Angle was fully justified in calling *The Real Lincoln* "Informal, interesting, [and] filled with welcome . . . detail," a worthy complement "to the great biography of which he was co-author."[20]

Born in 1857 in Greencastle, Indiana, Jesse Wilson Weik spent much of his life in that small town where his German-born father ran a grocery store and where young Jesse attended Depauw University (at the time called Indiana Asbury University), where he mastered Spanish and French to complement his German-language fluency. Upon graduation in 1875 he studied law, engaged in the real estate business, participated in Republican Party electoral efforts, pursued a master's degree, wrote freelance dispatches for the *Cincinnati Commercial,* and sought in vain to be named to the post of secretary to the governor of the New Mexico Territory.[21] In 1882, with the help of recommendations that described him as "industrious and energetic," "reliable and efficient," "*energetic, thorough-going, industrious, persevering* in whatever he undertakes," an "earnest enthusiastic republican," an "active and influential republican," "a Stalwart republican . . . untiring in his devotion to the party," a "young man with brains and energy and popular ways," with "remarkable clearheadedness, quick discernment and industrious habits," whose "appointment will tend to strengthen the Republican party," he secured a clerkship at the Interior Department's pension office in Washington, D.C., where he worked for a few months before being assigned as a special pension examiner in the Springfield, Illinois, office.[22] There he stayed from the fall of 1882 until the spring of 1885, when he returned to help his aging father run the grocery store. In 1891 he once again toiled for the pension bureau, but soon thereafter quit to establish the Greencastle Telephone Company.[23]

Those jobs interested him far less than did the life of Abraham Lincoln, whose corpse the eight-year-old Jesse had seen lying in state in Indianapolis. As Weik's daughter recalled, his "work on Lincoln was always the most important thing in his life—equaled only by his strong and humorous devotion to his family. This absorbing interest in Lincoln—a passion to preserve the homely truth of Lincoln *as a man*, freed from the myths and gossip that soon clustered about his memory—this interest in Lincoln was a saving thing, when the early death of my mother, with whom he was very much in love, came close to destroying his world."[24]

In college Weik had been inspired by a charismatic professor, John Clark Ridpath, author of *Ridpath's History of the World, Being an Account of the Ethnic Origin, Primitive Estate, Early Migrations, Social Conditions and Present Promise of the Principal Families of Men*, among other works, and whose vast admiration for Lincoln proved contagious to Weik.[25] In 1875, at Ridpath's suggestion, Weik wrote to Herndon asking for a Lincoln autograph.[26] For years that fateful letter remained unanswered. Meanwhile, Weik began making pilgrimages to Springfield, where he sought out Lincoln's brother-in-law, Clark M. Smith, who one day showed him the room over his store where Lincoln drafted his first inaugural address.[27]

Finally in 1881 the sixty-two-year-old Herndon replied at length to Weik's 1875 letter, describing his plans to write a biography of the sixteenth president and enclosing a page from Lincoln's schoolboy arithmetic book.[28] Thus began a decade-long correspondence that ended only with Herndon's death. When Weik was stationed in Springfield between 1882 and 1885, he visited Herndon and chatted about Lincoln. In 1885 the young Hoosier proposed collaborating with Herndon in writing a series of articles about Lincoln. The older man agreed and promptly deluged his friend with long letters about his former law partner. Along with Herndon's voluminous archive of interviews and correspondence with Lincoln informants that he had amassed in the 1860s and 1870s, those letters became the nucleus of the Herndon-Weik biography of Lincoln. Seeking to caulk gaps in the record compiled by Herndon, Weik continued the inquiries he had begun earlier. Over the next six years he spoke or corresponded with at least forty-four informants in Kentucky, Indiana, Illinois, Oregon, and elsewhere. In March 1887 he journeyed to Kentucky, which Herndon had failed to do.[29] (Herndon advised his collaborator that while there he should "scratch out the facts as a dog digs out a rabbit—coon or ground hog.")[30] The following summer Herndon spent a month in Greencastle where the two men drafted their biography of Lincoln, with Weik squeezing in time to write amid his duties in the grocery store and Herndon sweating in an overheated, poorly lit room on the second floor.[31] The following year they completed the manuscript, which was published in 1889 as *Herndon's Lincoln: The True Story of a Great Life, The History and Personal Recollections of Abraham Lincoln* by William H. Herndon and Jesse William Weik.[32] Two years later Herndon died.

When writing about Lincoln Weik was not uncritical in assessing the reliability of his informants. According to his daughter, he "viewed all testimony, written or oral, with an observing but skeptical eye. When he first took me with him to Springfield, on one of his frequent trips to look over old journals and recheck local records, he warned me to view what I saw and heard there with some caution. 'The whole town is full of Lincoln legends,' he told me. 'Every family has inherited one or two of its own. Some are fantastic. You have to sort out the truth from the cobwebs.'"[33] He was particularly suspicious of a Springfield resident, Henry B. Rankin, who claimed to have been a student in Lincoln's law office from 1856 to 1860. Weik's skepticism about Rankin is so well founded that Rankin's letter to him is not included in this volume.[34]

Weik often lectured on "The Boyhood and Early Manhood of Lincoln" and "Abraham Lincoln," employing some of Herndon's materials as props.[35] In 1899 he told an Indiana school administrator: "My production is peculiarly adapted to the entertainment of teachers and young people in the schools. . . . I carry with me many interesting souvenirs of Lincoln including pages from his school- and copy-books, besides numerous letters and documents all in the original, from which I read and which, after the lecture, the audience are free to examine. The effect produced on a young student in being privileged to hold in his hands a document written or a book once owned and studied by Abraham Lincoln cannot but be wholesome and elevating."[36]

When Lincoln's good friend and colleague at the bar Leonard Swett remarked that Herndon's biography had "failed to bring out as fully as he should the human side of Lincoln, the incidents of his domestic and home life, and especially a definite and searching insight into his activities as a lawyer," Weik resolved to write *The Real Lincoln* in order to provide "more local color, more of the details of his personal history as revealed by his neighbors," and to throw open "the doors of his office and of his home" and thus have "the light turned on so that we may indeed view him as a man."[37] He asked Indiana senator Albert J. Beveridge, whose four-volume biography of John Marshall was widely admired, to help persuade Houghton Mifflin (Beveridge's publisher) to bring it out.[38] In 1922 that company did release Weik's book, which incorporated many documents from the Herndon archive that had been left out of *Herndon's Lincoln*, supplemented with new information that Weik had gathered since the publication of that volume.[39] (In return for helping him secure publication with Houghton Mifflin, Weik allowed Beveridge to use the Herndon materials, a privilege he extended to few other researchers.)[40] Among Herndon's archive was a cache of legal papers of the firm Lincoln and Herndon, which allowed Weik to address Lincoln's career at the bar in detail. (For the surviving correspondence and interviews dating from 1892 to 1922 see the appendix, "Weik's Informants.") Some of the material presented in *The Real Lincoln* had appeared in various magazine articles Weik had published between 1897 and 1913.[41] In 1907 he lamented that "my bread-and-butter struggle does not allow me much time for magazine writing."[42] He also served on the commission to identify the route taken by the Lincoln family when they moved from Indiana to Illinois (the "Lincoln way").[43]

Weik then contemplated producing a biography of Herndon. Weik's daughter recalled that as "the years went on, he kept more and more to himself, made sensitive by local jests about his continued absorption in Lincoln." Beveridge—who reported that among the residents of Greencastle, Weik "well-nigh got the reputation of being a crank on Lincoln"[44]—was "working on his own Lincoln book and came down to consult Herndon's records, and to urge my father to do 'the study of Herndon no one else could do.' I knew my father wanted to do it; but he was of two minds about starting. He had of course the largest collection of Herndon papers right at hand. He loved and admired Herndon immensely for his honesty and dogged loyalty to the Lincoln of flesh-and-blood my father too revered; but he felt that some of Herndon's last writings were the product of powers that were clearly failing, and could not be relied on as history." For a long while "he pored over the problem, trying to work out a plan that would be fair to Herndon's memory. We moved east in the meantime to live. Publishers wrote inquiring about the project. I don't think he ever answered them. I must admit I prodded him about it too, seeing him sit every day at his desk, fingering through the Herndon papers."[45]

Eventually, however, Weik gave up the projected Herndon biography. In 1925 he moved to Larchmont, New York, to live with his daughter, who described him as "a strange mixture" who "liked people and congenial company, and to match stories with other good story-tellers. Yet the thing he valued most of all was his privacy," without which he could not write. "When at home he dressed like a farmer in blue overalls and they were often faded. He rose early and went to his garden, then after some hours would come in dripping wet and a little later go to his desk to study or write. His script was small, neat, near illegible to those not familiar with it, but he made few corrections of the first draft. At three o'clock in the afternoon he would go to the telephone company office, where a trusted bookkeeper kept the accounts and listened to complaints."[46]

A fellow native of Greencastle portrayed Weik as "of medium height" with "a massive head with white hair," "somewhat fleshy," "facile in conversation as with pen," "dignified yet sociable," a "neat dresser," "animated and outgoing," a "trifle puffy as he trudged up the Indiana Street hill to the post office," and an "articulate, companionable man" who "was usually surrounded by a wreath of friends when on the downtown streets."[47]

Jesse Weik died in Larchmont, New York, in 1930.

## EDITORIAL METHOD

In the appendix containing letters and interviews about Lincoln, words that cannot be deciphered with certainty have been included within brackets followed by a question mark [like this?] Contractions are retained. Raised letters have been reproduced as if they were not raised. When words are illegible, square brackets are supplied enclosing a blank space like this [ ]. Where the editor has inserted words into the text for clarification, they are placed within square brackets [like this]. When Weik or his informant inadvertently repeats a word, the second occurrence of the word is silently omitted. If a period is used when a comma is called for, a comma has silently replaced the period. Otherwise the original punctuation is unchanged.

Misspellings are retained without the cumbersome use of [*sic*]. Persons mentioned by informants are identified in endnotes when their names first appear, if any information about them has been found. No annotation is made for those about whom nothing has been discovered. Sources for annotations derived from manuscript collections, newspapers, and specialized monographs and biographies are identified, but not those taken from easily available published sources.

Several of Weik's informants provided biographical information about associates of Lincoln (such as Charles Constable, John Hanks, E. L. Baker, and Usher F. Linder), but gave no data about Lincoln himself. Such testimony has not been included in the appendix.

# Foreword

Not long after the appearance of Herndon's Life of Lincoln, in the preparation of which I collaborated with the author, I was asked by the late Leonard Swett to visit him when I next came to Chicago. In due time I complied with the invitation. It was not long after I had called until our conversation turned on the Life of Lincoln which was then undergoing the test of popular approval. It was soon apparent that Mr. Swett greatly admired Herndon and he was generous and complimentary in his allusions to the book; but while he expressed the belief that Herndon, of all persons who had attempted to narrate the story of Lincoln's life, was best qualified to tell all the truth and had religiously tried to do so, yet he felt that in some respects, due probably to his advanced age, he had fallen short of his full task. Mr. Swett intimated that he had talked to certain other friends, to whom he purposed sending me, who knew Lincoln personally, and they coincided with his view. He mentioned Joseph Medill, Horace White, Henry C. Whitney, Leonard W. Volk, the sculptor, and Alexander Hesler, the photographer, all of whom I interviewed. In addition he took me to see Lyman Trumbull, and I listened with deep interest to their recollections of Lincoln and Herndon. Regarding the need, in view of his unusual opportunities, of fuller revelations from Herndon, Swett and Trumbull agreed with each other, but in certain other respects, notably their estimate of Lincoln, they were not in complete accord. Trumbull, I regret to say, manifested an inclination to rob Lincoln of the credit of some of his achievements. I remember he criticized Nicolay and Hay because they claimed that Lincoln opened the way for the freedom of the slaves, whereas, as he contended, Congress had done it by two laws it passed before Lincoln issued the Emancipation Proclamation.

Mr. Swett's criticism of Herndon was that he had failed to bring out as fully as he should the human side of Lincoln, the incidents of his domestic and home life, and especially a definite and searching insight into his activities as a lawyer. He maintained that Mr. Lincoln, notwithstanding his brilliant career as a statesman, would never cease to be remembered as a lawyer and as such would be judged by the world; that therefore the more we learned of that phase of his life, the clearer and more impressive would be the portrait we should be able to transmit to posterity. Our knowledge, therefore, of all that Lincoln accomplished in the law office and the court-room, as well as how he did it, is in the highest degree essential.

Another criticism by Mr. Swett was that not enough attention had been given to Mr. Lincoln's Springfield environment—his connection with local affairs, commercial as well as political. We should know more about him as a fellow townsman—where and how he lived and how he spent his money. A great deal has been written regarding his public career, as statesman and Chief Magistrate during the most eventful period of our national history; but more remains to be said of that period of his evolution which antedates his elevation to the Presidency; in other words, there should be more local color, more of the details of his personal history as revealed by his neighbors—in short, the doors of his office and of his home should be made to swing open and the light turned on so that we may indeed view him as a man.

My visit to Chicago convinced me that Mr. Swett simply voiced the opinion of the friends of Lincoln whose names I have mentioned, as well as others whom I elsewhere encountered. Since then my earnest endeavor has been to learn and record the truth as it developed in a careful study of one of the greatest characters in human history, and to that end these pages have been written.

For the benefit of their ripe knowledge and discriminating judgment as well as the use of a generous array of letters, papers, and other valuable historical material, I am indebted to an army of friends. Among them may be named Charles A. Dryer, of Indianapolis; Dr. William W. Sweet, of DePauw University, Greencastle, Indiana; and Isaac R. Diller and the late John W. Bunn, of Springfield, Illinois. The full list is too large for individual mention, but each contributor may console himself with the reflection that he has added materially to a truthful history of *The Real Lincoln*.

Jesse W. Weik
Greencastle, Indiana
August 10, 1921

THE REAL LINCOLN

# THE REAL LINCOLN

∴

## CHAPTER I

Preliminary words — Beginning investigations at Springfield — Estimates of Horace White and Henry C. Whitney — Comparison of Lincoln and Herndon — Visiting places where Lincoln labored — Conference with Herndon — Preparing " The True Story of a Great Life "— Description of the Lincoln and Herndon library — Dismantling the law office.

ABRAHAM LINCOLN is rapidly nearing his place among the fixed stars; but before he is borne aloft in the nimbus of immortality which invariably overtakes a deservedly great and illustrious character, I feel emboldened to submit a few incidents gathered by me during a patient study of the man's history covering almost half a century. This array of material, including facts emanating from certain authentic and trustworthy sources, will, I hope, serve to bring out in sharper outline that portrait which, we are assured, some great artist, set apart for the task, is destined yet to produce. In thus acquainting the public with the results of my investigations I shall endeavor to avoid the expression of my own opinions, being content to impart the information as nearly as I can in the shape it came to me.

To begin with I do not feel justified in putting on record the facts and conclusions outlined in the following pages without first paying a merited tribute to the memory of William H. Herndon, who, of all persons, as Horace White has so fittingly observed, has "most thoroughly searched the sources of Lincoln's biography and most attentively, intelligently and also lovingly studied his character. He was generous in imparting his information to others. Almost every Life of Lincoln published since the tragedy at Ford's Theater has been enriched by his labors. He was nine years the junior of Lincoln. Their partnership began in 1843 and it continued until it was dissolved by the death of the senior member. Between them there was never an unkind word or thought. When Lincoln became President, Herndon could have had his fortunes materially advanced under the new Administration by saying a word. He was a poor man then and always, but he chose to remain in his more humble station and to earn his bread by his daily labor."

I can conceive of nothing more significant and illuminating than the following estimate of Herndon by one who was his associate at the bar and who, for upwards of thirty-five years, maintained with him the most intimate relations. In a letter to Herndon this gentleman — the late Henry C. Whitney, of Urbana, Illinois — says: "You saw Lincoln as he was and know him far better than all other living men combined. Armed with such knowledge it follows that you know better than others how to delineate him. You have the acuteness of vision that we attribute tc Lincoln; you acquired much of his analytical power by attrition and you thought deeply as he did. He had unbounded confidence in your intuitions and your adhesion to him. I shall never forget the day — January 6, 1859 — when the legislature of Illinois met in joint session and elected Stephen A. Douglas, instead of himself, to the United States Senate. I went to your office and found Lincoln there alone. He appeared to be somewhat de-

WILLIAM HENRY HERNDON

jected — in fact I never saw a man so depressed. I tried to rally his drooping spirits and thus extract all the comfort possible from the situation, but with ill success. He was simply steeped in gloom. For a time he was silent; finally he straightened up and thanked me, but presently slid back into his chair again, blurting out as he sank down, 'Well, whatever happens I expect every one to desert me now, but Billy Herndon.'"

As has been truthfully said, it was his unwavering and inflexible devotion to the truth that formed the predominating trait in the character of William H. Herndon. In this respect he resembled his illustrious law partner. Both men up to a certain point were very much alike; but there was a difference. Lincoln, deeply cautious and restrained, was prone to abstract and thoughtful calculation. Herndon, by nature forceful and alert, was quick, impulsive, and often precipitate. If he detected wrong he proclaimed the fact instantly and everywhere, never piling up his wrath and strength, as Lincoln did, for a future sweeping and telling blow. He never stopped to calculate the force, momentum, or effect of his opposition; but fought at the drop of the hat, and fought incessantly, pushing blindly through the smoke of battle until he was either hopelessly overcome or stood exultant on the hilltop of victory. Younger than Lincoln he was more venturesome, more versatile, perhaps, and magnificently oblivious of consequences.

Conscious of his limitations Herndon knew that he was too radical and bold to achieve success in politics and he therefore sunk himself in the fortunes of his more happily poised partner. In the end posterity will accept the verdict of Herndon's friends that, despite his faults, he was a noble, broad-minded man; incapable of a mean or selfish act, brave and big-hearted, tolerant, forgiving, just, and as true to Lincoln as the "needle to the pole."

Early in the seventies I opened up a correspondence with Herndon which ended only with his death and is represented by over five hundred pages of his manuscript now in my possession. After my graduation from college I journeyed from my Indiana home to Springfield to see him, and was so fascinated by his recital of Lincoln's life and activities that I adopted his suggestion and decided to remain there. For almost four years I traced Lincoln's footsteps viewing him from almost every possible angle. My researches were both continuous and painstaking; nor did I think of desisting until I had interviewed or communicated with almost every person then living in that region who had known or talked with Lincoln.

Shortly after my first meeting with Herndon, he piloted me to the dingy back room on the second floor of a store building facing the Court-House Square in Springfield which had sheltered him and his illustrious partner when they used it for their law office. "Here," he said, "is where we expounded the law to our clients, prepared our papers and charged up our fees." The room and furniture were strictly in keeping with the modesty of their fees. In the center was a table, leaning against the wall was an old sofa or lounge, and on the opposite side of the room stood the bookcase. An old wood-burning stove and four or five chairs completed the outfit. The bookcase contained not to exceed twenty volumes and of this number scarcely half were law books, the others miscellaneous, partly literary and partly official, and statistical reports. After a few hours spent in the old law office, Herndon took me to a room over another store building in an adjacent square where, as he related, Lincoln wrote his first Inaugural Address. The store-room below was occupied by Lincoln's brother-in-law, Mr. C. M. Smith, who conducted therein a dry-goods store. We were shown the table on which Lincoln did his writing and even the inkstand which, it was said, he had used. It was on this occasion that Herndon told me the story of the preparation by Lincoln of this, his first official document as President. Having but few books at his home Lincoln asked Herndon to procure certain volumes that he might consult them while he was at work preparing the Address. Herndon told me he was expecting a request for numerous books and pamphlets, but was surprised when Lincoln furnished him the list. It consisted of only four items: Jackson's proclamation against Nullification; Clay's famous speech on the Compromise of 1850; Webster's reply to Hayne, and a copy of the Constitution.

After visiting several points of interest in and about the court-house, Herndon and I returned to the law office where we spent the rest of the day. Lincoln had been but a few years in his grave so that the story of the association of himself and his partner, as it came from Herndon's lips, was a most vivid and entertaining recital. From this time forward I was destined to share to the end of his days the confidence and friendship of this rare and interesting man. From Herndon it was decreed I should learn what manner of man Lincoln was, how to measure him, to dissect his moral structure, to analyze his mental processes. I soon realized that no other man lived who comprehended so thoroughly the great character whose life I was trying to solve, who had dug so deeply and laid bare the springs of action, the motives that animated that clear head, brave heart, and strong right arm. It was plain that Herndon with implicit faith and fanatical devotion clung to Lincoln, and it therefore requires but little evidence to convince us that the latter, throughout the memorable and tempestuous times that made him great, bared his heart and soul to "Billy" Herndon.

In due time Herndon confided to me his plans. He had decided to relinquish the practice of law and move to the country. Once there, it was his purpose to write a number of articles for publication in a newspaper or magazine describing the youth and early manhood of Lincoln. Being somewhat infirm, as well as without experience in the art of narrative composition, he proposed that I should assist him and thus, by our joint efforts, we might produce a contribution to history the world would accept. After some reflection I decided to collaborate with him, but, later, when he had revealed to me the bountiful store of information he had accumulated, the project in my judgment began to broaden both in scope and importance. With the material already at hand and more of a like nature almost as accessible, I felt warranted in believing that a more interesting and pretentious work than a few columns of the regulation newspaper or magazine compilations of that period would be welcomed by the public, and I so insisted to Herndon. I was therefore not a little gratified a few days later when he announced that, after due deliberation, he had come around to my way of thinking.

Having determined to retire to the country he then asked me to help him classify and rearrange his papers, remove books, furniture, and other belongings — in short, dismantle the office generally. Although only preliminary to the details of research, verification, and composition, which were to engross our attention for the ensuing three or four years, I was soon made to realize that our joint labors had just begun. It only remains to add that, eventually, after a severe test of our zeal, vigor, and endurance, the time came when we were privileged to toss into the lap of an anxious and indulgent world three small volumes, depicting the life and achievements of Abraham Lincoln, under the significant if not euphonious title: "The True Story of a Great Life, by William H. Herndon." It may not be out of place to state here that prior to this, Ward H. Lamon had begun a "Life of Lincoln" obtaining from Herndon copies of numerous letters and papers which he was allowed to use. In the preparation of his manuscript Lamon was greatly aided by Chauncey F. Black, of Pennsylvania; in fact, as related by Herndon, Black really performed the better part of the work.

Elsewhere, in enumerating the contents of the Lincoln and Herndon law office, I have mentioned the bookcase standing against the wall on the north side of the room. It really surmounted a desk or table in which there were two small drawers, the whole being about eight feet high. There were five shelves; books occupied the lower three and those above were filled with a profusion of pamphlets, letters, and legal documents. Judging by the accumulation of dust which had settled on them Herndon's observation that the majority dated back to Lincoln's time was

an unnecessary deduction. On the floor near by stood a
wooden box into which Herndon explained he had been
placing papers of his own as well as matter concerning
Lincoln which he had gathered since the latter's death.
On the top of the bookcase I noticed a pasteboard box.
It was eighteen or twenty inches square and was minus a
lid. At the suggestion of Herndon I mounted a chair, lifted
the box from the place where it had evidently reposed for
many years and passed it down to him. After removing
the layer of dust which effectually covered it, he proceeded
to explore its contents, remarking that it was a box Lincoln
had used. It was filled with letters and papers tied in
bundles. One package he withdrew and untied. Beneath
the string was a paper label about five inches long containing these words in Lincoln's unmistakable and legible
handwriting: "*When you can't find it anywhere else look
into this.*" It was a collection of miscellaneous material set
aside by Lincoln. Among other things it contained numerous letters written to Lincoln during the campaigns of 1856
and 1858, some of which Herndon read and commented
on for my benefit; but the item which awakened his deepest interest was a couple of printed sermons, opposing the
extension of slavery, delivered by Theodore Parker of
Boston in the summer of 1858. Herndon told me that
these pamphlets were sent to him by Parker and that he
was so deeply impressed by them that he turned them over
to Lincoln. The latter folded and carried them in his
pocket to read. "That he did read them," said Herndon
after he had opened the package, "is shown by the fact
that he endorsed them by marking several paragraphs
with his pen." He then called my attention to two para-

graphs around which Lincoln had drawn his pen. In one of them Parker said: "Democracy is direct self-government, over all the people, for all the people, by all the people." In another place which Lincoln had underscored he said, "Slavery is in flagrant violation of the institutions of America — direct government, over all the people, by all the people, for all the people." Herndon insisted it was from this source that Lincoln drew the inspiration for the closing paragraph of his famous Gettysburg Address.

The limitations of time and space forbid a more extended description of the Lincoln-Herndon office, but I can hardly omit mention of another reminder which Herndon uncovered. When he was nearing the bottom of the box containing the array of miscellaneous matter just referred to, he withdrew from its depths a small leather-covered book about six by four inches in size, the two lids being fastened together with a brass clasp in front. After glancing through it for a few moments he gave it to me, saying as he placed it in my hands: "Here is the most important item in this entire collection. It reminds me more vividly of Lincoln than anything else we have thus far encountered. I am going to turn this over to you and I trust you will appreciate and preserve it, for, in its pages, you will find carefully stored all the ammunition Mr. Lincoln saw fit to gather in preparation for his battle with Stephen A. Douglas." He then explained that seeing the contest of 1858 approaching, Mr. Lincoln took this book, originally a blank book which had been used by himself and his partner to keep track of matters which concerned their business in the Supreme Court, and proceeded to paste on its pages newspaper clippings, tables of statistics, extracts from Judge Douglas's speeches, and other data bearing on the great and absorbing questions of the day. "When this little storehouse of political information was filled," observed Herndon, "Mr. Lincoln fastened the clasp, placed the book in his coat-pocket there to repose during the campaign and to be drawn upon whenever the exigencies of debate required it."

The book contained in the neighborhood of one hundred and eighty-five clippings, and the paste or mucilage used by Lincoln which had permeated the paper was so dark that it, in some cases, made the printed portions opaque and almost illegible. Among other things, Herndon called my attention to the order or arrangement of the material, contending that it was not only significant, but also decidedly Lincolnian. The first item, which was pasted on the inside of the front cover, was the second paragraph of the Declaration of Independence beginning with that immortal pronunciamento: "We hold these truths to be self-evident: that all men are created equal; that they are endowed by their Creator with certain inalienable rights; that among these are life, liberty, and the pursuit of happiness."

Lower down on the same page was this paragraph from a speech by Lincoln's great political exemplar, Henry Clay: "I repeat it, Sir, I never can, and never will, and no earthly power will make me vote, directly or indirectly, to spread slavery over territory where it does not exist. Never while reason holds her seat in my brain — never while my heart sends the vital fluid through my veins — NEVER."

Next in order and on the page following the quotation

The Chicago Times says the Declaration of Independence is an old instrument, and a cherished document. For over eighty years it has received the commendation and applause of all men who have read or heard it read. Since the exigencies of the black republican party has required the elevation of the negro to political equality with the white man, political doctors of that party have undertaken to give it new interpretations. We propose to state, first, the Declaration of Independence as adopted by congress, in 1776, and then, as succinctly as possible, the interpretations placed upon it by the democratic and black republican party. The second paragraph in the Declaration of Independence reads as follows:

"We hold these truths to be self-evident, that all men are created equal; that they are endowed by their Creator with certain inalienable rights; that among these are life, liberty and the pursuit of happiness. That to secure these rights, governments are instituted among men, deriving their just powers from the consent of the governed; that whenever any form of government becomes destructive of these ends, it is the right of the people to alter or to abolish it, and to institute a new government, laying its foundation on such principles, and organizing its powers in such form as to them shall seem most likely to effect their safety and happiness. Prudence, indeed, will dictate that governments long established should not be changed for light and transient causes; and, accordingly, all experience hath shown, that mankind are more disposed to suffer, while evils are sufferable, than to right themselves by abolishing the forms to which they are accustomed. But when a long train of abuses and usurpations, pursuing invariably the same object, evinces a design to reduce them under absolute despotism, it is their right, it is their duty, to throw off such government and to provide new guards for their future security."

"I repeat it, sir, I NEVER CAN, AND NEVER WILL, AND NO EARTHLY POWER WILL MAKE ME VOTE, DIRECTLY OR INDIRECTLY, TO SPREAD SLAVERY OVER TERRITORY WHERE IT DOES NOT EXIST. NEVER, WHILE REASON HOLDS HER SEAT IN MY BRAIN— NEVER, WHILE MY HEART SENDS THE VITAL FLUID THROUGH MY VEINS—NEVER!"

LINCOLN'S POCKET SCRAPBOOK CARRIED DURIN

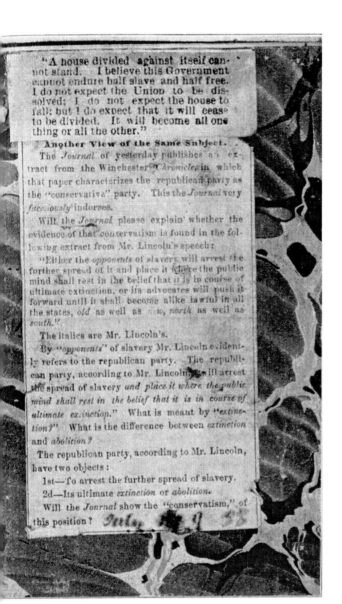

"A house divided against itself cannot stand. I believe this Government cannot endure half slave and half free. I do not expect the Union to be dissolved; I do not expect the house to fall: but I do expect that it will cease to be divided. It will become all one thing or all the other."

### Another View of the Same Subject.

The *Journal* of yesterday publishes an extract from the Winchester *Chronicle* in which that paper characterizes the republican party as the "conservative" party. This the *Journal* very *facetiously* indorses.

Will the *Journal* please explain whether the evidence of that conservatism is found in the following extract from Mr. Lincoln's speech:

"Either the *opponents* of slavery will arrest the further spread of it and place it where the public mind shall rest in the belief that it is in course of ultimate extinction, or its advocates will push it forward until it shall become alike lawful in all the states, *old* as well as *new, north* as well as *south."*

The italics are Mr. Lincoln's.

By "*opponents*" of slavery Mr. Lincoln evidently refers to the republican party. The republican party, according to Mr. Lincoln, will arrest the spread of slavery *and place it where the public mind shall rest in the belief that it is in course of ultimate extinction."* What is meant by "*extinction?"* What is the difference between *extinction* and *abolition?*

The republican party, according to Mr. Lincoln, have two objects:

1st—To arrest the further spread of slavery.

2d—Its ultimate *extinction* or *abolition.*

Will the *Journal* show the "conservatism," of this position?

from the Clay speech, Lincoln had inserted a portion of the opening paragraph of his famous speech delivered before the Republican State Convention which met in Springfield and nominated him as their candidate for United States Senator, June 16, 1858. It was in this speech he gave utterance to the doctrine that, so long as the slavery agitation was allowed to continue, this nation like "A house divided against itself cannot stand."

Part of this clipping included the comments of the local papers on the speech, but Lincoln chose the editorial notice, not of his own party's organ, the "Springfield Journal," but that of the "State Register," the opposition paper. He noted the date of its publication on the margin with pen and ink, and it doubtless served as a text for certain of his arguments during the campaign. With one exception the remaining portion of the material in the book is not especially noteworthy. That exception is an extract from an editorial printed in an Alabama newspaper — the "Muscogee Herald." It doubtless made something of an impression on Lincoln, for he had taken the precaution to record on the margin of the page the date of its appearance in the paper: August 7, 1856. It read as follows:

*Free society!* We sicken of the name. When it is but a conglomeration of greasy mechanics, filthy operatives, small-fisted farmers, and moon-struck theorists. All the Northern and especially the New England States are devoid of society fitted for well-bred gentlemen. The prevailing class one meets with is that of mechanics struggling to be genteel and small farmers who do their own drudgery, and yet who are hardly fit for association with a Southern gentleman's body servant. This is your *free society* which your Northern hordes are endeavoring to extend into Kansas.

Mr. Herndon smiled when he encountered this rank specimen of Southern journalistic expression. "Imagine the satisfaction," he exclaimed, "with which Mr. Lincoln, when he was addressing a crowd of greasy mechanics and small-fisted farmers who had emigrated from Ohio, Pennsylvania, and New York in quest of cheap homes, must have read this vivid and satirical allusion to the free society of the North. No wonder Douglas winced and threatened vengeance when he could get Lincoln 'down into Egypt' — in other words, southern Illinois."

# CHAPTER II

Lincoln's birth in Kentucky — Visiting his birthplace — Some of his early playmates — Interviewing Austin Gollaher and others at Hodgenville and Elizabethtown — Dr. Rodman's visit to Washington — Recollections of the artist Rowbotham — The removal to Indiana — Lincoln's schooling there — Incidents of his boyhood — Association with Dennis Hanks — Cutting wood at Posey's Landing — Letters of Dennis Hanks to Herndon.

OF his life in Kentucky Lincoln usually had but little to say; presumably, of course, because there was so little of it. Before he reached his ninth year his family had moved to Indiana, and although, in later years, he visited Louisville, Lexington, and possibly Frankfort, there is no evidence that he ever saw his birthplace or the scenes of his childhood in Kentucky again. When his nomination for President by the Chicago Convention in 1860 gave him national prominence, almost forty-five years had elapsed since his departure from Kentucky, and it is, therefore, not surprising that many of the people in the region where he was born were at a loss to determine who he was or whence he sprang; nor, during the few remaining years of his life, was the question of his exact identity and family descent, in the minds of some of these people, entirely free from obscurity and doubt.

For what we really know about Lincoln's birth and boyhood in Kentucky we owe more to the foresight and persistence of William H. Herndon than to any one else. Scarcely a month had elapsed after the tragedy at Ford's Theater, in April, 1865, before Herndon had set out for Kentucky and southern Indiana and begun an investigation so vigorous, conscientious, and exhaustive that the world will always be deeply in his debt. He was the first man on the ground and likewise the first man to meet and examine the few material and competent witnesses of Lincoln's advent into the world still living. He pursued his researches with rare vigilance and assiduity, toiling incessantly; nor did he cease his labors until he had dug to the very bottom in his search for the truth. Later, in compliance with his generous suggestion, I followed him, traversing the same path and visiting the same localities; and although I labored to the limit of my zeal and endurance I was never conscious of having added materially to the store of information he had already accumulated; nor of encountering anything of a valuable or interesting character which he had not unearthed himself. The truth is the field was so barren of material neither of us could gather much that was significant or trustworthy; but we consoled ourselves with the reflection that we had, to the point of exhaustion, explored every avenue that led to accurate or intelligent information.

Only four persons could be found who really knew and remembered Lincoln in Kentucky. One was Austin Gollaher, who was still living when I visited Larue County, and who seemed to have retained a more or less vivid recollection of his early playmate; but he was then well advanced in years and had already begun to view the past through the rosy mist of an old man's memory. About the only noteworthy thing he appeared to be able to recall was the published incident of his rescue of the boy Lincoln from the waters of Knob Creek into which he had fallen while trying to "coon" across that stream on a log. Another man — one met by Herndon — who knew Lincoln in Kentucky was John Duncan, a Baptist preacher, at that time in charge of Little Mount Church, the same church to which Thomas and Nancy Lincoln had belonged. One of the adventures in which both he and young Abe had leading parts — and I copy from the account in Duncan's handwriting, furnished to Herndon in 1865 and now in my hands — was this:

"Abe was very determined in pursuit of game, as an instance which I now recall will prove. He and I one day ran a ground-hog into a hole in the rocks. We worked a long time in an effort to get him out, but I finally became tired and gave up. Lincoln, however, ran to a blacksmith shop not far away and got the blacksmith to make a hook and fasten it to the end of a pole. The man came back with Abe and together they finally hooked the animal out of the hole."

Two other intelligent and dependable witnesses in Kentucky were interviewed by Herndon, both of whose statements or recollections in their own handwriting, turned over to Herndon in the summer of 1865, are still preserved. They were Presley Haycraft and John B. Helm. The first named, who was a brother of Samuel Haycraft, clerk of Hardin County, was a copyist in the latter's office. He was older than Lincoln and claimed to remember him well. He described him as a little "shirt-tail boy" in Elizabethtown who could be seen about the court-house and stores clinging closely to his mother's skirt. The fourth witness was John B. Helm who was a clerk or helper in his uncle's store, also in Elizabethtown, and who probably knew the Lincoln and Hanks families better than almost any other man in the village whom Herndon encountered. He describes young Abe as "a small boy who would sometimes come with his mother to the store to purchase their stock of family supplies. The little fellow, being a trifle shy, would frequently be seen sitting on a box or keg, and I have often dropped into his half-reluctant palm a lump of sugar which he would dispose of with as much relish as any other boy."

Though Lincoln in subsequent years failed to visit his birthplace, it does not follow that he forgot or viewed it with indifference; on the contrary, he retained and was prone to relate many interesting recollections of his associations there. From Dr. Jesse H. Rodman, of Hodgenville, who in 1865 represented Larue County in the legislature of Kentucky, I learned several characteristic and trustworthy incidents. During the war period a number of the leading citizens of Larue County, desirous of securing some concession or relief from a threatened draft on that county, held a meeting at Hodgenville and decided to send Dr. Rodman to Washington to call on the President and intercede with him in their behalf. Inasmuch as the appeal came from his native county, Lincoln, it was believed, might be moved to grant the desired relief. Meanwhile one of the President's friends went down to the farm on which he was born and cut from a tree growing there a limb or branch of the size required for a cane. This, together with a sum of money contributed by several persons about the court-house, was turned over to Dr. Rodman with directions, when he reached Washington, to have it mounted with a gold or silver head containing the names of the contributors engraved thereon. The whole was then to be presented to Lincoln. "Immediately on my arrival in Washington," related Dr. Rodman, "I called on the President and, after announcing the purpose of my visit as a representative of my fellow citizens in Larue County, ventured to tell him also the story of the cane, explaining that I had left the latter with a silversmith in the city to be mounted and properly engraved. The next day I called with the cane, to make the formal presentation. Lincoln seemed to be deeply pleased by this mark of appreciation on the part of his Kentucky friends and immediately asked how he was to learn who the donors of the cane were. Before I could answer that he would find their names on the metal head, he interrupted me, exclaiming laughingly, 'How absurd such a question. I ought to have known better than to ask it, for you have already answered it. I am like the Irishman who called on me when I was postmaster at New Salem, Illinois, and asked for his mail.

"'What name?' said I.

"'Sure,' said the Irishman, 'and the name is on the letter.'

"The President," continued Dr. Rodman, "ran over the list of early residents of the county, inquiring about the Brownfields, the Cesnas, the Friends, and other pioneer families, displaying a knowledge of persons and places more or less remarkable for one who, for so many years, had been away from his native heath. When I reached the name of Austin Gollaher he halted me. 'Is that old fox living yet?' he exclaimed. 'You may not believe it, but I would rather see him than any other man in Kentucky. Be sure to remember me to him when you reach home. I shall never forget an amusing but very scurvy trick he once played on me when we were boys. With weapons no more formidable than hickory clubs he and I had been playing in the woods and hunting rabbits. After several hours of vigorous exercise we had stopped to rest. After a while I threw down my cap, climbed a tree, and was resting comfortably in the forks of two limbs. Below me stretched out full length on the grass was Austin apparently asleep. Beside him lay his cap, the inside facing upwards. In the pocket of my little jacket reposed a paw-paw which I had shortly before found. The thought suddenly occurred to me that it would be great fun to drop it into Austin's upturned cap. It was so ripe and soft I could scarcely withdraw it whole from my pocket. Taking careful aim I let it fall. I had calculated just right; for it struck the cap center and I could see portions of soft yellow paw-paw spattering in every direction. I paused to observe the result, convinced that Austin would resent the indignity; but, strange to relate, the proceeding failed to arouse him. Presently I slid down the tree, but judge of my surprise on reaching the ground when I learned that, instead of sleeping, Austin had really been awake; and that while I was climbing the tree he had very adroitly changed caps, substituting my own for his, so that, instead of tormenting him as I was intending, I had simply besmeared my own headgear.'"

Elsewhere I have indicated that Herndon was the first visitor to Kentucky or southern Indiana in quest of intelligence or facts bearing on the events of Lincoln's early life. So far as it related to the collection of the requisite historical material, that statement is correct; but that Herndon was preceded a few weeks by a man whose mission, though nominally different, was along similar lines is also true. Joseph H. Barrett, who during the Civil War period was Commissioner of Pensions in Washington, had for some time been at work on a "Life of Lincoln"

which was published in the summer of 1865. In the earlier
part of the year his publishers, Moore, Wilstach & Bald-
win, of Cincinnati, had sent to Kentucky and Indiana an
artist, in the person of John H. Rowbotham, commissioned
to make pictures of important places and scenes in the
early life of Lincoln to be engraved and used in illustrating
the book. He was, in reality, the first man to penetrate
the backwoods of Kentucky and Indiana in search of
Lincoln data and material. Rowbotham began his travels
at Springfield, after first conferring with Herndon. As he
made his way through the territory assigned him he reported to Herndon, detailing his experiences frequently
from day to day. Having been told that the original log
cabin in which Lincoln was born was still standing near the
town of Hodgenville, he made his way there as speedily as
possible "fearing lest the structure might be burned, or
carried away piecemeal, by the army of relic hunters who
would soon be moving in that direction." When he arrived
there, however, he found, much to his surprise, that the
cabin was no longer in existence. When it disappeared no
one seemed to be able to tell.

"At Hodgenville, which is about ten miles northeast of
Elizabethtown," writes Rowbotham to Herndon June 24,
1865, "I inquired the way to Rock Spring farm, owned by
R. A. Creal, better known as 'Old Dickey Creal.' The farm
is about three miles southeast of Hodgenville on a good
straight road. The site of Mr. Lincoln's birthplace is on
this farm about five hundred yards from Mr. Creal's house.
It is situated on a knoll or rising ground and is now a bar-
ley field. The cabin has long since disappeared and gone to
decay, the only sign of its former existence being a few rocks

indicating where the chimney once stood. At the edge of the field are two old pear trees planted by Thomas Lincoln between which was a gateway leading to the house. Mr. Creal remembers the latter very well. Near the spot is a very romantic spring from which the farm takes its name and where, no doubt, Mr. Lincoln as a child often played."

While in Indiana Rowbotham visited Lincoln's home in Spencer County. "The home," he writes in another letter to Herndon, "lies a little off the Gentryville road on rising ground and is the most perfect reminiscence of Mr. Lincoln's early life. Here the family lived thirteen years. Mr. Lincoln's mother died here and is buried on the summit of a thickly wooded hill about a quarter of a mile from and immediately opposite the house. There is no stone to mark the spot, but it is well known. When you come, inquire for Josiah Crawford, John Romine, and old Mrs. Richardson, all of whom were at the burial of Mrs. Lincoln. Dennis Hanks was also present, but he is now in Illinois and you can see him yourself." There being, at that time, no stone, not even a board to mark the grave, Rowbotham was forced to the conclusion, expressed in one of his letters to Herndon, that "Mr. Lincoln does not appear to have cared for his home after the death of his mother."

Before young Lincoln had reached his tenth year his family moved to Indiana, and here, where they lingered till he had attained his majority, were the days of his wonderful boyhood spent. Here gathered those silent forces whose combination produced that unique character which stands

out in wonder and lofty eminence, one of the colossal
figures of modern history. It was these earlier years of
his life that had their lasting effect on the mind and temperament of this great mirthful but melancholy man.

The date of the removal from Kentucky to Indiana is
readily fixed by the statement of Mr. Lincoln in the sketch
of his life which he wrote and delivered to his friend Jesse
W. Fell, of Bloomington, Illinois, in 1859. "We reached
our new home," he relates, "about the time the State
came into the Union" — which would indicate the years
1816 to 1817. After describing the country as a "wild
region with many bears and other wild animals still in the
woods," he turns to the educational facilities of the period,
observing that "there were some schools, so called, but
no qualification was ever required of a teacher beyond
'readin', writin', and cipherin' to the Rule of Three.' If
a straggler supposed to understand Latin happened to sojourn in the neighborhood he was looked upon as a wizard.
There was absolutely nothing to excite ambition for education. Of course when I came of age I did not know much.
Still, somehow, I could read, write and cipher to the Rule
of Three; but that was all. I have not been to school since.
The little advance I now have upon this store of education
I have picked up from time to time under the pressure of
necessity."

The years of his residence in Indiana Lincoln never
failed to recall save with the deepest satisfaction. They
were indeed the formative period of his life and therefore
constitute an important epoch in his development. There
was a fascination in the rude companionship and boisterous horse-play of southern Indiana at that time which left

a deep impression on the tall, coarse-haired youth who grew to manhood in the hills and forests of this frontier region. When he neared the fame of later years he invariably located his best stories in the Hoosier State, and whenever he was heard to say, "That reminds me of an incident which happened when I lived in Indiana," his listeners would move their chairs closer together anxiously awaiting an interesting recital, bristling with wit and the expected "nib," or moral, which was so poignant it pierced the skin, or otherwise so effective it stung like the cracker of a whip-lash.

Though brief, Lincoln's school training really began in Indiana. True he was among the pupils at the schools in Kentucky taught by Zachariah Riney and Caleb Hazel, but his attendance was so short and irregular he hardly progressed beyond the alphabet — in fact, it may be truthfully said that he went largely as the companion of his only sister Sarah, who was two years his senior. The array of textbooks at his command was necessarily limited. We know he studied Webster's and, a part of the time, Dillworth's Speller, Pike's Arithmetic, and Murray's English Reader. Of the last-named book he was especially fond. Herndon told me that Lincoln once declared to him that "Murray's English Reader was the greatest and most useful book that could be put in the hands of a child at school."

He had neither grammar nor geography. The arithmetic he did not own, but he borrowed the book of a neighbor and laboriously copied a large part of it on sheets of paper about nine by twelve inches in size which he fastened together with twine sewed through the edge. His step-

PAGE FROM LINCOLN'S HAND-MADE ARITHMETIC, USED BY
HIM WHILE A SCHOOLBOY IN GENTRYVILLE, INDIANA,
SHOWING DOGGEREL IN CORNER

mother who, in 1865, was living at Charleston, Illinois, still had a portion of this hand-made book which she gave to Herndon. The latter turned several pages over to me, one of which contains the table of Long Measure with its quaint and primitive divisions of measurement:

> "Three barley-corns make one inch,
> Four inches one hand," etc.

It was in one of the lower corners of this sheet that young Abe had scrawled the four memorable lines of schoolboy doggerel:

> " Abraham Lincoln,
> His hand and pen,
> He will be good,
> But God knows when."

In some unaccountable way the young student secured a copy of Barclay's Dictionary which he doubtless frequently consulted, for when Herndon visited the stepmother the latter still had the volume with young Abe's name, in his own hand, written on the fly-leaf. At two places in the neighborhood where he lived in Indiana, the stepmother told Herndon, the boy was given access to books of a more literary character and he was occasionally permitted to take a volume home with him to read. This was at Josiah Crawford's and David Turnham's. From the first he obtained "The Kentucky Preceptor," out of which he learned the various poems and declamations he memorized and occasionally recited at school. At Turnham's there were two books to which he was especially attached and he read and re-read them. They were "Sinbad the Sailor" and "Scott's Lessons." These and the Revised Statutes of Indiana, which Turnham used in connection with the office of township constable, and which volume the latter turned over to Herndon in 1865, will indicate the probable scope of Lincoln's scholastic ventures up to this time.

With these primitive and unpretentious literary appliances Lincoln slowly acquired the rudiments of his education. All his school-days added together did not equal a year, and he not only was not privileged to attend a high or advanced school, but, until he was old enough to go to Congress, had never seen the inside of a college, academy, or high-school building. As Herndon very pertinently observed, it awakens the tenderest emotions to recall the story of this obscure but ambitious boy battling year after year against his evil star, wasting his ingenuity upon makeshifts and devices in a struggle to secure a training which to-day is not only easily within reach of the poorest and most indifferent lad in the land, but, under our generous educational system, is furnished to all without stint or reluctance.

The commonly accepted notion that Lincoln, especially during his sojourn in Indiana, was what would be called an intensive or industrious young man lacks more or less support. The truth is he had no fondness for the severe labor of the backwoods and no scruples against avoiding it whenever possible. Equally erroneous is the prevalent belief that he spent a large proportion of his time as a hired hand working for others. Service of that kind had no charms for him, and while it is true he occasionally labored for wages the instances were rare and invariably of brief duration. He was not much given to fishing, hunting, or sports generally, but much preferred reading and like diversions. He was an eager listener to debates and other wordy contests; was delighted with the arguments and contention evoked by a neighborhood controversy, and if a dispute was being aired in the squire's court he was certain to be on hand an earnest and absorbed listener.

Dilating on Lincoln's reputation as a physical laborer serves to recall an interview I had with Dennis Hanks. It was at Charleston, Illinois, where he was living in the fall of 1886. I write from notes of the conversation written at the time.

In August, 1826, Abe, Dennis Hanks, and Squire Hall — the last two having married daughters of Abe's stepmother, Sarah Bush Lincoln — all set out for Posey's Landing on the Ohio River, distant twelve miles from their homes at Gentryville, Indiana, to cut wood, it being reported that there was a brisk demand for that kind of fuel by the boats plying up and down the river. When they arrived they learned that the demand for wood had slackened materially and that, if they succeeded in securing an order for any, they would probably have to take their pay in merchandise, as there was then but a scant supply of cash in the community. How many days they tarried there Hanks did not indicate, but it was long enough to cut nine cords for which they were given nine yards of white domestic at twenty-five cents a yard. "Out of this," related Hanks, "Abe had a shirt made, and it was positively the first white shirt which, up to that time, he had ever owned or worn. It was also the first time he had ever hired out and worked away from home."

When he visited Indiana, Herndon learned that in 1827 Lincoln and his stepbrother, John D. Johnston, journeyed together to Louisville where they secured work for a brief time on the Portland Canal, then in process of construction around the falls of the Ohio. They were paid in silver dollars, probably the first silver money of any consequence Abe ever received. Naturally he was very proud of it and by virtue of frugal expenditures and determined self-denial managed to carry a goodly portion of it home with him when he returned to Gentryville.

Regarding the history of Mr. Lincoln's days while he lived in Indiana, including glimpses into the social conditions which prevailed there and thus had such a decided influence on his development into manhood, too much weight cannot be attached to the recollections of Dennis and John Hanks. Nor should the activities of Herndon in thus preserving their testimony be overlooked. Lincoln had hardly met his death in 1865 until Herndon was at work securing from both men all the information he could extract which tended to shed any light on the former's birth and boyhood. His method in dealing with Dennis was both systematic and effective. In addition to what the latter told him and which he carefully recorded at the time, Herndon induced him to put his testimony in writing also; but in order to keep him within certain limits and yet retain only so much as was essential to the continuity of the story, Herndon put his inquiry in the form of questions which he numbered, directing Dennis to number his answers also. There are many pages of these letters or statements, most of them dated and all of which were duly turned over to me. Knowing that I had spent more or less time with and had myself interviewed Dennis, Herndon seemed to think I was the proper depositary of the material both of us had gathered. These papers of Dennis, though written in defiance of the rules of grammar, capitalization, spelling, etc., are nevertheless of decided historic value. One dated December 24, 1865, is so characteristic and faithful a portrayal of life in Indiana when Lincoln lived there, I venture to reproduce it exactly as Dennis Hanks drew it, observing incidentally, that of the thirteen persons who formed the emigrant party that drove from Gentryville, Indiana, to Decatur, Illinois, in March, 1830, only two could write their names: Abraham Lincoln and Dennis Hanks:

December 24 1865.

you speak of my Letter written with a pencil. the Reason of this was my Ink was frose.

part first. we ust to play 4 Corner Bull pen and what we cald cat. I No that you No what it is and throwing a mall over our Sholders Backwards, hopping and half hamen, Resling and so on.

2nd what Religious Songs. The only Song Book was Dupees old Song Book. I Recollect Very well 2 Songs that we ust to Sing, that was

"O, when shall I see jesus and Rain with him aBove." the next was "How teageous and tasteless the hour when jesus No Longer I see."

I have tried to find one of these Books But cant find it. it was a Book used by the old predestinarian Baptists in 1820. this is my Recollection aBout it at this time. we Never had any other

the Next was in the fields

"Hail Collumbia Happy Land if you aint Broke I will Be Damned" and "the turpen turk that Scorns the world and Struts aBout with his whiskers Curld for No other man But himself to See" and all such as this. Abe youst to try to Sing pore old Ned But he Never could Sing Much.

# CHAPTER III

The question of Lincoln's birth and descent — The various books on the subject — Investigations by Herndon and the author in Kentucky and elsewhere — The Enloe tradition — The Lincoln family Bible record — Sarah Lincoln — The John L. Scripps incident — Herndon's story of his ride with Lincoln to Petersburg — Dennis and John Hanks, who they were and whence they sprang — Their letters to Herndon regarding the Lincoln family tree.

To what extent the knowledge of his lowly if not obscure origin contributed to the pensive and melancholy tendency in Lincoln's nature is a question not easily answered; but certain it is that much of the curious and absurd speculation regarding his genealogy, which has grown up in the popular mind, is largely due to his vague and evasive attitude when confronted by inquiries regarding his lineage or family history. In most instances the subject has been overlooked or glossed over by Lincoln's numerous biographers, but now that he has attained such enviable proportions among the other great figures in the temple of fame, and is therefore beyond "our power to add or detract," the feeling, gradually developed in the popular mind, that the truth should be known, cannot always be ignored. Nor can a portrait of the real Lincoln be deemed complete or exact which in any appreciable degree fails to bring out all the facts. The reading public has just been favored with "The Paternity of Abraham Lincoln," a book written by Dr. William E. Barton, who has for some time been a student of the subject mentioned in the title. It is a careful and exhaustive essay and will be warmly appreciated by the army of Lincoln students and admirers over the country.

Prior to 1858, Lincoln's achievements had not been noteworthy or momentous enough to attract, extensively, public attention, and it was not till after the debates with Douglas, and especially the Cooper Institute speech, that he began to attain anything like national recognition. When he was thus looming up large on the horizon, the people, manifesting the same degree of interest and anticipation with which they had awaited the history of every other man whose successful exploits had swept him into the limelight, naturally turned to him for the story of his life. At this juncture had he, with his accustomed spirit and candor, met the question squarely and imparted the facts as he understood them, the nebulæ which, for so many years, enveloped him would not have gathered, and the world would have been spared the nauseating and incredible "disclosures" which, under the guise of "revealing the true genesis of a wonderful man," have from time to time drifted into the open sea of public notice.

Among the books which attempt to settle the question of Lincoln's birth and family descent are "The Sorrows of Nancy," published in Richmond, Virginia, and written by a woman under the name of Lucinda Boyd; the "Sad Story of Nancy Hanks," a copyrighted pamphlet by William M. Coleman, of Dallas, Texas; "Truth Stranger than Fiction: or, The True Genesis of a Wonderful Man," by James Cathey, of Bryson City, North Carolina; and "The Parentage of Lincoln," a series of newspaper articles by D. J. Knotts, of Swansea, South Carolina, in which the author seeks to prove that Abraham Lincoln was the son of John C. Calhoun, who became intimate with Nancy Hanks and, for five hundred dollars, hired Thomas Lincoln to assume the paternity of the child and take the woman to Kentucky.

When, in obedience to the direction of Herndon, I visited Kentucky in quest of material for our contemplated Life of Lincoln, and especially as I neared the region of the latter's birthplace, a network of traditions confronted me. I dug my way patiently through clerks' records in obscure court-houses, read the faded pages of family history in musty old Bibles, deciphered curiously spelled and dimly written letters, followed down the never-ending lanes of neighborhood tradition and backwoods lore, interviewed witnesses of every age and condition in life — in short, searched for facts and data until I had apparently exhausted every available avenue to intelligent information. Each locality had its tradition, and many of them were curious and sometimes amusing. The rancor of sectional strife furnished an atmosphere in which some of these traditions, feeding on their own inconsistencies, grew to the dignity of colossal falsehoods. It is surprising how many at one time or another were current in central Kentucky. Herndon, who visited that locality in the summer of 1865, disposed of several, but even when I followed him later, some of them were still afloat in the currents and eddies of local history. The most persistently adhered to and the least preposterous of them was the Inloe or Enloe legend. I encountered it in both Hardin and Larue Counties, and it also bobbed up in other parts of the State. It is thus summarized by a man who lived in Elizabethtown, a member of one of the leading families and a lawyer, whose account, written and turned over to Herndon, lies before me:

"After Abe's birth a man by the name of Abraham Enloe living in this region claimed him as his son. Thomas Lincoln and Enloe had a regular set-to fight about the matter, in which encounter Lincoln bit off the end of Enloe's nose. Finally, Lincoln, to clear himself of Enloe, moved to Indiana. As far back as I can remember there lived in Hardin County three families of Enloes, all from North Carolina and all said to be cousins. Isham Enloe married a widow Larue and had a family of some distinction. Abe Enloe, another cousin, tall, dignified-looking man of fine personal appearance, very neat, silent, and reserved; more of a bookworm than anything else; married a Vernon — one of our best families — and was the father of a respectable family. Then comes our veritable Abe Enloe who claims to be the father of Lincoln. He was over six feet high and a fine specimen of physical manhood. I remember him with part of his nose bit off as one of the institutions of the county for thirty years. Very silent, very unobtrusive, never drunk nor boisterous, he seemed not to suffer in reputation by the conduct of his sisters who were more or less boisterous. I never had much to say to him except when I happened to sell him some article for his farm in my uncle's store. He may have been a man of destiny also and patiently filled the place assigned by Providence."

In addition to the Enloe story I devoted some time to the George Brownfield legend and to another which sought to fix the paternity of Lincoln on one of the Hardins. I was even provided with pictures of members of the Brownfield and Young families, all of them tall, muscular specimens, with unusually long arms, to impress me with the plausibility of the theory that, as Lincoln himself was a man of like physical proportions, he must have descended from the same family source. I listened to a long and carefully worded argument by a citizen of Mount Sterling, an editor and lawyer, claiming descent from the millwright Abe Enloe, at the town of Paris, and who sought to prove through that source his alleged kinship to Lincoln.

The books enumerated and the legends mentioned are not all the stories relating to Lincoln's ancestry that I encountered, but they are representative of their class and all fall to the ground when certain tests are applied. Aside from their inconsistencies there is an absence of proof in support of their ridiculous contentions beyond tradition or hearsay. Questioning the legitimacy of Lincoln's birth they overlook the well-established fact that he was the second child in the family, a sister older than himself, Sarah by name, having been born in 1807, whereas he did not see the light of day till 1809, almost three years after his parents' marriage. Moreover, as to the Enloe legend in particular, it is now known that at the time of the marriage of Thomas Lincoln and Nancy Hanks the latter was twenty-three years old and Abe Enloe, according to the recollection of some witnesses, hardly seventeen. Viewing the question as a whole there is no good reason to shake our faith in the conclusion that Abraham Lincoln was the lawfully begotten son of the above-named parents.

The family record in Thomas Lincoln's Bible by his son Abraham, and the only Bible record of the Lincoln family of which we have any knowledge, was, until recently, in the possession of Mr. C. F. Gunther, of Chicago. It covered

THE FAMILY RECORD IN THOMAS LINCOLN'S BIBLE, CHIEFLY IN ABRAHAM LINCOLN'S HAND

A piece is missing from the upper right-hand corner. The entries shown at the lower left-hand corner are from the back of the sheet.

but one sheet and was found by the author many years ago in the hands of a daughter of Dennis Hanks. The sheet had been detached from between the leaves of the book and had been folded in several places so long that the paper was gradually wearing away at the folds and the section in the upper right-hand corner — a piece about an inch and a half square — was missing. Possibly the latter was that part of the page which bore the record of the marriage of Thomas Lincoln and Nancy Hanks, although it is likewise possible that inscribed therein was the date of the birth of Thomas Lincoln as the head of the household. Within recent years documentary evidence has come to light establishing the fact that the marriage took place June 12, 1806. But did Mr. Lincoln know that? If, as Henry Watterson and others have stated, he died without knowing whether his parents were married or not, the query naturally arises, What did he write in the missing section of the Bible record? From the remaining portion of the latter we learn that "Sarah, daughter of Thomas and Nancy Lincoln, was born February 10, 1807," and that Abraham, son of the same parents, "was born February 12, 1809." Another son, Thomas, was born about 1812, but he lived a few days only. The record is silent as to his birth or death.

Sarah, the daughter, resembled her illustrious brother in but few particulars. She was short in stature and somewhat plump in build; her hair, according to her stepmother, was dark brown and her eyes gray. She was given the name Sarah at birth and was never called Nancy, as erroneously contended by certain biographers of Lincoln including Nicolay and Hay. When Herndon visited

Indiana he met several persons who knew and remembered the girl, including Elizabeth Crawford at whose house she frequently worked. Mrs. Crawford testified that she was slow and in some respects seemed to be lacking in spirit and initiative — in fact had, in a marked degree, the traits that characterized her father; just as her brother seemed to have inherited from his mother the quick perception, clear reasoning powers, and profound intellect that lifted him above the level of his surroundings. The sister was married to Aaron Grigsby August 2, 1826, and died in childbirth January 20, 1828. A beautiful granite monument was recently erected over her unmarked grave near the village of Gentryville, Indiana. As her death occurred before the removal of the family to Illinois, our knowledge of her is necessarily meager and dim. For the little we have been able to learn about her we are indebted to Dennis and John Hanks rather than to her illustrious brother, who seems to have been more or less silent regarding her. Herndon is authority for the statement that Lincoln seldom ever referred to her.

In tracing the line of Lincoln's ancestry we are not without certain authentic landmarks to guide us; and fortunately for all concerned their accuracy cannot well be questioned, for they were established by Lincoln himself. Late in the year 1859, when he was asked for the material and data usually expected of a man who has the presidential fever and whose career and deeds are entitled to more or less conspicuous mention in the newspapers, he made preparations, though with some reluctance, to comply with the request; but instead of dictating the required facts to another to put into shape for publication, as the average man of his standing would have done, he sat down one evening in his law office, after his partner, Herndon, had gone home, and with due care and deliberation wrote the story himself. After its completion he turned the paper over to a friend to be published or not as might seem to be for the best. With the exception of the few lines furnished to the compiler of the Directory of the Thirtieth Congress in 1847, this is the first attempt on Lincoln's part to acquaint the world with the facts and incidents of his personal career. Many years ago I had the original manuscript of this sketch in my hands. It covers several sheets of small note-paper and is a very clever, if not ingeniously worded, document. The writer, dwelling with pardonable pride on his paternal forebears, devotes the greater part of an entire page to the deeds and exploits of certain members of the Lincoln family, but scarcely two lines to the maternal side of the house. He even fails to state what his mother's name was, the only reference to her existence being the brief and incidental allusion that she "came of a family by the name of Hanks." Not long after this paper was written, a correspondent in Kentucky, in an effort to identify Lincoln with a branch of the Hanks family there, ventured to make certain inquiries into his antecedents. "You are mistaken about my mother" was his blunt reply, and beyond that he made no effort to enlighten his inquirer or otherwise add to his knowledge.

The above comprises all that the world knew of the history of Lincoln prior to the spring of 1860. Then came the great National Convention at Chicago. When it had adjourned the attention of the country was at once focused on the immortal Railsplitter at Springfield. All the roads now led to his house. Painters, sculptors, photographers, correspondents arrived by every train. They made his picture, they modeled his bust, they beset him at every turn. He received and with patient grace welcomed the well-nigh interminable line of callers that daily thronged through the doorway of the plain two-story house on Eighth Street. He told them amusing stories and sent them away laughing; but although ordinarily frank and communicative he seemed to draw within his shell whenever the conversation turned on himself or his family history. The situation was more or less delicate, to say the least. Meanwhile word reached him from sources he deemed it unwise to ignore and he was made to realize that the time for reticence and evasion had passed; in other words, that he must take the public into his confidence and tell the whole story.

It was at this juncture that John L. Scripps, the editor of the "Chicago Press and Tribune," appeared upon the scene. He was the authorized biographer of the nominee of the Chicago Convention. Of the visit of Mr. Scripps to Springfield to begin his work it is unnecessary to go into details. It suffices to say that in due time the biography — a pamphlet of thirty-two pages — appeared and was widely distributed. "Lincoln seemed to be painfully impressed," wrote Scripps in a letter to Herndon, after Lincoln's death, which has been turned over to me, "with the extreme poverty of his early surroundings — the utter absence of all romantic and heroic elements. He communicated some facts concerning his ancestry which he did not wish to have published and which I have never spoken of or alluded to before." To this man, therefore, Lincoln must have disclosed the facts he had been so persistently withholding from the public. But alas for us, what they were we shall probably never know, for, only a few months after Lincoln's death, the biographer to whom they were communicated himself died without revealing a word!

From Lincoln's halting and evasive demeanor, therefore, it soon became apparent that, somewhere in his ancestral line, there existed a lapse or hiatus or some equally embarrassing circumstance which he saw fit to withhold. The question naturally arose, Where and what was the trouble? We might still be in the dark and as far as ever from a solution of the difficulty but for the timely contribution of Herndon, who came nearer bearing the relation of confidant to Lincoln than any other man in Springfield outside of Joshua F. Speed. Herndon's testimony relates to a revelation made to him by Lincoln under the following circumstances:

"On the subject of his ancestry," writes Herndon, "I only remember one time when Mr. Lincoln referred to it. It was in the fifties when he and I were driving to court in Menard County. The suit we were discussing touched upon the subject of hereditary traits. During the ride he spoke of his mother, dwelling on her characteristics and mentioning or enumerating what qualities he believed he had inherited from her. Among other things I remember he said she was the illegitimate daughter of Lucy Hanks and a well-bred Virginia farmer or planter; he argued that from this last source came his power of analysis, his logic, his mental activity, his ambition, and all the qualities that distinguished him from the other members and descendants of the Hanks family. His theory was that, for certain reasons, illegitimate children are sometimes sturdier and brighter than those born in lawful wedlock; and in his case he believed that his better nature and finer qualities came from this unknown, broad-minded Virginian.[1] The revelation — painful as it was — called up the recollection of his mother, and, as the buggy jolted over the road, he added ruefully, 'God bless my mother; all that I am or ever expect to be I owe to her,' and lapsed into silence. Our interchange of ideas ceased and we rode on for some time without exchanging a word. Burying himself in thought and musing, no doubt, over the disclosure he had just made, he drew about himself a barrier which I feared to penetrate. His words and melancholy tone made a deep impression on me. It was an experience I can never forget. As we neared the town of Petersburg we were overtaken by an old man who entertained us with reminiscences of early days on the frontier. Lincoln was in turn reminded of several Indiana stories, and by the time we had reached the unpretentious court-house at our destination his sadness had passed away."

Fortunately for Herndon his narrative of what Lincoln told him — which may be the same thing Lincoln afterwards confided to John L. Scripps — does not lack for support; for, in its vital or material points, it is corroborated by the testimony of John and Dennis Hanks, the

---

[1] Of course this theory of hereditary or transmitted traits was not original with Lincoln; but it was most impressively illustrated in the history of his own, or rather, the Hanks family. Reared in extreme poverty and denied all early advantages, he was nevertheless able, by virtue of his profound intellect and sheer native powers, to rise to the loftiest niche any American has thus far attained; but, of the seven other children born to Lucy Hanks after the birth of her daughter Nancy — who was Abraham's mother — and their descendants, not one has ever been heard from.

two most competent of all the witnesses who have thus
far attempted to enlighten us regarding the question of
Lincoln's family descent. Their recollections, largely in
their own handwriting, were recorded within a year after
Lincoln's death, and, notwithstanding all that has been
said and written on the subject since then, their testimony remains practically uncontradicted. According to
Lincoln the two were cousins of each other and first cousins of his mother. Both were born in Kentucky — John,
February 9, 1802, and Dennis, May 15, 1799; both died
in Illinois; John, July 12, 1890, and Dennis, October 21,
1892.

Before proceeding further with their testimony, however, it will not be out of place to notice here the deductions of Mrs. Caroline Hanks Hitchcock, a lady in Cambridge, Massachusetts — descended from Benjamin Hanks,
of Plymouth — who, in 1899, wrote and published a book
entitled "Nancy Hanks — The True Story of Lincoln's
Mother," containing an account of the author's researches
into the early history of the Hanks family and preceded
by an introduction by Miss Ida Tarbell. The purpose of
the work, as stated, was to "clear the name of Nancy
Hanks Lincoln," and great stress is laid on the will of
Joseph Hanks executed January 9, 1793, in Nelson County,
Kentucky, and found by the author during a visit to that
State. In this will the testator, among other things, be-
queaths to his daughter Nancy "one heifer yearling called
Peidy," whereupon the author at once concludes that she
has accomplished her mission, proclaiming that her discovery "settles the question of Nancy Hanks' parentage,
showing that she had a father who recognized her in his

will with the same generosity that he did her brothers and sisters." Mrs. Hitchcock's motives are highly commendable and praiseworthy, but unfortunately for the accuracy of her deductions it happens that there were numerous Nancy Hankses in Kentucky in those days, and she fails to furnish the proof that the Nancy Hanks named by Joseph Hanks in his will was the same Nancy Hanks who was married to Thomas Lincoln. Two other facts tend to discredit her conclusion: Lincoln's mother was the daughter of Lucy Hanks, and the latter, we know, had a sister named Nancy. It will be observed that Joseph Hanks in his will makes no mention of a daughter Lucy and that his wife bore the name Nancy.

Dennis Hanks was the natural son of Charles Friend and Nancy Hanks. The latter after the birth of her son was married to Levi Hall and became the mother of several more children. Being as he himself states a "base-born" child, Dennis was not admitted to the Hall household, but was duly turned over to the sheltering care of his mother's sister Elizabeth, married to Thomas Sparrow. The latter were a childless couple and we are told cheerfully took the cast-off waif, caring for him as dutifully and affectionately as if he had been their own child. Nancy Hanks, the mother of Dennis Hanks, had a sister Lucy, who, in 1783, gave birth to a daughter, also called Nancy, to whom was reserved an illustrious maternity in the birth of her son Abraham Lincoln. Who the father of this last-named Nancy Hanks was no one, not even Mr. Lincoln himself, has thus far been able to tell; but we know that after her birth her mother, Lucy Hanks, was married to Henry Sparrow and became the mother of seven more children. The records of Mercer County, Kentucky, show that "the rites of marriage between Henry Sparrow and Lucy Hanks were duly solemnized by John Baily April 3, 1791." Nancy Hanks must, therefore, have been about eight years old when her mother was married to Henry Sparrow.

For the same reason that Dennis Hanks spent his early boyhood apart from the Hall family, his cousin, Nancy Hanks, was not suffered to remain in the same household with the children of her mother and Henry Sparrow. She, too, had been turned over to the fostering care of Thomas and "Betsy" or Elizabeth Sparrow and under their inviting roof-tree she for a time shared the fortunes and companionship of her cousin Dennis Hanks. That their foster-parents gave heed to their needs and zealously strove to promote their comfort and welfare is evidenced by the fact that both children seem in some way to have absorbed more of the rudiments of an education than any of their immediate kindred. Dennis Hanks, though of no greater native ability than his cousin John, had much the advantage of the latter in the matter of educational qualifications. His writing is legible and his letters and notes or statements, of which Mr. Herndon at one time had at least fifty pages, indicate a better knowledge of English than one could expect from a man whose early opportunities were so distressingly meager and adverse. A few extracts from his testimony, copied from the original manuscript, are more or less illuminative. They will serve to test his competency as a witness. Many of his letters are in response to specific inquiries propounded by Mr. Herndon, and when he replied he usually repeated the question adopting as nearly as possible the original phraseology regardless of its primitive spelling and rude capitalization. Thus, in February, 1866, writing from Charleston, Illinois, Hanks says:

Those questions you Propound is the Easiest for me to answer of all the Rest. I give it in full, Noing what I say. 1st What is the Name of A. Lincolns Mother?

Hir Name was Nancy Sparrow; hir fathers Name was Henry Sparrow, hir Mother was Lucy Sparrow, her Madin name was Hanks, sister to my Mother. 2nd. You say why was she cald Hanks?

All I can say is this She was Deep in Stalk of the Hanks family. Calling hir Hanks probily is My falt. I allways told hir She Looked More Like the Hankses than Sparrow. I think this is the way; if you call hir Hanks you Make hir a Base born Child which is not trew.

Of course no reasonable thinking person will doubt that Dennis Hanks not only knew who his own mother was, but who was the mother of his cousin Nancy as well. The same statement will apply to John Hanks; but the one difficulty with the testimony of both witnesses is, that while persisting in the declaration that Lincoln's mother was a daughter of Lucy Sparrow, and therefore should be called Sparrow, they overlooked the fact that, in thus endeavoring to preserve unbroken the Hanks ancestral line, they were in flat contradiction with the highest grade of evidence known to the law: a duly authorized public record. The clerk of Mercer County, Kentucky, certifies that Lucy Hanks and Henry Sparrow were married April 3, 1791; if, therefore, as these witnesses would have us believe, Lucy Hanks's daughter Nancy was not born till after the marriage to Henry Sparrow, she would have been scarcely fourteen years old at the time of her marriage to

Thomas Lincoln, whereas, on the contrary, she was then twenty-three, having been born in 1783.

February 22, 1866, Dennis Hanks writes Herndon again:

1st question, How comes it that Lincoln him Self Calls his Mother Nancy Hanks?

I say this I Dont Believe he ever Said so for his Mother was Nancy Lincoln; hir Madin Name was Nancy Sparrow. So what is the Use of all this?

Further along in the same letter he says:

You Say that you have Received a Letter from Charles Friend; he wished to No Sum of my ants and unkels. I will Say this a Bout it Billy. I am a Base Born Child. My mother was Nancy Hanks, The ant of A. Lincolns Mother; My first ant Lucy Sparrow, Next polly Friend, Next Elizabeth Sparrow, these on My Mothers Side and Abes; one ant on My fathers Side Married Zary Wilcox hir name was Sally Friend.

February 28, 1866, he writes:

Friend William those questions is Mity Easy to answer.

1st, Who was the Mother of Nancy Sparrow?

Now this is Abes Mother you asking a Bout. It was Lucy Hanks first and Next Lucy Sparrow My Ant.

2nd What was Miss Nancy Sparrows fathers Name?

It was Henry Sparrow. Lucy Hanks was his wife, the Mother of Abes Mother and my ant.

Did Mister Sparrow and his wife have any children except Nancy Sparrow?

I answer yes they had 8 children 4 Sons and 4 Daughters. James, thomas, Henry, George: girls Sally, Elizabeth, Nancy, all Born in Mercer county Kentucky.

3rd. Who did Jesse Friend Mary?

He married My ant polly Hanks, Abes Mothers ant. Thomas Sparrow married Elizabeth Hanks, A. Lincolns ant, Sister to Henry Sparrows wife Lucy Hanks; this is their first name.

Who did Levi Hall mary?

He married My Mother Nancy Hanks which was Lucy Hanks Sister, Henry Sparrows wife, Abes grand Mother.

4th Was you Raised by Charles friend or thomas Sparrow?
I was raised by thomas Sparrow on the Little South fork of
Nolin Kentucky.
5 Was thomas Sparrow Mr. Lincolns Mothers father?
I answer No Kin at all.

Further extracts from the written recollections of this
unique and willing witness would simply be confirmatory
of his original testimony. At the time of his death he was
the only man then living who had seen the infant son of
Thomas and Nancy Lincoln before he was a week old.
His narrative of this event, told in his crude and homely
style, is not without interest. "They told me the Lincolns had a baby at thur house," he related to the writer
at Charleston, Illinois, October 28, 1886, "and so I jest
run all the way down thar. I guess I was on hand purty
early, fur I rickolect when I held the little feller in my arms
his mother said, 'Be keerful with him, Dennis, fur you air
the fust boy he 's ever seen.' I sort o' swung him back
and forth; a little too peart, I reckon, fur with the talkin'
and the shakin' he soon begun to cry and then I handed
him over to my Aunt Polly who wuz standin' close by.
'Aunt,' sez I, 'take him; he 'll never come to much,' fur
I 'll tell you he wuz the puniest, cryin'est little youngster
I ever saw."

Dennis Hanks lived to be the last survivor of the little
band that gathered about the grave of Nancy Hanks Lincoln when she was laid to rest on the crest of that little
knoll in southern Indiana. He also witnessed the death
and burial of his own mother as well as that of his foster-
parents Thomas and Elizabeth Sparrow; in fact, it was
through his clear recollection of incidents and objects that
it has been possible with any degree of accuracy to deter-

mine the location of the grave of Nancy Hanks. In a
letter to Mr. Herndon, which bears no date, he writes:

You ask was Mr. Sparrow and Wife Buried on the same
Mound? I say yes, the Women was Side by Side; Abes Mother
in the Middle, first My ant, which was thomas Sparrows wife
on one side of Abes Mother and My Mother on the other side.
Levi Hall on the Side of his wife, which was My Mother, and
thomas Sparrow was on the side of his wife which was My ant,
the 5 together. Abes Mother Died first; they all Died Close together.

The association of John Hanks, the other witness referred to in these pages, with the other Hankses, the
Sparrows, and the Friends, was not so intimate or continuous as that of his cousin Dennis Hanks. About the
time of Mr. Lincoln's birth John Hanks left Hardin for
Grayson County in Kentucky. In 1822 he emigrated to
Spencer County, Indiana, buying a tract of land near
the Lincoln farm. Six years later he removed to Macon
County, Illinois, where he was living when Thomas Lincoln and his family, migrating from Indiana, joined him
in the spring of 1830. He made six flatboat trips to New
Orleans, one of them with Abraham Lincoln. He was a
soldier in the Black Hawk War and also in the Civil War,
serving as an enlisted man in the Twenty-First Illinois
Volunteers (General Grant's regiment) for three years.
Lincoln held him in high esteem. "I can say," wrote
Herndon in an endorsement on the margin of one of John
Hanks's statements, "that this testimony can be safely
relied upon. Mr. Lincoln loved this man — thought him
truthful, honest, and noble. Lincoln has stated this to
me over and over again."

While the recollections of John Hanks are not so voluminous and cover less range than the contributions of Dennis, yet he corroborates the latter on all vital and essential points, also resorting to the same artifice to legitimize the birth of Lincoln's mother by naming her Nancy Sparrow. His first letter, written at Decatur, Illinois, is dated May 25, 1865. After a brief sketch of Thomas Lincoln he says of the latter's wife: "Nancy Sparrow was the mother of Abraham Lincoln. Her mother's name was Lucy Hanks and was born in Virginia." In a subsequent statement he says: "Abe's mother was my first cousin. His grandfather and grandmother on his mother's side lived in Mercer County, Kentucky, about twenty-five miles south of his grandfather on his father's side. Dennis and I are cousins." In a letter still later he says: "Mr. Sparrow and Mrs. Sparrow never came to Illinois. Henry Sparrow was the husband's name. They lived and died in Mercer County, Kentucky."

The last letter from John Hanks was written at Linkville, Klamath County, Oregon, June 12, 1887, at which place he was then living. It was addressed to me. After a brief description of the physical make-up of Lincoln's mother, he says of her: "Her mother married Henry Sparrow. She was shrewd, not very much of a talker; very religious and her disposition was very quiet."

# CHAPTER IV

Removal of the Lincolns from Indiana to Illinois in 1830 — Thomas Lincoln sells the land to Charles Grigsby — Leaving Gentryville — Names of the emigrants and description of the journey — Reaching Macon County, Illinois — Abe leaves the family near Decatur and pushes out for himself — Thomas Lincoln and the Hankses — Story of Thomas Johnston jailed for stealing a watch and how Lincoln saved him — Recollections of Harriet Chapman who lived at the Lincoln home in Springfield.

THE year 1830 is a milestone in the life of Abraham Lincoln. It marks not only the time when he attained his majority and became his own master, but also when the Lincoln family made its last interstate removal: from Indiana to Illinois. This early migration westward is of such moment and historical importance that the legislatures of the two States have sought, through commissions selected for the purpose, to determine, and, by means of monuments and bronze tablets, to mark, the route over which these poor and luckless pioneers made their way from the village of Gentryville in Spencer County, Indiana, to their destination, a point several miles west of the town of Decatur in Macon County, Illinois.

In the year 1829 John Hanks had settled near the last-named place and was soon so well pleased with his new abode that he wrote to the Lincolns and Hankses in Indiana urging them to "pull up stakes" and follow. "The proposition," recites the Indiana Commission in their report, "met with the general consent of the Lincoln contingent and especially suited the roving and migratory spirit of Thomas Lincoln. He had been induced by the same rosy and alluring reports to leave Indiana. Four

times had he moved since his first marriage and in point
of worldly goods he was no better off than when he first
started in life. His land groaned under the weight of a
long neglected encumbrance, and like many of his neighbors he was ready for another change. Having disposed of
his eighty acres of land to Charles Grigsby for one hundred
and twenty-five dollars and his corn and hogs to his friend
David Turnham (the corn bringing ten cents a bushel and
the hogs being 'lumped'), he loaded his household goods
into a wagon drawn by two yoke of oxen and with his
family set out early in March, 1830, for the prairies of
central Illinois. The emigrant party comprised thirteen
persons and included Thomas and Sarah Bush Lincoln,
their two sons, Abraham Lincoln and John D. Johnston;
Squire Hall, his wife, Matilda Johnston, and son, John;
Dennis Hanks, his wife, Elizabeth Johnston, and four children: Sarah J., Nancy M., Harriet A., and John T. Hall and
Hanks had married the two daughters of Mrs. Lincoln.

"The journey was long and tedious, the streams swol-
len and the roads muddy almost to the point of impassa-
bility. The rude wagon with its primitive wooden wheels
creaked and groaned as it crawled through the woods
and now and then stalled in the mud. Many were the de-
lays, but none ever disturbed the equanimity of its passengers. They were cheerful in the face of adversity hope-
ful and determined; but none of them more so than the
ungainly youth in buckskin breeches and coonskin cap
who wielded the gad and urged the patient oxen forward.
As they entered the new State little did the curious people
in the various towns and villages through which they
passed dream that the obscure and penniless driver who

yelled his commands to the dumb oxen was destined to become the Chief Magistrate of the greatest nation of modern times."

As agreed upon by the authorities of Indiana and Illinois, the route through the two States leads as follows: In Indiana from Gentryville northward through Dale to Jasper; thence northwestwardly to Petersburg, thence to Vincennes. At the latter place the Wabash was crossed and they pushed on to Lawrenceville, Illinois; thence northwestwardly again to Palestine, York, and Darwin, where they left the Wabash and traveled northwestwardly again passing Richwoods, Dead Man's Grove in Coles County, Nelson in Moultrie County, finally reaching their destination, a few miles west of Decatur in Macon County, Illinois.

Here it was they pitched their tent. Abe helped John Hanks split the rails that brought him fame, and in various ways made himself useful. Realizing that he had attained manhood, he now began to measure himself along with other people. His family, all things considered, were indeed a sorry lot — his father poor, inert, and devoid of ambition and the other members equally dull, improvident, and shiftless. To be forced to spend the remainder of his days amid such unpalatable surroundings was a proposition from which he recoiled with feelings of commingled antipathy and regret. As he reasoned, other places existed where he could better his environment. The truth is the young eagle was anxious to try his wings! Therefore when he realized that his kindred, the ill-starred emigrants from Indiana, were now comfortably and, as he hoped, permanently settled, he left them, pushing on to another locality far enough away to avoid their illiterate if not unwelcome companionship.

It will not do to leave the impression that Lincoln was selfish and indifferent to the wants of his family. He never sought to evade the obligation to care for his father and stepmother — in fact, one of his last acts before leaving for Washington to be inaugurated President in February, 1861, was to visit his stepmother at Charleston, Illinois, and leave with her a generous sum of money to lighten the burden of her declining years and thus insure her every comfort. Likewise the letter by Lincoln to his stepbrother, John D. Johnston, in January, 1851, which Herndon caused to be published, forever dispels the imputation that he was callous or indifferent to the needs of his father.

And yet, although Thomas Lincoln lived for over twenty years in Coles County, Illinois, and within seventy-five miles of Springfield, he never visited his son there and, so far as is known, was never in the town. When Mr. Lincoln was wedded to Mary Todd, in November, 1842, not one of his kindred was present. Whether they were invited or not has never been determined. An idea of the moral and social status of the Hankses and Johnstons who formed Thomas Lincoln's household, and in whose company his son Abraham grew to manhood, may be gleaned from incidents suggested to me by Herndon and which I carefully investigated.

In a statement furnished to Herndon in 1865, Thomas L. D. Johnston, the son of Lincoln's stepbrother, John D. Johnston, says: "Mr. Lincoln took a fancy to my younger brother also named Abraham; wanted him to come to

HOUSE NEAR FARMINGTON, ILLINOIS, IN WHICH THOMAS LINCOLN LIVED, AND WHERE HE DIED IN 1851

Springfield, live at Lincoln's home, and go to school so as to get a fair start in the world; but when Mrs. Lincoln was consulted she objected so bitterly her husband was obliged to write to my brother and tell him the plan could not be carried out because of domestic opposition. He offered, however, to give my brother money to pay for his books and the schooling he received at home. He died in 1861 at the age of twenty-two."

Another episode came to me through Henry C. Whitney, who was a close friend of Mr. Lincoln, and for years a lawyer in Urbana, Illinois, later removing to Chicago. I investigated the story and learned that Mr. Whitney's version was fully corroborated by the court and county records.

"In the summer of 1856," he related, "when Mr. Lincoln was one of the electors-at-large on the Frémont presidential ticket, a boy was assisting a man to drive some horses to the northern part of Illinois. They stopped overnight at Champaign, and while there the boy went to a small watchmaker's shop, kept by an old and decrepit man named Green, upon an errand and managed to purloin a watch. The theft was discovered in time to cause the boy's arrest at the next stopping-place. He was brought before my father, a justice of the peace, and the case being made out the boy was committed; but the boy had asked that the case be held open till he could send for his uncle Abraham Lincoln to defend him. Meanwhile he was committed to jail to await the action of the grand jury.

"Not long after this occurrence I attended a meeting held at Urbana, the county seat at which Mr. Lincoln was one of the speakers. When he saw me he called me aside and whispered: 'There is a boy in your jail I want to see, but I don't want any one beside yourself to know it. I wish you would speak to the jailer and have him arrange to admit yourself and me to the jail after this meeting is over.' I then recalled the crippled boy, whereupon Lincoln explained that when his father married his second wife she had a son about his own age — John D. Johnston — and that they were raised together, slept together, and loved each other like brothers. The crippled boy was a son of that foster-brother and was rapidly going to the bad. 'He is under a charge of stealing a gun at Charleston,' said Lincoln sadly, 'and I'm going to help him out of these two cases, but that's the last. After that if he wants to continue his thieving I shall do nothing more for him.'

"The jail was a rude log cabin structure in which prisoners were put in through a trapdoor in the second story, there being no other entrance. So Lincoln and I were admitted into the small enclosure surrounding the jail, and as we approached the one-foot square hole through which we could converse with the prisoner, he heard us and set up a hypocritical wailing and thrust out toward us a very dirty Bible which Lincoln took and turned over the leaves mechanically. He then said: 'Where were you going, Tom?' The latter attempted to reply, but his wailing made it incoherent, so Lincoln cut it short by saying: 'Now, Tom, do what they tell you — behave yourself — don't talk to any one, and when court closes I will be here and see what I can do for you. Now stop crying and behave yourself.' And with a few more words we left. Lincoln was very sad; in fact I never saw him more so.

"At the fall term of the court Amzi McWilliams, the prosecuting attorney, agreed with us that if the Greens would come into court and state that they did not desire to press the case further he would file a *nolle pros*. That same evening Lincoln and others were to speak in a church in Champaign, and at my suggestion Lincoln and I left the meeting and made our way to the house where the Greens lived. They were a venerable old couple and we found them seated in their humble kitchen greatly astonished at our visit. I introduced Lincoln, who explained his position and wishes in the matter in a homely, plain way, and the good old couple assented. The next day they came into court and formally expressed themselves willing that the boy should be released, which, as the records of the court will show, was promptly done."

I cannot pass from the subject of Lincoln's family in the early days without mention of one member whom I personally knew and from whose lips I learned much that has escaped biographers and historians save what she imparted to Herndon. I refer to Harriet Chapman, a daughter of Dennis Hanks, who became the wife of Augustus H. Chapman and who died not long since in Charleston, Illinois, being past eighty years of age. The lady in her youth was for a time a member of Abraham Lincoln's household in Springfield. It was not long after Mr. Lincoln's marriage to Mary Todd when the children were still small. Mr. Lincoln had invited her to come to Springfield and make her home with him, with which generous invitation she finally complied. For the benefit of the author, who visited her at her home in Charleston several times, she described her departure and journey from the latter place to Springfield. Lincoln had been attending court in Charleston, and after the adjournment he drove to the home of Dennis Hanks from which point he and the girl set out for Springfield. The conveyance was a wheeled vehicle, a buggy, perhaps, drawn by a bay mare which Lincoln assured his fellow passenger he had named Belle. Sometimes, he said, he called her Queen. The ride through to their destination consumed parts of two days. Mrs. Chapman's account of the journey and her recollections of her home with the Lincolns was an entertaining and in some respects an amusing chapter. Her purpose was to attend school while in Springfield, and she lived with the Lincolns as a member of the household for about a year and a half; but in time her relations with Mrs. Lincoln became so strained, if not intolerable, she found it a relief at last to withdraw and return to her home at Charleston. The letters she wrote to Mr. Herndon between 1865 and 1868, and which are still in my possession, afford such characteristic and relevant glimpses into Lincoln's home life after his marriage to Mary Todd that I venture to quote a few lines.

In a letter written at Charleston, Illinois, November 21, 1866, she says: "You ask me how Mr. Lincoln acted at home. I can say, and that truly, he was all that a husband, father, and neighbor should be. Always kind and affectionate to his wife and child (Bob being the only one when I was with them) and very pleasant to all about him. Never did I hear him utter an unkind word to any one. For instance, one day he undertook to correct his child and his wife was determined that he should not, and attempted to take it from him; but in this she failed.

She tried tongue-lashing, but met with the same fate, for Mr. Lincoln corrected his child, as a father ought to, in the face of his wife's anger, and that too without changing his countenance once or making any reply to her. His favorite way of reading when at home was lying on the floor. I fancy I see him now lying full length in the hall of his old home. He would turn a chair down on the floor with a pillow on it. He was very fond of reading poetry and would often, when he appeared to be in a brown study, commence reading aloud 'The Burial of Sir John Moore,' and so on. He often told laughable jokes and stories when he thought we were looking sad and gloomy." The letter contains this additional paragraph: "Anything I can tell you regarding Mr. Lincoln will be cheerfully given, but I would rather omit further mention of his wife, as I could say but little in her favor."

In a letter dated December 10, 1866, she writes: "'Mr. Lincoln was remarkably fond of children. One of his greatest pleasures when at home was that of nursing and playing with his little boy. He was what I would call a hearty eater and enjoyed a good meal of victuals as much as any one I ever knew. I have often heard him say that he could eat corn cakes as fast as two women could make them, although his table at home was set very sparingly. Mrs. Lincoln was very economical; so much so that by some she might have been pronounced stingy. Mr. Lincoln seldom ever wore his coat when in the house at home and often went to the table in his shirt-sleeves, which practice greatly annoyed his wife who, by the way, loved to put on style."

# CHAPTER V

Lincoln's several proposals of marriage — Story of his failure to join Mary Todd at the Edwards home, January, 1841 — His letter to John T. Stuart — Invitation to John Hanks — Preparations for the marriage to Mary Todd — The story of the wedding — Judge Browne's amusing interruption — Conflicting views of Springfield people — Writer's visit to and interview with Ninian W. Edwards and wife — Refusal of Mrs. Simeon Francis to tell her story.

BEFORE I undertake to consider Lincoln as a lawyer, I venture to digress slightly in order that I may acquaint the reader with some of the things I have learned about him in another rôle. Adverting to the story of his activity and experience in the field of matrimony leads me to state that the honor which would have been Ann Rutledge's had she lived, and that Mary Owens and Sarah Rickard successively declined, was finally accepted by Mary Todd. Of all the women, contended Herndon, to whom Mr. Lincoln paid marked or serious attention, Mary Todd was, by far, the strongest, from an intellectual standpoint, and the most accomplished generally; and it only remains to add that she was also the only one whose keen vision penetrated the future and beheld in the homely face and awkward figure of her tall suitor the man of destiny.

No episode in Lincoln's life has occasioned greater diversity of opinion among the people of Springfield than the story of his marriage to Mary Todd as told by Herndon, who, in his account of the wedding, which was first scheduled to take place January 1, 1841, relates: "Nothing was lacking but the groom. For some strange reason he had been delayed. An hour passed and the guests as well as the bride were becoming restless. But they were all doomed to disappointment. Another hour passed;

messengers were sent out over town and, each returning with the same report, it became apparent that Lincoln, the principal in this little drama, had purposely failed to appear! The bride, in grief, disappeared to her room; the wedding supper was left untouched; the guests quietly and wonderingly withdrew; the lights in the Edwards mansion were blown out, and darkness settled over all for the night. What the feelings of a lady as sensitive, passionate, and proud as Miss Todd were we can only imagine — no one can describe them. By daybreak, after persistent search, Lincoln's friends found him. Restless, gloomy, miserable, desperate, he seemed an object of pity. His friends, Speed among the number, fearing a tragic termination, watched him closely in their rooms day and night. Knives and razors and every instrument that could be used for self-destruction were removed from his reach. . . . His condition began to improve after a few weeks, and a letter written to his partner, John T. Stuart, January 23, 1841, three weeks after the scene at the Edwards house, reveals more perfectly how he felt. He says: 'I am now the most miserable man living. If what I feel were equally distributed to the whole human family, there would not be one cheerful face on earth. Whether I shall ever be better, I cannot tell; I awfully forebode I shall not. To remain as I am is impossible. I must die or be better, as it appears to me. I fear I shall be unable to attend to any business here and a change of scene might help me. If I could be myself I would rather remain at home with Judge Logan. I can write no more.' "

Concerning this unusual if not dramatic episode in Lincoln's life, as described by Herndon, there remains but little for me to say. In view of the divided sentiment among the Springfield people regarding it I can only assure the reader that I have no theory of my own to establish, and shall content myself by presenting as briefly as I can such facts as I have been able to gather in an honest and impartial endeavor to ascertain the truth.

As shown by the records of Sangamon County, Illinois, Abraham Lincoln and Mary Todd were married in Springfield, Friday, November 4, 1842. Nowadays the average couple would shirk from plighting their vows on such an unlucky day as Friday, but to this pair the day had no such terrors. The ceremony took place at the residence of Ninian W. Edwards whose wife was an elder sister of Miss Todd. It was here that the latter had made her home since her arrival from Kentucky in 1839. The groom had passed his thirty-third birthday and his bride was approaching her twenty-fourth. None of Mr. Lincoln's immediate family, including his father, stepmother, stepbrother and stepsisters, all of whom lived in Coles County, distant about seventy-five miles, were present. Whether invited or not no one seems to know. The only invitation emanating from Lincoln of which I ever heard was the following characteristic note sent by him to his favorite cousin, John Hanks, who lived near the town of Decatur and who was his companion on the famous flatboat expedition to New Orleans in 1831:

DEAR JOHN —
  I am to be married on the 4th of next month to Miss Todd. I hope you will come over. Be sure to be on deck by early candle light.                    Yours

                                        A. LINCOLN

I did not see this note in the original. A lady living near Decatur, and who said she was a granddaughter of John Hanks, furnished me a copy.

The marriage of Mr. Lincoln and Miss Todd was solemnized by the Reverend Charles Dresser, the first Episcopalian clergyman to settle in Springfield. It was also among the earliest services there in accordance with the Episcopalian ritual; for Parson Dresser had officiated at only eight marriages prior to this one. Of course all the participants as well as all the witnesses have passed away. Until recently one of the latter, the late Dr. William Jayne, was still living in Springfield. He was a boy at the time, and though not an invited guest was sent to the house where the marriage took place the evening of the wedding and saw the guests as they arrived. The groom had two best men or attendants in the persons of James H. Matheney, a deputy in the county clerk's office — later county judge — and Beverly Powell, salesman in the leading store, very popular and conceded to be the best-dressed man in town. A few years later he returned to his birthplace in Kentucky. The maids of honor attending the bride were Miss Julia Jayne, afterwards the wife of Lyman Trumbull, United States Senator, and Miss Anne Rodney, sister of the wife of William L. May, formerly Congressman from the Springfield district.

In my time it has been my privilege to meet and interview a number of persons, both men and women, who witnessed the marriage, but the most accurate and trustworthy account of what took place on that now memorable occasion is the recollection of James H. Matheney, who, as stated, was Mr. Lincoln's close friend as well as groomsman. During my sojourn in Springfield many years ago I spent more than one pleasant afternoon with Judge Matheney. In the flower of his manhood he was in complete possession of all his faculties, and the facts were so fresh and so rigidly fixed in his mind he could recall with ease the minutest detail. Although generous in imparting his information, he had but one reservation and that was to refrain from making public some things he had communicated to me so long as he and the widow of Lincoln survived. As both have since passed away there can be no impropriety in putting on record the facts thus obtained.

The marriage was originally set for a day in the winter of 1840–41, probably New Year's Day, and Judge Matheney always insisted that he had been asked to serve as groomsman then; but Lincoln, for reasons unnecessary to detail here, having failed to materialize at the appointed time, an estrangement naturally followed and he was no longer enshrined in the affections of Miss Todd or *persona grata* at the Edwards home where, for a long time, she had been living. Without delving further into the merits of this luckless and regrettable episode, it suffices to add that in the course of time, through the intercession of the wife of Simeon Francis, editor of the "Springfield Journal," a reconciliation was effected and the couple duly brought together. Meanwhile, at frequent intervals, they were meeting each other as before, but never at the Edwards residence and probably without the knowledge of the Edwards family.

When the marriage was set for a second time it was planned to have it solemnized by the pastor at his own house in the presence of a few close friends; but a day or so before the appointed time, when Mr. Edwards first heard of it, he hunted up Lincoln and earnestly protested on the ground that he was the natural protector of Miss Todd; that she was in reality a member of his family, and that the marriage ceremony should take place, if at all, at his home. After some argument Lincoln and Miss Todd were finally won over to his view of the case; but the time was short, and there was great activity and hurried preparations at the Edwards mansion in consequence.

At that early day Springfield, although the capital of the State, could not boast of a confectioner, and the regulation caterer had not yet come into vogue. The town had two so-called bakeries, one being a concern operated by John Dickey whose leading products were "gingerbread and beer." Of course a bride's cake must grace the wedding supper, but as the two bakeries were scarcely able within the required time to produce one suited to the occasion, recourse was had elsewhere. As a last resort the services of a lady renowned for her skill in that line, the wife of a Springfield lawyer, were secured, and in due time a cake of the regulation size and quality decked the festal board. Meanwhile, in view of the limited hours ahead, certain other essentials were assigned to willing and helpful hands, so that, as we are assured by a lady who was present, "Mrs. Edwards, despite the hurry, had provided an elegant and bountiful supper, and the wedding itself was pretty, simple, and impressive."

The attendance was limited, probably not over forty persons being present. "For a time after the guests arrived," related Judge Matheney, "there was more or less stiffness about the affair due, no doubt, to the sudden change of plans and resulting 'town talk,' and I could not help noticing a certain amount of whispering and elevation of eyebrows on the part of a few of the guests, as if preparing each other for something dramatic or unlooked-for to happen. Things moved awkwardly — at least not naturally — until, during the ceremony, an interruption occurred so unusual and amusing it broke the ice, diverting the attention of the guests so effectually that the rest of the evening passed off literally as 'merry as a marriage bell.' In the company was a man named Thomas C. Browne, one of the judges of the Supreme Court of the State. He was a Tennesseean by birth, of the rough-and-ready order, corpulent as Falstaff, vain, coarse, and effusive. Despite his want of refinement, due to the lack of early training, he was, nevertheless, a good lawyer and a capable judge. During the ceremony, as provided by the ritual of the Episcopalian Church, Lincoln, the groom, placed the wedding ring on the bride's finger reciting very deliberately after the rector the words; 'With this ring I thee wed, and with all my worldly goods I thee endow.' To Browne, who stood near Lincoln and who, doubtless, had never before witnessed so elaborate and impressive a ceremony, the proceeding was ridiculous if not absurd; for, in a voice loud enough to be heard over the room, he blurted out, 'Lord A'mighty, Lincoln, the law fixes that!'"

And now at last, after numerous vicissitudes and strange chapters, Abraham Lincoln was safely married. A few days later he apprised his old friend Joshua F. Speed, then living in Louisville, and who, more than any other man, knew the inside of his courtship with Mary Todd,

JOSHUA F. SPEED AND HIS WIFE

of the auspicious beginning of his new life. "We are not keeping house," writes Lincoln, "but boarding at the Globe Tavern, which is very well kept by a widow lady of the name of Beck. Our room and boarding only costs us four dollars a week."

Mr. Herndon's version of the Lincoln-Todd courtship and wedding, as I have already stated, had the effect of evoking from many people in Springfield bitter criticism for his lack of taste in making the disclosure, and in some cases stout denial. The story first appeared in Ward Lamon's "Life of Lincoln," in which it was alleged that Lincoln disappointed Miss Todd, whom he had promised to wed, by failing to appear at the time and place agreed upon; that this led to an estrangement between them and that they remained apart for over a year or until reunited through the diplomatic instrumentality of Mrs. Francis. When I was in Springfield Herndon told me the story substantially as it appeared in the Lamon book and then advised me to interview Ninian Edwards and wife, both of whom were living and would no doubt communicate the facts as they recalled them. Accordingly a few days later, in obedience to the suggestion of Herndon, I visited the Edwards residence and found both husband and wife at home. This is what my diary records:

Thursday, Dec. 20, 1883.

Called on N. W. Edwards and wife. Asked about marriage Mary Todd to Lincoln — Mrs. E. said arrangements for wedding made — even cakes baked but Lincoln failed to appear. At this point Mr. Edwards interrupted — cautioned wife she was talking to newspaper man — she declined to say more — had said Mary greatly mortified by Mr. Lincoln's strange conduct. Later were reunited — finally married.

Herndon also furnished me the address of Mrs. Simeon Francis, who was then living in Oregon, and recommended that I apply to her for further information, as in view of her connection with the episode she could if she so desired relate the facts exactly as they occurred so that posterity might know the truth. Thus encouraged I wrote the lady three different times, reciting the story as it emanated from Herndon and others, and urging her in the interest of history to indicate whether Lincoln in his suit for the hand of Mary Todd had ignored the promise to meet her at the hymeneal altar on "that fatal 1st of January, 1841," or otherwise deceived her. She acknowledged the receipt of my letters, but in each case declined to deny the story or further enlighten me regarding the subject, on the ground that, as Lincoln and his wife were both dead, she felt a delicacy in disclosing to the world all the details of their courtship. I still have her letters.

# CHAPTER VI

Lincoln's attitude toward the ladies — His attentions to Sarah Rickard — What Mary Owens said about him — His conduct in the parlor — The stag literary society — How he, with the aid of Evan Butler and James Matheney, punished the drunken shoemaker — His bashfulness — Whitney's account of his embarrassment before the ladies at Urbana — The evening at Norman B. Judd's residence — What Mrs. Judd recollected — Lincoln's break at the concert — His attentions to the lady performer — What Davis and Swett said to him about it — His reply.

JUDGED by the literature of the day thus far, the world seemingly has come to the conclusion that Lincoln was both an ideal lover and a model husband, and yet, if history can be depended upon, it does not always happen that a man so profoundly intellectual as he was makes an exemplary husband or in every case an adorable and satisfactory lover. He may be princely in demeanor and angelic in temperament, but, in the language of a lady to whom Lincoln himself once offered his hand, he is generally "deficient in those little links that make up the chain of a woman's happiness."

While Lincoln was far from the conventional ladies' man, yet no one more deeply appreciated the charms of female society. It was David Davis who said that on more than one occasion he had heard Lincoln "thank God that he was not born a woman." Now when Lincoln said this he had in mind his own sympathetic and pliant nature, and he therefore feared himself when subjected to the plausible arguments and persuasive influences which, it is said, so often sweep a woman off her feet. This line of reasoning may, perhaps, serve to indicate the esteem in which he held woman's will and powers of resistance; but in saying what he did he certainly underrated his own strength and inflexibility, for we know that, when put to the test, no man ever lived who could say "no" more readily and abide by his decision with more resolution and firmness.

No doubt he longed for and enjoyed the attrition of social contact, and that included the company of the ladies, but even then we know he managed to hold himself in strict repression. Although a matchless story-teller and in other respects admirably entertaining, he was never prominent in the social life of early Springfield; but whether this was due to his shortcomings in the parlor and ballroom, his self-conscious lack of training generally, or to pure indifference, it is difficult to determine. Springfield, it should be remembered, though no larger or more important than the average inland prairie town in the early days of the West, had its aristocracy and social barriers as distinct and formidable as they are to-day. Evidence in support of this statement is found in a letter which Mr. Herndon once loaned me, written by Lincoln to Mary S. Owens, whose hand he sought in marriage. "There is a great deal of flourishing about in carriages here," he writes, "which it would be your doom to see without sharing in it. You would have to be poor without the means of hiding your poverty. Do you believe you could bear that patiently?"

In addition to Ann Rutledge, whose melancholy history, but for the indefatigable and exhaustive researches of Mr. Herndon, would probably never have been preserved, we know that, besides Mary Todd, Lincoln proposed also to Mary S. Owens and Sarah Rickard. With the story of one of these *affaires de cœur* I am somewhat familiar, because through the assistance of Mr. Herndon I was enabled to obtain the desired information from original sources, for at that time the lady interested was living and easy of access. In her interview she related that Mr. Lincoln was an unusually interesting talker with many winning and even fascinating traits. Just how ardent and demonstrative in his professions of love he was, the lady's intuitive modesty restrained her from indicating; but she insisted that in his conduct toward her no one could have been more thoughtful and considerate. He was delicate and attentive to the point of gallantry; made her several beautiful presents; attended her at numerous social functions and escorted her to the various public entertainments of the period. She recalled their having witnessed a dramatization or rendition of "The Babes in the Wood," and he accompanied her to the first real theatrical performance, with the regulation stage and curtain, ever given in Springfield. Her name being Sarah, Lincoln, in pressing his suit, urged that because the Sarah of Bible times became the wife of Abraham, therefore, she, Sarah Rickard, in view of that precedent, was foreordained to marry Abraham Lincoln! Droll and curious though this argument was, the lady admitted that it was not without some weight in her own mind, but that it failed eventually to win her consent because of the objection of an elder sister who contended that she was too young to think seriously of matrimony. But even that probably was not the real reason; for, in a letter from her which now lies before me, Sarah herself says: "Mr. Lincoln became daily more attentive and I found I was beginning to like him;

but you know his peculiar manner and general deportment would not be likely to fascinate a young lady entering the society world."

In this connection it will not be out of order to mention
that Joshua F. Speed, who was Lincoln's confidant in the
affair with Mary Todd, furnished Herndon, after Lincoln's death, with copies of all the letters the latter had
written him regarding that strange and tempestuous courtship. In transmitting the copies Speed asked that the
name of a certain lady which was frequently mentioned
therein should be omitted in case the letters ever became
public. In due time they appeared in Lamon's "Life of
Lincoln," but the name was carefully withheld. Not long
since among some other papers I found Speed's original
letter and thus learned that the name in question was
"Sarah." In all probability it was Sarah Rickard, but
why Speed wanted it omitted I have never been able to
learn.

It is hardly fair to assume, because he spent his
early days in the backwoods, that Lincoln was boorish
or lacked the essentials of true politeness, and yet his
conduct and bearing on some occasions were hardly calculated to win a woman's sincere admiration and approval.
This is very clearly demonstrated by an incident narrated
by Mary Owens, one of the two ladies to whom fate
reserved the distinction of having declined Lincoln's
hand. "On one occasion," she writes in a letter to Herndon, "we were going to a party at Uncle Billy Greene's.
Mr. Lincoln was riding with me and we had a bad branch
to cross. The other gentlemen were very officious in seeing that their partners got safely over. We were behind,

SARAH RICKARD

MARY S. OWENS

he riding in, never looking back to see how I got along. When I rode up behind him I remarked: 'You are a nice fellow! I suppose you did not care whether my neck was broken or not.' He laughingly replied (by way of compliment, I suppose) that he knew I was plenty smart to take care of myself."

Now Lincoln doubtless thought he was paying Miss Owens a delicate compliment when he credited her with "spunk" and judgment enough to look out for herself; but evidently the latter, whose notions of etiquette and propriety came from the refined associations of a wealthy Kentucky home, was not inclined to view his inattention in such a generous and forbearing light. And yet here is what she said of him in a letter to Herndon after Lincoln's death: "In many things Mr. Lincoln was sensitive to a fault. He told me this incident: He was crossing a prairie one day and saw before him a hog 'mired down,' to use his own language. He was rather 'fixed up' and resolved that he would pass on without looking at the shoat. After he had gone the feeling was irresistible and he had to look back; and the poor thing seemed to say wistfully: 'There, my last hope is gone!' Whereupon he got down and promptly relieved it from its difficulty."

While Lincoln has left us practically nothing from his pen by which to fix his real estimate of womankind, yet it cannot be truthfully said we are entirely without other sources of information. For instance, we know that, although given to the narration of an endless array of amusing and oftentimes equivocal stories, no man ever heard him question or reflect upon the "good name or fair fame" of any individual woman. He detested and never would repeat neighborhood scandal. The savory morsels which some people find so toothsome and delicious under their tongues were wholly unpalatable to him. If he happened to narrate a story in which the wit or weakness of woman was a factor, it was invariably located in the wilds of Kentucky or southern Indiana or some other region equally remote. Besides, the story itself was so ingeniously told and the point or moral so obvious and suggestive, no one present could identify the heroine by name because no name was used or needed. Thus, it will be observed the reputation of every woman he knew was safe in his hands.

In the winter of 1838, along with Evan Butler, James Matheney, Milton Hay — John Hay's uncle — and other habitués of the court-house, Lincoln joined in organizing a debating or literary society which met, usually in the clerk's office, once and sometimes twice a month. It was strictly a stag affair, the ladies not being represented. Among other things a poem was contributed by Mr. Lincoln. Its title, if it had any, has been forgotten, but James Matheney, who served as secretary, was able when I last saw him to recall a few verses. Here is one stanza which I have in his handwriting:

"Whatever spiteful fools may say,
Each jealous ranting yelper,
No woman ever went astray
Without a man to help her."

Notwithstanding his characteristically indulgent and forbearing nature, Herndon always contended that Lincoln had less charity or patience than the average person for the man who abused his wife or in any other way ignored his marriage vows. Not far from Hoffman's Row, the building in Springfield in which the early courts were held, lived a shoemaker who was given to the rather free use of intoxicants and who almost invariably wound up a spree by whipping his wife. One day Lincoln called the fellow aside, upbraided him for his brutality, and then admonished him that if he ever laid violent hands on his wife again a drubbing would be administered so vigorous he would not soon forget it. Meanwhile he apprised Evan Butler and James Matheney of his threat and invited them to join him in dealing out the requisite punishment if the offense should be repeated. "In due time," related Matheney to me, "the contingency arose. The drunken shoemaker had forgotten Lincoln's warning. It was late at night and we dragged the wretch to an open space back of a store building, stripped him of his shirt and tied him to a post. Then we sent for his wife, and arming her with a good stout switch bade her to 'light in' while the three of us sat on our haunches in solemn array near by to witness the execution of our judgment. The wife, a little reluctant at first, soon warmed up to her work, and emboldened by our encouraging and sometimes peremptory directions, performed her delicate task lustily and well. When the culprit had been sufficiently punished, Lincoln gave the signal 'Enough,' and he was released; we helped him on with his shirt and he shambled ruefully toward his home. For his sake we tried to keep all knowledge of the affair from the public; but the lesson had its effect, for if he ever again molested his wife we never found it out."

No better illustration of how Mr. Lincoln appeared socially, or rather how he demeaned himself in ladies'

company, is obtainable than the two incidents which
follow, and which, while emphasizing some of his singular
and characteristic traits, are also noteworthy in that they
come from truthful and unquestioned sources. One of
them was communicated to me both verbally and in writing by the late Henry C. Whitney. The testimony of this
witness, with whom I spent many hours in Chicago after
he had removed from Urbana, and who verified so much
that Herndon had told me, is of the highest value, because, for almost ten years prior to Lincoln's election to
the Presidency in 1860, he was much of the time in the
latter's company as the two made their way from county
to county on the circuit. "I well recollect," said Whitney, "that Mr. Lincoln was invited to join me and my
wife at tea one evening at the residence of Mr. Boyden,
the mayor of Urbana. He was in good spirits and seemed
to be at perfect ease during the meal and afterwards,
while I was in the room; but later I was called out for a
short time to meet a client who was awaiting me at the
front gate. When I returned, the party, meanwhile, having adjourned to the parlor, Mr. Lincoln's bearing and
manner had entirely changed; for some unexplained reason he was laboring under the most painful embarrassment
and appeared to be as demoralized and ill at ease as a
bashful country boy. Drawn up in his chair and gazing
alternately at the floor and ceiling, he would put his arms
behind him and then bring them to the front again as if
endeavoring in some way to hide them; meanwhile struggling, though in vain, to keep his long legs out of sight.
His discomfiture was so plain and unmistakable I could
not help pitying the poor fellow, and yet I could not

understand it unless it was because he was alone in a room with three women, for no one was present but Mrs. Boyden, my wife, and her mother." Evidently Sarah Rickard, who had declined to marry Lincoln, was not without a woman's intuitive discernment when she protested to Herndon that the former's "peculiar manner and general deportment were not calculated to fascinate a young lady entering the society world."

The second incident, which describes Lincoln under similar circumstances on another occasion, is equally well authenticated besides narrated by a woman herself. In September, 1857, Lincoln was in Chicago attending the United States Circuit Court where he was engaged in the trial of the noted Rock Island Bridge case. During his stay there he was invited to spend an evening at the home of Norman B. Judd, one of his valued friends, a lawyer and associated in the same case. Several ladies were present. What occurred and how Lincoln bore himself is so graphically and entertainingly told in an account written many years ago for Herndon by the wife of Mr. Judd, I feel that the portrait of Lincoln which I am trying to draw would be incomplete without it. After announcing the fact of Mr. Lincoln's arrival and describing the surroundings — they were sitting on the piazza in plain view of Lake Michigan with the full moon throwing "a flood of silvery light upon the dancing waves" — the writer undertakes to indicate the effect of the scene on her visitor.

"Mr. Lincoln, whose home," she writes, "was far inland from the Great Lakes, seemed stirred by the wondrous beauty of the scene and by its very impressiveness was carried away from all thoughts of the earth. In that

high-pitched but smooth-toned voice he began to speak of
the mystery which for ages enshrouded and shut out those
distant worlds above us from our own; of the poetry and
beauty which was seen and felt by seers of old when they
contemplated Orion and Arcturus as they wheeled seemingly around the earth in their mighty course; of the discoveries since the invention of the telescope which had
thrown a flood of light and knowledge on what before
was incomprehensible and mysterious; of the wonderful
computations of scientists who had measured the miles of
seemingly endless space which separated the planets in
our solar system from our central sun and our sun from
other suns which were now gemming the heavens above us
with their resplendent beauty.

"When the night air became too chilly to remain longer
on the piazza, we went into the parlor where, seated on
the sofa his long limbs stretching across the carpet and
his arms folded about him, Mr. Lincoln went on to speak
of the discoveries and inventions which had been made
during the long lapse of time between the present and
those early days when man began to make use of the material things about him. He speculated upon the possibilities of the knowledge which an increased power of the
lens would give in the years to come, and then the wonderful discoveries of late centuries, as proving that beings
endowed with such capabilities as man must be immortal
and created for some high and noble end by Him who had
spoken these numberless worlds into existence.

"We were all indescribably impressed," continues Mrs.
Judd, "by Mr. Lincoln's conversation. After he had gone
Mr. Judd remarked: 'The more I see of Mr. Lincoln the

more I am surprised at the range of his attainments and the wonderful store of knowledge he has acquired in the various departments of science and learning during the years of his constant labor at the bar. A professor at Yale could not have been more entertaining and instructive.'"

Lincoln was never oracular, though when not unduly embarrassed he was easily the leader in conversation. Like all truly great men he was a good listener. He loved to slip away from his fellow lawyers, while out on the circuit, to attend a concert, panorama, or other like entertainment at the town hall or academy. He had an insatiable fondness for negro minstrelsy and seemed to extract the greatest delight from the crude jokes and harmless fun of the black-faced and red-lipped performers. Frequently, as if awakened from a spell of abstraction by something exuberantly funny, he would blurt out in a laugh louder than any one around him. Herndon told me that he and Lincoln, on their way homeward from the office one night, passed a public hall in which a church or benevolent society was giving an entertainment. They decided to go in. Although they entered the room at the same time, they were not seated together — Lincoln having slid over to a seat next to the wall and somewhat in the rear. Among other things on the programme they heard for the first time the story of "Miss Flora McFlimsy With Nothing to Wear" rendered by an elocutionist. The piece, then newly published and rather popular, was a long one, containing over three hundred lines of rhyme. In one place near the middle and not intended to be especially humorous, some one in the audience broke out in a guffaw, as loud as it was sudden and unexpected. Everybody turned in his seat and gazed in the direction whence the disturbance came. There sat Lincoln looking sheepish and guilty. Something in the piece had struck his funny-bone and, despite his surroundings, had forced the interruption from him. Realizing that every eye was now focused on him he slid down in his seat and blushed like a school-girl.

Mr. Whitney told me that a company of singers known as the Newhall Family traveled over Illinois in *antebellum* times giving concerts. "If they struck a town where Lincoln happened to be," said Whitney, "he would invariably arrange his affairs so that he could be at the church or town hall in time to attend their entertainment. No trial, consultation, or business engagement of any kind was allowed to interfere. To most of us the thing for a time seemed more or less strange until finally the real reason developed. It was Lincoln's predilection for a woman. One of the performers was a Mrs. Hillis. She was not especially prepossessing in appearance, although a good singer, but she had somewhere made the acquaintance of Lincoln and appeared to manifest a decided fancy for him. She would give him a smile of recognition if she saw him in the audience, and the two often were seen talking to each other if they chanced to meet, as they sometimes did, at the tavern or elsewhere. The attraction was a little unusual for Lincoln, who was particularly thoughtful in matters of that kind. Finally when Judge Davis, Leonard Swett, and others equally close to him became aware of it, they began to prod him about it and with mock gravity ventured to remind him of his duty as

a married man, the danger of entangling alliances, etc.
'Don't trouble yourselves, boys,' was his retort; 'there's
no danger. She's actually the only woman in the world,
outside of my wife, who ever dared to pay me a compliment, and if the poor thing is attracted to my handsome
face and graceful figure it seems to me you homely fellows
are the last people on earth who ought to complain.'"

Mr. Whitney's account of the foregoing episode is confirmed by the testimony of no less a person than Mrs.
Hillis herself. She was, as Mr. Whitney relates, a member
of the Newhall Family, a somewhat noted company of
singers which, in the fifties, made the rounds of the various
towns in Illinois, Michigan, and Indiana, giving concerts
extending over a period, sometimes of two days, and, in
some instances, almost a week at a stretch. The troupe
consisted of the parents, two sisters, a brother, and a
brother-in-law. It was before the day of the modern railroad so that most of their traveling was done by stage or
private conveyance. After her marriage Miss Newhall, the
lady mentioned, bore the name Lois E. Hillis. Being an
accomplished musician she frequently taught music and,
late in the eighties, she communicated to William J. An-
derson, one of her pupils, an account of her experiences as
a concert performer which he promptly reduced to writing
and carefully preserved. In her reminiscences Mrs. Hillis
described her first meeting with Mr. Lincoln and how he
impressed her and her sister as well as the other members
of the concert company. She related that one evening at
the hotel where Lincoln had for some time been a so-
journer, one of the group of lawyers gathered there,
anxious for a little fun at Lincoln's expense, arose and

exclaimed: "Now, Lincoln, you have been listening to and for almost a week enjoying the delightful music produced by these ladies, and it therefore only seems fair to the rest of us that you should, in turn, entertain them by singing some of the songs for which you are already famous." Of course this demand elicited the approval of everybody present, but it only served to evoke from Lincoln a refusal to comply. He protested that he had never sung a song in his life and loudly declared that he did not propose to jeopardize his reputation as a musician by attempting it then.

"Meanwhile, my sister and I," relates Mrs. Hillis, "were anxious that Mr. Lincoln should sing. Each of us, for some reason, had taken a great liking to him. We had, it is true, heard him speak several times, but that did not impress us so much as his pleasing personality and his happy manner toward women. He listened for a while to our urgent solicitation, and then, with a threatening look at the other lawyers who were enjoying his embarrassment, he turned on his heel and announced that as the hour was late he was going upstairs to bed. There was a melodeon in the room at which I was sitting, and just as he passed I looked up into his face and said:

" 'Mr. Lincoln, if you have a song that you can sing, I know that I can play the accompaniment. If you will just tell me what it is, I can follow you even if I am not familiar with it.'

"Although visibly embarrassed, he laughed and exclaimed:

" 'Why, Miss Newhall, if it would save my soul, I could n't imitate a note that you would touch on that instrument. I never sang in my life; and those fellows know it. They are simply trying to make fun of me!'

"Noticing my disappointment, he paused a moment and said:

" 'But I 'll tell you what I am willing to do. Inasmuch as you and your sister have been so kind and entertained us so generously, I shall try to return the favor. Of course I can't produce music, but if you will be patient and brave enough to endure it, I will repeat for your benefit several stanzas of a poem of which I am particularly fond.'

"Then stepping to the doorway which led from the parlor to the stairway and leaning against the casing, for he seemed too tall for the frame, and half closing his eyes, he repeated the lines of 'O, Why Should the Spirit of Mortal Be Proud!'

"It was the first time we had ever heard Mr. Lincoln recite the poem, and it was, indeed, so impressive that when he had finished, all occasion for joking and raillery had passed away. I remember I was so deeply moved that I could scarcely restrain my tears. As he passed me on his way upstairs I ventured to ask him who wrote the poem.

" 'My dear Miss Newhall,' he answered, 'I regret to say that I do not know. But if you really like it, I will write it out for you to-night before I go to bed, and leave a copy on the table so that you may have it to read when you sit down to breakfast.'

"The next morning I was sitting at the breakfast-table eating by candlelight. I recall very distinctly that I was eating pancakes, and was in the act of cutting one, holding it with my fork while I wielded the knife, when I became conscious that some one was behind and bending over me. A big hand took hold of my left hand, covering it on the table, and with his right hand, over my shoulder, he laid down a sheet of paper covered with writing, in front of my plate. I realized it was Mr. Lincoln. He told me that he was due to leave town in a few minutes, and as he moved away, he looked back, waved his hand, exclaiming, 'Good-bye, my dear!' and passed through the door. It was the last time I ever saw him."

# CHAPTER VII

Lincoln's passion for women — How he dealt with them — Herndon's testimony — Interviewing one of Lincoln's female clients — Her story of his conduct — Lincoln on the circuit — Avoiding social functions — Fondness for concerts and like entertainments at the town hall — Accompanying Henry C. Whitney to the negro minstrel show in Chicago — Efforts of author to determine if Lincoln attended lecture by Thackeray in St. Louis — Lincoln's status as a married man — His wife's temperament and its effect on him — Her traits of character — Her management of the household — Her experience with Springfield tradesmen.

MENTION of Lincoln as a society or family man serves to recall some of the things illustrating that phase of his make-up which came to the surface before his intimates and professional brethren — the most competent of witnesses — had all passed away. Following is the written testimony of Herndon, of deep significance and value, because it is exactly as recorded by him:

"Mr. Lincoln had a strong, if not terrible passion for women. He could hardly keep his hands off a woman, and yet, much to his credit, he lived a pure and virtuous life. His idea was that a woman had as much right to violate the marriage vow as the man — no more and no less. His sense of right — his sense of justice — his honor forbade his violating his marriage vow. Judge Davis said to me in 1865, 'Mr. Lincoln's honor saved many a woman,' and this is true to the spirit. This I know on my own knowledge. I have seen Lincoln tempted and I have seen him reject the approach of woman."

In this connection I venture to relate an experience of my own. One day in Springfield I was sitting in the room which Lincoln, for a few days prior to his removal to

Washington in February, 1861, had used as an office,
when I was joined by Mr. Herndon who had asked me to
meet him there. In due time our conversation drifted toward Lincoln, a subject of such intense and engaging interest that sunset found us still absorbed in the discussion of
that great and marvelous character. Herndon did most
of the talking, nor did he manifest the slightest sign of impatience at the fusillade of curious and unusual questions
I asked him. I remember among other things how admirably he enlightened me regarding Mr. Lincoln's moral and
professional standards, his personal habits, his conduct
and bearing in court, including the narration of some of his
apt and incomparable stories. He even went so far as to
imitate Lincoln's voice and gesture in the delivery of a
speech. To me it was a revelation so vivid and fruitful I
felt, when we separated for the day, almost as if I had
been in Lincoln's presence.

"In order that you may judge of Mr. Lincoln's habits
in dealing with people professionally," said Herndon, "including his demeanor and conduct toward the fair sex, and
thus enable you to determine how near the truth my estimate of the man is, I am going to send you to a woman who
was once a client of ours and who, if you succeed in finding
her and induce her to talk, can tell you how Mr. Lincoln
behaved as a man and lawyer as well as how he treated
her." Mr. Herndon further explained that at an early day
the woman, handicapped by a shady reputation, had landed
in court charged with keeping a house of ill-repute or some
like offense, had counseled with Lincoln and himself and
retained them to represent her. "She is well along in
years," continued Herndon, "and although I have not seen

her for a long time I have been assured on reliable authority that now and for some time past she has been leading a correct and becoming life."

In compliance with Mr. Herndon's suggestion I started out in search of the woman and after diligent inquiry located her. At first, when I sought to interrogate her, she was somewhat reticent if not really unresponsive, but when I explained that Mr. Herndon had sent me to see her with the assurance that her name should not be used, she gradually relented and eventually answered all my questions. She admitted that she had employed Lincoln and Herndon to look after her interests when her case came up in court. The first thing done was to ask for a change of venue, which, having been granted, she and the witnesses, some of whom were female inmates of her own household, others sundry gentlemen of gay and sportive tendency, were obliged to travel a short distance over the country to another court. "There was a good crowd of us," she related, "and a livelier delegation never drove over the prairies. As to the behavior and actions of Mr. Lincoln, I must say it was in every respect correct so that I can recall nothing improper or out of place about it. Of course he talked to me a good deal, and for that matter to the other ladies too."

"Where and when was it he talked to you?" I asked.

"Sometimes in the office, sometimes in the court-house, and sometimes elsewhere."

"Did he ever talk with you alone?"

"Yes, I have frequently been in his office and spoken to him when no one else was there."

"What did he talk about?"

"Usually about business; also many other things that

suggested themselves. The truth is he was an interesting talker on all subjects."

"How did he conduct himself? Was he agreeable?"

"To me he seemed always a gentleman. I could see nothing wrong or unpleasant about him."

"Did you hear him tell any stories?"

"Yes; a good many."

"Were any of these stories told when you and he were alone?"

"Yes; and I remember that he told some when one or more of the ladies who accompanied me were present."

"What kind of stories were they?"

"Various kinds. Of course I can't describe them now, but I remember that they were all very much alike in one particular and that is that they were usually funny."

"Were any of them suggestive or objectionable?"

"No, I do not think they were."

"Then what would you say about their propriety; that is, would you consider what he said unfit to be told in polite society or in the company of ladies?"

The last question was evidently more or less of a tax on the old woman's memory or perhaps her conception of propriety; for she hesitated a few moments, as if buried in thought, before she answered; but she soon rallied and then responded:

"No, although some of the things he said were very amusing and made me as well as the others laugh, I do not think it would be fair to call them improper; in fact, I believe they could with safety have been told in the presence of ladies anywhere." At this point the witness halted again, but only an instant; for she promptly recovered her equanimity and concluded her testimony with the following emphatic and sententious declaration which I have never forgotten: "But that is more than I can say for Bill Herndon."

While out on the circuit the lawyers of Lincoln's day were frequently invited to spend the evening at some hospitable home, attend a ball, or take part in the various social functions of that period. Judge Davis was a frequent attendant, but Lincoln avoided them whenever he could. The interchange of ideas and small talk generally one encounters on such occasions seemed to have no charm for him. "I have known him," said Whitney, "to sit in his room all alone an entire evening while the rest of us were away at a ball or party somewhere, and when we returned we would find him rolled up and sound asleep in his bed. The only place besides the tavern or some inviting lawyer's office he cared to visit of an evening was a public entertainment at the town hall, and even in that event he would often try to slip away from the rest of us so that on his arrival there he could drop into a seat in an obscure nook or corner of the room and enjoy the show without being seen."

Mr. Lincoln's partiality for the time-honored concert or dramatic exhibition at the academy or town hall — a predilection so pronounced that David Davis and certain other friends could never agree whether it was a weakness or only a peculiarity — calls to mind another penchant of his, and that is the conventional negro minstrel show. Of this type of entertainment, which I have alluded to before, he was inordinately fond. "In the latter part of March, 1860," wrote Mr. Whitney to me several years ago, "I remember Mr. Lincoln was in Chicago attending the United States Court, where I met him. It was less than two months before the convention which nominated him for President. Three tickets to Rumsey and Newcomb's Minstrels, a high-toned troupe, having been presented to me, I hunted up Lincoln and asked him if he would like to go to a 'nigger show' that night. He assented rapturously exclaiming: 'Of all things I would rather do to-night that certainly is one.' He and I witnessed the performance and I never saw him enjoy himself more than he did that night. He applauded as often as anybody and with greater animation. The nondescript song and dance of 'Dixie' was sung and acted by the troupe, the first time I ever saw it, and probably the first time it was sung and acted in Illinois. I can remember well the spontaneity of Lincoln's enthusiasm and the heartiness of his applause at the music and action of this rollicking and anomalous performance. Little did we think that this weird and harmless melody would erelong be transformed into a fierce battle-cry by whose inspiration slaughter and carnage would be carried into the ranks of those who bared their bosoms to save the nation's life. Little did we think of this as he clapped his great brawny hands in true rustic heartiness and exclaimed in riotous enthusiasm: 'Let's have it again! Let's have it again!'"

Several years ago my friend General James Grant Wilson, of New York, a great admirer of the renowned Thackeray, and who was then at work on his book "Thackeray in the United States," wrote me a letter in which he said that Thackeray gave one of his readings before a crowded house in St. Louis March 26, 1856, and it had been reported that

Lincoln was in the audience. Having been told that Lincoln occasionally visited St. Louis, General Wilson, trusting that the report was true, was anxious to state in his book that the former was present and heard the famous Englishman deliver his lecture to a St. Louis audience; but before committing himself he took the precaution to write to me asking me to make careful inquiry and report to him whether he could make the desired statement and be safely within the bounds of truth. Unless it could be shown that Lincoln was on hand and heard Thackeray as indicated, General Wilson said he preferred not to mention the incident. In due time I set out to learn the truth, making a thorough and industrious canvass. I interviewed all the few remaining friends and associates of Lincoln, then living in Springfield or elsewhere, that I could find who were in a position to know the facts, but was unable to find one who could recall the circumstance or otherwise enlighten me. Not content with personal interviews I patiently examined the files of the Springfield and St. Louis papers, only to realize that they, too, were void of information. Unfortunately it was after the death of Mr. Herndon so that I was unable to obtain the testimony of one witness whose credibility as well as competency could not be questioned. Among other things I examined the records of the various courts Lincoln was in the habit of attending, hoping thereby to determine Lincoln's whereabouts on March 26, 1856 — the date mentioned by General Wilson; but they failed to reveal anything of great moment or value beyond the fact that a document in Lincoln's handwriting, a declaration or bill, was filed in the Circuit Court at Bloomington, Illinois, dated

March 28, 1856. But this was far from conclusive, for it did not necessarily follow that he was in Bloomington that day, much less did it prove that he was in St. Louis listening to Thackeray's lecture on George III two days before.

My inquiry was so vigorous and persistent that it was not long until almost every old friend of Lincoln in Springfield had been subjected to an interview and thus learned what I was striving to accomplish. This was especially true of the older generation of lawyers, all of whom seemed deeply interested and generously coöperated with me in my quest of the truth. I recall one man, close to Lincoln, who was of material aid to me. One day he ventured to ask me who or what it was that prompted me to dig into the matter so deeply; also, in case I reached a definite and satisfactory conclusion, what I purposed doing with the information thus obtained. I told him I had been asked to make the investigation by a literary gentleman in New York who wished to know whether Lincoln while in St. Louis on one occasion attended a lecture by the talented English writer Thackeray, but that after careful and patient inquiry I was unable to determine whether he was actually present and heard the lecture or not.

"Tell your literary friend," he said, "that you have talked with a man in Springfield who, for many years, was a close friend of Lincoln and who insists that if he, Lincoln, was in St. Louis and the wonderful Mr. Thackeray was billed to lecture in one public hall and Campbell's or Rumsey's Negro Minstrels were to hold forth in another hall on the same evening, it would have been folly to look for Lincoln at the lecture. Instead of the latter the 'nigger show' would have caught him every time."

The marriage of Mr. Lincoln and Mary Todd was, indeed, an important and eventful chapter in the lives of both. Whether it was a wise and judicious union is a question on which the people of Springfield have never been able to agree. A few persons — and among them are some of Lincoln's closest friends — were disposed to look upon it as a piece of accidental good fortune. Their theory was that Lincoln's success and political ascendancy was due more to the influence of his wife than to any other single agency; that her unrestrained temper, her willful and turbulent nature effectually debarred him from the full measure of domestic happiness — in other words, forced him out into the angry sea of politics and public applause. Instead of evenings engrossed in the comforts of his own fireside, he was a great part of the time away from his home, discussing public questions with the politicians and lawyers, who thronged the offices in the court-houses, exchanging views with and telling stories to the farmers at the stores or the loungers at the tavern, and otherwise mingling with his fellow citizens of every grade, rank, and station. The result of this continuous rubbing of elbows with the so-called plain people was that Lincoln in the course of time was more generally and widely known than almost any other man in his part of the country. His wife, therefore, was a material though possibly an unintentional aid in his promotion.

If, on the other hand, as contended by certain of his friends, he had married some more placid and adjustable woman, one who would have been content to minister and defer to him because of his acknowledged intellect and brilliant promise of leadership, the result, doubtless, would have been different. For although it would have been the wife's delight to see that he had clean clothes when he needed them; that his slippers were in their accustomed place; that he was warmly clad and had plenty to eat; and although the privilege of ministering to his wants may have been to her a pleasure rather than a duty; yet the probability is he would have been satisfied with the modest emoluments of a country lawyer's practice, deaf to the siren call of politics, and buried in the delights of an inviting and happy home. Such, at least, was the opinion of Herndon, whose theory thus expressed was confirmed by David Davis, Milton Hay, and James Matheney, three close, unerring, and loyal friends of Lincoln, and with all of whom I talked regarding the latter's domestic history.

Judge Davis laid great stress on the fact that Lincoln seemed to prefer life on the circuit because it occasioned prolonged absence from his home. He told me that on the circuit the lawyers as the week neared its close were in the habit of expediting business so as to be able to leave at the earliest moment and thus reach home in time to spend Sunday with their families. They all went but Lincoln; he was proverbially slow and would linger behind pleading an accumulation of unfinished business or something equally commonplace and improbable as an excuse for not going. The next Monday, when the other lawyers returned, they would invariably find Lincoln still there anxiously awaiting their reappearance. It was more or less unusual. Davis professed to believe that "Lincoln was not happy domestically," in proof of which he alluded to the fact that often as he had been in Springfield Lincoln had never entertained him, nor, so far as he could learn, any other visiting lawyer at his home.

Speaking of Lincoln and his wife Milton Hay, the uncle of John Hay, said: "If he had married a woman of more angelic temperament and less social ambition, he, doubtless, would have remained at home more and been less inclined to mingle with the people outside. She had a very extreme temper and made things at home more or less disagreeable. This probably encouraged Mr. Lincoln to seek entertainment elsewhere. Mentally she was a bright woman with decided aristocratic pretensions, but she was of very saving habits. In dealing with others she was very determined; not easily moved or thoughtful about what she should say or do."

Judge Matheney agreed with Davis and Hay. He told me also that although in worldly matters Lincoln was as prudent and careful as the average man, yet he never succeeded in acquiring very much property. Compared to his second partner, Stephen T. Logan, David Davis, and a few other associates of like standing at the bar, he was poor. At the time of his election in 1860 the house in which he lived was the only real estate he possessed and his personal accumulations did not exceed ten thousand dollars. His tastes were proverbially simple; he indulged in no excesses and his expenditures were kept at the minimum. His wife, on the other hand, had a weakness for certain luxuries, but they were modest and only few in number. She loved fine clothes, but in other respects she was close and in no sense extravagant. In support of Judge Matheney's testimony illustrating the economical trait in the Lincoln family, I was shown a book kept by a Springfield merchant containing the Lincoln account. I copied the record of purchases made by Mrs. Lincoln in 1860 during the greater part of which year her husband was engaged in his canvass for the Presidency. A list of the items will not only serve to indicate the character and extent of her outlay, but also prove to be of more or less interest to the ladies; especially those who are prone to wonder what change, if any, in his wife's conduct or style of living a man's elevation to the Presidency brings about.

In the case of Mrs. Lincoln the following entry is a record of her first purchase after the news of her husband's nomination at Chicago:

Abraham Lincoln
To  1 Silk Parasol                    $5.00
"  11 y'ds Calico                     $1.38

Meanwhile the need of more elaborate raiment with which to bedeck the first lady of the land began to assert itself. Accordingly, a few days later, occurs this:

A. Lincoln per wife
To 1    Mantle                       $18.00
"  8½   yds Cable Cord                  1.06
"  1    pair Kid Gloves                  .85

And this:

Mrs. A. Lincoln
To  1    Eng. Straw Bonnet           $5.00
"   1    Rouch                         .25
"  23    yds Cotton Flannel           3.83
"   2    Hats                         1.50
"  1¾ yds Pld. Linen                   .66

As the summer wore on came this:

Hon. A. Lincoln
To 6¼ yds Bon Silk                   $5.31
"   9   "  Thread Edg.                2.25
"   ¾   "  Linen Cambric               .75

And shortly before election day, this:

Abraham Lincoln
To 3 yds Plaid Satteen                        .75
" 1 Silk French Umbrella                      5.75
" 1 Straw Tassel                              .25

The last entry, dated December 31, was recorded only a few days before Lincoln left Springfield for Washington and included these items:

A. Lincoln
To 1   Wh. Rouch                              .60
" 1     "      "                              .20
" 1   BB    "                                 .40
" 1¾ yds French Merino                        1.75
" ¾ " Marcelline                              .45
"     Sewing Silk                             .25

Another tradesman's account book I examined was that of a druggist, the man who supplied the Lincolns with their "medicines, perfumes, and hair tonics." I append this list bought in 1852:

A. Lincoln
Aug.  7 To Prescription                       .15
"    11 " Cal Powders                         .10
"    14 " Pennyroyal                          .10
"    23 " Bot. Carminative                    .25
"    30 "  "  "                               .50

Farther along in the book I found and copied numerous items added to the Lincoln account, but when the owner, who gave me the book to examine, observed that I had reached the page on which was entered, " 1 Bottle Brandy," charged to Lincoln, he asked for its return and declined to allow me to copy further. I remember an entry in one place showing the sale of a bottle of perfume beneath which was penciled this notation: "Returned by Mrs. L.," which prompted a gentleman who accompanied me to relate that his father, who was formerly connected with the store, told him that he was once instructed by the proprietor not to honor Mrs. Lincoln's order for perfume because she had so often broken the seals and, through a messenger, returned bottles of the preparation she had opened, claiming that the contents were inferior or otherwise not as represented, and thus preventing their sale to others.

"Notwithstanding her love of fine apparel," is the statement of a lady relative, "Mrs. Lincoln was not only economical, but close; but in order that she might gratify her passion for the ornamental her economy and self-denial ended at the kitchen. As a rule servants were conspicuous about her household only when she entertained. She was not noted for her skill as a cook, but was unusually neat with the needle. She had an ungovernable temper, but after the outburst she was invariably regretful and penitent."

My inquiry into the domestic history of the Lincolns in Springfield convinced me that Mrs. Lincoln was, in some respects, of great value to her husband, in that she protected him from imposition. "She was an excellent judge of human nature," said Herndon; "a better reader of men's motives than her husband and quick to detect those who had designs upon and sought to use him. She was, in a good sense, a stimulant. Firm in her belief that he would ultimately attain immortal fame she kept him from lagging, was constantly prodding him to keep up the struggle. She coveted place and power; wanted to be a leader in society, and her ambition knew no bounds. Realizing that Lincoln's rise in the world would elevate and strengthen her, she strove in every way to promote his fortunes, to keep him moving, and thereby win the world's applause."

# CHAPTER VIII

Further accounts of Mrs. Lincoln — Herndon's account of the dance with her — The serenade — Riding with the Bradfords — Her difficulties with the servants — Her husband's ingenious scheme to retain them — The government of the children — Lincoln taking them to the office on Sunday — His control over them — Playing chess with Judge Treat — An interesting glimpse by a law student — Description of the office — How Lincoln dressed — How he spent the day — His habits of study — Escorting Mrs. Lincoln to a ball — Her husband's consideration for her — His action when a storm threatened.

OUTSIDE of her husband and kindred it is fair to assume that Mr. Herndon knew Mrs. Lincoln more thoroughly and comprehended her peculiar construction better than almost any other person in Springfield. The popular notion fathered by numerous writers that the two were hostile to each other and at outs most of the time has no sure foundation on which to rest. That they did not invariably and completely agree on all subjects is doubtless true, but it does not necessarily follow that they hated each other. In fact the correspondence between them, much of which I have been privileged to read, as well as the many facts I gathered during my association with Mr. Herndon, convince me to the contrary. I cannot, therefore, resist the conclusion, regardless of the things which have found their way into the columns of some of our newspapers and magazines, that Mr. Herndon and Mrs. Lincoln, all things considered, held each other in generous and reasonable esteem.

"Mary Todd," wrote Mr. Herndon, "was a woman of more than average attainments, having had the benefit of a thorough education, excellent social training, and the most refined surroundings. She was a good writer, could

MARY TODD LINCOLN

express her thoughts in chaste and perfect English; understood French and was otherwise highly endowed. Of all the ladies to whom Mr. Lincoln paid court she was undoubtedly the most versatile and accomplished. An animated and interesting talker, she was also a shrewd observer, and in some respects a better and more intuitive judge of men than her husband. But unfortunately for her and those with whom she came in contact, she seemed to lack the very elements calculated to win the reverence and retain the affection of a man of Mr. Lincoln's type. Not entirely free from an appearance of haughty disdain, she was devoid of patience, tolerance, and self-control. In her letters, some of which were addressed to me and others which I have read, she invariably speaks of her husband in the most endearing and affectionate language; and yet I am sure her fearless, austere, and caustic nature greatly marred the blissful companionship which should have existed between her and her imperturbable and kindly natured helpmate."

Miss Todd came to Springfield from her Kentucky home about the time the place became the capital of the State, and she was promptly and cordially welcomed into the highest and most approved social circles. A comely and attractive figure she soon had a number of admirers. Among the latter was Mr. Herndon, who was about her age. This is his account of their first meeting: "It was at an evening party and I danced with her. I was charmed with her, and after the dance I thought it would be seemly and proper to compliment her on her superb poise and graceful bearing, meanwhile suggesting that her movements on the floor, as she glided through the waltz, were fairly serpentine — alluding, of course, to the ease with which a serpent, gracefully turning corners and making its way around obstructions, moves over the ground. Of course it was a hideous and unpardonable comparison, and later, when I became better acquainted with the lady and her responsive temperament, I used to wonder how I happened to escape so well; for, strange to say, she simply drew back and glared at me a moment — with a look too I shall never forget — and moved to another part of the room."

The recollection by Judge Matheney of Mrs. Lincoln was equally vivid and interesting because, in view of his intimacy with Mr. Lincoln, he was in a position to learn things which, but for his keen observation and wonderful memory, might not have been preserved. Here is one incident he related to me in March, 1883, which was before Herndon's death:

"Soon after Miss Todd came to Springfield our crowd of young fellows decided to serenade her — a custom very much in vogue in those days. We had flutes, violins, and other old-time instruments and produced what we regarded as very creditable music. The next evening Miss Todd attended a social gathering where she met a young man — his name was Peck, I believe — who was a member of the party of musicians that serenaded her the night before. On being introduced to him she indulged in several sneering allusions to the music and mentioned that she had met him before, referring, of course, to the serenade. Stung to the quick by her uncomplimentary and sarcastic suggestion Peck was nevertheless equal to the emergency. 'That music,' he retorted, 'was not intended for you, Miss Todd; that was for Sally' — the colored servant at the Edwards mansion."

John S. Bradford, at one time State Printer, told me this incident in his office in Springfield and I made a note of it at the time: "Some years ago when I had invested in my first carriage I invited Mrs. Lincoln to accompany me and my family in a drive to the country. We drove to the Lincoln residence, and when the madame came down the front steps to join us in the carriage, she appeared to be very nervous and more or less wrought up. What had caused her agitation she failed to disclose. We suspected that there had been a collision or disagreement of some kind with her servant, for, just as she settled back in her seat, she exclaimed with a sigh: 'Well, one thing is certain; if Mr. Lincoln should happen to die, his spirit will never find me living outside the boundaries of a slave State.'"

Among the people of Springfield, rich and poor alike, those who opposed as well as those who supported his political principles, Lincoln, so far as I could determine, was held by his fellow citizens in unquestioned esteem. In my long sojourn there I found but one man who condemned or even belittled him. That man, I regret to say, was the one who related the incident just described. For a long time I could not understand it; but finally, through Herndon, I learned the reason. In March, 1842, Lincoln was retained by one William Darmody and brought suit against Bradford for slander, the grievance being that the latter had publicly denounced Darmody, characterizing him as a "damned rogue." Lincoln lost the suit, and although he conducted the case with due regard to the professional ethics involved, as shown by the record, Bradford never forgave him. This explains why Bradford could not agree with his neighbors and thus endeavor to find in Lincoln's life and morals something to commend.

Reverting to a further contemplation of Mrs. Lincoln, it may not be out of place to suggest that, as a rule, she experienced the utmost difficulty in retaining a household servant beyond a brief or nominal period. On account of her frequent and violent outbursts of temper, she was in bad repute with the domestic servant population of Springfield. At the joint suggestion of Mr. Herndon and Judge Matheney I met and talked with a woman who claimed in her girlhood days to have lived as a servant in the Lincoln household. When she entered Mrs. Lincoln's employ she had been apprised, she said, of that lady's peculiarities, and was warned that, like the other girls who had preceded her at the Lincoln home, a few days, possibly a month at the most, would mark the limits of her stay; but, to the surprise of all, she remained a much longer period, in fact, upwards of two years. The secret of her steady and unbroken service came out with the explanation that Lincoln himself gave her additional compensation each week — generally a dollar — conditioned on her determination to brave whatever storms that might arise. This arrangement was discreetly kept from Mrs. Lincoln, but that extra payment each week gave the servant the requisite courage, whenever she and Mrs. Lincoln happened to clash, as they sometimes did. "At last, however," said the woman, "the madame and I began to understand each other. More than once, when she happened to be out of the room, Mr. Lincoln with a merry twinkle in his eye patted me on the shoulder urging me to 'Stay with her, Maria; stay with her.'"

Over his household Lincoln exercised no supervision of any kind. The government of the family or domestic machine was entirely in the hands of his wife. His children did much as they pleased. Many of their antics he ostensibly approved and he restrained them in nothing. He never reproved nor gave them a fatherly frown. Parental discipline or punishment, if needed, had to come from another source.

"He was the most indulgent parent," is the testimony of Mr. Herndon, "I have ever known. When at home on Sunday he frequently brought his two younger sons, William and Thomas, or 'Tad,' down to our office while his wife was at church. The boys were absolutely unrestrained in their amusements. If they withdrew all the books from the shelves, bent the points of the pens, overturned the inkstands, scattered papers over the floor, or threw pencils into the spittoon, it never disturbed their father's serenity or good nature. Absorbed in thought he apparently never observed their mischievous and destructive pranks, and even if brought to his attention he virtually encouraged their repetition by failing to manifest the least sign of impatience or disapproval.

"Mr. Lincoln could sometimes be seen, also on Sunday, in his shirt-sleeves drawing his children in a little wagon up and down the pavement in front of his house. So abstracted and lost to the surroundings was he that if, perchance, one of the little fellows happened to roll overboard, as they sometimes did, he would pull steadily ahead, his eyes fixed on the ground, in a brown study regardless of the child's lamentations. His attention being called to the mishap by a passer-by, he would turn back, pick up the youngster, try to soothe or pacify it, and then resume his perambulation as unconcernedly as if nothing unusual had happened. But at this juncture Mrs. Lincoln would be espied a few steps down the street, hastening home from church. Almost instantly there would follow a loud protest from a woman's shrill and angry voice. The scene would change. All steps now turn to the Lincoln mansion. The front door swings open and an abashed but indulgent father, looking neither to the right nor left, hastens up the steps and disappears within."

In the winter of 1883 I spent a good portion of one afternoon with a gentleman who was present and heard Lincoln's first oral argument before the Supreme Court of Illinois. It was Samuel H. Treat, who had himself been on the Supreme bench and at the time of my visit was serving as Judge of the United States District Court. His recollection of the political campaign of 1846, when Lincoln defeated the redoubtable Peter Cartwright for Congress, was to me an especially interesting chapter. He said he admired Lincoln and he entertained me with several vivid and characteristic episodes in which the latter figured. I tried to draw out his opinion of Mrs. Lincoln, but with poor success, for, beyond the simple admission that he was acquainted with her coupled with the names of three or four other persons who, he claimed, could adequately describe her "if they dared to," he declined to commit himself.

On the afternoon just mentioned when I visited him Judge Treat told me, among other things, that one morning Lincoln came to his office and joined him in a game of chess. The two were enthusiastic chess-players and when the opportunity offered indulged in the game. On the occasion named they were soon deeply absorbed, nor did they

realize how near it was to the noon hour until one of
Lincoln's boys came running in with a message from his
mother announcing dinner at the Lincoln home, a few steps
away. Lincoln promised to come at once and the boy left;
but the game was not entirely out; yet so near the end
the players, confident that they would finish in a few moments, lingered a while. Meanwhile almost half an hour had
passed. Presently the boy returned with a second and more
urgent call for dinner; but so deeply engrossed in the game
were the two players they apparently failed to notice his
arrival. This was more than the little fellow could stand;
so that, angered at their inattention, he moved nearer,
lifted his foot, and deliberately kicked board, chessmen, and
all into the air. "It was one of the most abrupt, if not
brazen, things I ever saw," said Treat, "but the surprising
thing was its effect on Lincoln. Instead of the animated
scene between an irate father and an impudent youth which
I expected, Mr. Lincoln without a word of reproof calmly
arose, took the boy by the hand, and started for dinner.
Reaching the door he turned, smiled good-naturedly, and
exclaimed, 'Well, Judge, I reckon we'll have to finish this
game some other time,' and passed out. Of course I refrained from any comment," continued Treat, who, by the
way, was old and had never been blessed with a child, "but
I can assure you of one thing: if that little rascal had been
a boy of mine he never would have applied his boots to
another chessboard."

Lincoln was a man of marked personality. He was generous and sympathetic; was willing to help if help was
needed, but in manner restrained and somewhat slow to

volunteer. The recipient of every one's confidence he rarely gave his own in return. People oftentimes mistook his dignified composure for indifference.

"If a man betrayed undue familiarity," said Herndon, "Mr. Lincoln drew about himself a shield, a sort of charmed circle which effectually barred too near approach. Though oftentimes abstracted, he was not repellent; but there was something in his face and manner that restrained even the boldest and most venturesome man. It can hardly be said that he had a confidant nor did he unbosom himself to others. Notwithstanding the long and close association between us, if a cloud hovered over and depressed him, as it unfortunately sometimes did, he made no mention of it, and I am sure that I was equally careful to refrain from alluding to it in his presence. To me he was ever imperturbable and mysterious. If in Springfield, and not out on the circuit, he usually reached our office about nine in the morning, although, sometimes, he came as early as seven; and on one or two occasions I recall he was there soon after daylight. The cause of these early appearances at the office could not be learned from anything he said, but that did not prevent me from making deductions of my own. The main piece of furniture in the office was an old sofa or lounge on which he would throw himself, one foot on a chair, the other on the edge of the table, and begin to read. Stretched out thus and generally reading aloud, he would succeed in monopolizing practically a fourth of the room. After a while he would exclaim, 'Billy' — he always called me Billy — and begin to relate a circumstance suggested by something he had been reading and which had happened in Indiana or 'down in Egypt.' That incident would lead

to another and still another, and the array of stories would
follow each other until a large part of the morning was thus
consumed. His narratives were almost invariably so witty
and amusing they kept all of us in the office laughing, a
result which no one enjoyed more heartily than he. At
two o'clock he would return to the office. If no important
or pressing matters claimed his time, he would draw his
chair up to the table on which rested his elbow, place his
chin in the palm of his hand, his gaze fixed on the floor or
through the window into space, and linger thus absorbed
for hours or until interrupted by callers or the demands of
his profession. On these occasions he was grave, taciturn,
unresponsive. But the most significant and noteworthy
thing about him was his look of abstraction and melancholy. It was as painful as it was inescapable. I have often
watched him in one of these moods. Bent over in his chair,
lost to the world in thought, he was the most striking picture of dejection I had ever seen. When in one of these
moody spells neither of us spoke. Occasionally it would
become necessary to trouble him with a question without
eliciting a response. Meanwhile I would forget that I had
asked him; but to my surprise a few moments later (once
it was over fifteen minutes) he would break the silence and
give me an appropriate and satisfactory answer. Apparently he had, for the time, pushed my question aside.

"A large part of the time he read aloud. It annoyed me
more or less, and I sometimes left the room under pretense of a call elsewhere if I suspected a long chapter ahead;
but he was my senior by almost ten years and so much
superior in every other respect I would not for the world
have given evidence of any objection or even indifference.

I remember once in answer to my inquiry why he read aloud he said: 'I catch the idea by two senses; for, when I hear what is said and also see it, I remember it better even if I do not understand it better.' At his home when reading he would lie on the floor, his head resting against a chair placed upside down, the inclined surface serving as a pillow. He was not a general reader, save in his endeavor to keep abreast of the times through the developments in the political world. In quest of knowledge or information his reading seemed to be characterized by marked concentration of thought, the study of some special subject — in other words, his reading like his efforts in other lines always had a definite end in view. He was practical, strong, and reflective."

A faithful and interesting glimpse of Lincoln comes from Gibson W. Harris, a student in his office after the dissolution of the partnership with Judge Logan, and who later moved to Cincinnati where he lived many years.

"In 1845," relates Harris, "I was inducted into the office of Lincoln & Herndon as student and clerk. The office was in a room in the upper floor of a building which housed the post-office. Across the hall the Clerk of the United States District Court held forth. The furniture, somewhat dilapidated, consisted of one small desk and a table, a sofa or lounge with a raised head at one end, and a half-dozen plain wooden chairs. The floor was never scrubbed. If cleaned at all it was done by the clerk or law student who occasionally ventured to sweep up the accumulated dirt. Over the desk a few shelves had been enclosed; this was the office bookcase holding a set of Blackstone, Kent's Commentaries, Chitty's Pleadings, and a few other

books. A fine law library was in the Capitol building across
the street to which the attorneys of the place had access.

"And now as to Mr. Lincoln himself: The blue jeans in
which he was clad the first time I saw him in 1840 had been
discarded in favor of broadcloth shortly before his marriage.
The day I entered his office in 1845 he had on a black suit
— coat and trousers of cloth and vest of satin; and the
buckram stock about his neck was covered with black silk
forcing him to carry his head more erect than would an ordinary tie. In summer he was accustomed to wear shoes
known as the Wellington style; but in winter he wore
boots. He had great fondness for chess or checkers and also
liked tenpins; but cared nothing for fishing or hunting.

"It would not be fair to speak of Mr. Lincoln as an idler
save in his aversion to bodily labor. His brain was a singularly active one — seemed never to rest, never to tire; yet
as a formal student he struck me as actually lazy. Days
of leisure came frequently, and on such occasions he might
sometimes be seen sitting in his chair with his feet on the
office table reading the office copy of Byron or Burns. He
would read for an hour or two, then close the book and
stretch himself at full length on the office lounge, his feet
projecting over the end, his hand under head, and his eyes
closed, and in this attitude would digest the mental food
he had just taken. He read but little at the office, and I
have never imagined there was much burning of the midnight oil at his home. The truth is he never studied hard at
any period of his life. He did not need to study hard. With
him a single reading was sufficient to afford a clear insight
into any ordinary subject.

"I was well acquainted with Mrs. Lincoln and was frequently at her house, being sent there now and then by her husband on errands from the office. On two occasions, I remember, I was her escort at a ball, instead of her husband, who, because of absence from home, was unable to accompany her. I found her to be a good dancer; she was bright, witty, and accomplished, being able to speak French fluently. The sportive title or nickname she gave me was Mr. 'Mister,' but her husband invariably addressed me by my first name. She rarely visited the office. She was a member of the Presbyterian Church, but the statement that Mr. Lincoln attended divine service nearly every Sunday he was in Springfield may have been true of later years, but to predicate it of the period when I was in office, in the forties, would be more or less of an exaggeration. Mr. Lincoln showed great consideration for his wife. She was unusually timid and nervous especially during a storm. If the clouds gathered and the thunder rolled, he knew its effect on his wife and would at once hasten home to remain there with her till the skies cleared and the storm was safely over."

# CHAPTER IX

A Springfield lawyer's opinion of Lincoln's mental equipment — Outline of his physical organization — His appetite — How he ate an apple — His predisposition to melancholy — Description of his figure — His head, arms, and legs — His countenance, his walk, and other physical attributes — His mental processes — His perception, judgment, and conscience — His indifference as to forms or methods — A profound reasoner — Remorseless in analysis — A giant intellect and in full comprehension of his own ability.

IN his physical organization, according to John T. Stuart and Herndon, both of whom were his law partners and therefore observed him at very close range, Lincoln was something of a riddle. Likewise to those who viewed him from another angle he was still difficult of comprehension. Here is an analysis of his mental structure by a fellow lawyer. It was written in 1866 and the original manuscript is still in my possession. Although I have thus far withheld the writer's name, I feel free to state that he was a Springfield man, but not a partner of, nor intimate with, Lincoln. After reciting that he had been asked to put in writing his opinion of the mind of Lincoln he says:

"I consent to do so without any other motive than to comply with the request of a brother lawyer, for if I know myself, no other motive would induce me to do it, because, while Mr. Lincoln and I were always good friends, I believe myself wholly indifferent to the future of his memory. The opinion I now have was formed by a personal and professional acquaintance of over ten years, and has not been altered or influenced by any of his promotions in public life. The adulation by base multitudes of a living and pageantry surrounding a dead President do not shake my

well-settled convictions of the man's mental caliber. Phys-
iologically and phrenologically the man was a sort of mon-
strosity. His frame was large, long, bony, and muscular; his
head small and disproportionately shaped. He had large,
square jaws; large, heavy nose; small, lascivious mouth,
and soft, tender, bluish eyes. I would say he was a cross
between Venus and Hercules. I believe it to be inconsist-
ent with the laws of human organization for any such
creature to possess a mind capable of anything called great.
The man's mind partook of the incongruities of his body.
He had no mind not possessed by the most ordinary of men.
It was simply the peculiarity of his mental and the oddity
of his physical structure, as well as the qualities of his heart,
that singled him out from the mass of men. His native
love of justice, truth, and humanity led his mind a great
way in the accomplishment of his objects in life. That
passion or sentiment steadied and determined an otherwise indecisive mind."

The following extract from a lecture by Herndon soon
after Lincoln's death contains an analysis of the latter's
physical and mental equipment so unerring and yet so profound there is abundant reason why it should be preserved.
Its value to history arises from the fact that it was prepared for delivery to audiences in central Illinois composed
largely of Lincoln's neighbors, people the most competent of all to test its accuracy and truthfulness. Among
other things he said:

Mr. Lincoln was wiry, sinewy, and raw-boned — thin through
the breast to the back and narrow across the shoulders. Standing, he leaned forward; was somewhat stoop-shouldered, in-
clining to the consumptive in build. His usual weight was

Surveyor for Rufus Goolsby- the West Part of the North East quarter of Section 30 in Township 19 North of Range 6 West. Begining at a White oak 12 inches in diameter bearing N34E 84 Links, White oak 10 inches S58W. 98 Links- thence South a White oak 19 inches. N36.20 Links 40 chains to a White oak 19 inches- thence East 20 chains to a Black oak 19 inches S54W. 16 Links- thence North 40 chains to a Post thence West 20 chains to the begining

Channon
Hercules Demoning

J. Calhoun S.L.C.
By A Lincoln

CERTIFICATE OF SURVEY WRITTEN BY LINCOLN WHEN HE WAS DEPUTY SURVEYOR UNDER JOHN CALHOUN IN 1834

about a hundred and eighty pounds. His organization worked slowly. His blood had to run a long distance from his heart to the extremities of his frame, and his nerve force had to travel through dry ground a wide circuit before his muscles were obedient to his will. His structure was loose and leathery, his body shrunk and shriveled, he had dark skin, dark hair, and looked woe-struck. The whole man, body and mind, worked against more or less friction and creaked as if it needed oiling.

His circulation was low and sluggish, so that there was after all only limited wear and tear of his bodily tissues. Hence he had no very strong appetite for stimulating drinks or tonics. "I am entitled to little credit for not drinking," he once said to me when I asked him about whiskey, "because I hate the stuff. It is unpleasant and always leaves me flabby and undone." He had a good but moderate appetite for food and was satisfied with almost anything that would allay hunger. He ate slowly and mechanically, never complaining of the food if it was bad nor praising it if good. On the circuit and elsewhere I sat down with him times without number, but I never knew him to manifest any objection to the food that graced the table, although some of our colleagues would often swear at it. He adored the vegetable world, but in his own selection of things to eat he was decidedly mixed. He loved a good cup of coffee, but he was especially fond of an apple. His manipulation of an apple when he ate it was unique. He disdained the use of a knife to cut or pare it. Instead he would grasp it around the equatorial part, holding it thus until his thumb and forefinger almost met, sink his teeth into it, and then, unlike the average person, begin eating at the blossom end. When he was done he had eaten his way over and through rather than around and into it. Such, at least, was his explanation. I never saw an apple thus disposed of by any one else.

The most marked and prominent feature in Lincoln's organization was his predisposition to melancholy or at least the appearance thereof as indicated by his facial expression when sitting alone and thus shut off from conversation with other people. It was a characteristic as peculiar as it was pronounced. Almost every man in Illinois I met, including not only Herndon, but John T. Stuart, Samuel H. Treat, James C. Conkling, James H. Matheney, David Davis, Leonard Swett, and Henry C. Whitney, reminded me of it. No one was able to determine what caused it. Stuart and Swett attributed it to defective digestion — in fact, Stuart told me and Herndon that Lincoln's liver failed to function properly. "It did not secrete bile," he said, "and his bowels were equally inactive. It was this that made him look so sad and depressed. That was my notion, and I remember I talked to him about it and advised him to resort to blue-mass pills which he did. This was before he went to Washington. When I came on to Congress in 1863, he told me that for a few months after his inauguration as President he continued the pill remedy, but he was finally forced to cease because it was losing its efficacy besides making him more or less irritable."

My inquiry on this subject among Lincoln's close friends convinced me that men who never saw him could scarcely realize this tendency to melancholy, not only as reflected in his facial expression, but as it affected his spirits and well-being. Robert L. Wilson, who was a member with Lincoln of the Illinois Legislature in 1836, wrote thus to Herndon February 10, 1866:

"Mr. Lincoln told me that although he appeared to enjoy life rapturously, still he was the victim of terrible melancholy. He sought company and indulged in fun and hilarity without restraint or stint as to time; but when by himself he told me that he was so overcome by mental depression he never dared carry a knife in his pocket; and as long as I was intimately acquainted with him previous to his commencement of the practice of the law he never carried a pocket-knife."

The above is copied from the original manuscript signed by Wilson, delivered to Herndon, and by him turned over to me. Along with it came this reference to Lincoln's peculiarity in Herndon's hand:

"As to the cause of this morbid condition, my idea has always been that it was occult and could not be explained by any course of observation and reasoning. It was ingrained, and being ingrained could not be reduced to rule or the cause assigned. It was necessarily hereditary, but whether it came down from a long line of ancestors and far back or was simply the saddened face of Nancy Hanks cannot well be determined. At any rate, it was part of his nature and could no more be shaken off than he could part with his brains. Simple in carriage or bearing, free from pomp or display, serious, unaffected, Lincoln was a sad-looking man whose melancholy dripped from him as he walked."

How Lincoln impressed Herndon may be judged from the following fragments of his lecture:

In person and physique it can hardly be said that Mr. Lincoln was either dapper or handsome. Somewhat ill-proportioned in figure, his movements seemed labored if not at times more or less awkward. He had a sad and rugged face which defied artistic skill to soften or idealize. It was capable of few expressions, but they were abundantly suggestive and unusual. When in repose his face was grave and thoughtful, pervaded by a look of dejection as painful as it was prominent; it brightened like a lighted lantern when animated. His dull eyes would sparkle with fun or express as kindly and tender a look as ever mounted a face when moved by some matter of human interest or sympathy. There was more difference between Lincoln grave and Lincoln animated in facial expression than almost any other man of his day.

His forehead was narrow but high; his hair dark, coarse and rebellious. His cheek-bones were high, sharp, and prominent; his jaws were long; nose large and a little awry toward the right eye; chin sharp and upcurved. His eyebrows cropped out like a huge rock on the brow of a hill; his face was sallow, shrunk, and wrinkled, with here and there a hair on the surface and his cheeks leathery. His ears were large and ran out almost at right angles from his head, caused partly by heavy hats and partly by nature; his lower lip thick and undercurved while his chin reached for the lip upcurved; his neck slender and trim neatly balancing his head; there was the lone mole on the right cheek and Adam's apple on his throat.

His head was long and tall from the base of his brain and from the eyebrows. His head ran backwards, his forehead rising at a low angle like Clay's, and unlike Webster's, which was almost perpendicular. The size of his hat measured at the hatter's block was seven and one eighth, his head being from ear to ear six and one half inches and from the front to the back of the brain eight inches. Thus measured it was not below the medium size. The look of gloom or sadness, so often noted in the many descriptions of his countenance, was more or less accentuated by a peculiarity of one eye, the pupil of which had a tendency to turn or roll slightly toward the upper lid, whereas the other one maintained its normal position equidistant between the upper and lower lids.

His legs and arms were very long and in undue proportion to the rest of his body. Sitting in a chair he was not taller than ordinary men; it was only when he stood up that he loomed above them. He walked like an Indian, with even tread, the inner sides of his feet being parallel, betokening caution. He put the whole foot flat down on the ground, not landing on the heel; he likewise lifted it all at once, not rising from the toe; hence there was no spring to his step as he moved up and down the street.

Thus stood, walked, and looked this unusual man. True he was plain, unprepossessing, yea even commonplace, but when that gray eye and every feature of that earnest and deeply thoughtful face were lighted up by an inward soul reflecting the fires of righteous zeal and determination, then it was that these apparently homely features beamed rather than repelled or sank beneath the sea of inspiration that sometimes flooded his face. In fact, there were times when it seemed to me as if Lincoln's soul was fresh from the hands of Him who gave it being.

Mr. Lincoln's perceptions were slow, cold, and exact. Everything came to him in its precise shape and color. No lurking illusion or other error, false in itself and clad for the moment in robes of splendor, ever passed undetected or unchallenged over the threshold of his mind — that point which divides vision from the realm and home of thought. He saw all things through a perfect moral lens. There was no diffraction or refraction there; nor was he impulsive, fanciful, or imaginative. He threw his whole mental light around the object and in time substance and quality stood apart, form and color took their respective places, and all was clear and exact in his mind. He was pitiless and unrelenting in his search for the truth. His skill in the association of ideas was as marvelous as his memory was tenacious and unerring. His language indicated oddity of vision as well as expression. In his search for words he was sometimes hard pressed to give proper expression to his thoughts; first, because he was in no sense a master of the English language, and secondly, because in the vast store of words there were so few at his limited command that represented the exact shade of meaning he intended to convey. This will account for the frequent use by him of stories and maxims with which to impress the truth of his convictions upon the minds of his listeners.

Mr. Lincoln in mental action was causative; his mind apparently with an automatic movement ran behind facts, principles, and all things to their origin — their first cause. He was remorseless in his analysis of everything he sought to determine. He would stop in the street and study a machine. He would whittle things to a point and then count the numberless inclined planes and their pitch making the point. Mastering and defining this, he would cut that point back and get a broad transverse section of his pine stick and peel and define that. Clocks, omnibuses, and language, paddle-wheels and idioms never escaped his observation and analysis. Before he could form an idea of anything, before he expressed his opinion, he must know it in origin and history, in substance and quality, in magnitude and gravity. He must know his subject inside and outside, upside and downside.

All facts and principles had to run through the crucible of an inflexible judgment and be tested by the fierce fires of an analytical mind; and hence when he spoke his utterances rang out with the clear ring of genuine gold upon the counters of the understanding. His reasoning through logic, comparison, and analogy was unerring and deadly; his adversaries dreaded his originality of idea, condensation and force of expression, not less than they writhed under the convincing effect of singularly significant and apt stories. Woe be to the man who hugged to his bosom a secret error if Abraham Lincoln ever suspected or started in chase of it! Time and all the legerdemain of debate could hide it in no nook or angle of space in which he would not detect and expose it.

Though accurate in perception, a profound thinker as well as analyzer, his judgment on some occasions and in certain questions was pitiably weak. It might be said that his mind was in some respects slow and ponderous, not quick or discriminating; but when it came to the concentration of his great powers of reasoning, from cause to effect, the supremacy of truth, his deductions could not be overcome. When his mind could not grasp premises from which to argue, he was weaker than a child, because he had none of the child's intuitions — the soul's quick vision of the assembled facts. To that extent Mr. Lincoln was lacking in his mental structure. He was on the alert if a principle was involved or a man's rights at stake in a transaction; but he could see no harm or impropriety in wearing a sack-coat instead of a swallow-tail at an evening party, nor could he realize the offense of telling a coarse or questionable story if a preacher happened to be present.

He did not care for forms, ways, methods — the non-substantial things of this world. He could not, by reason of his structure and mental make-up, be much concerned about them; nor did he manifest an intense interest in any individual man — the dollar, property, rank, order, manners, or similar things; neither did he have any avarice or other like vice in his nature. He detested somewhat all technical rules in law and the sciences, contending they were, as a general thing, mere forms founded on arbitrary ideas and not on reason, truth, and the right. What satisfied a small or narrow and critical mind did not always suit Mr. Lincoln any more than a child's clothes would his body. As a rule he took but slight interest in purely local affairs; was hardly ever present at a town meeting, and the few gatherings which he did attend almost invariably were political conventions. He seemed not to care who succeeded to the presidency of this or that society or railroad company; who made the most money; who was going to Philadelphia and what were the costs of such a trip; who among his friends got this office or that — who was elected street commissioner or health inspector. No principle of justice, truth, or right being involved in these things, he could not be moved by them. It only remains to say that he was inflexibly steadfast in human transactions when it was necessary to be so and not otherwise. One moment he was as pliable and expansive as gentle air; the next as firm and unerring as gravity itself.

Mr. Lincoln's understanding, his conscience, yea, everything, yielded submissively to the despotism of his reason. His analytical power was profound. In his mental organization logic occupied the throne. His vision was clear; his pursuit of the truth intense and unremitting. His conscience ruled his heart; he was always just before he was generous. But above and beyond everything else it was plain to his friends that his strength lay in his ability to reason. From that height he came down with crushing and irresistible force. The tallest intellects in the world bowed to him, and it is, therefore, no stretch of the truth to declare that, when viewed from the elevated standpoint of reason and logic, he was easily one of the greatest intellects the nation has produced. Another strong point in his construction was his knowledge of himself; he understood and comprehended his own capacity — what he did and why he did it — better, perhaps, than any other man of his day. He had a wider and deeper conception of his environments and limitations than men who made greater pretensions or had enjoyed the benefits of more thorough training.

Viewing his life as a whole the student of history will be sure to conclude that the elements which predominated in Mr. Lincoln's peculiar character were: first, his great capacity and power of reason; second, his conscience and excellent understanding; third, an exalted idea of the sense of right and equity; fourth, his intense veneration of the true and the good. Whatever of life, vigor, and power of eloquence his peculiar qualities gave him; whatever there was in a fair, manly, and impartial administration of justice under law to all men; whatever there was in a strong will in the right, governed by tenderness and mercy; whatever there was in toil and sublime patience; whatever there was in these things or a wise combination of them Lincoln is justly entitled to in making up the impartial verdict of history. These limit and define him as a lawyer, an orator, a statesman, and a man. They developed in all the walks of his life; they were his law; they were his nature — they were Abraham Lincoln.

# CHAPTER X

Behind the door of Lincoln's home — What the neighbors saw and heard — The testimony of James Gourley — Lincoln's garden and dooryard — The ups and downs of life at the Eighth Street home — How Lincoln and his wife agreed — What Josiah P. Kent saw and remembered — Mrs. Lincoln and the iceman — The family carriage — Buying a ticket to the circus — Juvenile pranks at Lincoln's expense — Mrs. Lincoln's peculiarities of temperament.

IN order to bring out in sharper outline the human side of Lincoln, to learn more definitely how he lived and bore himself with the door of his home closed against the intrusion of an anxious but heartless world, Mr. Herndon was good enough to put me on the track of much rare and authentic information which, otherwise, might not have reached the public. Among other things I remember he gave me the names and whereabouts of certain neighbors of Lincoln, urging me to "run them down and pump them dry," as he expressed it, a suggestion which I promptly undertook to carry out. Judged by their opportunities and the angle from which these people viewed Lincoln, I could not but agree with Herndon that their testimony was of unquestioned value and importance. One of Lincoln's closest neighbors was James Gourley, a shoemaker, who lived in a house adjoining the Lincoln homestead on the east. The Lincolns and Gourleys were on the best of terms, which is evidenced by the fact that one of the first persons in Springfield selected by Lincoln for a position in Washington after he became President was a son of Gourley.

"I lived next door to the Lincolns for nineteen years," said Gourley, "and knew the family well. The truth is I knew him as early as 1834. At that time he was living in New Salem, where he was postmaster. He used to come from there afoot to Springfield and wind up at Stuart and Dummer's office, where he borrowed books and took them back with him. Even then he was a great story-teller, and when he was at Stuart's office as I have told you he always had a crowd about him. In those days I used to run foot-races, and I recall that E. D. Baker challenged me and I ran a race with him. Baker was a close friend of Lincoln, but notwithstanding the friendship between them Lincoln backed me and I beat Baker. In the course of time Lincoln moved here to Springfield and finally became my neighbor. He used to come to our house, his feet in a pair of loose slippers, and wearing an old, faded pair of trousers fastened with one suspender. Sometimes he came for milk. Our rooms were low, and one day he said: 'Jim, you'll have to lift your loft a little higher: I can't straighten out under it very well.' To my wife, who was short in stature, he used to say that little people had some advantages: they required less 'wood and wool to make them comfortable.'

"As I remember Mr. Lincoln he was a poor landscape gardener and his yard was graced by very little shrubbery. He once decided to plant some rosebushes in the yard, and called my attention to them, but in a short time he had forgotten all about them. He never planted any vines or trees of any kind; in fact seemed to take little, if any, interest in things of that kind. Finally, however, yielding to my oft-repeated suggestion, he undertook to cultivate a garden in the yard back of his house; but one season's experience in caring for his flowers and vegetables sufficed to cure him of all desire for another. In other respects he was more or less domestic in his tastes. He kept his own horse; feeding and caring for the animal when at home. He fed and milked his own cow and even sawed his own wood.

"Like all families the Lincoln's had their ups and downs, too, but viewing, as a whole, the almost twenty years I lived beside them, I think it is safe to say they agreed moderately well. As a rule Mr. Lincoln yielded to his wife — in fact, almost any other man, had he known the woman as I did, would have done the same thing. She was gifted with an unusually high temper and that invariably got the better of her. She was also very excitable and when wrought up frequently had hallucinations. I remember once when her husband was away from home she conceived the notion that some rough characters had designs on her and her hired girl. She had worked herself up to a furious pitch, weeping and wailing loud enough to be heard by the neighbors, and even asked me to spend the night at her house guarding the premises and thus protect her and her girl. Of course I expressed a willingness to do whatever she asked, although I knew the whole thing was imaginary as well as absurd. This was not the only time her demonstrations were loud enough to be heard by some of the neighbors. If she became excited or troublesome, as she sometimes did when Mr. Lincoln was at home, it was interesting to know what he would do. At first he would apparently pay no attention to her. Frequently he would laugh at her, which is a risky thing to do in the face of an infuriated wife; but generally, if her impatience continued, he would pick up one of the children and deliberately leave home as if to take a walk. After he had gone, the storm usually subsided, but sometimes it would break out again when he returned.

"Notwithstanding her unfortunate temper and her peculiarities generally, I never thought Mrs. Lincoln was as bad as some people here in Springfield have represented her. The truth is she had more than one redeeming trait. She and I rarely ever differed — in fact, we were good friends. Although I do not believe she could plead justification for many of the uncalled-for things she did, yet, when I hear her criticized by some people, I cannot but recall what she once said to me about her husband, which was, that if he had been at home as much as he ought, she could have been happier and loved him more."

Another man to whom I had been referred by Herndon and other old residents of Springfield was Josiah P. Kent. Although not so well advanced in years as Gourley, he lived as near and knew the Lincolns quite as well, especially during the closing years of the family's stay in Springfield. At first he seemed a little reluctant to express himself, and it was only after a second visit coupled with the urgent suggestion of an old friend that he was induced to unbosom himself. His home, he told me, was in the same block with the Lincoln residence, and he was at the latter so often and so much of the time he became virtually a member of the household.

"It was largely at the instance of my mother," he said, "that I went there. She arranged with Mrs. Lincoln that I should help the family by doing the various things a young man of my age should do to befriend a neighbor. It was late in the fifties when Robert was away attending college in the East. Mr. Lincoln was also away from home a good deal, so that my willingness and service to the family were deeply appreciated. I spent many a night at the house, sleeping usually in the same room which Robert had occupied. I took care of the horse and in general made myself useful about the premises. In the course of time Mrs. Lincoln induced her husband to purchase a carriage after which I was duly installed as coachman. In order to keep up with the fashion of that day, she hired me to drive her about town on certain days, usually for a few hours, in the afternoon, going from house to house where she made her calls. For this service I was to receive twenty-five cents each time I made the drive. One day I remember she offered an additional quarter of a dollar if I would go down to see Myers, the iceman — there was only one dealer in ice in those days — and learn why he had ceased bringing her ice. I saw the man and he told me he had ceased supplying the lady with his commodity because she lost her temper a day or two before, accused him of cheating in weight, and abused him so loudly he had resolved never to call at her house again. After an ingenious explanation and prolonged entreaty on my part, however, he finally relented, and the next day appeared at the Lincoln house with the required allotment of ice.

"Meanwhile a circus was advertised for Springfield and I wanted to go. I had taken Mrs. Lincoln on one drive which, with the amount due me for visiting and influencing the iceman, made a total of fifty cents — the price of a ticket to the show. The good lady had not yet paid me, and I did n't have the courage to ask her for it. But the circus was due the next day. Meanwhile a friend told me that Mr. Lincoln had just reached town and advised me to state the case to him and ask for the money. Being more or less desperate, I finally resolved to do it. Arrived at a certain street corner I lay in wait for Mr. Lincoln, who was sure to pass by on his way home. In due time he appeared. I accosted him and having summoned all my courage blushingly told my story. He eyed me closely and seemed deeply interested especially when I mentioned the approaching circus. 'Fifty cents,' he said, 'is rather small pay for the service you seem to have rendered Mrs. Lincoln and you should have been paid long ago.' He smiled and drew from his pocket the money; but it was not the expected fifty — it was seventy-five cents. 'What's the extra twenty-five cents for?' I asked. 'That's interest on your investment,' he laughed, and then resumed his walk toward home.

"Mr. Lincoln was well liked by the boys of our neighborhood notwithstanding the many pranks we played on him in some of which his own boys occasionally joined. He seemed to understand as well as enjoy boy nature perfectly. We were in the habit, after dark, of hiding behind a certain fence along which people walked on their way home from downtown. We had a lath which we would poke between two pickets just high enough above the ground to knock off the headgear of the passer-by. Concealed from sight behind the fence we carried on our sport without detection. One evening as usual we heard footsteps coming down the sidewalk, and although it was too dark — there were no street lights then — to determine who it was, we jumped behind the fence and prepared for action. The lath did its work and off came a tall stiff hat. The victim was no less a person than Mr. Lincoln. We suppressed our giggles the best we could and prepared for the punishment, or at least the rebuke, which we felt sure would follow; but to our surprise Mr. Lincoln simply picked up his hat, and although he could not see us, he laughed, exclaimed, 'Boys, you ought to be ashamed to impose on an old man,' and resumed his saunter down the street as if nothing unusual had happened.

"After the Lincolns had had their carriage for some time, or until the novelty of owning one had passed away, I conceived the idea of trying to borrow it for an afternoon's use myself. Accordingly I applied to Mr. Lincoln for it, but refrained from telling him where I wanted to drive or who, if any one else, I expected to take with me. The truth is I intended to fill the conveyance with boys — including in the number one of Mr. Lincoln's — and drive the outfit to a well-known swimming hole some distance from town. When I asked Mr. Lincoln he declined, saying that there were two things he would not lend: his wife and his carriage; but he added that I might have the use of his horse and harness. After he was gone, and without his knowledge, but with the aid of another, we slipped the carriage out, filled it with boys, and started away; but just after we had passed the edge of town the horse became frightened and ran away, throwing most of us out and damaging the vehicle. A near-by blacksmith was secured who repaired the break, and after much effort we succeeded in getting the carriage back home. Among other things I remember we carefully painted the place which the blacksmith had marred in making his repairs, and then threw dust over it to give it the appearance of age and thus remove the sign of fresh paint; in fact, we made every effort possible to keep all knowledge of the accident from Mr.

Lincoln. We probably succeeded, for if he learned the story he never mentioned it to us."

Beyond what is here recorded Mr. Kent had but little more to communicate regarding Mrs. Lincoln herself. The incidents of her home life as he detailed them were far from voluminous; nor did he comment very freely on her attitude and bearing toward her husband. On that phase of the subject he was more or less non-committal. He insisted that Maria Drake, the girl who, for a long time, was an inmate of the Lincoln home, could shed more light than any one else, but she having married William Clark and moved to the Far West many years before, was no longer accessible. Brief and definite though Kent's recollection of Mrs. Lincoln was, I found that he agreed substantially with the other neighbors. "She was not only nervous and high-tempered," he said to me, alluding to Mrs. Lincoln, "but very demonstrative, quick of action, and at times loud. It was never difficult to locate her. It mattered not who was present when she fell into a rage, for nothing would restrain her. The iceman could testify to that. Her voice was shrill and at times so penetrating, especially when summoning the children or railing at some one whose actions had awakened her temper, she could easily be heard over the neighborhood. When thus aroused and giving vent to her feelings, it is little wonder that Mr. Lincoln would suddenly think of an engagement he had downtown, grasp his hat, and start for his office by the shortest and most direct route he knew."

# CHAPTER XI

Lincoln as a lawyer — Estimates of David Davis and others — First leaning toward the law manifested in Indiana — Borrowing books of Judge Pitcher, of Rockport — Attending squire's court at Gentryville — Studying law books after reaching New Salem — Admission to the bar at Springfield — His opinion of examinations — Story of an applicant he himself examined — The note to Judge Logan — Hawthorne *vs.* Woolridge, his first case: its history and termination — Scammon *vs.* Cline, his first case in the Supreme Court — His last appearance in court — His three partnerships — His wonderful ability as a reasoner — The scope and extent of his practice — Range and size of his fees — His skill and care in the preparation of papers — The trial of Bailey *vs.* Cromwell proving that a negro girl was not a slave — Also Carman *vs.* Glasscock involving the navigability of the Sangamon River.

NOTWITHSTANDING the copious and unprecedented array of matter that has been apportioned to an eager world regarding the life of Lincoln, it cannot be said that his biographers have provided as broad and exhaustive an account of his varied achievements as we are entitled to have. This is especially true of our conception of him as a lawyer; for it was in the law office and the court-room that many of his peculiarities and traits of character were brought to the light. When delving into this phase of his activities I found that, among his colleagues at the bar and others equally competent to judge, no two agreed in their estimate of his genius and ability. Two men who have written books describing him as a lawyer put him at the very head of the list, whereas David Davis and William H. Herndon, who knew him longer and more intimately, probably, than all the other lawyers at the Springfield bar, each qualified what they said about him. "He could hardly be called very learned in the profession," said Davis, "and yet he rarely tried a cause without fully understanding the law applicable to it. At the same time it can be said that he read law books but little save when the cause in hand made it necessary." In October, 1885, Herndon put this in writing: "Although only moderately well read in the elementary books he studied so thoroughly certain special and adjudicated cases until he developed into a good practitioner. To that extent, therefore, it is fair to call him a case lawyer. Apparently he cared but little for forms, rules of pleading, or practice. He went in for substance mainly; but in the end became a good *nisi prius* lawyer and a better Supreme Court lawyer." Here is the tribute of Samuel C. Parks, one of his colleagues: "Lincoln's conscience, reason, and judgment worked out the law for him. It would 'not do to call him a great lawyer, for he was not; but it is fair to state that he was a good lawyer under conditions. He was not as quick as some men — in fact, required more time to study his case and thus arrive at the truth. But above all things he must feel that he was right. For a man who was for a quarter of a century both a lawyer and a politician, he was the most honest man I ever knew. He was not only morally honest, but intellectually so. At the bar he was strong if convinced that he was in the right, but if he suspected that he might be wrong he was the weakest lawyer I ever saw."

Though Lincoln was not a profound lawyer in the sense that the jurist John Marshall was, or, possibly, as able and successful a *nisi prius* practitioner as was Stephen T. Logan, yet, from an intellectual standpoint, he was greater than either. For clear reasoning power, merciless analogy, and lucidity of statement he had no superior at the Illinois bar, and yet the truth is there never was, either in Illinois or elsewhere, just such a lawyer. He said once he had never read a law book through in all his life, and yet it is the testimony of his colleagues that he was a most adroit and oftentimes dangerous antagonist. In the language of David Davis: "That man who laughed at a contest with the clear head, the brave heart, and the strong right arm of Abraham Lincoln always had to have his laugh first; for after the contest had ended and the man woke up with his back in a ditch, laughing was too serious a matter." Whatever he may have lacked of the delicate polish which comes of collegiate training was counterbalanced by his wonderfully well-developed reasoning powers. "All facts and principles," said Herndon, "had to run through the crucible of an inflexible judgment and be tested by the fierce fires of an analytical mind, and hence, when he spoke, his utterances resounded with the clear ring of genuine gold on the counters of the understanding. His reasoning through logic, analogy, and comparison was unerring and deadly. His adversaries dreaded his originality of idea, condensation and force of expression, not less than they writhed under the convincing effect of his singularly significant and apt stories. Woe be to the man who hugged to his bosom a secret error if Abraham Lincoln ever set out to uncover it. All the ingenuity of delusive reasoning, all the legerdemain of debate, could hide it in no nook or angle of space in which he would not detect and expose it."

Who or what really prompted Lincoln to adopt the law as his calling through life has never been determined. Along with numberless others I confess I have often wondered what would have happened, or what, if any, differ-

ence it would have made in the world's history if, instead
of making a lawyer of himself, he had taken to medicine,
the pulpit, or some other one of the learned professions. It
is known that very early in life, while living in Indiana, he
evinced a pronounced fondness for the argumentative dis-
putations which so often took place at the store and the
blacksmith shop in Gentryville; and when the stage was
set for a lawsuit before the village squire, "Abe Lincoln was
sure to be on hand an eager and attentive listener." Many
years ago, when I was at Mount Vernon, Indiana, I learned
from Judge John Pitcher, that between the years 1820 and
1830, when he was living and practicing law in the town of
Rockport, the county seat of Spencer County, Indiana,
Abraham Lincoln on several occasions came down from his
home in the village of Gentryville, distant about fifteen
miles, and talked to Judge Pitcher about books, asking
how to read them and how in other ways to obtain or at
least improve his education. "I counseled with him," said
Pitcher, "and loaned him several books, some of them being law books, which he took home with him to read. I
understood he wanted to become a lawyer and I tried to
encourage him." The specific names or titles of the volumes which Judge Pitcher loaned young Lincoln the
former did not indicate, but we have the best of authority for believing that the first law book to which he had
access was the Revised Statutes of Indiana, a small volume
loaned to him by his boyhood friend, David Turnham.
This statement is confirmed by Lincoln's stepmother, who
was visited by Herndon at her home near Charleston,
Illinois, in the summer of 1865, and later by a son of Turnham whom I met several times during my sojourn in south-

JUDGE JOHN PITCHER

ern Indiana. It is said — but it is only a tradition and not verified — that while still a young man in Indiana, Lincoln would occasionally journey to Boonville, the county seat of Warrick County, also about fifteen miles from Gentryville, to attend sessions of the court, and that on one occasion he was so profoundly impressed by the argument of John A. Brackenridge, who appeared for the defense in a murder trial, that he sought the latter after court adjourned and congratulated him on the brilliance and effectiveness of his speech.

In that characteristic bit of autobiography which Lincoln wrote and turned over to Jesse W. Fell, of Bloomington, Illinois, in 1859, he relates that from 1832 to 1838, which he terms his legislative period, he studied law, which would indicate that, although he may have leaned toward the law while still living in Indiana, from which State he emigrated in 1830, he did not decide upon it as a profession, at least did not enter on a systematic study of its principles, till after he had reached and located in the village of New Salem, in Illinois. It is probable that during his service in the Black Hawk War, where he became acquainted with Major John T. Stuart, who was then a practicing lawyer in Springfield, he apprised the latter of his ambition; at any rate, after the war was over and both had returned to their respective homes, Lincoln would frequently trudge down to Springfield from New Salem to borrow or return Stuart's law books.

Lincoln's induction into the legal arena was unattended by any display, ceremony, or noteworthy circumstance. The first step in the formal process of which there is any evidence is the following entry found in the records of the Circuit Court of Sangamon County, Illinois, dated March 24, 1836: "It is ordered by the Court that it be certified that Abraham Lincoln is a person of good moral character." The next item appears in the records of the Supreme Court of Illinois, where it is shown under date of September 9, 1836, that he was licensed to practice in all the courts of the State by two justices of the Supreme Court. On March 1st of the following year the clerk entered his name on the roll of attorneys and he thus became a full-fledged lawyer. After March 1, 1841, the Supreme Court adopted a rule requiring all applicants for admission to the bar to present themselves in person for examination in open court. Whether Lincoln underwent any examination either private or in open court is not known. The truth is he never put much faith in the propriety or efficacy of the conventional examination. He believed there were other if not better ways of determining a man's fitness for a given task or position than the regulation test questions. "I personally wish," he said in a letter addressed to the Secretary of War, November 11, 1863 —just eight days before he delivered the Gettysburg Address — "Jacob Freese, of New Jersey, to be appointed colonel for a colored regiment, and this regardless, whether he can tell the exact shade of Julius Cæsar's hair."

Before the close of the fifties Lincoln was a member of a committee appointed by the Supreme Court of Illinois to examine applicants for admission to the bar. At the town of Bloomington he was approached one day by Jonathan Birch, a young man who for some time had been a student in the office of a practicing attorney there, and desired to undergo the required examination. It happens that I knew the applicant well, for he later removed to Indiana where I was born; was my neighbor, my legal adviser, and for upwards of forty years one of my most trusted and intimate friends. He told me that when the matter of his examination was presented to Lincoln, he was directed by the latter to meet him at the hotel in the evening after court had adjourned for the day. "At the appointed time," said Mr. Birch when he related the incident, "I knocked at the door of his room and was admitted. Motioning me to be seated he began his interrogatories at once without looking at me a second time to be sure of the identity of his caller. 'How long have you been studying?' he asked. 'Almost two years,' was my response. 'By this time it seems to me,' he said laughingly, 'you ought to be able to determine whether you have in you the stuff out of which a good lawyer can be made.' Then he asked me in a desultory way the definition of a contract and two or three other fundamental questions, all of which I answered readily and, as I thought, correctly. Beyond these meager inquiries, as I now recall the incident, he asked nothing more. Meanwhile, sitting on the edge of the bed he began to entertain me with recollections — many of them characteristically vivid and racy — of his own practice and the various incidents and adventures that attended his start in the profession. The whole proceeding was interesting and yet so unusual, if not grotesque, I was at a loss to determine whether I was really being examined or not. In due time we went downstairs and over to the clerk's office in the court-house, where he wrote a few lines on a sheet of paper which he enclosed in an envelope and directed me to report with it to Judge Stephen T. Logan,

the other member of the examining committee at Springfield. The next day I went to Springfield where I delivered the note as directed. On reading it Judge Logan
smiled and, much to my surprise, gave me the required
certificate or license without asking a question beyond
my age, residence and the correct way of spelling my
name. The note from Lincoln read":

MY DEAR JUDGE —
    The bearer of this is a young man who thinks he can be a
lawyer. Examine him if you want to. I have done so and am
satisfied. He's a good deal smarter than he looks to be.
                                                    Yours
                                                        LINCOLN

On March 1, 1837, when he had gone through the various steps and become a fully accredited practitioner by
the action of the clerk of the Supreme Court in entering
his name on the roll of attorneys in the State, Lincoln
was still a resident of the village of New Salem. A month
and half later he had removed to Springfield. Years ago
Herndon gave me the papers, in Lincoln's handwriting,
containing the history of the first suit or court proceeding
in which Lincoln figured or with which he seems to have
had any connection. As it was his first venture in that line
and naturally throws more or less light on his evolution as a
lawyer, it is noteworthy enough to warrant a brief account
of its origin and termination. It was an action or, more
strictly speaking, three actions growing out of one episode
or transaction, and was brought by James P. Hawthorn
through his attorneys, Walker & Hewitt, in the circuit court
of Sangamon County, Illinois. Of the three causes one was
what is known among lawyers as an action on assumpsit,
or breach of contract, another for trespass *vi et armis*, and

PAGE OF THE RECORDS OF THE CIRCUIT COURT OF SANGAMON COUNTY, ILLINOIS, FOR MARCH 24, 1836, SHOWING THE COURT ORDER CERTIFYING TO LINCOLN'S GOOD MORAL CHARACTER ON HIS ADMISSION TO THE BAR

the third in replevin. With the exception of the replevin suit, which was not brought till in the fall, the declaration or complaint in each case — which was the initial proceeding in a lawsuit of that day — was filed July 1, 1836. This was before Lincoln had appeared before the two justices of the Supreme Court to secure his license to practice. John T. Stuart, looking forward to an election to Congress and who was soon to invite Lincoln to enter a partnership with him, had been retained by the defense; but, although the pleadings in one or two instances bear Stuart's signature, they are almost without exception in Lincoln's characteristic and legible handwriting. Stuart soon became absorbed in his race for Congress; at any rate, it was but a brief time until Lincoln assumed active charge of the defendant's interests. Stephen T. Logan, destined also several years later to become a partner of Lincoln, was the judge, and William Butler, at whose home Lincoln was a boarder and so continued till his marriage to Mary Todd, was the clerk.

The suit in assumpsit was based on Wooldridge's failure to furnish Hawthorn, the plaintiff, "two yoke of oxen to break up twenty acres of prairie sod-ground"; also because of his refusal to allow Hawthorn to have access to a tract of ground on which the latter had contracted with him to raise a crop of "corn or wheat at the option of the plaintiff"; for all of which he demanded a hundred dollars. The trespass case was of greater weight and importance. The declaration sets out in detail what happened when Hawthorn, despite the threats and protests of Wooldridge, undertook to reach the disputed cornfield. The situation became more or less dramatic. It was charged of Wooldridge, Lincoln's client, that: "He struck, beat, bruised and knocked him (Hawthorn) down; plucked, pulled and tore out large quantities of hair from his head; that with a stick and his fists he struck plaintiff a great many violent blows and strokes on and about his face, head, breast, back, shoulders, hips, legs, and divers other parts of his body; that he struck, shook, pulled, pushed and knocked plaintiff to the ground; violently hit, kicked, struck and beat him a great many other blows and strokes; and also then and there, with great violence, forced, pushed, thrust and gouged his fingers into plaintiff's eyes; by means of which assault and consequent illness, injuries, loss of time and expense for medical attention said plaintiff demands damages in the sum of five hundred dollars and other proper relief." The replevin suit demanded the return of "one black and white yoke of steers, one black cow, and calf and one prairie plow," together with twenty dollars damages for the unlawful detention of the same. The exceedingly modest demand for money reparation in all these cases would seem to indicate that the modern damage suit, which has gradually attained such profitable proportions, had not yet come into vogue.

With three suits against his first client on hand at one time we may well imagine that Lincoln, the young barrister, was in many respects a busy man. The record shows, as his first step, a plea filed October 5, 1836, containing the conventional denial of the alleged trespasses in support of which he puts himself "upon the country." On the same day, with a view either to gain time or in some way embarrass the plaintiff, or both, he files the affidavit of his client reciting the fact that, as the plaintiff is a young man

without family or property, and the court officers are in
danger of losing their fees, he should therefore be required
to furnish a bond for costs. On the following day, much to
the surprise of the defendant and his counsel, the required
bond for costs was duly executed and filed. The skirmish
for vantage-ground was now becoming brisk and animated. The next move on Lincoln's part was to draw up
and file an account which he undertakes to "exhibit and
prove as an offset" to the demand on assumpsit containing
sundry items illustrative of commercial values then current
on the frontier. With the exception of one line added by
Stuart the entire account is in Lincoln's hand as follows:

James P. Hawthorn to David Wooldridge Dr.

| | |
|---|---:|
| To Boarding from the first of April until the first day of November 1835 at $1–50 cents per week being 30 weeks 4 days | $45.75 |
| To use of waggon & team from first of April till first of November 1836. | $90.00 |
| 1834 | |
| To 11 bushels of wheat @ 75 | 8.25 |
| 1836 Jan'y 8 Cash lent | 100.00 |
| " May & June Breaking 10 acres of Prairy | 20.00 |
| | $264.00 |
| To money lent to enter land, afterwards entered in the name of your brother | 50.00 |

What next followed before the final encounter we do not
know, for the record is silent. The cases were now at issue,
but for some reason, which even Mr. Herndon did not
know, the term of court was suffered to adjourn without
conclusive action. The next term found the combatants
still apart and seemingly reluctant to measure arms. But
meanwhile the peacemaker had not been idle, for March 17,
1837, the parties by their counsel came into court with a report of the settlement of all pending litigation and asked

that the case be dismissed. The record shows that this was promptly done. In the assumpsit case judgment by agreement was entered against the plaintiff for costs; in the replevin case against the defendant; and in the trespass case that item was equally divided between the two. The judge duly signed the record, the parties in all probability withdrew from the old court-house in Hoffman's Row, and thus ended Abraham Lincoln's first lawsuit.

The first case in the Supreme Court of Illinois in which Lincoln appeared was that of Scammon vs. Cline, reported in 3rd Ills. p. 456. It was an action relating to the conflict of jurisdiction between two counties in the State, Boone and Jo Daviess. Mr. Scammon, the plaintiff in error, was himself a lawyer of more or less prominence in Chicago. Mr. Lincoln appeared for the other side, but his plea, a denial, was in the handwriting of his friend James H. Matheney. The case was begun during the April, 1839, term of the Boone Circuit Court. The opinion of the Supreme Court reversing the judgment of the lower court was rendered February 24, 1841.

The last public appearance of Lincoln in the trial of a cause was in the United States District Court in Springfield June 20, 1860. This was in the month following his nomination at Chicago, after which event we may well conclude that he was so deeply absorbed in the race for President he could ill afford to give any time to the practice of law. The action, entitled Dawson vs. Ennis, included a demand of ten thousand dollars damages for the sale, in Morgan County, Illinois, in violation of an agreement to the contrary, of an improved double plow on which a patent right had been obtained. The declaration was written

James P. Hawthorn to David Wooldridge Dr.

To Boarding from the first day of April until
the first of November 1835. at $1-50 cents per week
being 30 weeks & 4 days                          $ 45.75

To use of waggon & team from first of Ap-
ril till first of November 1836                   $ 90.00

1834 To 11 bushles of wheat @ 75.                    8.25

1836. Jan 8 Cash lent                              100.00

Andy & Jms. Breaking 10 acres of Prair[ie]         30.00

To Money lent to enter land, expences     $ 264.00
entered in the name of your
brother                                             50 00

James P. Hawthorn
        vs                    }    In Trespass
David Wooldridge

The defendant, David Wooldridge, being
sworn says that he verily believes that the said
plaintiff is unable to pay the costs of this suit, and
that the officers of this court will be in danger of
of losing their costs in said suit unless the said
plaintiff be ruled to give security therefor. He states
that said plaintiff is a young man and without family
and that he has not, to this said defendants knowledge,
any real, or personal property out of which the costs
could be made.
                                        David Wooldridge

PAPERS IN LINCOLN'S FIRST CASE, HAWTHORN *vs.* WOOLDRIDGE

and signed by Mr. Lincoln, who appeared for the plaintiff along with John A. McClernand and Isaac J. Ketcham, of Jacksonville. John M. Palmer represented the defense. On June 20, 1860, as noted, Lincoln argued the cause of the plaintiff, whereupon the court took the case under advisement. The record shows no further action till March 9, 1861, when a finding was made for the defendant and judgment entered against Lincoln's client for costs. It will thus be seen that, when we view Lincoln's legal career as a whole, we can hardly resist the conclusion that he was practically unsuccessful both in his first and last suit.

A word as to Lincoln's law partnerships, of which there were three. The first, with John T. Stuart, began April 27, 1837, and continued till April 14, 1841. It was promptly followed by the second with Stephen T. Logan, which terminated September 20, 1843. Immediately thereafter Lincoln was joined by William H. Herndon, and that partnership continued till, in the language of Herndon, it was "dissolved by the bullet of John Wilkes Booth in April, 1865."

As indicative of his regard for his law partners it may be said that in the spring of the year following his inauguration as President, he directed the Secretary of War to appoint Judge Logan one of three commissioners authorized to investigate and audit all unsettled claims against the War Department at Cairo, Illinois. The other members of the commission were George S. Boutwell, of Massachusetts, and Charles A. Dana, of New York. Mr. Dana related that after the commission had been at its labors two days Judge Logan was compelled by illness to resign. The next year Lincoln tendered Herndon a similar appointment, describing it in his telegram as "a job at St. Louis at $5 a day and mileage," but which Herndon delicned. So far as known Lincoln made no offer to Stuart, due probably to the fact that the latter was elected to Congress in 1862 and therefore disqualified from holding any other office.

We have the warrant of Herndon for the statement that Lincoln was one of the clearest and most unerring thinkers the bar of Illinois ever produced. Of course, his integrity, his humanity, his kindness have not been overlooked; in fact, have in some instances been overplayed; but too much cannot be said of his wonderful intellect and profound ability in the realm of reason. Of this pronounced and marvelous equipment Lincoln was duly aware; more than that, it can be truthfully said, he was not only conscious but in reality more or less vain of it. It will be remembered that during a ride with Herndon to Petersburg Lincoln, after relating to his partner the history of his mother's origin and descent, alluded to his unusual analytical and reasoning powers, that which distinguished him from so many other men, frankly contending that he inherited it from his mother. According to the testimony of Herndon, Lincoln did not say this boastfully, but because both he and Herndon knew that his strength in this regard was conceded to him by practically every other member of the bar. All of which emphasizes the axiom enunciated by John Hay that no really great man was ever modest.

Although a good lawyer it is doubtful if Lincoln held the law in any higher esteem than his colleagues; in fact, it looked, sometimes, as if he lost sight of its standing or value as a profession and viewed it rather as a vocation — simply as a means of gaining a livelihood. Judges Logan and Davis were more deeply absorbed in it as a profession, but it was only that it might yield them greater financial returns, because both of them were careful and ambitious men, both accumulating comfortable fortunes. On the other hand, with a strong and ineradicable bent in the direction of politics, Lincoln seemed to care less for the material end of things. Before me lies one of Lincoln's account books, a glance over which will indicate the scope and extent of his practice. On the first page it is marked, "Day Book of Lincoln & Herndon"; and in another place, "Lincoln & Herndon's Fee Book." The entries are mostly in Lincoln's hand. It comprises the record of a hundred and eighty-two cases. In one of them the fee charged is only $2.50; in two it is $3; in sixty-four, $5; in five, $7; in sixty-three, $10; in five, $50; in one, $100, and in the remainder from $15 to $25. The total is slightly in excess of $2000 representing over three years' business. The book illustrates the crude and primitive way in which Lincoln and his partner kept trace of their business. Here is one entry:

Scott *vs.* Busher (for Def't.)
  To attending case in Menard Cir. Court if it ends where it is.
  Paid.                                                         $20.00

Here is another — tried before a justice of the peace:

Negro *vs.* Robert Smith (for Deft.)
  To attending case of Negro Bob.   J.P.                        $5.00

This is how they kept the record of their partnership accounts:

Stevenson & Wardwell *vs.* Garrett (for Defts)
  To attending case in Sup. Court Dec. Term 1846               $10.00

Roswell Munsill *vs.* Temple (for Plff in Error)
    To attending case in Sup. Court,
    By note $10.00. Note mislaid and cannot be found.
    Later — paid cash in full of note

Mrs. Little *vs.* Little's Estate (for Deft)
    To attending to case before J. Probate                 $10.00
    (Dan & Sam Little bound for this)

Across the lines of this entry are written "Incorrect," and
again "Not Right."

G. B. Merryman *vs.* Lake (for Plff)
To attending to case — Cir. Court                          $10.00
    (½ goes to Logan)

A few items from the account or fee book kept by the
firm of Stuart & Lincoln, a portion of which I was enabled
to secure in Springfield many years ago, may not be without
interest. The entries are all in Lincoln's hand and relate
to cases in which both he and Stuart were interested and
within a year or more after their partnership was formed.
A glance at the fees set down opposite each case will serve
to indicate how lucrative the practice of the newly established firm was. In the absence of evidence to the contrary, it is fair to assume there was an equal division of the
proceeds. Following is copied from one page of the book:

E. C. Ross
    To Stuart & Lincoln                                    Dr.
1837 — April — To attendance at trial of right of J. F. Davis
        property before Moffett                            $5.00

Mather Lamb & Co.
        To Stuart & Lincoln                                Dr.
1837 — April — To attendance at trial of J. F. Davis prop-
        erty before Moffett                                $5.00

Lucinda Mason
        To Stuart & Lincoln                                Dr.
1837 — Oct — To obtaining assignment of Dower              $5.00

Matter, Saml & Co

To Stuart & Lincoln      Dr

1837 - Aprile - To attendance at trial of right of
J. F. Davis' property before Moffett    $ 5.00


William Herndon

To Stuart & Lincoln     Dr.

1837 - Oct? To Attachment case against Smith   $5.00


Wiley & Wood

To Stuart & Lincoln     Dr

1837-8 To defence of Chancery case of Ely   $50.00
Credit by coat to Stuart —      15.00
                    $ 35.00


Peyton L. Harrison

To Stuart & Lincoln     Dr

1838 March - To case with Dickinson —   $10.00


Allen & Stone

To Stuart & Lincoln     Dr

1838. Oct? To case with Carter   $2.50


ITEMS FROM STUART AND LINCOLN'S FEE BOOK

Wiley & Wood
        To Stuart & Lincoln                    Dr.
1837-8 To defence of Chancery case of Ely                    $50.00
        Credit by coat to Stuart                             15.00
                                                            $35.00


Peyton L. Harrison
        To Stuart & Lincoln                    Dr.
1838 — March —
        To case with Dickinson                              $10.00


Allen & Stone
        To Stuart & Lincoln                    Dr.
1838 — Oct
        To case with Centre                                 $2.50


A word as to the size of the fees Lincoln was in the habit of charging his clients. In this respect he was exasperatingly modest. His associates at the bar, including Judge Davis, were out of patience with him. "Think," exclaimed one of them whom I knew in Springfield in the early eighties, "of a lawyer carrying a case through the Supreme Court for the paltry sum of ten dollars, and yet that seemed to be the limit of his charges." The following letter serves to indicate Mr. Lincoln's estimate of the value of a professional man's services:

SPRINGFIELD ILLS, Feb'y 21, 1856

MR. GEORGE P. FLOYD,
   Quincy Ills.
DEAR SIR:
   I have just received yours of the 16th with check on Flagg & Savage for twenty-five dollars. You must think I am a high-priced man. You are too liberal with your money. Fifteen dollars is enough for the job. I send you a receipt for fifteen dollars and return you a ten-dollar bill.
                        Yours truly
                                A. LINCOLN

The current impression that Lincoln chose Herndon as his law partner, because he could draw up the required papers and thus divide the office work, is a great popular misconception. Lincoln was not only the better office man of the two, but when at home really performed a large part of the clerical and office work. When it came to drawing up a paper, either a document to be used in court or to file away for preservation, Lincoln had no superior. He was careful to the point of punctiliousness. And this is all the more remarkable when we reflect that many of his colleagues were trained, college-bred men; whereas his entire attendance at school did not exceed eleven months; and he not only had never been permitted to enter college, but had never seen the inside of a college, academy, or high-school building till after he was old enough to go to Congress or practice law.

He rarely ever used a lead-pencil, preferring pen and ink. His penmanship as compared to Herndon's and the average lawyer of his day was small, uniform, and always legible. Herndon literally slung his ink over the page; Stuart's writing was both cramped and uneven; Davis's loose and irregular; and Judge Treat's so stilted and angular it was difficult to read. But it was not alone in penmanship that Lincoln excelled; he almost invariably spelled correctly. He sometimes spelled wagon with two *g*'s (and by some it has even been held that that is not always incorrect), but unlike many of his colleagues he rarely ever spelled judgment with two *e*'s. In the matter of punctuation he was likewise painstaking and correct. He never omitted a comma, and he used the semicolon with discrimination and taste. He had one peculiarity; frequently at the end of a sentence or paragraph using a short dash to indicate a full stop instead of the conventional period. To the writer, who has examined the court records of the various counties in Illinois in which Lincoln practiced law, and who has read so many pages of his manuscript as well as the thousands of pages written by his colleagues, a majority of whom paid no attention to punctuation, the matter of his accuracy and conformity to the rules of grammar becomes all the more wonderful and impressive. If so many of his associates at the bar who had enjoyed the benefits of college training displayed such indifferent scholarship and lack of skill, the question arises: Where did Lincoln acquire his genius and sagacity?

Of the one hundred and seventy-six cases which Mr. Lincoln either individually or in association with his partners carried through the Supreme Court of Illinois, he won ninety-two; of the twelve cases tried in the United States District and Circuit Courts (of which, however, only ten were decided), he appears to have won seven; and of the three cases in the Supreme Court of the United States, he was successful in two. It would be difficult, if not well-nigh impossible, at this late day to fix accurately the limits of his practice in the lower or courts of original jurisdiction in Illinois. The famous Eighth Circuit over which he traveled so long consisted in 1853 of eight counties: Sangamon, Logan, McLean, Woodford, Tazewell, DeWitt, Champaign, and Vermilion. In 1857 Sangamon, Woodford, and Tazewell were transferred to another circuit. The zenith of his practice was during the partnership with Herndon and between the years 1852 and 1858. After that the siren voice of politics began to lure him away from the profession.

In order to illustrate the character and scope of his practice and thus determine the kind of lawyer he was, a brief
retrospect of some of the most notable cases in which he
appeared is essential.

Bailey *vs.* Cromwell, an action appealed from Tazewell
County, reached the Supreme Court of Illinois in December, 1839, two years after his admission to the bar. Mr.
Lincoln represented the appellant and Stephen T. Logan
the other side. Of his conduct of this case Mr. Lincoln was
more or less proud, and the case itself has been generously
and frequently cited in the appellate courts of other States.
It was in the presentation of this cause that Mr. Lincoln
maintained that it was a presumption of law in the State
of Illinois that every person is free without regard to color;
that where the consideration of a promissory note was
shown to have been a negro girl, and that, at the time of
the sale, it was agreed between the parties that before the
payment of the note should be demanded the payee should
produce the necessary papers and indenture to prove that
the girl was a slave or bound to service under the laws of
the State of Illinois, and such papers were not produced,
though demanded, there was no consideration for the note,
and that it was therefore void, as the sale of a free person
was an illegal transaction.

The case of Carman *vs.* Glasscock, another one of Lincoln's early ventures, was tried in the Circuit Court of
Sangamon County, also in 1839. It related to a controversy over a fish-trap dam erected across the Sangamon
River; and incidentally the question of the navigability of
the latter stream. The brief of Lincoln's argument was
more or less suggestive of the flatboat ride on the bosom

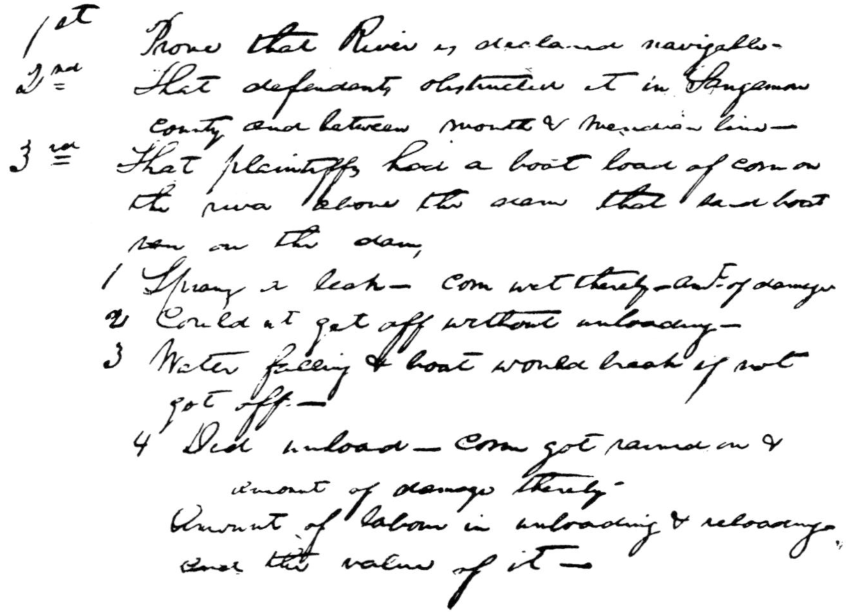

of the river which he and John Hanks took when they floated down to New Orleans in 1831. The original, which is in Lincoln's hand and is still preserved, reads as follows:

1st   Prove that River is declared navigable —

2nd.  That defendants obstructed it in Sangamon county and between mouth & meridian line —

3rd.  That plaintiffs had a boat load of corn on the river above the dam; that said boat ran on the dam,

    1 Sprang leak — corn wet thereby — am't of damages

    2 Could n't get off without unloading —

    3 Water falling & boat would break if not got off —

    4 Did unload — corn got rained on & amount of damage thereby —

    Amount of labor in unloading & reloading and the value of it.

# CHAPTER XII

Green *vs*. Green, Lincoln's first divorce case—His dislike for divorce suits—His magnanimity in the trial of Samuel Rogers *vs*. Polly Rogers — His comment on the Miller *vs*. Miller petition — A pitiful story of marital discord — A slow collector — Rarely enforced collection of fees by suit — When in partnership with Logan brought one suit for fee — Retained by Illinois Central Railroad to enjoin McLean County from assessing road for taxation — Lincoln's letter to Brayman — Gains case in Supreme Court — Lincoln sues railroad company for his fee — History of transaction — Dividing fee with Herndon — One of Lincoln's first suits for personal injury — The Horological Cradle case — The slander suit of McKibben *vs*. Hart — Turning the fee over to his father — The Spink *vs*. Chiniquiy case settled by Lincoln — The Dungey *vs*. Spencer case as recalled by Lawrence Weldon — Fixing Lincoln's fee — Linder *vs*. Fleenor — How Lincoln proved the marriage — Dorman *vs*. Lane — Proposal by Lincoln to his associates that they join him and donate fees as a wedding present.

ACCORDING to Herndon there was one kind of practice to which Mr. Lincoln as a lawyer was not favorably inclined, and that was suits for divorce; in fact, whenever practicable, he tried to discourage that sort of ligitation. Of course he sometimes appeared in divorce proceedings, but it was always with more or less reluctance. The first action brought by him to dissolve the "marriage bond," as he termed it, was that of Nancy Green *vs*. Aaron Green filed in the Sangamon Circuit Court September 4, 1837. Lincoln represented the wife, and succeeded in securing the divorce on the ground of desertion or abandonment for a given period. A year later, in the same court, he appeared in another case, that of Samuel Rogers *vs*. Polly Rogers, but this time in behalf of the husband. An affidavit executed by Lincoln in connection with the case indicates to what extent he could be chivalrous or forbearing when his professional duty required him to espouse the cause of a man in a contest with his wife. Following is a copy of the original document which has been preserved:

State of Illinois
Sangamon County

A. Lincoln being first duly sworn says that he was employed as counsel in the case of Samuel Rogers *vs.* Polly Rogers for a Divorce; that he, the affiant, drew up the complainant's bill; that said complainant at that time told this affiant that he could prove that the said defendant had been guilty of adultery with one William Short while she lived with said complainant; but that affiant advised said complainant not to make the charge in his bill as there was other sufficient grounds upon which to obtain a divorce, to-wit, absence of more than two years.

A. LINCOLN

Sworn to and subscribed before me this 20th day of October 1838

WM. BUTLER CLERK

There is also in existence an affidavit by Samuel Rogers, the complainant, in which he recites that the charge of adultery was omitted from his bill at the instigation of his counsel, Mr. Lincoln, who opposed the allegation "for no other cause than through tenderness to defendant's character." One can hardly read Lincoln's affidavit in this case without wondering how many lawyers of this day and generation would, under like circumstances, be equally considerate and magnanimous.

While on the subject of divorce suits I can hardly refrain from adverting to one that deeply impressed and awakened Lincoln's sympathetic interest. It was brought by him during the partnership with Judge Logan, entitled George Miller *vs.* Elizabeth Miller, and was tried in Menard County. When one has read the lament of the luckless and discouraged husband he can doubtless account for Lincoln's sympathy, and appreciate the significance of the brief memorandum penned on the back of one of the pleadings prepared by him for his use in the suit: "A pitiful story of marital discord." In his petition, written by Lincoln, the husband recites that he and Elizabeth Miller were married in Bath County, Kentucky, in 1829; that

after said marriage they continued to live together as man and wife, he doing and performing all the duties of an affectionate husband for two or three years when unhappy differences arose and without the fault of your orator she, the defendant, left the bed and board of your orator and went to her relatives; a short time passed and a reconciliation which your orator fondly but vainly hoped would be permanent took place between the defendant and him and she returned to his house; but in a short time she left again and after that frequent temporary reconciliations and separations occurred between them extending in time to the year 1834 when it was agreed between them that they would remove separately to Illinois, there meet, be finally reconciled and live together as man and wife; that they did so remove to Sangamon county, Illinois, where they soon met and, being encouraged by the defendant, your orator set about making preparation to live with her by procuring a house etc. when in a short time, without the fault of your orator, difficulties again arose extending in time up to the year 1836 when she, the defendant, announced to your orator her determination never to live with him again. Thus matters passed till the year 1841 when the defendant and your orator again met in Kentucky and at her instance agreed that on their return to Illinois they would meet and live in peace. Your orator further charges that he did in good faith endeavor to put said last named agreement into execution, but that on meeting the defendant in Menard county, Illinois, where she now resides and has resided since the formation of the county in the fall of 1841, she again announced to your orator her determination never to live with him again, since which time your orator has abandoned all hope of a reconciliation. And so your orator charges that the said defendant has wilfully deserted and absented herself from him without any reasonable cause for more than two years. In tender consideration of all which your orator prays that on a final hearing of this cause your Honor will decree that the bonds of matrimony heretofore and now existing between said defendant and your orator be forever dissolved; and that your Honor will grant such other and further relief as equity may require.

Mr. Herndon is also authority for the statement that Lincoln was a poor collector. He disliked to attempt to collect his fee by suit; but there is abundant evidence that his partners were not quite so indulgent. In July, 1845, he filed a suit in the Sangamon Circuit Court against James D. Smith, executor of the last will and testament of William Trailor, deceased, in which a demand is made for the payment of one hundred dollars, being a fee due "For defending said Trailor against a charge of murdering one Fisher." The action was brought in the name of Logan & Lincoln and the declaration or complaint is in the handwriting of the latter. Another suit of like nature, a relic of the partnership with Herndon, was brought in the same court five years later. The defendant was John B. Moffett and the declaration was written by Lincoln, who describes the plaintiffs as "Abraham Lincoln and William H. Herndon doing business in the name of Lincoln & Herndon." The demand is based on an account containing two items; one, a fee of one hundred dollars for bringing a suit in the Sangamon Circuit Court and fifty dollars for carrying it through the Supreme Court; but the record shows that the plaintiffs recovered judgment for only seventy-five dollars and costs.

A third suit, brought by Lincoln for an attorney fee, and the most noteworthy in his career, will require more extended mention. In the summer of 1853 the authorities of McLean County, Illinois, believing that all the land in that county should pay its proportionate share of taxes, decided to place on the assessment rolls all the property in that county belonging to the Illinois Central Railroad Company. This was done in the face of the fact that, by the action of the Illinois legislature, that corporation had been granted exemption from taxation conditioned that it should pay seven per cent of its gross earnings into the State treasury. The railroad company at once brought suit to enjoin the county from collecting the tax and to that end sought to retain the services of Lincoln in their behalf. as the following letter will show:

Pekin, Ills. Oct. 3, 1853

M. Brayman Esq.
Dear Sir:
Neither the county of McLean nor any one else on its behalf has yet made any engagement with me in relation to its suit with the Illinois Central Railroad, on the subject of taxation — I am now free to make any engagement for the Road; and if you think fit you may "count me in." Please write me on receipt of this — I shall be here at least ten days.

Yours truly<br>A. Lincoln

Lincoln was duly employed and four days after the above letter was written, Mr. Brayman, who was of counsel for the railroad company, sent to Lincoln, through the Marine Bank of Springfield, a retainer fee of two hundred and fifty dollars. In the lower court the case went against the railroad company and an appeal was promptly taken to the Supreme Court at Springfield. "At the hearing in the Supreme Court," relates Mr. James F. Joy, who was the general solicitor for the railroad, "both Lincoln and myself argued the case for the appellants, he being the junior and I the senior counsel. John T. Stuart and Stephen T. Logan, both former partners of Lincoln, represented the appellee. The case was long under advisement, and later the court complied with my request and gave us a rehearing. Mr. Lincoln and I did the best we could in the reargument with the result that the case was decided in our favor."

Later when it came to settling the question of attorneys' fees, Lincoln, on learning that the railroad company had paid Mr. Joy twelve hundred dollars, wrote the latter that for his services he would like to have the company give him a particular section of land, describing it, saying that for once in his life he thought he was entitled to a large fee. This the officers of the road declined to do, claiming that the land was covered by a mortgage or some other encumbrance. It was then that he rendered a bill for five thousand dollars, less the retainer fee of two hundred and fifty dollars already advanced, which the company also declined to pay. "I think there would have been no difficulty with Mr. Lincoln's bill," related Joy, "if I had charged as, perhaps, I ought to have done, five thousand dollars. The time for such fees as the lawyers now ask had not arrived, and my own charge for the arguments in the case was only twelve hundred dollars. I think now my charge was a small one for the service rendered. The railroad company, after declining to pay Mr. Lincoln the five thousand dollars he demanded because they thought the fee was too large, then made him this proposition: 'Bring suit against the company for the amount demanded and no attempt will be made to defend against it. If by the testimony of other lawyers it shall appear to be a fair charge and there shall be a judgment for the amount, then we shall be justified in paying it.' "

In compliance with the recommendations of the railroad officials Lincoln brought the required suit for his fee in the Circuit Court of McLean County. Several years ago I read the declaration in his own handwriting. It was then on file in the court-house at Bloomington. Following is a copy of his account or demand as made out and presented to the company as well as the written opinion of six of his fellow lawyers who certified to the reasonableness of his fee:

The Illinois Central Railroad Company
To A. Lincoln      Dr.

To professional services in the case of the Illinois Central Railroad Company against the County of McLean argued in the Supreme Court of Illinois and decided at the December Term 1855        $5000

We, the undersigned, members of Illinois Bar, understanding that the above entitled cause was twice argued in the Supreme Court; and that the judgment therein decided the question of the claim of counties and other minor municipal corporations to tax the property of said Railroad Company and settle said questions against said claim and in favor of said Railroad Company are of opinion that the sum above charged as a fee is not unreasonable.

GRANT GOODRICH
N. B. JUDD
ARCHIBALD WILLIAMS
N. H. PURPLE
O. H. BROWNING
R. S. BLACKWELL

Of the six men who thus approved Lincoln's claim, one became a Congressman and later an ambassador to a European court; one a United States District Judge in a

The Illinois Central Railroad Company
To A. Lincoln Dr.

To professional services in the case
of the Illinois Central Railroad Company against the County of McLean,
argued in the Supreme Court of
the State of Illinois, and decided
at December Term 1855 $5000-00.

We the undersigned members of the Illinois Bar, understanding that the above
entitled cause was twice argued in the
Supreme Court; and that the judgment
therein decides the question of the claim
of Counties and other minor municipal
Corporations, to tax the property of said
Railroad Company, and settles said
question against said claim, and in favor of said Railroad Company, are of opinion that the sum above charged, as a
fee, is not unreasonable.

Grant Goodrich
N. B. Judd
Archibald Williams
N. H. Purple
O. H. Browning
R. S. Blackwell.

LINCOLN'S BILL AGAINST THE ILLINOIS CENTRAL RAILROAD COMPANY,
WITH COPY OF OPINION SIGNED BY FELLOW LAWYERS

Western State; another a United States Senator and also a member of the President's Cabinet at Washington; and the remainder were three of the ablest and most successful lawyers of the Illinois bar. When the case was called in court the railroad company suffered the judgment to go by default, and later, within the period fixed by law, paid to the clerk of the court the required five thousand dollars less the two hundred and fifty dollars already advanced to Lincoln as a retainer. Although the name of Herndon does not appear in the record of the case as of counsel, it does not follow that he had no part in it or that Lincoln was disposed to overlook him. "The judgment was finally paid," related Herndon, "and Lincoln gave me my half. He brought the money down from Bloomington one evening and sent me word to come to the office. It was after dark and when he had pushed my share of the proceeds across the table to me, he covered it for an instant with his hand, smiled, and said: 'Billy, it seems to me it will be bad taste on your part to keep on saying the severe things I have heard from you about railroads and other corporations. The truth is, instead of criticizing them, you and I ought to thank God for letting this one fall into our hands.'"

As this was the largest attorney fee ever received by Mr. Lincoln, it may not be amiss to note also the smallest one; which was two dollars and a half paid to him for his services in a suit in the fall of 1838, one half of which went to his partner, John T. Stuart. In another case the firm of Stuart & Lincoln made a charge of fifty dollars, but their clients were either reluctant or unable to pay the entire sum in cash; for the record of the transaction in the book, entered by Lincoln, shows that a coat, furnished to Stuart and valued at fifteen dollars, was accepted as a partial payment.

By the time Mr. Lincoln was nearing the end of his career as a practicing lawyer, the modern damage suit against common carriers and other corporations, especially where based on personal injury, was coming into vogue. Lincoln's experience in that line, as indicated by several cases to which Herndon called my attention, was necessarily limited. One of the earliest was an action brought by him during the partnership with Stuart in which George Stockton demands of James Tolby a hundred dollars for damages to "a cooking stove" in transit between Beardstown and Springfield. Tolby drove "a conveyance for hire" between the points named and was therefore liable as a common carrier. Another case, and probably the first personal injury suit he ever brought against a common carrier, was that of Grubb *vs*. Fink and Walker tried in 1852. The defendants were operating a stage-coach between Rushville and Frederick which overturned one day resulting in a serious injury to one of the passengers. In his account of the accident Mr. Lincoln is sufficiently careful and minute in his averments. After describing the plaintiff's long list of "cuts, bruises, wounds, and divers broken bones," he recites the payment by him of large sums of money paid for the services of physicians and surgeons in the endeavor to be cured of the fractures, bruises, and injuries, and concludes with a demand for damages of one thousand dollars. Another action, that of Jasper Harris *vs*. Great Western Railway Company, was tried in Sangamon County in 1854. The plaintiff was a brakeman whose "right foot, ankle, leg, and thigh while in the service of said company, were so greatly torn, crushed and broken that amputation of his said right limb above the knee was necessary." It was Lincoln's first suit against a railroad company for personal injury and included a demand for ten thousand dollars in damages. The declaration, though signed Lincoln & Herndon, was written by Lincoln, and when contrasted with the phraseology of a bill of complaint as lawyers now word such things is about as crude and primitive as the machinery and appliances of that early period appear when compared to the ponderous and elaborate equipment now in use by the railroads of this day.

Perhaps no case in which Lincoln figured awakened his interest more readily and completely than an action, entitled Hildreth *vs.* Turner, appealed to the Supreme Court of Illinois from Logan County in the spring of 1854. It related to the validity of a patent, but involved no great legal principle and was otherwise of no especial significance save as Lincoln's connection therewith gave it prominence. In February, 1853, one Alexander Edmonds, a mechanical genius in the town of Mount Pulaski, invented what he called "The Horological Cradle," a contrivance to be "rocked by machinery with a weight running on one or more pulleys; the cradle constituting the pendulum and which, being wound up, would rock itself, thus saving the continual labor to mother and nurses of rocking the cradle." The brief description by the inventor suffices to indicate the objects and character of the proposed apparatus, but notwithstanding its doubtful value from a practical standpoint there was something about it that attracted the interest and attention of Mr. Lincoln. Eventually a disagreement between the inventor of the machine and a man who was induced to advance capital for its manufacture led to a lawsuit in which Lincoln & Herndon represented one side of the controversy when it reached the Supreme Court. "Although Lincoln and I were duly retained," related Herndon, "Mr. Lincoln, owing to his natural bent for the study of mechanical appliances, soon became so enamoured of the case that he assumed entire charge of our end of it. The model of the machine was for a time exhibited in a store window in town and eventually reached our office where Mr. Lincoln became deeply absorbed in it. He would dilate at great length on its merits for the benefit of our callers or any one else who happened into the office and manifested the least interest in it. Although the papers in the case indicated that Lincoln & Herndon were of counsel, I recall that I had but little beyond a nominal part in it. All the papers were drawn by Mr. Lincoln himself, a division of our labors to which I readily consented because, in view of my apparent lack of faith in the enterprise, I apprehend he suspected I was willing that he should assume the entire responsibility of winning or losing the suit."

The record of the case recites that the inventor professed to have obtained a "patent for said invention and had been exhibiting a model of the same; that the patent right would be valuable and could be sold for a large amount of money, etc."; but before the case was decided it was discovered that Edmonds had no letters patent for the cradle, its machinery or mode of operation, but only for an ornamental design for a "horological cradle" as set out in the specifications. The court ruled against the patentability of the contrivance, holding that every one should be presumed to know that a baby cradle would not be patentable by the description so far as the application of its use is concerned.

While the case was under consideration by the Supreme Court, the model was brought into the room and set to going — a proceeding in which Lincoln was plainly interested as shown by his willingness to enlighten the judges, some of whom ventured to make inquiries regarding the *modus operandi*. Although the inventor claimed to have disposed of his rights in the States of Mississippi, Georgia, Alabama, Florida, and South Carolina for ten thousand dollars, he made no mention of his interest in Illinois, Indiana, Missouri, and other near-by States, probably because the people in those localities, like Herndon, had seen the device at a range close enough to make them more or less cautious in the investment of their surplus capital.

On the way to his office from the court-room after the case was over, Lincoln was halted by an old friend in the person of John W. Bunn, the banker, who related the incident to me shortly before his recent death in Springfield. "Mr. Lincoln," said Bunn, "was telling me about the case and included a description of the apparatus, although I had seen the model of it in operation in a store window several times. After agreeing with him that it was rather an ingenious piece of mechanism, I then ventured to ask him how to stop the thing when in motion. 'There's the rub,' he replied, laughing, 'and I reckon I'll have to answer you as I did the judge who asked the same question. The thing's like some of the glib and interesting talkers you and I know, John; when it gets to going it doesn't know when to stop.'"

The shrinkage in a lawyer's practice in Lincoln's day attributable to the lack of bodily injury suits was more than counterbalanced by the then popular slander suit. It was a most abundant source of litigation and hardly a term of court was allowed to pass without one or more actions of that kind. The money demand for damages was invariably large, and even though the injured party sometimes recovered judgment for the full amount demanded, he frequently waived payment of all but a nominal sum. Of these primitive and sprightly contests Lincoln had his proportionate share. In Coles County, Illinois, in the fall of 1843, in conjunction with Usher F. Linder, he appeared for the plaintiff in the slander suit of Bagley vs. Vanmeter. Evidently Lincoln's prospects, so far as a generous fee is concerned, were not very encouraging, for a document written by him and signed by his client, the plaintiff, has been found in which the latter, referring to the judgment in his behalf which he expects, makes the following pertinent reservation regarding the pay due his attorneys: "I assign twenty dollars to Usher F. Linder and thirty dollars to Logan & Lincoln if said judgment shall amount to so much." Unfortunately for all concerned, when the records were all made and the money paid in, the judgment yielded a total of eighty dollars. In the case of Thomas McKibben, who brought suit against Jonathan Hart demanding two thousand dollars damages because the latter had called him a horsethief, Mr. Lincoln represented the plaintiff. Trial took place during the May term, 1845, of the Circuit Court of Coles County, Illinois. Mr. Lincoln's father, Thomas Lincoln, lived a few miles south of Charleston, the county seat, which will doubtless account for the fact that the latter's son figured so frequently in the litigation of that locality. In the case mentioned, Lincoln secured for his client a judgment for about two hundred dollars, of which thirty-five dollars was assigned to him for his fee and which he deposited with the clerk of the court with instructions to pay the same to his father. In due time Thomas Lincoln trudged over to Charleston, where the money which, doubtless, was a welcome addition to the old gentleman's meager income, was turned over to him. The receipt, drawn up by the clerk, was duly signed, but the name, Thomas Lincoln, was written by his stepson, John D. Johnston.

One of the most noted actions for slander in which Mr. Lincoln participated was that of Spink *vs.*Chiniquiy begun in Kankakee County, Illinois, a case in which Charles Chiniquiy, a priest, was sued for having falsely charged that Peter Spink, one of his parishioners, had been guilty of perjury. The parties and most of the witnesses were French Catholics. Mr. Lincoln and Leonard Swett represented Father Chiniquiy. It was a well-known and warmly contested case. "Father Chiniquiy was plucky," related Henry C. Whitney who was present and remembered the trial, "and plead justification; and preparations were made for a 'fight to the finish,' not only by the two principals, but by the two respective neighborhoods in which they lived, for eventually almost everybody became involved. A change of venue brought the case to Champaign County, and when the term came on the principals, their lawyers and witnesses and an immense retinue of followers, came to Urbana. The hotels were monopolized and a large number camped out. After a tedious and long-drawn-out trial the jury disagreed. Next term the crowd in no wise diminished returned, camp outfits, musicians, parrots, pet dogs, and all. The prospect was that all their scandal would have to be aired again; but Mr. Lincoln, who abhorred that class of litigation, in which there was no utility, and dreading the outlook, set to work and finally effected a compromise."

The formal decree reciting the terms of the settlement of the case which follows was prepared by Lincoln and is an excellent specimen of his concise and orderly presentation of a legal proposition:

Peter Spink
   vs.
Charles Chiniquiy.

This day came the parties and the defendant denies that he has ever charged, or believed the plaintiff to be guilty of Perjury; that whatever he has said from which such a charge could be inferred, he said on the information of others, protesting his own disbelief in the charge; and that he now disclaims any belief in the truth of said charge against said plaintiff. It is therefore, by agreement of the parties, ordered that the suit be dismissed, each party paying his own cost — the defendant to pay his part of the cost heretofore ordered to be paid by said plaintiff.

Two more slander suits, in which Lincoln had a part and which were carefully explained to me by Herndon, I ought not to omit. One was the case of Dungey *vs.* Spencer tried at the town of Clinton, in Dewitt County, in the spring of 1855. Lincoln represented Dungey, the plaintiff, and Lawrence Weldon, afterwards a member of the United States Court of Claims, the defendant. The basis of the action, as set out in the declaration in Lincoln's hand, and for which several thousand dollars in damages was asked, was the charge that the defendant "in the presence of divers good citizens falsely and maliciously spoke and uttered of and concerning the plaintiff, these false scandalous, malicious, and defamatory words: 'Black Bill (meaning the plaintiff) is a negro and it will be easily proved if called for.'" It was a family quarrel, Dungey, who was a Portuguese and somewhat dark complexioned, having married Spencer's sister. The law of Illinois made it a crime for a negro to marry a white woman, and hence the words were slanderous. It is unnecessary to dwell on the details of the trial. It suffices to state that Lincoln won, recovering for his client, the plaintiff, a judgment for six hundred dollars, of which amount the latter on the advice of his counsel remitted four hundred dollars; the defendant meanwhile assuming payment of Lincoln's fee and the costs of the suit.

"At this juncture," related Mr. Weldon later in life, "Mr. Lincoln proposed to leave the question of the amount of his fee to my associates, Mr. C. H. Moore and myself. We protested against this and insisted that he should fix the amount of his own fee. After a few moments' thought he said: 'Well, gentlemen, don't you think I have honestly earned twenty-five dollars?' We were astonished, and had he said one hundred dollars it would have been nearer what we expected. The judgment was a large one for those days: he had attended the case at two terms of court, had been engaged for two days in a hotly contested suit, and his client's adversary was going to pay the bill. The simplicity of his character in money matters is well illustrated by the fact that for all this service he only charged twenty-five dollars."

"In his argument to the jury," continued Weldon, "Mr.

Lincoln was both entertaining and effective. A dramatic and powerful stroke was his direct reference to Spencer's accusation that Dungey was a 'nigger.' It had a curious touch of the ludicrous by his pronunciation of a word which, instead of detracting, seemed to add to the effect. I hear him now as he said: 'Gentlemen of the jury, my client is not a Negro, though it is no crime to be a Negro — no crime to be born with a black skin. But my client is not a Negro. His skin may not be as white as ours, but I say he is not a Negro, though he may be a Moor.'" The humor in the situation was due to the fact that the lawyer who assisted Mr. Weldon on the other side of the case was Mr. C. H. Moore, an attorney living in the village of Clinton where the case was tried, and when Mr. Lincoln's attention was called to his play upon words by Judge Davis he smiled and replied: "Of course, your Honor, I mean a Moor, not our friend C. H. Moore; and I therefore repeat that my client may be a Moor but he is not a Negro."

The recollection by Mr. Weldon of Lincoln's proverbially generous treatment of his clients in the matter of fees prompts me to repeat an incident narrated to me by John W. Bunn, the veteran banker, who was also a client and close friend of Lincoln and who outlived all the other financiers of Lincoln's day in Springfield. "On the way from his home to the office or *vice versa*," said Mr. Bunn to me, "Mr. Lincoln and I frequently walked a short distance together. One morning he was telling me about a lawsuit the day before in which he succeeded in gaining possession of a farm for one of his clients. For his services he had made a charge of two hundred dollars, but said he had been thinking the matter over and was beginning to wonder if that wasn't, after all, rather too stiff a fee. He asked my opinion, but before I could answer we espied, a short distance ahead of us, Ben. Edwards, the lawyer who represented the other side of the case, and lost it. When we overtook him Lincoln, curious to learn whether the fee he charged equaled or exceeded that of his opponent, ventured to inquire how he fared in settling with his client. 'Very well,' answered Edwards. 'My man said that inasmuch as we had lost he hoped I would be proportionately merciful when I fixed my fee. And I was: for I let him off for three hundred dollars.'"

The record of one slander suit tried by Lincoln I read with not a little interest. It is not especially noteworthy, but I cannot refrain from referring to it because the vital incident around which it revolves, as outlined by Lincoln in one of his own written pleas, took place within a few feet of the very spot where I was born in the town of Greencastle, Indiana. As I gathered the facts from the original papers in Herndon's hands, it developed that early in the summer of 1847 John Linder, in the Circuit Court of Coles County, Illinois, brought an action for slander against Abraham N. Fleenor, claiming a thousand dollars in damages. The grievance against Fleenor was that he had falsely charged Linder with perjury, because the latter, a short time previously, had testified before the Grand Jury that Levi B. Fleenor and Emeline Fleenor, a woman with whom he was living as a wife, were not married to each other. Lincoln was retained by the defendant, and in his plea, after reciting how "wilfully, maliciously and corruptly" the plaintiff had testified that the said Levi B. and Emeline Fleenor had not been married to each other, concluded the paragraph by the direct and unqualified averment, "when in truth the said Levi B. Fleenor and the said Emeline had theretofore been married to each other in the said town of Greencastle in the State of Indiana." This last allegation Linder, the plaintiff, promptly denied, adding that the parties could not have been so married without his knowing it; that they did not stop in Greencastle more than fifteen minutes (they were migrating overland from Indiana to Coles County, Illinois), and that the said Emeline did not leave the wagon during the interval, thus implying that, as the contracting parties did not stand on *terra firma*, there could have been no binding marriage. But the logic of this proposition did not commend itself to Lincoln, and its only effect was to evoke from him a repetition of the statement that the marriage did take place in the town of Greencastle as alleged. Even though the dainty foot of the gentle Emeline may not have been lifted from the wagon during the fifteen minutes' sojourn in the Indiana village, it did not necessarily follow that an accommodating parson or squire was not conveniently near by and himself standing on the ground so as to solemnize properly the marital union which, according to the contention of Lincoln and his client, undoubtedly followed.

It is unnecessary to dwell further on the details of this quaint, pioneer controversy beyond relating that a judgment was rendered against Lincoln's client for a thousand dollars, of which amount nine hundred and fifty dollars was remitted, thus leaving due a net balance of only fifty dollars. The averments in Lincoln's hand were not facts of his own knowledge, but, like many other allegations incorporated in an attorney's plea, were based entirely on information furnished by his client. In this case the client, doubtless, misrepresented the facts; for a careful and thorough examination of the public records at the town of Greencastle, Indiana, fails to reveal any evidence of the marriage of the said Levi and Emeline Fleenor or any other members of the Fleenor family.

Another story of a Lincoln lawsuit and I pass to other incidents. The case of Dorman *vs.* Lane, appealed from Gallatin County, reached the Supreme Court of Illinois in 1842 and was in court for a long time. Briefly told, Rebecca Daimwood, an orphan girl, believing she had been defrauded in the settlement of her father's estate, brought suit against John Lane, her guardian, to recover certain lands sold by him, ostensibly, for her maintenance. Samuel D. Marshall, a Shawneetown lawyer, gained the case for the girl in the lower court, but Lane promptly appealed to the Supreme Court, whereupon Lincoln was retained to assist Marshall in the girl's behalf. Lyman Trumbull appeared for Lane. "The action was warmly contested," said Franklin M. Eddy, son of Henry Eddy, one of the lawyers associated with Trumbull, "but Lincoln, unaided, beat them all as the record of the Supreme Court easily proves." Meanwhile Miss Daimwood had married William Dorman, a young farmer, and he therefore became a party to the litigation.

In due season the case was disposed of and the time came for the lawyers to put their heads together and reach some understanding regarding the size of their respective fees. As the case progressed, Mr. Lincoln, aside from his professional relation, had become more or less interested in the fortunes of Rebecca and her young husband. Though the latter was poor, he was also both deserving and ambitious; and, in addition, there were in the bearing and history of the two some things that in various ways appealed to Lincoln's sympathy and sense of justice. When, therefore, Marshall reminded him that their clients, Dorman and his wife, were anxious to learn how much of a fee he was expecting from them, Lincoln answered that, so far as his connection with the case extended, there would be no charge; that if in this case he had gained any substantial advantage the thanks of his grateful clients were sufficient remuneration for what he had accomplished. Having thus expressed himself, he authorized Marshall to assure the newly married couple that they might appropriately consider his service in their behalf as a willing though somewhat belated wedding present.

"Dorman was a very strong Democrat," is the testimony of Frank M. Eddy, of Shawneetown, "but always voted for Samuel D. Marshall when he was a candidate for office. Dorman named his youngest boy by Rebecca for Marshall, and I heard him on more than one occasion say that, had his wife lived to bear him another son, he would have been named Abraham Lincoln. When Mr. Lincoln was a candidate for President in 1860, Dorman, in spite of his many Democratic friends, voted for him, and when the latter protested he only answered: 'Lincoln and Marshall recovered my wife's land and would not charge me a cent. Of course I honor them for it, and I intend to vote and fight for them as evidence of my gratitude.' I heard this from Dorman's lips many times, especially in 1860 when Mr. Lincoln first ran for President."

# CHAPTER XIII

Lincoln seldom wrote briefs or legal arguments — Scarcely ever made notes — Of the few briefs he reduced to writing Herndon preserved but a portion — One was a petition for rehearing in Patterson *vs.* Edwards tried in the Supreme Court in 1845 — Slander suit between two women — Notable specimen of Lincoln's reasoning — Smith *vs.* Smith, suit on election bet — Vigorous denunciation of those who bet on elections — Hurd *vs.* Rock Island Bridge Company tried by Lincoln in United States Circuit Court in Chicago — Record of Lincoln's argument before the jury as delivered, preserved, and reproduced by Robert R. Hitt, the shorthand reporter — How Lincoln talked when he faced a jury — What he thought of Judge McLean.

ALTHOUGH skillful and efficient if not voluminous in the matter of drawing up pleadings and preparing papers generally, Mr. Lincoln rarely wrote out his speeches, briefs, or legal arguments; in fact, so reluctant was he to put his spoken utterance in manuscript form that in many instances he even neglected to prompt his memory by making notes. The result is that much of what has been put forth portraying his methods and achievements as an advocate or public speaker is in a large degree based, not on what he had taken the pains to commit to writing, but on the personal recollection of others who claim to have been present and heard him when he expressed himself in public. In this way it is possible that some of the things he is reported to have said have not been as faithfully and accurately reproduced as if preserved in his own handwriting. When I was in Springfield and began my inquiry into Lincoln's history as a lawyer, I was impressed by this fact, and therefore in my quest of information was never satisfied till I had reached original sources. To that end, through the good offices of Mr. Herndon and others equally indulgent and trustworthy,

I was granted access to and permitted to copy certain of the very briefs which Mr. Lincoln deemed of sufficient interest and importance to preserve in his own penmanship. Although limited in number they are characteristic specimens of his method of reasoning and style of expression as well as unquestioned evidence of his actual utterance. In presenting them thus publicly I presume I should beg the indulgence of such persons as may question their propriety, for some of them may touch upon delicate and suggestive topics. We should remember they are a part of Lincoln and should, for that reason, be preserved. It is possible they may not please or attract every reader, but they cannot fail of their effect on the lawyers of the land and that vast army of other people who will not be content till they see Lincoln "just as he was."

Without further explanation or apology I venture to quote from Lincoln's brief in the case of Patterson *vs.* Edwards appealed to the Supreme Court of Illinois. It was a suit between two women in which one charged the other was the mother of a negro child. The court having ruled against his client Lincoln petitioned for a rehearing. Following is a portion of his argument copied from the original draft in Lincoln's handwriting which lies before me as I write:

In the Supreme Court of the State of Illinois, December term
A.D. 1845. Patterson & wife vs. Edwards & wife. Error to
Mason.

And now we, the defendants in error, present this, our petition, for a rehearing in this cause. This court reversed the judgment of the court below;

First: Because the court below denied the motion for a new trial — and

Secondly; Because the court below denied the motion in

arrest of judgment. To entitle ourselves to a rehearing, it is incumbent on us to make it appear *probable*, at least, that the court below decided correctly on *both* of these points.

And first as to the question of new trial. In reversing the judgment on this point, the court seem to proceed on the supposition that the words *alleged* and the words *proved* are not the same — that there is a *material* variance. That there is a literal variance is certain; but is it a *material* one? The words alleged are: "Mrs. Edwards has raised a family of children by a negro, and I can prove it." If we change the language from the second person, past tense, as detailed by the witnesses, to the first person, present tense, as spoken by Mrs. Patterson, the words proved by Mrs. Seymour, to have been spoken by Mrs. Patterson are: "I did tell Julius Scoville that Mrs. Edwards has had children by a negro, and it is true"; and those proved by Mrs. Edwards are, "Your mother has had children by a negro, and all her children are negroes."

Now in what particular, this court regards these words as *proved* materially variant from those *alleged* the opinion does not state: but merely states the undeniable doctrine that it is not sufficient to prove *equivalent* words. What in the sense of the law are *equivalent* words? We understand *equivalent* words to be the words amounting to something very near the charge and quite as bad as the charge alleged; while we understand words amounting to the *identical* charge alleged, as being, in the sense of the law, not *merely equivalent* words but *the* words alleged, notwithstanding a slight literal or verbal variance — we insist that a variance to be material in law, must be a variance in *sense*. If we are right in this, we ask 'Is there any difference *in sense* between saying a woman has *raised* children by a negro, and saying she *had* children by a negro?

On the question of variance we refer the court to

1 Starkie on Slander side pages 369 to 383 inclusive & notes. Also 2 Cowen 479–83.

But if there is a material variance, and the evidence was therefore improper to be received under the issue, still, could the party opposed, permit it to go to the jury, without objection, let us rest without supposing it necessary to introduce other evidence, take the chance of a verdict and after losing make the objection for the first time by motion for a new trial? Let it be borne in mind that the objection is not to *proper* evidence *insufficient in amount* but to *improper* evidence.

On this point we refer to 1 Bibb 248, 4 Wendell 277–283.

But if the variance is *material* and the objection might properly be taken for the first time, by a motion for a new trial, ought the court below to have allowed the motion without our attention and the court's attention being particularly drawn to the point by *reasons in writing*, according to the statute? We insist that by our statute, upon principle and upon analogous decisions, a court ought not to allow a new trial, unless the ground on which it is sought, be specifically pointed out. On page 491, Sec. 20 of an old revised code is the following, to wit: "And if either party may wish to except to the verdict, or for other causes to move for a new trial, or in arrest of judgment, he shall, before final judgment be entered, give, by himself or counsel to the opposite party, or his counsel, the points in writing, particularly specifying the grounds of such motion and shall also furnish the judge with a copy of the same, etc."

Upon principle we say, that it is unfair to the court below, to reverse his judgment upon a point never presented to the judge's consideration; that it is unfair to us to do here, at our delay, trouble and expense what might have been done in the court below, upon the ground being fairly shown; and further, that it is probable the variances, such as it appears in the Bill of Exceptions, did not really exist; but that it got into the Bill only by the carelessness of the court below and of us; no such point being supposed to be involved. It is hardly necessary to add that no such reasons in writing, as we hold to be necessary appear by the record. For decisions bearing on this point we refer to 1 Bibb 142, 1 Scam. 233, 4 Wendell 484–9. In this last case the court say: "If counsel will not discriminate in their objections, so as to draw the attention of the court to what is conceived to be objectionable in the decision made, they are precluded from urging it as a cause for reversing the judgment."

On the question of arrest of judgment this court declared that the words "Mrs. Edwards has raised a family of children by a negro" do not, "in their plain and popular sense, or in common acceptation, *necessarily* amount to charge of adultery." Wherein these words vary from, or fall short of such a charge, the opinion does not state. Whether the court believe that these words do not mean, that Mrs. Edwards had raised a family of children, of whom she was the *mother*, and a negro was the *father;* or whether, admitting this, the court believe she may have been the wife of the negro, and therefore, may have borne children by him without adultery, the opinion shows nothing from which we can judge. Until the decision of this court, we had never supposed there could be a rational doubt that these words would be construed by all who might hear them, as the declaration construes them. We have thought, and still do think, that if twelve plain men should enter this room and each, out of the hearing of the others should be told these words, not one of them would fail to attach to them the very meaning that the declaration attaches to them. But we may be mistaken; and we now proceed to treat them as being of more doubtful import than we had thought. The opinion says the words "do not *necessarily* amount to a charge of adultery etc." We say, as matter of law, that to sustain the judgment of the court below, they *need* not *necessarily* to amount to such a charge. We say they need only be *capable* of the meaning attached to them by the declaration; even though the contrary meaning were more probably the true one. In this, we do not speak without the books. We will furnish the court, if they desire, with a new edition, in two volumes, of Starkie on Slander, and refer to Volume 1 — side pages 44 to 51 inclusive. The construction of words of doubtful meaning is there fully discussed. It is there shown that there *was* an *old*, and *is a new* rule on the subject; that the old rule was to construe words in *mitiori sensu*, or, in the most favourable sense for the defendant, which they were capable of bearing, never allowing a plaintiff to have a judgment, unless the words *necessarily* amounted to the charge he alleged in his declaration; that this old rule has been exploded nearly or quite a hundred years; and a new rule fully established. A train of decisions under each rule is given; and on side pages 59 & 60 the author sums up in these words.

From these cases containing the opinion of some of the most enlightened judges of their own, or any other times, it may be collected; 1st That when words are capable of *two constructions* in what sense they were meant, is a matter of fact to be *decided by the jury.* 2nd That they (the jury) are to be guided, in forming their opinion by the impression which the words or signs used were calculated to make on the minds of those who heard or saw them, as collected from the whole of the circumstances.

3rd  That such words or signs will, after verdict for the plaintiff be considered by the court to have been used in their worst sense. See notes also. Also see 2 Cowen 479 to 82 where the court say — "But aside from the difficulty as to the remedy, it is a sufficient answer to this application that the words proved would admit of some doubt as to their meaning, and where there is room for the least criticism upon their import, it is properly a question for the jury, whose decision is conclusive." For these reasons your petitioners pray for a rehearing of said cause.

LINCOLN p. q.

The brief of another argument by Lincoln is worthy of our attention, because, when we read his observations and moral reflections outlined therein, we are no longer at a loss to determine what he thought of gambling, and more particularly his attitude regarding the sinfulness, if any, of betting on elections. His deductions in the suit of Smith *vs.* Smith, which was appealed to the Supreme Court of Illinois from Bond County, are both pertinent and suggestive. After relating that in November, 1856, two days after the presidential election, Isaac Smith, the plaintiff in error, made a bet of one hundred and ten dollars with one Moffett, against a buggy owned by the latter, that the vote of Fillmore as a candidate for President of the United States was not behind the other candidates in the State of New York, he continues:

The defendant attempts to defend his wrong by proving a bet on the Presidential election in this wise: He says he bet some money with Moffett against the buggy of Moffett on the *Presidential Election in the State of New York;* that the money and buggy were put into the hands of a stake-holder; and that the stake-holder about the 14th day of November, 1856, decided the bet in the favor of the defendant below. The defendant took the buggy away from the place where the plaintiff left it at the time of the trade. See Record — page 9. The trade between Moffett and plaintiff below was for the buggy in controversy. Now it appears that Moffett's and the plaintiff's trade about and for the buggy and note was before the bet. *This does not appear* from absolute figures, but it is necessarily so, as the witnesses in spirit state it. But suppose this is not so, yet *it is positively true* that the plaintiff below and Moffett traded as aforesaid long before the stake-holder had decided the question and long before the defendant below took possession of the buggy.

And now this question is presented: Is this gambling debt contrary to the laws of this state, or public policy, or morality; and this being the case, as we think it is, the seller of the buggy had a right to *repent of the law's violation* and to *revoke the bet;* and the power conferred on the stake-holder so long as the Presidential question in the State of N. Y. was an open and undecided question by the stake-holder.

1st — This is gambling and comes within the provisions of our statute against gambling. See Rev. Statute pages 177–263; 2 Carter (Indiana) 499 and 2 Vol. Freeman's Digest 1570–71. We think that betting on Presidential elections over the Union, or in *particular states thereof*, comes within the spirit of the laws; and if not such betting is contrary to public policy and morality and therefore void, or, at least, voidable; i.e. that bets may be *revoked while the decision is pending.*

2nd. — And now for the revocation argument: A bet may be revoked because it is contrary to the law of this state or its *public policy or public morality.* See 9 Barlow 315; 18 Penn 329; 12 B. Monroe 140–141; 11 Cushing 357. This bet was revoked by the sale to the plaintiff below, long before the decision of the question by the stake-holder, *and this repenting and revoking the law allows — yea favors.*

Following this comes a long list of authorities including various court decisions relied upon by Mr. Lincoln unnecessary to enumerate here. The remaining item that merits our attention is the closing paragraph of the brief. It is in the form of a moral essay, but is in the handwriting of Herndon who also signs the firm's name to the document. Whether it expresses Lincoln's real ideas, or those of Herndon, or both, does not appear; but viewed at this distance we cannot deny that it has the right ring. It reads as follows:

This Union is a brotherhood of states and it is said that if it is to fall it will be caused by fraud, force and wrong upon the ballot-box. Once make Missouri, Kentucky and Indiana interested by bets in Illinois elections, though for President, and you hold out inducements to raids, ruffianism, etc. The same with reference to elections in Indiana, Kentucky and Missouri and the people of Illinois will overrun those states. Build up good communities; do as you would be done by and all is safe and right. Let the court put its face against betting on all elections in this Union; but upon totally foreign countries leave it as at common law though barbarous. The complicated relations of these 32 states to each other and the Union create a peculiar public policy. Read 3 Scammon again and reverse or modify it.

Respectfully
LINCOLN & HERNDON

Notwithstanding the varied and interesting incidents of Lincoln's life which I have gathered and tried to preserve, I cannot but feel that any delineation of his character as a lawyer will be incomplete if it does not throw the required light on his qualification and equipment as an advocate — if it fails to indicate how he appeared and what he said when he looked into their faces and sought to convince the twelve men who confronted him from the jury box. Thus far I have been content to quote from the briefs of arguments carefully written out by him before they were read to learned and dignified judges; but now I beg the indulgence of the reader if I venture to present, as accurately as human agency can reproduce it,

his language when he addressed the jury in the famous
Rock Island Bridge case, tried in the United States Circuit Court in Chicago in September, 1857, Judge John
McLean, of the Supreme Court, presiding. In order to
keep within proper bounds it will be necessary to abridge
Lincoln's speech somewhat, but even then I fear I shall
make serious inroads on the reader's patience.

As the suit was, in reality, one of the most memorable
Lincoln ever tried, a few words of explanation are essential. The action was entitled Hurd *vs*. Rock Island
Bridge Company, and grew out of the opposition by the
steamboat people interested in the navigation of the Mississippi River to the construction of a bridge across that
stream. The bridge between Rock Island and Davenport
was built and in use only a short time when the steamboat
Effie Afton passing up, proceeded some two hundred feet
above the head of the long draw pier when one of her
wheels stopped, and the other being continued, the boat
turned around against the tendency of the current and
brought up against the bridge at the pier next east of the
draw pier. A stove was overturned by the shock, burning
the boat, and the span against which it struck. The result
was a suit by the steamboat people against the owners
of the bridge, which included the railroad company, for
damages, on the ground that the bridge was an obstruction to navigation. The counsel for the plaintiff included
H. M. Wead, of Peoria, Illinois, and T. D. Lincoln, of
Cincinnati, Ohio, a prominent admiralty lawyer famil-
iarly known as "Tim" Lincoln, and Corydon Beckwith, of
Chicago, afterwards a member of the Supreme Court of
Illinois. The counsel for the defendant consisted of Nor-

man B. Judd, of Chicago, Joseph Knox, of Rock Island, and Abraham Lincoln, of Springfield.

"The case was of absorbing interest to the river towns," says John T. Richards, formerly President of the Chicago Bar Association, "as well as to those centers of population whose future prosperity was dependent upon the development of railroad transportation. The people of the country were divided in accordance with local self-interest. The people of St. Louis, Cincinnati, and other towns similarly situated believed that if the railroad companies were permitted to build bridges across the navigable rivers of the country they would lose the commercial advantages which they enjoyed from traffic upon the Mississippi and Ohio Rivers; and the owners of the steamboats, who for many years had enjoyed a monopoly of the transportation of freight from points west of the Mississippi, foresaw that if the railroads were to be allowed to transport freight from the vast territory west of that great artery of commerce across that river and through to the eastern seaboard without the expense of reloading on the banks of the streams over which it must pass to reach its destination, that monopoly would be destroyed. Hence the interests referred to combined in the case against the bridge company for the purpose of preventing the building of other bridges which would interfere with river traffic."

The newspapers of Chicago, Cincinnati, and St. Louis gave unusual publicity to the "Effie Afton Case," the name by which the suit was popularly known. "Some idea of the bitterness of the contest," writes Frederick Trevor Hill, "may be gathered from the fact that the railroad charged the steamboat captain with being bribed to run

his vessel against the bridge and thus make a case of obstructed navigation. This accusation was, of course,
angrily denied; but when the bridge was accidentally
burned all the river craft gathered at the spot and let their
whistles loose in sheer joy at the disaster. Under these
circumstances it required a cool head and an even temper
to carry the day, and Lincoln was to equal the occasion."

For such portions of Lincoln's argument on this occasion as are here quoted credit is due Robert R. Hitt,
the shorthand reporter representing the "Chicago Press
and Tribune," who was present, heard Lincoln and took
down his speech. Mr. Hitt assured the writer and Mr.
Horace White, for many years editor of the "Tribune,"
that he reported it for the paper with unusual fidelity and
that when he had elaborated his notes he was sure his
version of the speech was as nearly word for word the
language of Lincoln as he knew how to preserve and record it. As it is probably the only published utterance of
Lincoln prior to 1860, with the exception of his debate
with Douglas, his lecture on "Discovery and Invention"
in 1859, and the Cooper Institute address, which ap-
proaches the literal reproduction of his spoken words, it
cannot fail to interest the man who never saw Lincoln and
who is, therefore, all the more anxious to learn how the
latter expressed himself when he undertook to convince
a jury of his peers. As already indicated the limitations of
space forbid the insertion of the entire speech, but certain
portions are so edifying and characteristic they cannot
well be omitted.

After the usual recognition of the judge and jury, Lincoln
began:

It is foreign to my purpose to pursue or assail anybody, and although I may seem to grow earnest I shall try not to be offensive or ill-natured. There is some conflict of testimony in this case, but one quarter of such a number of witnesses seldom agree, and even if all were on one side some discrepancy might still be expected. We are to try to reconcile them and to believe that they are not intentionally erroneous as long as we can.

Following this Lincoln called to mind the opposition to the bridge which developed at St. Louis because that place felt that it was adverse to her commerce and would divert a portion of it from the river.

It would not be pleasing to me, [he continued,] to have one of these great channels extending from where it never freezes to where it never thaws blocked up; but there is a travel from east to west whose demands are not less important than those of the river. It is growing larger and larger, building up new countries with a rapidity never before seen in the history of the world. This current of travel has its rights as well as that north and south. If the river had not the advantage in priority and legislation we could enter into free competition with it and we could surpass it. This particular railroad line has a great importance and the statement of its business during a little less than a year shows this importance. It is in evidence that from September 8, 1856, to August 8, 1857, 12,586 freight cars and 74,179 passengers passed over this bridge. Navigation was closed four days short of four months last year, and during this time while the river was of no use this road and bridge were valuable. There is, too, a considerable portion of the time when floating or thin ice makes the river useless while the bridge is as useful as ever. This shows that this bridge must be treated with respect in this court and is not to be kicked about with contempt. The other day Judge Wead alluded to the strife of the contending interests and even a dissolution of the Union; but the proper mode for all parties in this affair is to "live and let live" and then we will find a cessation of the trouble about the bridge.

And now I ask what mood were the steamboat men in when this bridge was burned? Why, there was a shouting and ringing of bells and whistling on all the boats as it fell. It was a jubilee, a greater celebration than follows an exciting election.

After describing the difficulty of navigation following the burning of the bridge, alluding to the "tapering off" of the dangers, and predicting that as the boatmen "get cool the ratio of accidents will decrease," Lincoln proceeds to pay his respects to the opposing counsel as follows:

Judge Wead said while admitting that the floats went straight through there was a difference between a float and a boat, but I do not remember that he indulged us with an argument in support of this statement. Is it because there is a difference in size? Will not a small body and a large one float the same way under the same influence? True a flatboat will float faster than an eggshell might be blown away by the wind, but if under the *same influence* they would go the same way. Logs, floats, boards, various things, the witnesses say, all show the same current. Then is not this test reliable? At all depths, too, the direction of the current is the same. A series of these floats would make a line as long as a boat and would show any influence upon any part and all parts of the boat.

At this point in his argument Lincoln evidently fell back on his knowledge and the experience he gained when he floated down the Mississippi on a flatboat to New Orleans with John Hanks a quarter of a century before.

I will now speak of the angular position of the piers. What is the amount of the angle? The course of the river is a curve and the pier is straight. If a line is produced from the upper end of the long pier straight with the pier to a distance of three hundred and fifty feet and a line is drawn from a point in the channel opposite this point to the head of the pier, Colonel Nason says they will form an angle of twenty degrees. But the angle if measured at the pier is seven degrees; that is, we would have to move the pier seven degrees to make it exactly straight with the current. Would that make the navigation better or worse? The witnesses of the plaintiff seem to think it was only necessary to say that the pier formed an angle with the current and that settled the matter. Our more careful and accurate witnesses say that though they had been accustomed to seeing the piers placed straight with the current, yet they could see that here the current had been made straight by us in having made this slight angle; that the water now runs just right; that it is straight and cannot be improved. They think that if the pier was changed the eddy would be divided and the navigation improved.

I am not now going to discuss the question of what is a material obstruction. We do not greatly differ about the law. The cases produced here are, I suppose, proper to be taken into consideration by the court in instructing a jury. Some of them I think are not exactly in point, but I am still willing to trust His Honor, Judge McLean, and take his instructions as law. What is reasonable skill and care? This is a thing of which the jury are to judge. I differ from the other side when it says that they are bound to exercise no more care than was taken before the building of the bridge. If we are allowed by the legislature to build the bridge which will require them to do more than before, when a pilot comes along it is unreasonable for him to dash on heedless of this structure which has been *legally put there*. The Afton came there on the 5th and lay at Rock Island until next morning. When a boat lies up the pilot has a holiday, and would not any of these jurors have then gone around to the bridge and gotten acquainted with the place. Pilot Parker has shown here that he does not understand the draw. I heard him say that the fall from the head to the foot of the pier was four feet. He needs information; he could have gone there that day and seen there was no such fall. He should have discarded passion and the chances are that he would have had no disaster at all. He was bound to make himself acquainted with the place.

McCammon says that the current and the swell coming from the long pier drove her against the long pier; in other words, drove her toward the very pier from which the current came! It is an absurdity — an impossibility. The only explanation I can find for this contradiction is in a current which White says strikes out from the long pier and then like a ram's horn turns back, and this might have acted somehow in this manner.

It is agreed by all that the plaintiff's boat was destroyed and that it was destroyed upon the head of the short pier; that she moved from the channel where she was with her bow above the head of the long pier till she struck the short one, swung around under the bridge, and there was crowded and destroyed.

I shall try to prove that the average velocity of the current through the draw with the boat in it should be five and a half miles an hour; that it is slowest at the head of the pier and swiftest at the foot of the pier. Their lowest estimate in evidence is six miles an hour; their highest twelve miles. This was the testimony of men who made no experiment, only conjecture. We have adopted the most exact means. The water runs swiftest in high water and we have taken the point of nine feet above low water. The water when the Afton was lost was seven feet above low water, or at least a foot lower than our time. Brayton and his assistant timed the instruments, the best instruments known in measuring currents. They timed them under various circumstances and they found the current five miles an hour and no more. They found that the water at the upper end ran slower than five miles; that below it was swifter than five miles; but that the average was five miles. Shall men who have taken no care, who conjecture, some of whom speak of twenty miles an hour, be believed against those who have had such a favorable and well-improved opportunity? They would not even *qualify* the result. Several men have given their opinion as to the distance of the steamboat Carson and I suppose if *one* should go and *measure* that distance you would believe him in preference to all of them.

These measurements were made when the boat was not in the draw. It has been ascertained what is the area of the cross-section of this stream and the area of the face of the piers and the engineers say that the piers being put there will increase the current proportionately as the space is decreased. So with the boat in the draw. The depth of the channel was twenty-two feet, the width one hundred and sixteen feet; multiply these and you have the square feet across the water of the draw, viz.: 2552 feet. The Afton was thirty-five feet wide and drew five feet, making a fourteenth of the sum. Now, one fourteenth of five miles is five fourteenths of one mile — about one third of a mile — the increase of the current. We will call the current five and a half miles per hour. The next thing I will try to prove is that the plaintiff's boat had power to run six miles an hour in that current. It has been testified that she was a strong, swift boat able to run eight miles an hour upstream in a current of four miles an hour and fifteen miles downstream. Strike the average and you will find what is her average — about eleven and a half miles. Take the five and a half miles which is the speed of the current in the draw and it leaves the power of that boat in that draw at six miles an hour, 528 feet per minute, and 8 4/5 feet to the second.

Next I propose to show that there are no cross-currents. I know their witnesses say that there are cross-currents; that, as one witness says, there were three cross-currents and two eddies; so far as mere statement without experiment and mingled with mistakes can go they have proved. But can these men's testimony be compared with the nice, exact, and thorough experiments of our witnesses. Can you believe that these floats go across the currents? It is inconceivable that they could not have discovered every possible current. How do boats find currents that floats cannot discover? We assume the position, then, that those cross-currents are not there. My next proposition is that the Afton passed between the S. B. Carson and the Iowa shore. That is undisputed.

Next I shall show that she struck first the short pier, then the long pier, then the short one again, and there she stopped. How did the boat strike when she went in? Here is an endless variety of opinion — the testimony of eighteen witnesses. But ten of them say what pier she struck; three of them testify that she struck first the short, then the long, and the short for the last time. None of the rest substantially contradict this. I assume that these men have got the truth because I believe it an established fact. My next proposition is that after she struck the short and long pier and before she got back to the short pier, the boat got right with her bow up. So says the pilot Parker: "that he got her through until her starboard wheel passed the short pier." This would make her head about even with the head of the long pier. He says her head was as high or higher than the head of the long pier. Other witnesses confirmed this one. The final stroke was in the splash door aft the wheel. Witnesses differ but the majority say that she struck thus.

At this point the court adjourned, and on the following day, shown by the record to be Wednesday, September 23, 1857, Lincoln resumed his argument assuring the court that he would conclude as soon as possible. From the model of a boat he explained where the splash door is just behind the wheel, adding that the current as represented would drive an ascending boat to the long pier, but not to the short pier as the other side had contended. Continuing his argument he said:

The boat struck on the lower shoulder of the short pier, as she swung around, in the splash door; then as she went on around she struck the point or end of the pier where she rested. Her engineers say the starboard then was rushing around rapidly. Then the boat must have struck the upper point of the pier so far back as not to disturb the wheel. It is forty feet from the stern of the Afton to the splash door and thus it appears that she had but forty feet to go to clear the pier. How was it that the Afton with all her power flanked over from the channel to the short pier without moving one foot ahead? Suppose she was in the middle of the draw, her wheel would have been thirty-one feet from the short pier. The reason she went over thus is her starboard wheel was not working. I shall try to establish the fact that the wheel was not running and that after she struck she went ahead on this same wheel. Upon the last point the witnesses agree that the starboard wheel was running after she struck and no witnesses say that it was running while she was out in the draw flanking over.

Other witnesses show that the captain said something of the machinery of the wheel and the inference is that he knew the wheel was not working. The pilot says he ordered the engineers to back her up. The engineers differ from him and said they kept on going ahead. The bow was so swung that the current pressed it over; the pilot pressed the stern over with the rudder, though not so fast but that the bow gained on it, and only one wheel being in motion, the boat nearly stood still, so far as motion up and down is concerned and thus she was thrown upon this pier.

The Afton came into the draw after she had just passed the Carson, and as the Carson no doubt kept the true course the Afton, going around her, got out of the proper way, got across the current into the eddy, which is west of a straight line drawn down from the long pier, and was compelled to resort to these changes of wheel which she did not do with sufficient adroitness to save her. Was it not her own fault that she entered wrong, so far wrong that she never got right? Is the defense to blame for that?

At this point Lincoln unbent slightly and indulged in a brief witticism, a thing he rarely attempted in public save occasionally in a talk to a country jury.

For several days we were entertained with depositions about boats "smelling a bar." Why, then, did the Afton after she had come up smelling so close to the long pier sheer off so strangely? When she had got to the center of the very nose she was smelling, she seemed suddenly to have lost her sense of smell and to have flanked over to the short pier.

It is suggested as a way out of the difficulty that a tunnel be built under the river; but that is not practicable, for there is not a tunnel that is a successful project in this world. A suspension bridge cannot be built so high but that the chimneys of the boats will grow up till they cannot pass. The steamboat men will take pains to make them grow. The cars of a railroad cannot without immense expense rise high enough to get even with a suspension bridge or go low enough to get through a tunnel; such expense is unreasonable.

The plaintiffs have to establish that the bridge is a material obstruction and that they have managed their boat with reasonable care and skill. As to the last point high winds have nothing to do with it, for it was not a windy day. They must show due skill and care. Difficulties going downstream will not do; for they were going upstream. Difficulties with barges in tow have nothing to do with the accidents, for they had no barge.

Here Lincoln paused, but whether due to a suggestion or intimation from the court we do not know. At any rate, fixing his eyes on the jury he said:

Gentlemen, I have not exhausted my stock of information and there are more things I could suggest regarding this case, but as I have doubtless used up my time, I presume I had better close.

In due time Judge McLean delivered his charge to the jury and they retired. At eight o'clock they returned with the report that they were unable to agree. The court, believing that even if given more time they would never agree, dismissed them. They stood: three for the boat and nine for Lincoln's clients, the bridge people.

In September, two years before this, the noted McCormick *vs.* Manny patent infringement was tried before Judge McLean in the United States Circuit Court in Cincinnati. Lincoln was present having been retained by the defendant Manny. It will be recalled that owing to the determination of his associates, Edwin M. Stanton and George Harding, of Philadelphia, to make the two speeches allowed the defense, he was successfully ignored. He remained in Cincinnati throughout the trial, but took little part in the proceedings. When he returned home he told the Springfield lawyers, Herndon among the number, that McLean, although of decided mental vigor, was, nevertheless, a man of limited perception. "If you pointed your forefinger and a darning needle at him at the same time," said Lincoln, "he never could make up his mind which was the sharper."

# CHAPTER XIV

Life on the circuit — The Eighth Circuit described — Lincoln only lawyer who traveled over all of it — His horse and buggy — The landlord's welcome — Life at the tavern — Lincoln's dress — Leonard Swett's introduction to Lincoln and Davis — Lincoln's methods described by Henry C. Whitney — Joins Leonard Swett in defense of a murderer — His record in fugitive slave cases — Explanation by John W. Bunn of his few appearances in court in behalf of runaway slaves — Account by J. Birch of Lincoln lounging in the county clerk's office — Also his physical appearance and habits in political campaigns — The Wright case — Befriending the Matheney heirs — Forcing the foreign impostor to disgorge his gains — Fee paid by Jacob Bunn and how Lincoln applied it.

MR. LINCOLN always divided his life as a lawyer into two periods or epochs; one preceding and the other following his single term in Congress. His legal career, therefore, dates from the spring of 1849, when, believing himself politically dead, he returned to the law and began the struggle in dead earnest again. His business was largely confined to the circuit, a mode of practice almost unknown to the present generation of lawyers. The now historic Eighth Circuit over which he traveled included fourteen counties in central Illinois, comprising eleven thousand square miles or almost one fifth of the area of the State.

"For many years," relates a survivor of the circuit days, "there were no railroads and but few bridges over the streams. Courts were held in the various counties twice a year lasting from three days to a week. After court adjourned in one county, the judge rode to the next county seat and was followed by the State's attorney, whose authority extended over the whole circuit, and by some of the lawyers to a few of the counties near their homes." Mr. Lincoln was the only lawyer who rode the entire circuit, visiting practically all the courts, which lasted about three months in the spring and three in the fall. When the courts opened in Christian, Menard, and Logan Counties, which adjoined Sangamon, where Lincoln lived, Herndon, his partner, sometimes accompanied him, but to points beyond he usually drove alone or, occasionally, with the judge. While Herndon spent the greater part of the time in Springfield in charge of the firm's local practice and to keep track of matters in the Supreme Court, Lincoln was out on the circuit beating the bushes for more business.

"Most of the lawyers," related George P. Davis, the son of Judge David Davis, "rode horseback; but after a few years my father, who was the circuit judge, and Mr. Lincoln were able to afford a buggy. My father, who was a very heavy man, used two horses. Mr. Lincoln had a one-horse open buggy and drove his own steed, 'Old Buck,' as I remember his name. In the fall of 1850 my mother went around the circuit with my father and Mr. Lincoln took me in his buggy. I have a distinct recollection of the horse, the buggy, and Mr. Lincoln, although I cannot now relate much of what he said on the trip."

Following the court around on the circuit was, no doubt, one of the greatest pleasures Lincoln enjoyed; in fact, it is now known that he declined an offer to enter a promising if not lucrative law partnership in Chicago after the debates with Douglas because, as he contended, it would confine him to the office and thus keep him off the circuit. Seated in his one-horse buggy behind a sorry-looking animal he would set out from Springfield to be gone for weeks at a stretch. The lawyers, as he drove into each successive town, eagerly anticipating a new stock of stories, were anxious to greet him, and the landlords, so we are told, hailed his coming with delight. He was one of those gentle, uncomplaining beings whom the servants at the inns generally put off with the most indifferent accommodations. He said once he never so completely felt his own insignificance as when he stood face to face with a real, live city hotel clerk.

"He was never," said one of his colleagues, "seated next to the landlord at a crowded table and never got a chicken liver or the best cut from the roast. He never complained of the food, bed, or lodging. If every other fellow grumbled at the bill of fare which greeted us at many of the dingy taverns where we sojourned, Lincoln said nothing; yet he loved the life and never went home without reluctance."

When the court moved from one county to another there was great bustle and activity at each successive place. Men came together when court-time rolled around to meet the celebrities at the bar, to buy supplies, to negotiate loans, to sell live stock, to hear the lawyers "plead," and, in fact, for almost every imaginable purpose. The best room at the tavern was reserved for the judge and such choice spirits among the lawyers as he might draw about him. The other lawyers slept two in a bed, and two or more beds were frequently crowded into one room. At meals the judge, lawyers, jurors, suitors, witnesses, court-officers, and prisoners out on bail ate together at a long dining-table. "I well remember," relates one of this promiscuous company, the late Henry C. Whitney, of Champaign, Illinois, "a term of court at one place where a prisoner on trial for perjury used to spend the evenings with us in Judge Davis's room, and another place where the prisoner, then on trial for larceny, not only spent his evenings in our room, but took walks with us and ate in our immediate company."

In this crude and nomadic life Lincoln spent almost half of each year. Without the conveniences of the modern lawyer, stenographer, typewriter, without books even, he moved from court to court, his papers in his hat or coat-pocket, his business in his head. The consideration and trial of each case began and ended with itself, and each successive county brought new business and new clients.

In the matter of dress, when on the circuit and away from home, Lincoln, though properly clad, was far from fastidious. His personal habits were of the simplest character. Henry C. Whitney, who was with him in the latter half of the fifties hardly less than David Davis, Leonard Swett, and Herndon, thus describes him: "His hat was brown and faded and the nap invariably worn or rubbed off. He wore a short cloak and sometimes a shawl. His coat and vest hung loosely on his giant frame and his trousers were usually a trifle short. In one hand he carried a faded green umbrella with his name, A. LINCOLN, in rather large white cotton or muslin letters sewed on the inside. The knob was gone from the handle and, when closed, a piece of cord was usually tied round it in the middle to keep it from flying open. In the other hand he carried a literal carpet-bag in which were stored the few papers to be used in court, and underclothing enough to last till his return to Springfield."

He is thus described by the son of David Davis: "He was careless about dress, though he was always clean. I thought his clothes were too short for him, especially his coat. For a necktie he wore an old-fashioned stiff stock which encircled his neck. When he became interested in his speech he would frequently take it off, unbutton his shirt, and give room for his Adam's apple to play up and down. He had a high-pitched voice, but it could be heard a great distance, every word of a sentence being equally clear. He was frequently at my father's house, and in 1858, the year of the debates with Douglas, spent a long season with us. On one of his visits I had a new autograph album in which he wrote as follows: 'My young friend George Perrin Davis has allowed me the honor of being the first to write his name in this book. A. Lincoln. Bloomington Ills. Dec. 21 1858.'"

I cannot pass from this phase of Lincoln's development without putting on canvas a copy of his portrait drawn for me several years ago by one who also traveled the circuit with him and who in every way was closely allied to him. I refer to Leonard Swett. "I shall never forget," Mr. Swett once told me, "the first time I saw Mr. Lincoln. I had expected to encounter him at Springfield, but he was absent from home, nor did our meeting occur till later. It was at the town of Danville. When I called at the hotel it was after dark, and I was told that he was upstairs in Judge Davis's room. In the region where I had been brought up, the judge of the court was usually a man of more or less gravity so that he could not be approached save with some degree of deference. I was not a little abashed, therefore, after I had climbed the unbanistered stairway, to find myself so near the presence and dignity of Judge Davis in whose room I was told I could find Mr. Lincoln. In response to my timid knock two voices responded almost simultaneously, 'Come in.' Imagine my surprise when the door opened to find two men undressed, or rather dressed

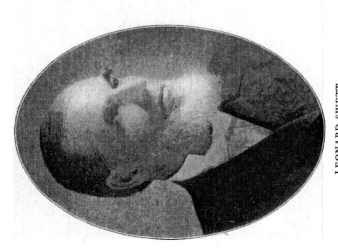

LEONARD SWETT
August 23, 1887

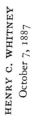

HENRY C. WHITNEY
October 7, 1887

for bed, engaged in a lively battle with pillows, tossing them at each other's heads. One, a low, heavy-set man who leaned against the foot of the bed and puffed like a lizard, answered to the description of Judge Davis. The other was a man of tremendous stature; compared to Davis he looked as if he were eight feet tall. He was encased in a long, indescribable garment, yellow as saffron, which reached to his heels, and from beneath which protruded two of the largest feet I had, up to that time, been in the habit of seeing. This immense shirt, for shirt it must have been, looked as if it had been literally carved out of the original bolt of flannel of which it was made and the pieces joined together without reference to measurement or capacity. The only thing that kept it from slipping off the tall and angular frame it covered was the single button at the throat; and I confess to a succession of shudders when I thought of what might happen should that button by any mischance lose its hold. I cannot describe my sensations as this apparition, with the modest announcement, 'My name is Lincoln,' strode across the room to shake my trembling hand. I will not say he reminded me of Satan, but he was certainly the ungodliest figure I had ever seen."

I attach much importance to the recollection and testimony of Henry C. Whitney, who, in the decade prior to the Civil War, practiced law in Champaign County, Illinois, where he was both intimately acquainted, and, from a professional standpoint, frequently associated, with Lincoln. After Lincoln became President, Mr. Whitney removed to Chicago, where, in the eighties, I spent a good deal of time with him. It was from and through him that I gathered a fund of material regarding Lincoln's life as a circuit-court lawyer which has proved to be of decided historic value. He was a close friend of Herndon, maintaining that the latter was as useful as he was true to Lincoln, and insisting that, notwithstanding his weaknesses, Lincoln's faith in him remained unshaken to the last. The greater part of what Mr. Whitney communicated to me he put in writing, all of which I have carefully retained.

Among other things I remember he contended that the estimate of Lincoln by some writers who seek to prove that, as a lawyer, he was in the habit of surrendering his fee and retiring from every case in which there was any doubt of his success, was a great popular misconception. "Mr. Lincoln would advise with perfect frankness about a potential case," he once said, "but when it was *in esse*, then he wanted to win as badly as any lawyer; but unlike lawyers of a certain type he would not do anything mean, or which savored of sharp practice, or which required absolute sophistry or chicanery in order to succeed. In a clear case of dishonesty he would hedge in some way so as not himself to partake of the dishonesty. In a doubtful case of dishonesty, he would give his client the benefit of the doubt, and in an ordinary case he would try the case so far as he could like any other lawyer except that he absolutely abjured technicality and went for justice and victory denuded of every integument.

"As attorney for the Illinois Central Railroad I had authority to employ additional counsel whenever I chose to do so, and in Judge Davis's circuit I frequently applied to Lincoln when I needed aid. I never found him unwilling to appear in behalf of a great 'soulless corporation.' In such cases he always stood by me, and I always, of course, tried to win. There was nothing of the milksop about him, nor did he peer unnecessarily into a case to find some reason to act out of the usual line; but he had the same animus ordinarily as any other lawyer. I remember a murder trial in which he was joined with Leonard Swett and myself for the defense. Swett was a most effective advocate, and when he closed in the afternoon I was full of faith that our client would be acquitted. Lincoln followed the next morning, and while he made some good points the honesty of his mental processes forced him into a line of argument and admission that was very damaging. We all felt that he had hurt our case. In point of fact our client was convicted and sent to the penitentiary for three years. Lincoln, whose merciless logic drove him into the belief that the culprit was guilty of murder, had his humanity so wrought upon that he induced the Governor to pardon him after he had served one year."

Although humane and prone to right a wrong whenever possible, it cannot be said that Lincoln sought cases of injustice to remedy or went out of his way to befriend or defend the weak man from the heartlessness of his oppressor. Of course he opposed slavery, but he himself was no more aggressive in defense of the slave than others whose sentiments on that subject were less widely known. Herndon, for instance, was far more radical and venturesome. Before me lie the papers disclosing the history of three cases tried in the Springfield courts, in each of which a negro sought to obtain his freedom. In the case of Emily Logan *vs.* Marcus A. Chinn, venued from Morgan to Sangamon County in 1840, the woman sued out a writ of *homine replegiando*, seeking to recover her freedom from

Chinn who claimed her as a runaway slave from Kentucky. The case was closely contested, but the jury decided in the slave's favor, thus relieving her from further surveillance. Stephen T. Logan represented the defendant, Chinn, and Baker & Edwards the woman. Another action which was tried early in 1850 grew out of the detention, in the Springfield jail, of five negroes, three men and two women, believed to be runaway slaves. One of the men, called Hempstead Thornton, was described as a "negro supposed to be forty or fifty years old, with one leg off," and another one, "twenty-five or thirty years old, with one short leg supposed to be occasioned by the white swelling." The women were described as copper-colored. By the order of J. W. Keyes, justice of the peace, the negroes, "being runaway slaves and believed to be without free papers," were turned over to a constable to be placed in jail. The latter official Strother G. Jones, made this return on his writ:

Executed by taking into possession the within named persons supposed to be runaway slaves, four of whom escaped from my custody on taking them before the court on the 16th inst., and the other, the oldest, a one-legged negro, was taken from my possession by the Sheriff of Sangamon County by virtue of process from the Supreme Court.

The proceeding occasioned deep interest among the people of Springfield and a decided conflict of opinion developed, but Thornton, in response to his appeal for a writ of habeas corpus, was taken before the Supreme Court, and, the facts being inquired into, he was awarded his liberty and discharged.

Another fugitive slave case was that of Edgar Canton, a negro about fifty-five years of age, who was apprehended in Springfield February 11, 1860, and arraigned before

United States Commissioner Corneau, charged with being the property of George M. Dickinson, of Shelby County, Missouri, from whom he ran away in the fall of 1856. More or less feeling arose, and although it was contended that no proof of the existence of slavery in Missouri had been offered or introduced, and the court, therefore, had no right to presume from historical knowledge that Missouri was a slave State, Commissioner Corneau held against the negro, who had a wife and two children in Springfield, and delivered him over to Dickinson to be transported to Missouri.

In no one of these fugitive slave cases did Lincoln take any part, nor did he, apparently, interest himself in other cases of like nature. As I have already intimated, it cannot be said that he upheld slavery, for we know he opposed it, but even then we should not forget that he was a lawyer and stood on high professional ground. An attempt was made to promote the cause of freedom by organizing and maintaining a colonization society in Springfield, but, judged by the local newspapers, there is nothing to indicate that Lincoln gave the movement more than passing notice. As a lawyer, it is true he did in the Bailey *vs.* Cromwell case seek to convince the court that the girl in question was not a slave, but it should also be borne in mind that in the equally noted Matson case, tried in Coles County, where a company of negroes had been imprisoned in the jail as fugitive slaves, he was still a lawyer and accepted a fee, not from the negroes seeking their freedom, but from Robert Matson, who claimed to be their owner and endeavored to return them to their Kentucky home.

Regarding Lincoln's political notions John W. Bunn

once made for my benefit this rather pertinent observation: "The reason Mr. Lincoln appeared in so few suits in behalf of runaway negroes was because of his unwillingness to be a party to a violation of the Fugitive Slave Law, arguing that the way to overcome the difficulty was to repeal the law. I have heard him make that suggestion, and I remember that in one case at least he advised that a few dollars be paid to buy off those who were holding the negro."

Elsewhere I have recorded the experience of Jonathan Birch, an old friend of mine who was licensed to practice law on an examination by Mr. Lincoln at Bloomington, Illinois, where the young man had for some time been a student in the office of his brother, one of the prominent practitioners of the place. Mr. Birch's description of Lincoln as he observed him in the court-room, the clerk's office, and other places where he held forth while out on the circuit, was to me an unusually interesting recital. Many years ago when Mr. Herndon spent a portion of one summer with me at my Indiana home, he and Mr. Birch, who was my neighbor, frequently met. I was present when they talked with each other, and I recall that what Mr. Birch, who was the embodiment of truthful and conscientious statement, said about Lincoln was verified by Herndon. Some of the things related by Birch merit repetition. Alluding to his observation and recollection of Lincoln at Bloomington and other near-by points on the circuit, he said to me once:

"Having no office of his own, Mr. Lincoln, when not engaged in court, spent a good deal of his time in the clerk's office. Very often he could be seen there surrounded by a group of lawyers and such persons as are usually found about a court-house, some standing, others seated on chairs or tables, listening intently to one of his characteristic and inimitable stories. His eyes would sparkle with fun, and when he had reached the point in his narrative which invariably evoked the laughter of the crowd, nobody's enjoyment was greater than his. An hour later he might be seen in the same place or in some law office near by, but, alas, how different! His chair, no longer in the center of the room, would be leaning back against the wall; his feet drawn up and resting on the front rounds so that his knees and chair were about on a level; his hat tipped slightly forward as if to shield his face; his eyes no longer sparkling with fun or merriment, but sad and downcast and his hands clasped around his knees. There, drawn up within himself as it were, he would sit, the very picture of dejection and gloom. Thus absorbed have I seen him sit for hours at a time defying the interruption of even his closest friends. No one ever thought of breaking the spell by speech; for by his moody silence and abstraction he had thrown about him a barrier so dense and impenetrable no one dared to break through. It was a strange picture and one I have never forgotten.

"In his physical make-up Mr. Lincoln could not be said to be a man of prepossessing personal appearance; but his splendid head and intellectual face made up in a large measure for all his physical defects, if such they might be called. When intellectually aroused he forgot his embarrassment, his eyes kindled, and even in his manner he was irresistible. It is well known that he was more or less careless of his personal attire, and that he usually wore in his

great canvass with Douglas a linen coat, generally without
any vest, a hat much the worse for wear, and carried with
him a faded cotton umbrella which became almost as famous in the canvass as Lincoln himself.  Late one afternoon during this canvass I boarded the train at Bloomington, soon after which Mr. Lincoln himself entered the same
car in which I was seated, wearing this same linen coat and
carrying the inevitable umbrella.  On his arm was the cloak
that he was said to have worn when he was in Congress
nine years before.  He greeted and talked freely with me
and several other persons whom he happened to know, but
as night drew on he withdrew to another part of the car
where he could occupy a seat by himself.  Presently he
arose, spread the cloak over the seat, lay down, somehow
folded himself up till his long legs and arms were no longer
in view, then drew the cloak about him and went to sleep.
Beyond what I have mentioned he had no baggage, no
secretary, no companion even.  At the same time his opponent, Judge Douglas, was traveling over the State in his
private car surrounded by a retinue of followers and enjoying all the luxuries of the period.

"It was during this canvass, with every fiber of his being tremulous with emotion, I heard him, in one of his
speeches denouncing the extension of slavery, passionately
exclaim: 'That is the issue that will continue in this country when these poor tongues of Judge Douglas and myself
shall be silent.  It is the eternal struggle between these two
principles — right and wrong — throughout the world.
They are the two principles that have stood face to face
from the beginning of time; and will ever continue to struggle.  The one is the common right of humanity and the other

the divine right of kings. It is the same principle in whatever shape it develops itself. It is the same spirit that says,
"You toil and work and earn bread and I'll eat it." No
matter in what shape it comes, whether from the mouth of
a king who seeks to bestride the people of his own nation
and live by the fruit of their labor, or from one race of men
as an apology for enslaving another race, it is the same ty-
rannical principle.' The melting pathos with which Mr.
Lincoln said this and its effect on his audience cannot be
described."

While it is true that Lincoln was always mindful of his
prerogatives as a lawyer, and as a rule sought to conform
to the ethics of the profession, it cannot be said that he was
cold and inexorable — invariably deaf to the appeal of a
human heart. As he reasoned he might be rigid and he
should be just, but he need not be without sympathy or
inhumane. This is admirably demonstrated in the Wright
case, reported by Herndon, in which Lincoln espoused
the cause of a widow who had been victimized by a money
shark, recovered all the damages asked for, declined to
charge for his services, and even offered to pay his client's
board while attending court.

One incident in Lincoln & Herndon's law practice, and
which was revealed to me by Herndon, brings into view
so vividly Lincoln's innate honesty, admirable courage,
and love of fair play, I feel I ought not to omit it. Charles
Matheney, the owner of a piece of land near the limits of
the city of Springfield, sold it to a woman — a client of
Lincoln who lived in another part of the State. In the deed
of conveyance the tract was described as a given number
of acres at a fixed price per acre.

"Some years after the sale," related Herndon, "the lady wrote to Mr. Lincoln apprising him of her desire to have the land surveyed and laid off into lots. Mr. Lincoln therefore procured a compass, chains, etc., and made the required survey. When he had finished and was making his calculations, he found that Matheney, the former owner through some oversight or erroneous description had lost about three acres of land and that the woman had gained it. He at once notified his client of the discovery and advised her that in morals and equity she ought to rectify the mistake by paying to the Matheney heirs (for in the meantime Charles Matheney had died) what was justly due them according to the actual number of acres and the price per acre originally agreed upon. The woman, probably because it was a closed incident, declined to make the desired restitution. Lincoln wrote her again, reciting what, in his judgment, was both right and equitable and emphasizing the additional fact that Matheney's heirs were poor and needy. His appeals finally reached the woman's heart and she relented; for in a short time he was surprised to receive from her a generous remittance in satisfaction of the claim. With the funds thus obtained he started out in quest of the Matheney heirs and never rested till he had located them and paid to each one his proportionate share of the proceeds. I helped him divide and distribute the money, and I remember the incident well, especially his zealous and persistent efforts to awaken the woman's sense of duty if not gratitude."

An incident dealing with Lincoln's activities as a lawyer, and obtained from trustworthy and unquestioned sources, I cannot well refrain from narrating; and yet it relates not so much to his professional experience as it serves to bring out the inherent and charitable forbearance that oftentimes characterized him when brought face to face with the delinquencies and shortcomings of some of his friends.

An Englishman, who posed as a nobleman or man of wealth and had purchased some land and cattle below St. Louis, succeeded in leaving there without having met all his financial obligations. He reached Springfield, where he stopped for a brief time on his way to Bloomington. Meanwhile a claim for a large sum of money followed him and was put in the hands of Jacob Bunn, the pioneer banker of Springfield, for collection. Fearful lest the stranger might press on to Bloomington without paying, Mr. Bunn induced his brother John W., his book-keeper and assistant, and Lincoln to keep an eye on him. The two sat up the better part of one night in front of the hotel where the man had lodged with directions to halt him if he should attempt to leave town. Meanwhile a rumor was current that a warrant for his arrest had followed him from the south and application for his apprehension or extradition had been made to the Governor. By this time the stranger, realizing, doubtless, that he was being closely watched, and anxious to avoid serious or embarrassing consequences, called Lincoln aside and offered to produce a thousand dollars provided the claim against him was surrendered and he was otherwise undisturbed. Lincoln conferred with Jacob Bunn, the offer was accepted, the money paid over, and the man proceeded on his journey. After he had gone, Bunn asked Lincoln about his fee, but the latter declined to make any charge, saying that he had served more as a

detective or officer than as a lawyer and adding that if at
any time in the future he felt that he was entitled to a fee
he would make a demand on Bunn for it.

"Thus the matter stood for a long time," related Bunn,
"and had almost dropped from my recollection when early
one morning, before I had eaten my breakfast, Mr. Lincoln called at my house, reminded me of the transaction,
and asked me if I would pay him a hundred dollars and consider it his fee in that case. I complied promptly, assuring
him I was glad to do so. Meanwhile I ventured to inquire why he had delayed asking for so long a time, and
especially what had prompted him to make the demand at
such an unusually early hour, reminding him that he was
entitled to his money and could have had it long before.
His answer was that he wanted the money, not for himself,
but for another who was in trouble and needed his help.
This awakened both my interest and curiosity, whereupon
he explained that three of his friends had spent the night
in a drunken spree, had broken in almost the entire front
of a grocery or saloon and otherwise committed acts of
such vandalism that before daylight the sheriff was forced
to apprehend them; that they were then in the latter's office
and would speedily be placed in jail unless some one should
appear and settle for the damage done. In a few moments
I secured the money and turned it over to him. He seemed
more or less relieved, and hurriedly left to interview the
sheriff and as soon as possible secure the release of his err-
ing friends. I did not press him for names, but in a short
time learned that two of his friends were the sons of
wealthy parents and the third, unfortunately, was his law
partner. Lincoln was poorer than any of them, and yet,

notwithstanding their wealth and disgraceful conduct, he seemed to regard it his duty to crawl out of his bed before daybreak and hasten to their rescue. I doubt if another man in Springfield would have done it. No wonder he sometimes thanked God he was not born a woman!"

# CHAPTER XV

How Lincoln whiled away his spare moments in Springfield — Places he was in the habit of frequenting — An evening in the office of Colonel W. B. Warren, Clerk of the Supreme Court — Incidents of Lincoln's stay at Urbana in the spring of 1856 — Stealing the hotel gong — Apprised of his vote for Vice-President at the Republican National Convention in Philadelphia — Leaving Urbana for Springfield — Riding in the omnibus — Whitney's recollection of Lincoln's modest fees — His financial accumulations — The bank account of Lincoln & Herndon.

How and where Lincoln spent his time when he was in Springfield and not traveling over the circuit is admirably told in a reminiscence by Mr. Herndon written and turned over to me by the latter not many months before his death. I had been trying to learn from him something additional about Lincoln's habits, what he did when he was not in the office, whether he was given to lounging in stores or other places where people in small towns frequently congregate — in short, how and where he spent his idle or unemployed moments. He said that Lincoln was never a lounger; that prior to 1858, by which time he had begun to attain more or less political prominence, there were only two or three places in the business part of Springfield, outside of certain law offices, he frequented, and even then his visits were never long. One of these was a drug-store, in the ownership of which his brother-in-law, Dr. Wallace, was interested. He also oftentimes stopped in at the combined store and bank of Jacob Bunn, which place he passed going to or from his home. He hardly ever visited stores to make purchases because his wife exercised undisputed control of that part of the domestic economy. But there was one place in which, as a *raconteur*, he shone and delighted to linger, and that was the court-house.

"From 1852 to 1854," said Herndon, "I assisted Colonel W. B. Warren, of Jacksonville, who was Clerk of the Supreme Court — in other words, served as his deputy, which I could do without interfering with my law practice — and thus had an excellent opportunity to meet not only the Springfield lawyers, but those from other parts of the State as well. The Supreme Court chamber was in the northeast corner of the State House, and adjoining it on the south was the library where the lawyers usually studied their cases, made their abstracts, and prepared their briefs. Not all of them were absorbed in study, for some, less diligent than others, chatted, told stories, and in divers ways consumed the time. With but few exceptions they drank their toddy, making frequent visits to a jug of good liquor which Colonel Warren usually hid from sight, but which was never so cleverly concealed that the wise ones could not find it.

"As a rule the lawyers who wanted to study were at work the greater part of the day, but after sunset their application gradually slackened and a good part of the evening was given over to social relaxation and breezy conversation. In the gathering were numerous story-tellers, but none of them equaled Lincoln, who was invariably the central figure and by far the most entertaining and inimitable performer in the aggregation. No one enjoyed the occasion more than he. His accumulation of stories was both unique and inexhaustible. One suggested another and they followed in rapid succession. As one man used to say, 'Where he learned them and where they would end no one could tell.' Lincoln drank none of the whiskey, pushed aside study, banished his melancholy, and joined in the general merriment. As the evening wore on the lawyers closed their books, and one after another threw aside their notes and unfinished briefs. From now on everything bespoke of fun and good humor; so much so, in fact, that Judge Caton and some of his colleagues on the bench would quit the room in which they had been studying or consulting, and, one after another, slyly slip into the library so as not to miss the stream of amusing recitals which they knew Lincoln would be pouring out for the delight and entertainment of the anxious group gathered about him.

"Meanwhile I was at my tasks, preparing records, issuing writs, and in every way endeavoring to assist Colonel Warren; but often my progress was provokingly slow, for these gatherings rarely adjourned before midnight, and occasionally, especially if Lincoln chanced to be in good trim and the supply of good cheer in that memorable jug had not run out, continuing still later. Sometimes after one of these festive and companionable evenings Lincoln and I would leave for our homes at the same time walking to a certain spot where our paths diverged. I recall one occasion. It was much past midnight and Lincoln was still jolly and bubbling over with the merriment and amusing incidents of the evening. Joyous and light-hearted, free from the look of dejection which so often beclouded his face, I believe I never saw him in happier spirits. Presently we reached the corner where we separated, each headed for his home. In a few minutes Lincoln would reach the two-story frame house at the corner of Eighth and Jackson Streets, and I confess I tried to picture to myself his changed attitude and expression and the scene that would ensue after he had crossed his threshold at that unseemly hour and undertook to square himself with that capricious little wife whose chief asset was a piercing voice and a fiery temper."

By the time 1856 rolled around, the calls for Lincoln to take part in the political campaign of that year became so numerous and persistent that his friends began to wonder if he could afford any longer to ignore the demand. He was still actively engaged in his chosen profession, but there was a charm about the attrition of a political campaign which he was daily finding it more difficult to resist. At the Republican National Convention, which was held in Philadelphia that year, he received 110 votes for Vice-President, a fact which serves to indicate that he was growing in popular favor. At the very time the convention met, Lincoln was at the town of Urbana, Illinois, attending an extra session of the Circuit Court. Henry C. Whitney who, with David Davis and Leonard Swett, was oftener and longer with Lincoln while making the rounds of the circuit than any one else, told me once a reminiscence of the court at Urbana at this time, well worth recording.

"Judge Davis," said Whitney, "held the court, and Lincoln, who had two or three cases to try, was there also. At the judge's request I secured a room for him, also for Lincoln and myself, at the American House, a primitive hostelry kept by one John Dunaway. The building had three front entrances from the street, but not a single hall downstairs; one of these entrances led directly into the ladies' parlor, and from it an entrance was obtained to the dining-room and from another corner a flight of stairs conducted us to our room. Close by the front and dining-room doors hung a gong which our vulgar boniface, standing in the doorway immediately beneath our windows, was in the habit of beating vigorously as a prelude to our meals. It was frequently very annoying, and so often disturbed our slumbers in the early dawn that we decided one morning it must be removed or forever silenced. By a majority vote Lincoln was chosen to carry out the decree. Accordingly, shortly before noon, he left the court-room, hastened to the hotel, passed through the dining-room, and, in a mischievous prank, took the offensive and noisy instrument from the place where it hung and quietly secreted it between the top and false bottom of a center table where no one would have thought of looking for it. In a short time I encountered Dunaway, our host, coming down from our room, where he had been and still was searching anxiously for the gong which some ruthless hand had, alas, abstracted. I passed on, and when I reached our room I realized I was in the presence of the culprit, for there sat Lincoln in a chair tilted awkwardly against the wall after his fashion, looking amused, sheepish, and guilty, as if he had done something ridiculous as well as reprehensible. The truth is we all enjoyed the landlord's discomfiture, and even Judge Davis, who urged Lincoln to restore the gong, was amused. Presently, however, Lincoln and I repaired to the dining-room, and while I held the two contiguous doors fast Lincoln restored the gong to its accustomed place, after which he bounded up the stairs two steps at a time, I following. The next day when the Chicago paper came in — it usually arrived about noon — it brought the news that Lincoln had received 110 votes for Vice-President at the Philadelphia Convention the day before. The announcement created something of a stir. Lincoln and Davis had left the court-room and had gone down to the hotel, where I joined them a few minutes later, bringing with me Judge Cunningham's copy of the 'Chicago Press' which I read to them. Of course Davis and I were more or less jubilant. Alluding to Lincoln's rude and undignified prank with the hotel gong, Davis laughed and with harmless irony admonished him: 'Great business for a man who aspires to be Vice-President of the United States.' But the news of the honor shown him at the Philadelphia Convention made but slight impression on Lincoln. Apparently he was unmoved, if not indifferent, his only response being: 'I reckon it's not me. There's another Lincoln down in Massachusetts. I've an idea he's the one.'

"The term of court that week at Urbana was decidedly prosaic, and the cases tried, usually by the court without the aid of a jury, were meager both in amount and incident. In due time Lincoln was ready to return home. He had collected twenty-five or thirty dollars for that term's business, and one of our clients owed him ten dollars which he felt disappointed at not being able to collect; so I gave him a check for that amount and went with him to the bank to get it cashed. T. S. Hubbard was the cashier who waited on us. I never saw Lincoln happier than when he gathered his little earnings together, being, as I now recollect it, less than forty dollars, and had his carpet-bag packed ready to start home."

Mr. Whitney, the narrator of the preceding incidents, was one of Lincoln's favorites among the lawyers of central Illinois. Judged by Lincoln's letter to him prior to 1860, which he permitted me to read, along with other facts of equal convincing value, one cannot doubt that he enjoyed Lincoln's full confidence.  A native of New England he emigrated to central Illinois early in the fifties.

"Very soon thereafter," he once said to me, "I became acquainted with Lincoln.  It was about the time of my first appearance at the bar.  I did not feel the slightest delicacy in approaching him for assistance; for it seemed as if he invited me to familiarity if not close intimacy at once; and this from no selfish motive at all — nothing but pure philanthropy and goodness of heart to a young lawyer just beginning his career.  He sat on the bench for the judge a while that term; and my first motion in court was made before him.  The next day he made some arrangements for his horse and buggy and took the train to fill an appointment farther north.

"I saw him start for the train.  He was obliged to ride over two miles in an old dilapidated omnibus, and being the sole occupant of the conveyance had somewhere procured and held in his hand a small French harp with which he was making the most execrable music.  I rallied him on this, to which, stopping his concert, he replied: 'This is my band; Douglas had a brass band at Peoria, but this will do me.' He resumed his uncouth solo as the vehicle drove off, and the primitive strains, somewhat shaken up by the jolting conveyance, floated out upon the air till distance intervened."

The recollection by Mr. Whitney of the extent of Lincoln's earnings on the circuit naturally led to the contemplation of his financial status generally.  When I inquired into that subject in Springfield I soon learned that as customers or patrons of the banks Lincoln & Herndon never rose above the lesser lights.  As a firm they were anything

but substantial depositors — in fact, the balance occasionally placed to their credit was usually so meager they could
scarcely be listed among the depositors, save in name. A
bank attaché told me that if, in the course of business,
Lincoln & Herndon received a check or draft it was rarely
ever deposited with the bank to be placed to the firm's credit
and drawn upon as is customary among bank patrons;
but instead one or the other of the two constituting the
firm, as soon as a remittance reached them, took it to the
bank, drew the requisite cash, and promptly returned to
the office to divide the proceeds with his partner. It will
thus be seen that their partnership, so far as the division
of earnings was concerned, was settled every day before the
sun went down. It was a simple but effective way of keeping their books balanced.

"While Lincoln and I were partners," wrote Mr. Herndon to me several years ago, "we kept no books as to our
partnership, though we did, of course, keep due account of
our transactions so far as other interests were involved.
Lincoln did the major part of the circuit work while I remained in Springfield to look after the local end of the business. Occasionally I was out on the circuit with him, but
never for long periods. At such times all moneys paid to
either of us was immediately divided. What Lincoln collected on the circuit, when I was back in Springfield, he
would bring home with him. If, when he returned, it happened I was not in the office, he would withdraw from his
pocket-book my share, wrap the money in a paper with a
slip attached, containing my name and a memorandum
indicating whence it came, and place it in a certain drawer
where I would be sure to find it. If, on the other hand, I

was in the office when he arrived he would open his pocket-book and make the requisite division. He was so prompt and his rule was so invariable I ventured once to ask him why he was so timely and particular in the matter. 'Well, Billy,' he answered, 'there are three reasons: first, unless I did so I might forget I had collected the money; secondly, I explain to you how and from whom I received the money, so that you will not be required to dun the man who paid it; thirdly, if I were to die you would have no evidence that I had your money. By marking the money it automatically becomes yours and I have no right in law or morals to retain or use it. I make it a practice never to use another man's money without his consent.'"

Late in the fifties, when he had attained the proportions of a United States Senator, Lincoln opened an individual bank account. He began to deposit his personal funds with the Marine Bank, one of the leading financial concerns of Springfield, presided over by his old friend and client Jacob Bunn. A brief perusal, however, of such of the old books as have been preserved proves that his transactions were of exceedingly modest proportions. Among his checks which were shown me, one of the largest — given, probably, for improvements to his residence — did not exceed two hundred dollars. As it was drawn by Lincoln immediately after the famous Rock Island Bridge suit it is fair to infer that it represented a portion of the fee paid him for his services in that case.

# CHAPTER XVI

Instances of Lincoln's weakness — His unwonted faith in certain friends — His blindness to their faults — His failure to redeem Herndon — Joining the charmed circle at the tavern — His bland and inexplicable confidence in the ability and moral influence of Ward Lamon — Appoints him United States Marshal of the District of Columbia — Lamon's attempt to influence General Frémont — Scheme to transport troops to West Virginia — The pretended Lamon's Brigade — Investigation by Congressional committee which denounces Lamon in scathing report — Notwithstanding opposition of fifteen Senators Lincoln adheres to him — Mark W. Delahay another instance of Lincoln's misplaced confidence — Surprise of John J. Ingalls — Lincoln finally appoints him United States Judge for the District of Kansas — Congressional committee visits Kansas to investigate Delahay's moral and official conduct — Delahay resigns to avoid impeachment — Lincoln's appointment of Simon Cameron and the trouble it gave him — Herndon's letter to Henry Wilson — Lincoln's real estimate of Douglas — What he told C. H. Moore about Douglas — Incidents of the joint debate — The recollections of Horace White.

No portrait of Lincoln, no delineation of his character can be deemed accurate or complete which does not take into the account certain attributes — more properly speaking, weaknesses — which were well known to many of his close friends. As one of the latter, Leonard Swett, said to me: "If Lincoln had some faults, we should not forget that Washington had more: few men less." It was the bard of Avon who makes one of his characters say:

The web of our life is of a mingled yarn, good and ill together; our virtues would be proud, if our faults whipped them not; and our crimes would despair, if they were not cherished by our virtues.

This sapient reflection can most fittingly be applied to Lincoln. True his delinquencies were not glaring, as compared to those of many others, but they were none the less inherent and characteristic. As I have elsewhere noted, both David Davis and Herndon insisted that Lincoln's wife was a better reader of men and in some respects a safer guide than he. In the selection of his associates, those on whom, when in doubt or danger, he expected to rely, we cannot avoid the conclusion that he was either so blinded by his affection for them that he could not see their shortcomings, or so indifferent, if not perverse, that he cared nothing for public opinion. There is abundant ground for the belief expressed by the late Horace White that there was a certain degree of moral obtuseness in Abraham Lincoln which the public do not recognize and will refuse to believe in the present generation.

Take, for example, the case of his law partner Herndon. It cannot be denied that he was conversant with the latter's bibulous and unfortunate habits. Although Herndon was able if not more or less brilliant, Lincoln knew that he was headed downhill, and yet there is no evidence that he sought to restrain him or even criticized him for his moral laxity. Advice and admonition from Lincoln might have been efficacious in Herndon's reformation; it undoubtedly would have steadied him, but often though he yielded to temptation and fell from grace Lincoln said nothing. Instead of chiding and repelling him as a mark of his disapproval of his conduct, Lincoln seemed to cling to him all the closer. He was ten years older than Herndon and knew that the latter looked up to and believed in him; he also had due regard for Herndon's ability. On the whole, therefore, had he made the proper effort, it would seem as if he might have saved him. An instance cited by Henry C. Whitney is further illuminative of Lincoln's peculiarities. "He did not like the man regarded as the best lawyer in a neighboring county seat," said Whitney, "nor, for that matter, did the latter like him; but a drunken fellow, who turned lawyer later in life and settled there, Lincoln used to seek and play billiards with by the hour."

On the circuit where he spent half of his time, Lincoln's closest and most confidential friend was Ward H. Lamon, or "Hill" Lamon as he was commonly known to his associates. Lamon lived at Danville and was a mediocre lawyer. He suffered himself in later years to be advertised to the world as Lincoln's law partner and he was sometimes associated in lawsuits with Lincoln, as the records of the courts in Vermillion and also in McLean County, Illinois, indicate; but the partnership was invariably limited to the case in hand. After the separation from Stuart and Logan in succession Lincoln's only partnership was with Herndon, who remained in charge of the firm's business in Springfield.

When in his rounds over the circuit Lincoln reached Danville, where Lamon held forth, it was the signal for a jolly if not uproarious time. Usually after dark when the business of the court for the day was over, a certain crowd of companionable brethren gathered in Lincoln's and Judge Davis's rooms at the hotel. It was Lamon's business to provide a pitcher of good liquor, which duty having been performed, the fun for the evening was due to begin. Davis scarcely imbibed, but Lamon and certain others were far more generous in their potations. In time Lincoln or Davis, realizing that Lamon was "mellow" enough, would exclaim, "Now, Hill, let us have some music," whereupon Lamon would respond by rendering the plaintive strains of "The Blue-Tailed Fly," or "Cousin Sally Downard," or some other ballad of equal interest but less propriety. Thus the hours flew by, and in proportion as the fluid in the pitcher diminished the hilarity increased. Occupying a seat in this charmed circle and joining heartily in the rude and equivocal merriment was Lincoln himself, who, strange to relate, never touched a drop of the liquor; and this, as John Hay said, "not from any scruples or from principle, but simply because he did not like wine or spirits."

The confidence and intimacy between Lincoln and Lamon began early and continued without interruption. Notwithstanding the feeble esteem in which Lamon was held by others, as well as the many things Lincoln himself must have known about him, Lincoln closed his eyes to the man's imperfections and clung tenaciously to him. Nothing, it seemed, could shake his faith in him. Among Lincoln's earliest official acts as President was the appointment of Lamon United States Marshal of the District of Columbia, which office Lamon was still holding at the time of Lincoln's death. In the fall of 1861 Lamon turned up in St. Louis, and on the strength of his close relations with Lincoln attempted to secure from General Frémont an order authorizing a regiment, the 39th Illinois Volunteers, to be sent to Williamsport, Maryland, to join the so-called General Lamon's Brigade in West Virginia — a military organization having its existence only in Lamon's brain. His "unwarranted and scandalous assumption of authority" prompted an investigation by Congress. The Special Committee reported as follows: "The cost of the transportation of the regiment from St. Louis to Williamsport, Maryland, would be about thirty thousand dollars and there is no law authorizing the transfer of troops from one

department to another without the special order of the Secretary of War or Commander-in-Chief. Edward Castle, in
charge of railroad transportation in the Western Department, says that on October 26, 1861, Lamon was introduced
to him as a brigadier-general from Washington, D. C.,
and that he was wearing the uniform of such a military
officer. Lamon's object was to have Castle send him next
day by special express train from St. Louis to Springfield
at the expense of the Government. Castle, who was much
flattered by Lamon's attentions, ordered an engine and car
and took Lamon and several friends. In going to St. Louis
to see Frémont, Castle not only provided it should be free
of expense, but directed the express messenger to 'show
General Lamon every attention and contribute to his comfort.'"

In its report the Special Committee insisted that the removal of the regiment desired by Lamon had no other object beyond that gentleman's personal gratification. "At
such a time," is the language of the report, "when every
dollar in the Treasury is needed to crush the Rebellion, we
submit that thirty thousand dollars is too large a sum to be
expended for the purpose of flattering the vanity of any
single individual. The removal of the regiment not only
without authority of the law, but inexpedient and without justification and thirty thousand dollars of the public
money worse than squandered, Lamon had no authority
to travel in special trains at public expense, and he should
be called on to refund the amount paid for special trains
which took him and his friends from St. Louis to Springfield, Illinois. If he should not do so the Treasury Department should ascertain what the amount is and deduct

from his salary as Marshal of the District of Columbia. It turns out from a letter of the Secretary of War that this gentleman, who proclaimed himself a brigadier-general and who was wearing the insignia of that distinguished rank, had no such an appointment. All such pretenses are unfounded as was also the pretense that the President told him he might take this regiment. He seems to have made use of his official position as Marshal of the District of Columbia and his assumed position as a brigadier-general to secure his object of removing the regiment and traveling in special trains at public expense. Instead of devoting his attention to the duties of his position, instead of watching and protecting the interests of the Government in the sphere of duty assigned him, he has been engaged in the business described by the committee above."

In January, 1862, Senator Grimes of Iowa exposed the fraud in a speech in open Senate, denouncing Lamon so scathingly that it caused a coolness between himself and Lincoln during the remainder of the latter's life. Senator Wilson of Massachusetts said that Lamon was so notoriously unfit for his office that he and fourteen other Senators voted against the confirmation of his appointment. And this is the man who, in February, 1861, when the President-elect was spirited through Philadelphia on his way from Harrisburg to Washington, was, on account of his spotless and sterling manhood, selected by Lincoln as his trusted companion rather than Colonel E. V. Sumner and Major David Hunter, military officers of approved courage and high standing who had been sent to Lincoln by General Scott for that purpose. A few weeks later, and after the inauguration, when the situation regarding

Fort Sumter was becoming daily more acute, Lincoln caused Lamon to be sent to Charleston, South Carolina, on what the latter said was "a confidential mission of great delicacy and importance." Nicolay and Hay say that he came with an "ostensible Government mission, was looked upon as the real Presidential messenger, was treated to a formal audience with Governor Pickens and permitted to make a visit to Fort Sumter, meanwhile, hobnobbing with the young Secessionists at the Charleston Hotel."

Another notable instance of Lincoln's susceptible nature and misplaced confidence was Mark W. Delahay. a mediocre, if not obscure, lawyer who, during Lincoln's earlier years, flourished in the neighborhood of Jacksonville and Petersburg in Illinois. Delahay laid claim to an intimate personal and professional acquaintance with Lincoln, in support of which he would relate numerous stories to impress his hearers with the importance of that relation. "It so happened that at my attendance at court in Menard County," was one of his recitals, "Mr. Lincoln was absent during the early part of the term, much to the regret of a number of young men who had been indicted for playing cards and were expecting Lincoln to represent them; but on account of his absence I was employed to assist in their defense. Mr. Lincoln's love of joking, for which he became famous in the latter days of his life, was quite as marked during the earlier period. He used to relate to his friends at the bar, and after he became President, some incidents connected with my defense of these young men. Sometimes he would tell it as upon 'a young lawyer' or sometimes on 'Delahay.' The prosecuting attorney in framing the indictments alternately charged the defendants with playing a certain game of cards called 'Seven-Up,' and in the next bill charged them with playing cards at a game called 'Old Sledge.' Four defendants were indicted in each bill. The prosecutor, being entirely unacquainted with games at cards, did not know that both 'Seven-Up' and 'Old Sledge' were one and the same. On the trial on the bills describing the game as 'Seven-Up' Delahay's witnesses would swear that the game played was 'Old Sledge,' and *vice versa* on the bills alleging the latter. The result was an acquittal in every case under instructions of the court. The prosecutor never found out the dodge until the trials were over and immense fun and rejoicing were indulged in as the result."

Late in the fifties Delahay turned up in Kansas, where he became more or less conspicuous in the politics of that locality. He was a candidate or applicant for almost every office from county surveyor to United States Senator. In 1859 Lincoln visited Kansas and made a few speeches there, being for a time a guest at Delahay's home. This so stimulated the latter's confidence in his own importance that he tried, unsuccessfully, to be chosen a delegate from Kansas to the Chicago Convention in 1860. He had divulged to Lincoln his ambition in that direction, but he was so impecunious he was unable to bear the expense of a trip to Chicago, and after Lincoln's death a letter was found, written by him to Delahay, in which he offered to furnish him a hundred dollars for that purpose. Lincoln's faith in the man continued unabated, a fact demonstrated by another letter of Lincoln written in March, 1861, less than ten days after his inauguration as President. It was addressed to Delahay and virtually turned over to him the federal patronage of Kansas, a proposition which so profoundly awakened the interest of the late Senator John J. Ingalls of that State that he visited me at my home several years ago in an endeavor, as he claimed, to learn the truth regarding the story. "I knew Delahay well," said Ingalls, "but he was so weak and debased I cannot think that Lincoln, who also knew him, believed in or trusted him." Convinced that Ingalls questioned the current story, I withdrew from the place where it had been stored Lincoln's original letter to Delahay and gave it to Ingalls to read. I shall never forget the look of astonishment that spread over his face as he read it.

In 1859 Delahay aspired to a seat in the United States Senate from Kansas and promptly invoked Lincoln's aid. He evidently wanted Lincoln to intercede with General James H. Lane in his behalf. Instead of approaching Lane directly, as Delahay asked, Lincoln sought to accomplish the desired end by a somewhat circuitous, but equally effective route. He wrote Delahay a letter in which he committed himself to his candidacy, at the same time telling him he might show the letter to General Lane and thus gain the latter's support — a suggestive specimen of Lincoln's subtlety as a politician. In April, 1861, Lincoln appointed Delahay Surveyor-General of Kansas and Nebraska, which office he seems to have filled till October 5, 1863, when Lincoln appointed him United States District Judge for Kansas. His daughter, Mary E. Delahay, is authority for the statement that Lincoln offered to appoint him Minister to Chile, which post he declined. But despite his political ambition, his ability and pretensions, Delahay was both debased and corrupt. It is hard to believe that Lincoln was not aware of it, for eventually Delahay's conduct became so flagrant and notorious that a committee of the lower House of Congress at Washington, consisting of Messrs. Bingham of Ohio, Butler of Massachusetts, Mercer of Pennsylvania, Peters of Maine, Wilson and Voorhees of Indiana, and Eldredge of Wisconsin, were appointed to impeach him. The committee journeyed to Kansas, where it examined numerous witnesses and otherwise endeavored to investigate the record and conduct of the accused judge.

The testimony showed that Delahay was a confirmed drunkard and frequently sat on the bench and presided at trials in a maudlin, befuddled condition. In some instances at the hotel and other public places where he appeared he reeled and had to be assisted in moving from one point to another. He even staggered on one occasion in an attempt to cross the floor of the court-room and he was drunk on the bench within sixty days after his appointment by Lincoln in the fall of 1863. On another occasion he was sentencing a man who had been found guilty of an offense wherein the law fixes the minimum penalty at two years' imprisonment and a fine of a thousand dollars; but Judge Delahay reduced the fine one half and refused to add any further penalty, after which he turned to the astonished crowd in the court-room and exclaimed: "You have been a long time impeaching old Mark Delahay. Now would be a good time to try him!" On numerous occasions he would interrupt attorneys in court, admonishing them that they must either "fish or cut bait." A. L. Williams, the United States District Attorney, testified that late in the year 1863 Delahay was drunk in court. When sentencing criminals he could not remember names or offenses for which convicted. "I delayed bringing up defendants for several days at times," continued Williams, "for the express purpose of having them sentenced by a sober court. After the death of my father, who was Delahay's predecessor on the bench, I went to see Lincoln and told him of Delahay's unfitness. I also spoke to several Senators expressing my disapproval. I felt aggrieved that the position my father had so honorably filled should be occupied by such an inferior if not disreputable successor."

The most suggestive, if not damaging, thing which awakened the doubt and attention of the Congressional committee arose from reports floating about regarding the disposition of what was known as the Confiscation Fund — moneys in Kansas as well as other Northern States belonging to Rebels subject to confiscation, and which were duly turned over to the United States authorities. In the case of Delahay, owing to his vicious habits and his questionable record generally, it became noised about that he was unable in certain instances to account satisfactorily for all sums that passed through his hands. However, there was no legal evidence that Delahay was guilty of retaining confiscation funds, but, owing probably to the fear that the committee might strike paying dirt and in order to avoid embarrassing if not scandalous disclosures generally, Delahay felt impelled to act. To meet the array of testimony piling up against him was an ordeal from which he revolted. He therefore took the bull by the horns and averted further inquiry by resigning.

After Delahay was out of office he prepared a lecture on Lincoln, a copy of which I ran across among some papers turned over to me by Mr. Herndon several years ago. I loaned it to Horace White, who read it and then wrote me: "I thank you for sending me Delahay's lecture on Lincoln, which I have read and return herewith. There is one passage in it which would make a horse laugh if he knew Delahay as we knew him. It is the one where he eulogizes Lincoln's 'unerring judgment of men and his intuitive knowledge of character.'"

The most glaring instance of Lincoln's weakness in judging of individual men, their character or fitness, — in other words, his lack of acumen, — was the appointment, knowing his record and what manner of man he was, of Simon Cameron to a place in his Cabinet. In the words of Mr. White: "It was the most colossal blunder of Lincoln's public life — if it is proper to call it a blunder; for it may have a worse name in history a hundred years hence." The Cameron incident has been so exhaustively dealt with by Nicolay and Hay and other historians of the Civil War period but little remains for me to add. "There is, however, another fact in this connection," wrote Mr. White in a letter to me shortly before his death, "which somebody else will bring out in the course of historical criticism. That is that after Cameron came back from Russia Lincoln was just as friendly to him as though nothing had happened to force him out of the Cabinet. He appointed him Minister to Russia with all his imperfections in his head and received him back in the same way; and if I recollect rightly employed him in running political errands just prior to the National Republican Convention of 1864. That I call moral obtuseness of the same kind as his intimacy with Lamon, Delahay et al."

In their knowledge of Lincoln, in their analysis of his growth, his unfolding in "morals and motives," no two men I met in Illinois impressed me more profoundly than Herndon and Horace White. One, a lawyer, the other an able editor, and both so situated that they could observe Lincoln at closer range than the majority of his other friends, they nevertheless seem to have viewed him from somewhat different angles. Herndon's estimate of the President-elect as outlined in his letter to Henry Wilson of Massachusetts, in December, 1860, is one of the cleverest bits of character delineation one is likely to encounter. Herndon admitted that Lincoln in his ability to read men, to decide many of the questions of administration or of political economy, questions which no man can demonstrate, was, in a sense, weak and his friends could rule him. "But when on justice, right, liberty, the Constitution and the Union," he says in his letter to Wilson, "then you may all stand aside: he will rule then and no man can move him — no set of men can do it. There is no fail here. This is Lincoln, and you mark my prediction. You and I must keep the people right: God will keep Lincoln right."

Mr. White viewed Lincoln through the eyes of a trained newspaper student. Being the correspondent and ultimately one of the editors of the "Chicago Tribune," which was so potent a force in moulding public opinion during the decade when Lincoln, as a leader, was in the making, he was close to the latter. He enjoyed his confidence, frequently accompanied him, sometimes lodging in the same room, in his travels over the State as a campaign speaker. His observation and judgment of Lincoln are therefore not without their weight.

"The popular conception of Mr. Lincoln," said White, "as one seeking honors, but not avoiding public duties is a *post-bellum* growth very wide of the mark. He was entirely human in this regard, but his desire for political preferment was hedged about by a sense of obligation to the truth which nothing could shake. This fidelity to the truth was ingrained and unchangeable. He was one of the shrewdest politicians of the State. Nobody had more experience in that way, nobody knew better than he what was passing in the minds of the people. Nobody knew better how to turn things to advantage politically and nobody was readier to take such advantage, provided it did not involve dishonest means. He could not cheat people out of their votes any more than out of their money.

"Mr. Lincoln never gave assent so far as my knowledge goes to any plan or project for getting votes that would not have borne the full light of day. At the same time he had no objection to the getting of votes by the pledge of offices, nor was he too particular what kind of men got the offices. His preference was always for good men; but he could not resist pressure where persons were concerned even though his conscience told him he was doing wrong. In the case of Simon Cameron it was impossible for Lincoln to retain him after the House had censured him. He could not have carried on the Government with such a burden and blot. Yet Lincoln whitewashed him by giving him the Russian mission, and after he came back Lincoln made him his friend and confidential agent in politics. I remember well how Lincoln fell in the estimation of the best men in Congress in consequence of his association with Cameron after the latter came back from Russia."

At this point in my story I hope it will not be considered amiss if I digress slightly in order to comply with the request of an old friend who earnestly besought me not to omit suitable mention of Lincoln's real estimate or appreciation of Stephen A. Douglas. In order to obey the mandate and quiet the apprehensions of this anxious old friend, I made a careful and conscientious inquiry and dug deeply enough into the subject to convince me that, in so far as the personal relations of Lincoln and Douglas toward each other were concerned, no differences between them worthy of note existed. Moreover, a careful study of their famous joint debate in 1858 warrants the conclusion that in every regard Lincoln treated his competitor with the proper degree of dignity and respect. I was always impressed by Herndon's conclusions regarding Douglas. He said: "He was full of political history, well-informed on general topics, eloquent almost to the point of brilliancy, self-confident to the point of arrogance, and a dangerous competitor in every respect. What he lacked in ingenuity he made up in strategy, and if in debate he could not tear down the structure of his opponent's argument by a direct and violent attack he was by no means reluctant to resort to a strained restatement of the latter's position or the extravagance of ridicule. As a lawyer I found him to be broad, fair, and liberal-minded. Although not a thorough student of the law his large fund of common sense kept him in the front rank. Usually he was both just and generous and, so far as I knew, never stooped to gain a case. Lincoln, I remember, viewed him very much as I did. Although not in every respect commendatory Lincoln's estimate of Douglas could not be called unfair. The truth is I recall but two men that Lincoln really praised: Jefferson and Clay; and of the very few I heard him condemn Douglas was one.  I remember an incident in our office once when some one present exclaimed, 'It's a lie,' alluding to a statement made by a man who had just left the room. 'A lie!' interrupted Lincoln. 'Did you ever read the "Life of Patrick Henry"?' alluding to Wirt's 'Life' of Henry which some people regard as a great exaggeration."

Mention of Lincoln's opinion of Douglas carries me back several years to a time when I was in the town of Clinton, Illinois, and visited Mr. Clifton H. Moore, one of Lincoln's associates in the days when he rode the circuit. An able and successful lawyer Mr. Moore was also something of an authority on the development of Illinois, because, during the period when Lincoln and Douglas were contending for leadership in their respective parties, Mr. Moore was himself a political factor of no mean proportions. An enthusiastic adherent of Lincoln he was also acquainted with and well qualified to pass on the record and merits of Douglas. "In the summer of 1858," said Mr. Moore to me, "Douglas made a speech at Pontiac during the course of which he ventured to quote from Holland's 'Life of Van Buren.' A day or so later Lincoln passed through here and among other things told me that Douglas in his speech at Pontiac had seriously misquoted Holland, a fact he could easily establish if he only had Holland's book; but unfortunately not a copy was to be found in Clinton. The next morning he pushed on to Bloomington. He was still so wrought up over Douglas's misrepresentation that David Davis was finally induced to send a man on horseback to Springfield with a note from Lincoln asking for the book. In due time the messenger returned with the desired volume which he turned over to Lincoln, who took it with him, threatening to confront Douglas with it at the earliest opportunity."

As indicative of Lincoln's real opinion of Douglas, Mr. Moore related this circumstance which so deeply impressed me that I made a note of it at the time: "On the day Mr. Lincoln delivered his speech at Clinton during the campaign of 1858 he was in my office; and I shall always remember with regret one thing he said about Douglas, which was this: 'Douglas will tell a lie to ten thousand people one day, even though he knows he may have to deny it to five thousand the next.'"

It was in the domain of political agitation that Lincoln mistrusted Douglas. It was there the latter manifested his dexterity and lack of rectitude; and it was done so invariably and unmistakably there is little wonder that Lincoln eventually lost faith in him. It will be remembered that in the fall of 1854 Douglas deceived Lincoln, if he did not actually break his word, when he journeyed to the town of Princeton and there renewed his campaign, colliding in debate with Owen Lovejoy, in violation of an agreement or understanding to the contrary made with Lincoln a few days before at Peoria. "Upon being charged afterwards with his breach of word," related Herndon, "Douglas responded that Lovejoy 'bantered and badgered' him so persistently he could not resist the encounter. The whole thing, I remember, thoroughly displeased Lincoln."

When I reminded Horace White, who heard every one of the Lincoln-Douglas debates, of the incident just related he said: "The fact I had in mind when I spoke of Douglas's unveracity in stump speaking was a statement he made at the Ottawa joint debate in which he said that Lincoln as a young man 'could ruin more liquor than all of the boys in town together.' This was said in order to draw Lincoln into a personal controversy. Everybody who knew Lincoln knew that he never used liquor or tobacco at all. He said to me once that he had never taken a drink of any alcoholic beverage in the past twenty years. That he should have been a drunkard before 1838 is impossible. Not only was Douglas's statement essentially false as to Lincoln, but it would have been a true description of himself (Douglas) at the time of the Ottawa debate. The fact was that Douglas at that time was drinking himself to death — an end which he reached three years later. The pen of the historian has not touched upon that fact as yet.

"I have no doubt whatever that Douglas made that false statement about Lincoln to get a denial from him that he was a drinking man, in which event he would have enlarged upon it and given particulars which he could easily have invented and would have assured Lincoln that he did not wish to injure him, etc., leading off the debate into a personal quagmire as was his habit when he was getting the worst of it. But Lincoln was too smart. He never noticed the charge at all. So Douglas never repeated it."

The joint debate between Lincoln and Douglas in 1858 has been so exhaustively treated in the volume issued by the Illinois State Historical Library in 1908, and so vividly portrayed by Horace White who heard all the speeches, it would savor of supererogation were I to attempt a further or more comprehensive account of it. It suffices to say that, viewed from various angles, it was one of the greatest forensic combats the country has known.

Having so effectively demonstrated his ability to cope with Douglas in 1854 when, to use a homely figure of speech, he "ran the latter into his hole," Lincoln was ready if not really anxious to measure swords with him in 1858. That he was sure of himself is illustrated by the surprisingly meager preparations he seems to have made for a joust with an adversary as daring and resourceful as Douglas. In another chapter I have alluded to the reference-book filled with sundry notes and newspaper clippings which he carried with him during the canvass. Although small enough to fit comfortably into his coatpocket it contained all the ammunition he saw fit to store away and hurl at Douglas when scheduled to meet him in combat. I once showed it to Mr. White, who recognized it, but assured me that Lincoln was so conversant with the various phases of the dominant questions and otherwise so well equipped he could recall but two instances when Lincoln felt impelled to read from or otherwise refer to it.

The debate itself was conducted on an animated and yet magnanimous plane. Notwithstanding the multitude of ardent supporters who gathered about the speakers and the spirited feeling which naturally was awakened, the two contestants, as a rule, kept within decent and reasonable bounds. In some respects it was a test of patience and forbearance hardly short of sublime. Mr. Lincoln bore himself with dignity and composure. His nearest approach to an exhibition of anger or irritation was at the debate at Charleston. There, in answer to the "old charge revived by Judge Douglas" against Lincoln for opposing the Mexican War, the latter caught Mr. Orlando B. Ficklin, who was sitting on the platform, by the collar and led him forward. Lincoln was visibly agitated, in fact deeply aroused by Douglas's innuendo. "I do not mean to do anything with Mr. Ficklin," he exclaimed, "except to present his face and tell you that *he personally knows it to be a lie.* He was a member of Congress at the only time I was in Congress, and he knows that whenever there was an attempt to procure a vote of mine which would endorse the origin and justice of the war, I refused to give such endorsement and voted against it; but I never voted against the supplies for the army, and he knows as well as Judge Douglas that whenever a dollar was asked by way of compensation or otherwise for the benefit of the soldiers, *I gave all the votes that Ficklin or Douglas did and perhaps more.*" (*Loud applause.*)

Mr. White further explained that Lincoln, who was expecting Douglas to repeat at Charleston, or, as he termed it, renew the old charge regarding his vote on the Mexican War, had prepared himself accordingly. The "Congressional Globe" or some like public document contained his record on the subject with which he intended to confront Douglas when the proper time came, but the desired volume had inadvertently been left in a law office downtown and about a mile away from the Fair Ground where the debate was being held. A boy was dispatched thither to get it; but before the messenger returned, Lincoln without waiting for the book became aroused, and noting the presence of Mr. Ficklin on the stand led him forward and the dramatic incident just related followed.

A glance at the map of Illinois will suffice to convince the reader that of the seven places where Lincoln and Douglas were scheduled to measure swords in joint debate, Charleston, the fourth in the list, was the point farthest east. Consequently it was nearest to the Indiana line, and thither the multitudes from the Hoosier State, scarcely less anxious to greet the doughty gladiators than their Illinois brethren, gradually wended their way. The newspapers of the period report that among the crowds which reached Charleston before and on the day of the debate one delegation "comprising eleven cars of passengers on the Alton road came from Terre Haute alone." The leading band in the parade hailed from Bowling Green, also in western Indiana. Three of the most adept fife-and-drum musicians as well as certain other persons came from my own home — the town of Greencastle, only a few miles east of Terre Haute. Of the latter one was Dillard C. Donnohue, a lawyer and partner of John P. Usher, afterwards Secretary of the Interior in President Lincoln's Cabinet. In 1860 Donnohue was a delegate to the Chicago Convention and voted for Lincoln, who, when he became President, rewarded him by sending him on a diplomatic mission to the West Indies. In later years, he often entertained me with interesting recollections of the Lincoln-Douglas debates. One incident impressed me. He related that while at Charleston he was a guest of the Capitol House where Mr. Lincoln was also quartered before and after the debate. Of course the latter was always surrounded by a crowd of listeners and, as contended by Donnohue, was thoroughly out of patience with Douglas because of his conduct that day. He made no concealment of his indignation. It will be remembered that Mrs. Douglas, described by Horace White as "a lady of attractive presence and queenly face and figure," was in the habit, as the campaign progressed, of accompanying her husband to most of his appointments. This circumstance evidently did not escape the notice of Lincoln, who doubtless knew the lady and realized the extent of her influence over her husband; for when alluding to Douglas for the benefit of the crowd gathered about him at the hotel, Mr. Donnohue said he heard Lincoln make this statement: "I flatter myself that thus far my wife has not found it necessary to follow me around from place to place to keep me from getting drunk."

# CHAPTER XVII

Lincoln as a student — The effect of a college education — Comparison of John Fiske's and Lincoln's conception of social evolution — Lincoln takes up Euclid — Reading "The Annual of Science" — Studying higher mathematics — His attempt to square the circle — His self-confidence and secretiveness — His mechanical bent — Securing a patent — Working on the model of his invention at Walter Davis's shop — Explaining it to his partner and callers at his office — Preparing his lecture on "Discoveries and Inventions" — Delivers it at Jacksonville and Springfield — What some of his colleagues thought about it — Several paragraphs of the lecture — Account by S. H. Melvin of what Lincoln did with the manuscript — Herndon also enters the lecture field — Delivers his effort entitled "The Sweep of Commerce" before an audience in Cook's Hall in Springfield — What the "Journal" said about it.

THERE is no gainsaying the assertion that Lincoln was in the main a profound student. A natural logician and patient investigator he was so relentless and unerring in his pursuit of knowledge that the question naturally arises: "What effect would the discipline and attrition of a college training have had upon him?" I have met people who pretend to believe that instead of strengthening, it would have weakened him. "If he had been trained in a university before his style of expression had crystallized," said Herndon, "his utterances, though conforming to the tenets of modern and so-called artistic criticism, would have been rounded and the sharp edges which so unmistakably betoken his individuality would have disappeared beneath the gloss of conventionality. His mental evolution was through thought to Æsop's Fables, through these to general maxims, from maxims to stories, jokes and jests; from these to clear, strong Anglo-Saxon words of power. I have heard Lincoln substantially state this, including what he believed was the probability of the weakening process — the methods of a classical or college education."

Illustrative of this element in Mr. Lincoln's makeup and style of expression as compared to that of a profoundly scientific and college trained mind, attention is called to the "Formula of the Law of Progress" as laid down by John Fiske in his book on "Cosmic Philosophy": "The evolution of Society is a continuous establishment of psychical relations within the community in conformity to the physical and psychical relations arising in the environment; during which both the community and the environment pass from a state of relatively indefinite, incoherent homogeneity to a state of relatively definite coherent heterogeneity; and during which the constituent units of the community become even more distinctly individuated."

So much for a university-trained philosopher's conception of social evolution! But note how Lincoln, a clearheaded, self-educated man illustrates the law of progress: "Many independent men everywhere in these States a few years back in their lives were hired laborers. The prudent, penniless beginner in the world labors for wages a while, saves a surplus with which to buy tools or land for himself, then labors on his own account another while, and at length hires another new beginner to help him. This is the just and generous and prosperous system which opens the way to all, gives hope to all, and consequent energy and progress and improvement of condition to all."

The failure of Lincoln to return to Congress after the end of his first and only term in 1849 marks the beginning of an important epoch in his development. Believing he

for what they have already done, we apprehend they are
to be able to proceed — The precise amount of cost already
incurred we have not now at hand, but it will not
greatly vary from $40 — We will direct the Sheriff to col-
lect the balance —

As to the real estate, we can not attend to it, as agents, &
we therefore recommend that you give the charge of it, to Mr.
Isaac S. Britton, a trust-worthy man, & we show the have an
hope for such brandish.

Yours &c
Logan & Lincoln

PART OF A LETTER OF LINCOLN'S TO A CLIENT (ROWLAND SMITH & CO., APRIL 24, 1844), SHOWING ERRORS IN HIS USUALLY CORRECT SPELLING

was politically moribund and yearning to broaden his knowledge, he turned most heartily to intensive study.

"He secured a copy of Euclid," related Herndon, "and took it with him on the circuit. Of nights and at odd times he would bury himself in the study of the problems of the great Greek geometrician. Occasionally I traveled with him, occupying the same bed, he reading by the light of a tallow candle. Sometimes the bedsteads were slightly short so that his feet would extend a trifle over the footboard. Thus engaged he would study for hours. Having apparently abandoned all thought of ever rising above the waves of the political sea, he became not only deeply studious and abstracted, but markedly reticent if not gloomy.

"One day about this time I purchased at Bradford & Johnson's book-store in Springfield a copy of a work called 'The Annual of Science,' as I now recall the name, and was reading it when Lincoln came in the office. In answer to his query: 'Billy, what are you reading?' I handed it to him. He looked over it for a while and then returned it with the suggestion that so far as he could observe it was constructed on the right principle. 'Unlike many books of its class,' he said, 'it recites the failures as well as the successes of life. Too often we read only of successful experiments in science and philosophy, whereas if the history of failure and defeat was included there would be a saving of brain work as well as time. The evidence of defeat, the recital of what was not as well as what cannot be done serves to put the scientist or philosopher on his guard — sets him to thinking on the right line.' In the afternoon he picked the book up again and later took it home with him to read that night. The next morning when he had returned to the office he told me the book pleased him so much he had decided to buy himself a copy. I thus began to realize that he was gradually being led to the study of profound questions, for he was also steadily delving into the mysteries of mathematics and the abstruse sciences. A few days later I found him already in the office and deeply engaged when I arrived. This was unusual, for I almost invariably preceded him there. He was sitting at the table and spread out before him lay a quantity of blank paper, large heavy sheets, a compass, a rule, numerous pencils, several bottles of ink of various colors, and a profusion of stationery and writing appliances generally. He had evidently been struggling with a calculation of some magnitude, for scattered about were sheet after sheet of paper covered with an unusual array of figures. He was so deeply absorbed in study he scarcely looked up when I entered. I confess I wondered what he was doing and what had occasioned his profound application at the office so early in the morning; nor was my curiosity allayed till a later hour in the day when he arose from his chair, apparently headed for the court-house. It was then that he enlightened me by announcing that he was trying to solve the difficult problem of squaring the circle. In a short time he returned to the office and resumed his study. For the better part of the succeeding two days he continued to sit there engrossed in that difficult if not undemonstrable proposition and labored, as I thought, almost to the point of exhaustion. He talked but little about it to me or to others, so far as I could observe, but it was evident he was toiling with all his might. I have been told that the so-called squaring of the circle is a practical impossibility, but I was not aware of it then, and I doubt if Lincoln was. His attempt to establish the proposition having resulted in failure, we, in the office, suspected that he was more or less sensitive about it and were therefore discreet enough to avoid referring to it.

"Mr. Lincoln was peculiar in that he had absolute confidence in his own powers, which will account for the fact that he never asked for advice nor sought the opinion of another for his guide. He was the most self-reliant man imaginable, standing by himself, steadfast in purpose and idea. You had to judge him by what he said. The embodiment of honesty he told the truth always in so far as he declared himself, but there were times when he was so guarded in his utterances he apparently talked without saying anything. Profoundly secretive but philosophical, he was a wily man in mental reservation, begotten by the eternal silence."

Although successful as a railsplitter, it cannot be said that Lincoln leaned toward agriculture or manifested a fondness for farm work. Instead he evinced a decided bent toward machinery or mechanical appliances, a trait he doubtless inherited from his father who was himself something of a mechanic and therefore skilled in the use of tools. It will be remembered that it was during his journey homeward from Washington after the adjournment of Congress in 1849, when he saw a steamboat stranded on a sandbar, that he conceived the idea of an apparatus designed to lift the vessel off or over the offending shoals; and later, after he had returned to Springfield he was granted a patent on a device of that kind which he had invented. "I well remember," related Herndon, "when Lincoln was at work on his patent. He was very much taken up with the project and, for a time, would slip away from the office and hurry down to the shop of Walter Davis, a Springfield mechanic, where, with the aid of the latter and the use of his tools, he gradually constructed the model and sent it to Washington. I often saw him tinkering in Davis's shop and, on one or two occasions, owing to his absence from the office, I had to go down there and confer with him regarding matters of business. When the model was done it was brought to the office, and, with the enthusiasm of the average inventor, Lincoln would expatiate on the marvels and merits of the device for the benefit of the few persons who dropped in and were sufficiently interested to listen to his vivid and rosy predictions. Of course he talked to me about it, and although I could not, with propriety, appear to ignore it, yet it was so impractical, if not visionary, I experienced the greatest difficulty in concealing from others my lack of faith in it." Another contrivance which evoked Lincoln's study and attention was the invention of one Alexander Edmonds and known as the Horological Cradle. It brought on a lawsuit in which Lincoln was more or less conspicuous and is elsewhere described in these pages.

Herndon never gave utterance to a more truthful declaration than when he contended that as a lawyer and politician Lincoln was both profound and successful, but that in certain other respects he was proportionately weak; and by that he doubtless meant that it was as an inventor and lecturer that he failed to measure up to the required standard. Lincoln's desire to test his skill and ability on the lecture platform did not manifest itself until after his debate with Douglas in 1858. In its issue of February 14, 1859, the "Springfield Journal" contains this announcement: "Mr. Lincoln delivered a lecture at Jacksonville last Friday night on the subject of 'Discoveries and Inventions.' It was received with repeated and hearty bursts of applause." On the editorial page of the "Jacksonville Sentinel" this notice appeared: "Hon. Abraham Lincoln delivered a lecture on last Friday evening before one of the literary societies of the pupils of Illinois College; subject, 'Discoveries and Inventions.' We learn that the lecturer drew largely from his fund of spicy anecdotes and the lecture proved highly entertaining."

The late William Jayne, who was one of the founders of the Phi Alpha Society before whom the lecture was delivered at Jacksonville, told me that the audience was small and the receipts at the door proportionately disappointing, a fact that Mr. Lincoln could not fail to note. When the committee, after the lecture, met him, he relieved their embarrassment, saying: "Don't be discouraged, boys. Pay my railroad fare and fifty cents for my supper at the hotel and we'll call it square." A few days later this item appeared in the "Springfield Journal": "Hon. A. Lincoln will lecture before the Springfield Library Association at Concert Hall Monday night February 21st 7.30 o'clock. Admission twenty five cents. Geo. S. Roper, Cor. Sec." — accompanied by the following editorial mention: "It will be seen by notice in another column that the gentleman lectures before the Library Association at Concert Hall this evening. Let one and all compliment him with a full audience. His lecture we are assured will be an intellectual feast."

Beyond the above items the papers of the period contain no further mention of the lecture enterprise. That it did not awaken any unusual degree of public interest or approval and probably failed even to meet Mr. Lincoln's expectations is demonstrated by a letter written by him, March 28, 1859, to a friend in a near-by town in which he says: "Your note inviting me to deliver a lecture at Galesburg received. I regret to say I cannot do so now; I must stick to the courts awhile. I read a sort of lecture to three different audiences last month and this; but I did so under different circumstances which made it a waste of no time whatever." In response to another invitation he writes, April 16, 1859: "Yours of the 13th is just received. My engagements are such that I cannot at any very early day visit Rock Island to deliver a lecture or for any other object."

The truth gradually dawned on Lincoln, and he soon realized that of his many and varied accomplishments lecturing was not one of them; so also concluded many of his friends and professional associates. Some of them, including David Davis and Leonard Swett, the latter of whom told me of the circumstance, ventured to prod him about it, but fearing that he might be sensitive over it they soon desisted. Henry C. Whitney told me that on one occasion he was emboldened to joke with Lincoln about the lecture, but the latter interrupted him, saying good-naturedly, "Don't, Whitney; that plagues me." Herndon told me that he went to Concert Hall in Springfield and listened to Lincoln when he delivered the lecture, and remembered vividly the day before when he was preparing it at the office, noting down various items on stray pieces of paper which were folded and reposed in one of his pockets or found an equally convenient lodgment inside his hat. The whole was finally put into connected manuscript form which he read. As a whole it was in some respects commonplace, and so unlike Lincoln that it failed to draw from his friends the endorsement or applause which he so anxiously awaited. Realizing that he would not be classed among the stars of the Lyceum he soon disappeared from the field. "If Lincoln's address over the death of Clay in 1852," said Herndon, "demonstrated that he was not a eulogist, his effort at Concert Hall in Springfield a few years later proved that he was not a lecturer."

Before I pass from the subject, and in order the reader may be his own judge of Lincoln's fitness and aptitude as a platform speaker, I venture to set out here a few pertinent facts regarding his effort on "Discoveries and Inventions" together with a portion of the lecture itself copied from the original manuscript. The latter paper belonged to the late Dr. Samuel H. Melvin, a former resident of Springfield who removed to California and died there in 1898. Shortly before his death, in explanation of how he came into possession of the manuscript he made the following statement:

"In the month of February, 1861, being at that time a resident of Springfield, Illinois, I called one evening at the residence of my friend John Todd, who was an uncle of Mrs. Abraham Lincoln. While there Mr. Lincoln came in bringing with him a well-filled satchel, remarking as he set it down that it contained his literary bureau. He remained fifteen or twenty minutes conversing mainly about the details of his prospective trip to Washington the following week, and told us of the arrangement agreed upon by the family to follow him a few days later. When about to leave he handed the grip to Mrs. Grimsley, the only daughter of Dr. Todd, remarking as he did so that he would leave the bureau in her charge; that if he ever returned to Springfield he would claim it, but if not she might make such disposition of its contents as she deemed proper." (Here follows a brief account of Mr. Lincoln's assassination, over four years later, coupled with the announcement that Dr. Melvin was chosen a member of the committee of twelve Springfield citizens sent to Washington to accompany home the remains of the late President.) "A few days after the body was laid to rest," continued Dr. Melvin, "I again called upon my neighbors, the family of Dr. Todd. Scenes and incidents connected with the assassination of the dead President were discussed and the remark made by Mr. Lincoln on his last visit to the house was referred to as indicating a presentiment that he would not return alive. This recalled the fact of his having left his so-called literary bureau and his injunction as to its disposition. Mrs. Grimsley brought the grip from the place where it had been stored and opened it with a view to examining its contents. Among them was found the manuscript and attached to it by means of a piece of red tape was another of like character. They proved to be the manuscripts of two lectures which he had prepared and delivered within a year prior to his election to the presidency — one at Jacksonville and a few days later at Decatur, the other at a hall in Springfield at which I was present. Mrs. Grimsley told me to select from the contents of the bureau any one of the manuscripts it contained; and supposing at that time

~~Beaver and musk-rats build houses, but they build no better now, than they did five thousand years ago—Ants, and honey-bees, lay up their winter stocks of provision, but they do so, no wiser better, or less laboriously, than they did in the day of creation~~— Man is not the only animal who labor; but he is the only one who improves his workmanship— This improvement, he effects by Discoveries, and ~~Inventions~~— His first important discovery was the fact that he was naked; and his first invention was the fig-leaf apron— This simple article— the a=pron— made of leaves, seems to have been the origin of clothing— the one thing for which nearly half of the toil and care of the hu=man race has ever since been suspended— The most important improvement ever made in connection with clothing, was the invention of spinning, and weaving— The spinning jenny, and power-loom, invented in modern times, though great improvements, do not, as inventions, rank with the ancient arts of spinning, and weaving— Spinning and weaving brought into the department of clothing such abundance and variety of material— Wool, the hair of several species of animals, hemp, flax, cotton, silk, and perhaps other articles, were all suited to it, affording garments not only adapted to wet and dry, heat and cold, but also susceptible of high degrees of ornamental finish— Exactly when, or where, spin=ning and weaving originated is not known— At the first interview of the Almighty with Adam and Eve after the fall, He made "coats of skins, and clothed them" Gen: 3-21—

PAGE OF LINCOLN'S MANUSCRIPT OF HIS LECTURE "DISCOVERIES AND INVENTIONS"

that the two manuscripts belonged to the same lecture I selected them. On subsequent examination I discovered that while they both treated on the same subject (Discoveries and Inventions) they were separate lectures. Twenty-five years later I disposed of one of the manuscripts to Mr. C. F. Gunther, of Chicago. The other, it is my hope and desire, shall remain in possession of my family and its descendants."

Which one of the two manuscripts mentioned by Dr. Melvin contains the text of the Springfield lecture delivered by Mr. Lincoln no one at this day seems to be able to determine. The manuscript sold to Mr. Gunther has already been published and what follows is copied from the other one:

Beavers and musk-rats build houses but they build no better ones than they did five thousand years ago. Ants and honeybees lay up their winter stock of provisions but they do so no wise better or less laboriously than they did at the dawn of creation. Man is not the only animal who labors; but he is the only one who *improves* his *workmanship*. This improvement he effects by *Discoveries and Inventions*. His first important discovery was the fact that he was naked; and his first invention was the fig-leaf apron. This simple article the apron — made of leaves, seems to have been the origin of *clothing* — the one thing for which nearly half of the toil and care of the human race has ever since been expended. The most important improvement ever made in connection with clothing was the invention of *spinning and weaving*. The spinning jenny and power-loom, invented in modern times though great *improvements* do not *as inventions rank* with the ancient arts of spinning and weaving. Spinning and weaving brought into the department of clothing such abundance and variety of material. Wool, the hair of several species of animals, hemp, flax, cotton, silk and perhaps other articles were all suited to it, affording garments not only adapted to wet and dry, heat and cold, but also susceptible of high degrees of ornamental finish. Exactly *when* or *where* spinning and weaving originated is not known. At the first interview of the Almighty with Adam and Eve after the fall He made "coats of skin and clothed them" (Gen. 3:21).

The discovery of the properties of *iron* and the making of *iron tools* must have been among the earliest of important discoveries and inventions. We can scarcely conceive the possibility of making much of anything else without the use of iron tools. Indeed an iron *hammer* must have been very much needed to make the *first* iron hammer with. A *stone* probably served as a substitute. How could the "*gopher wood*" for the Ark have been gotten out without an axe? It seems to me an axe or a miracle was indispensable. Corresponding with the prime necessity for iron we find at least one very early notice of it. Tubal-Cain was "an instructor of every artificer in *brass* and *iron*" (Gen. iv: 22). Tubal-Cain was the seventh in descent from Adam; and his birth was about one thousand years before the flood. After the flood frequent mention is made of *iron* and *instruments* made of iron.

As man's *food* — his first necessity — was to be derived from the vegetation of the earth it was natural that his first care should be directed to the assistance to that vegetation. And accordingly we find that even before the fall, the man was put into the garden of Eden "to dress it and to keep it." And when afterwards, in consequence of the first transgression, *labor* was imposed on the race as a *penalty* — a *curse* — we find the first born man — the first heir of the curse — was a "tiller of the ground." This was the beginning of agriculture; and although both in point of time and of importance it stands at the head of all branches of human industry it has derived less direct advantage from Discovery and Invention than almost any other. The plow, of very early origin; and reaping and threshing machines, of modern invention are, at this day, the principal improvements in agriculture. And even the oldest of these, the plow, could not have been conceived of until a precedent conception had been caught and put into practice — I mean the conception or idea of substituting other forces in nature for man's own muscular power. These other forces, as now used, are principally the *strength* of animals and the *power* of the wind, of running streams and of steam.

Of all the forces of nature, I should think the *wind* contains the largest amount of *motive power* — that is power to move things. Take any given space of the earth's surface — for instance Illinois; and all the power exerted by all the men and beasts and running water and steam over and upon it shall not equal the one hundredth part of what is exerted by the blowing of the wind over and upon the same space. And yet it has not so far in the world's history become proportionately valuable as a motive power. It is an *untamed* and *unharnessed* force; and quite possibly one of the greatest discoveries hereafter to be made will be the taming and harnessing of it. That the difficulties of controlling this power are very great is quite evident by the fact that they have already been perceived and struggled with more than three thousand years; for that power was applied to sail-vessels, at least as early as the time of Isaiah.

The advantageous use of *Steam-power* is, unquestionably, a modern discovery. And yet, as much as two thousand years ago the power of steam was not only observed, but an ingenious toy was actually made and put in motion by it at Alexandria in Egypt. What appears strange is, that neither the inventor of the toy, nor any one else, for so long a time afterwards, should perceive that steam would move *useful* machinery as well as a toy.

The criticism of Herndon that Lincoln's lecture was a commonplace effort and in some respects beneath the latter's standard of excellence is hardly warranted and may not after all have been strictly in accordance with his original estimate. It is possible Herndon may have cherished the idea that he could surpass Lincoln's effort — in fact, there is evidence that he was so pleased with his partner's success and confident of his own ability in the same line that he decided to venture upon the platform himself. Accordingly in the number of the "Springfield Journal" issued March 15, 1860, appeared this item:

W. H. Herndon will lecture before the Springfield Library Association at Cook's Hall this evening. His subject will be

"The Sweep of Commerce." He will no doubt handle it in an able manner. Let there be a large audience, for the treasury of the Library Association is not quite full and every twenty-five-cent piece left at the door of the hall this evening will be so much clear gain to the association.

The character and extent of the people's response to Herndon's effort is indicated by the following editorial in the next day's "Journal":

The lecture by Mr. Herndon at Cook's Hall last night was altogether too good for the size of the audience which did not number one hundred persons. The subject of the lecture was "The Sweep of Commerce" and ample justice was done to it by the talented lecturer. We cannot close our eyes to the fact that a generous outpouring of people gathered night before last to hear Lola Montez, a woman who has violated every known rule of life, mocked the sacredness of the marriage relation and publicly set at naught all that is beautiful and modest in womankind. The lecture by Mr. Herndon was for the most part historic and could not fail to interest all, and when the lecturer indulged in anticipations of the future or moralized on the past it was in the clear and comprehensive view of a man who has studied well his subject and shown himself capable both to please and interest.

# CHAPTER XVIII

An epoch in Lincoln's life — His political baptism — Signs the call for the Bloomington Convention — Herndon's account of the incident — How Stuart tried to retard him — Lincoln announces himself — His speech at the Bloomington Convention — The prediction of Jesse K. Dubois described by Whitney — Lincoln invited to speak in New York — Effect on his neighbors in Springfield — What John T. Stuart said — The Cooper Institute address — His speeches in New England — How he impressed the Eastern people — Mentioned for President by the press — County convention in Springfield endorses him for President — He attends the Decatur meeting where John Hanks brings in the famous rails — Crowds of Lincoln's friends head for Chicago leaving him at Springfield — The Chicago Convention — What Lincoln was doing at home — The nomination on Friday — How Lincoln received the news — The account by Clinton L. Conkling — The effect at Springfield — Marching to Lincoln's house — His speech — Arrival of notification committee from Chicago — Incidents of their visit — The notification ceremony in the parlor of Lincoln's home — Incidents of the campaign — All paths lead to Springfield — The great rally in August — Letter of John Hanks supporting the claims of his cousin Abe Lincoln — Some local campaigners — Herndon's speech at Petersburg — Comments of the local papers.

HAVING devoted more or less space to an account of Mr. Lincoln's activities as a lawyer, lecturer, and inventor, it follows that in order to acquaint the reader with a comprehensive review of the real man, his evolution as a political leader should not be omitted. In the endeavor to arrive at the truth in this regard, however, I shall avoid as fully as I can the repetition of the things with which the public is already familiar and in relating the story of his development view him through the eyes of his neighbors and close friends. This and a retrospect of conditions as reflected in the local press cannot fail to add to the interest of the narrative.

Those who have carefully studied the life of Lincoln will, I believe, agree with his biographers that the year of

1854 marks the beginning of an eventful epoch in his career. We have his own testimony that for a period of five
years prior thereto beginning with the close of his only
term in Congress in 1849 he had practically forsaken politics and concentrated his energy and masterly ability on
the practice of law. And doubtless he would have continued thus politically inactive during the remainder of his
days but for a circumstance mentioned in the notes prepared by him for an autobiography in which he makes the
sententious declaration that "in 1854 his profession had
almost superseded the thought of politics in his mind when
the repeal of the Missouri Compromise aroused him as he
had never been before."

His first decisive and noteworthy utterance after the
great bolt from the political sky was the speech at Springfield October 4, 1854, in answer to one by Stephen A. Douglas at the same place the day before. Twelve days later he
repeated it at Peoria. On this occasion he wrote it out in
full and, fortunately for history, it was published word for
word in the Springfield papers. It was a profound and
masterly argument. "After the lapse of more than a
quarter of a century," wrote one of his biographers, "the
critical reader finds it a model of brevity, directness, terse
diction, exact and lucid historical statement and full of
logical propositions so short and strong as to resemble
mathematical axioms. Above all it is pervaded by an elevation of thought and aim that lifts it out of the commonplace of mere party controversy. The main broad current
of his reasoning was to vindicate and restore the policy of
the fathers of the country in the restriction of slavery. But
running through this like a thread of gold was the demon-

stration of the essential injustice and immorality of the system."

It is unnecessary to recount here the various steps by which Lincoln rose to the eminence of political leadership he was destined to attain. He was still but a unit in that great but unorganized army of Whigs and Democrats who, like himself, were aroused by the repeal of the Missouri Compromise. The Republican Party as an organization had not yet come into existence, but events were crystallizing — gradually assuming form and shape. Although the political sea until then had been pervaded by a calm, it was an ominous circumstance, for often a calm is but the precursor of a storm. Lincoln's attitude and conduct at this particular juncture is of the profoundest significance and necessitates the recital of a brief but interesting chapter of history.

Early in the spring of 1856 at the head of its editorial column the "Springfield Journal" carried a notice or proclamation signed by a number of Sangamon County people urging the propriety of a "county convention to be held at Springfield on Saturday, May 24, to appoint delegates to the Bloomington Convention." It made no pretense of representing an organization and nothing was said to indicate the political complexion of those who were to attend the convention beyond the brief declaration that it was to be a gathering of those who were "opposed to the repeal of the Missouri Compromise, opposed to the present Administration, and in favor of Washington and Jefferson." This call, when turned over to the newspaper, bore the signature of one hundred and twenty-nine citizens of Springfield and near-by territory. Among them were two of Lincoln's law partners and men like William Jayne, James C. Conkling, and Edward L. Baker. The first name on the list was that of Abraham Lincoln followed immediately by William H. Herndon. Being thus so near the head of the list it is manifestly fair that the latter should be allowed to give his version of the episode as follows:

"Tossed about with the disorganized elements that drifted together after the angry political waters had subsided, it became apparent to Mr. Lincoln that if he expected to figure as a leader he must take a stand himself. Mere hatred of slavery and opposition to the injustice of Kansas-Nebraska legislation was not all that was required of him. I ventured to warn him against his apparent inaction, seeing that the needs of the hour were so pressing, insisting that he must be a Democrat, a Know-Nothing, or Republican, or forever float about on the sea without a compass, rudder, or sail; but about the only response I could evoke was that I was 'too rampant and spontaneous.' At length, however, he decided to declare himself, and it came about in this way: Believing the times were ripe for more advanced movements in the spring of 1856 I drew up a paper for the friends of freedom to sign calling a county convention in Springfield to select delegates to the forthcoming Republican State Convention in Bloomington. The paper was freely circulated and generously signed. Lincoln was absent from town at the time and, believing I knew what his feeling and judgment on the vital questions of the hour was, I took the liberty of signing his name to the call. The whole was then published in the 'Springfield Journal.' No sooner had it appeared than John T. Stuart, who, with others, were endeavor-

# THE JOURNAL.

## SPRINGFIELD:

### FRIDAY EVENING, MAY 16, 1856.

## To the Citizens of Sangamon County.

The undersigned, citizens of Sangamon county, who are opposed to the Repeal of the Missouri Compromise, and who are opposed to the present Administration, and who are in favor of restoring the administration of the General Government to the Policy of Washington and Jefferson, would suggest the propriety of a County Convention, to be held in the City of Springfield, on SATURDAY, the TWENTY-FOURTH day of MAY, 1856, to appoint Delegates to the Bloomington Convention.

| | | |
|---|---|---|
| A Lincoln | J A Dikeman | E R Wiley |
| Wm H Herndon | Nicholas Dunnuck | S B Moody |
| Z A Enos | Oliver P Hall | P L Harrison |
| N W Matheny | J N Fullinwider | M O Reeves |
| John Irwin | William Henricks | Wm H Boyd |
| Walter Davis | James Jamison | Jas Wier |
| Pascal P Enos | David Hall | S M Parsons |
| W H Ballhache | Allen Hall | S S Sabin |
| E L Baker | E T Dikeman | Frank Hoppin |
| William Jayne | James McBride | Dan'l Hoppin |
| Geo W Chatterton | J G Elkin | W S Pickrell |
| J D Harper | Thos S Kizer | P Van Bergen |
| Thomas M Helm | A T Thompson | Geo Pasfield |
| E B Hawley | J A Jenkins | W Fisher |
| S F Paden | Morris Bird | A Y Ellis |
| Fred I Dean | J B Fosselman | A J Ashton |
| Amos Camp | H W Owen | P Breckenridge |
| J A Hough | J A Mason | Thos Cantrall |
| H B Grubb | Chas Fisher | W L Gookins |
| Geo A Black | A H Saunders | A A McQuesten |
| J B McCandless | Elijah Tomlinson | Job Flesher, jr. |
| A E Constant | D Humphreys | L S Conant |
| J R Mingle | J R Saunders | Jay Slater |
| John Ranson | J L Lanterman | John Smith |
| Joseph W Arnold | J C Planck | J Cantrall |
| Sam'l Cunningham | Alfred A North | S B Fisher |
| E R Ulrich | Charles Dunn | Grover Ayers |
| David A Martin | A W French | Wm Perce |
| Geo S Roper | J A McCandless | Hal Reily |
| H Post | R J McCandless | G Jayne |
| B Coon | Wm S Wallace | G A Sutten |
| Isaac A Hawley | S T Logan | John Cook |
| A J Sell | Rob Irwin | J W Moffett |
| R Churchill | C Birchall | C C Brown |
| S C Whitney | Wm F Elkin | B Moore |
| A M Watson | William Butler | Jno W Weber |
| T S Little | Jas C Conkling | George R Weber |
| J A Pickrell | Jno Williams | Jacob Lewis |
| W Hathaway | B P Fox | A H Lanphear |
| Enos Bradley | Joseph Thayer | E C Matheny |
| Elisha Dunnuck | P C Canedy | Thos J Knox |
| Alex Armstrong | S Smith | John Armstrong |
| B Turley | A Millington | John Branson |

ing to retard Lincoln in his advanced ideas, rushed into the office and asked if Lincoln had 'signed that Abolition call in the Journal.' I answered in the negative, but added that I had signed his name myself. To the question, 'Did Lincoln authorize you to sign it?' I returned an emphatic 'No.' 'Then,' exclaimed the indignant Stuart, 'you have ruined him!' But I was by no means alarmed at what others deemed inconsiderate and hasty action. I thought I understood Lincoln thoroughly, but in order to vindicate myself if assailed I sat down, after Stuart had rushed out of the office, and wrote Lincoln, who was then in Tazewell County attending court, a brief account of what I had done and how much stir it was creating among his friends and others at home. If he approved of my course I asked him to telegraph or write me at once. In due time came the answer: 'All right; go ahead. Will meet you — radicals and all.' Stuart subsided; and the pretended conservative spirits in and about Springfield no longer claimed to control the political fortunes of Abraham Lincoln."

It would be next to impossible to trace the development of Lincoln as a politician without some account of the Republican State Convention at Bloomington May 29, 1856, referred to in a previous paragraph. Descriptive of this great meeting Herndon once said: "The convention adopted a platform ringing with strong anti-Nebraska sentiment and there gave the Republican Party its official christening. The business of Convention being over, Mr. Lincoln, in response to the repeated calls, came forward and delivered a speech of such earnestness and power that no one who heard it will ever forget the effect it produced. I have heard or read all of Mr. Lincoln's great speeches, but I give it as my opinion that the Bloomington speech was the grand effort of his life. Heretofore he had simply argued the slavery question on grounds of policy — the statesman's grounds — never reaching the question of the radical and the eternal right. Now he was newly baptized — freshly born; he had the fervor of a new convert; the smothered flame broke out; enthusiasm unusual to him blazed up; his eyes were aglow with an inspiration; he felt justice; his heart was surcharged with sympathy and he stood before the throne of the eternal Right. His speech was full of fire and energy and force; it was logic; it was pathos; it was justice, equity, and truth. I attempted for about fifteen minutes, as was usual with me, to take notes, but at the end of that time I threw my pen and paper away and lived only in the inspiration of the hour. If Lincoln was six feet four usually, he was seven feet high at Bloomington that day and inspired at that. From that day to the day of his death he stood firm in the right. He felt his great cross, had his great idea, nursed it, kept it, taught it to others, in his fidelity bore witness of it to his death, and finally sealed it with his precious blood."

Being admonished that his account of Lincoln's speech, in the opinion of some persons, appeared unusually graphic if not overdrawn, Herndon answered: "The description was used by me in a lecture in 1866 and to some persons may seem more or less vivid if not extravagant in imagery, but, although more than twenty years have passed since it was written, I have never seen the need of altering a single sentence. I still adhere to the truthfulness of the scene as originally depicted."

In my travels through Illinois I have met and talked with

many persons who heard Lincoln's Bloomington speech. They included Leonard Swett, Joseph Medill, David Davis, and Henry C. Whitney, and all agreed that it was a wonderful and memorable effort. I was much impressed by Whitney's recollection. He said that soon after the speech, as he descended the stairway from the convention hall, Jesse K. Dubois, of Lawrence County, Illinois, who had just been nominated State Auditor, caught him by the arm and exclaimed: "Whitney, that is the greatest speech ever made in Illinois and puts Lincoln on the track for the presidency." A little later Whitney caught up with Lincoln, who was on his way to the residence of Judge David Davis, where both were guests, and told him what Dubois had said. "He walked along for a few moments," related Whitney, "without saying a word, but with a thoughtful, abstracted look; then he straightened up and made a remark about some commonplace subject having no reference to the matter we had been discussing. Did he recognize in this burst of enthusiasm from Dubois the voice of destiny summoning him to the highest responsibility on earth? If so, well for him was it that he did not also see the towering granite tomb only nine years distant, consecrated by a flood of human tears."

No single factor, however, did so much to strengthen Lincoln or rather to promote his fortunes as the speech he delivered at Cooper Institute in New York, February 26, 1860. When it became known in Springfield that he had been invited to speak in New York, it occasioned unwonted surprise. Inviting a man of no more pretensions than Lincoln, hailing from a place as obscure as Springfield, to deliver an address before a cultured audience in

the great metropolis was indeed an extraordinary and unusual occurence. No wonder Lincoln ordered a new suit of
clothes for the occasion. Comments were numerous and
varied. The following which appeared February 23, 1860,
in the "Illinois State Register," the Democratic organ in
Springfield, shows what Lincoln's political adversaries at
his home thought of him as a lecturer:

*Significant:* The Hon. Abraham Lincoln departs to-day for
Brooklyn under an engagement to deliver a lecture before the
Young Men's Association in that city in Beecher's church. Subject: not known. Consideration: $200 and expenses. Object:
presidential capital. Effect: disappointment.

As a rule the people of Springfield were loyal to Mr.
Lincoln, applauded his efforts, and rejoiced in his success.
There were, of course, a few exceptions. John T. Stuart,
unfortunately, was one. Recalling Lincoln's lecture at
Concert Hall the year before, which he characterized as a
weak effort, Stuart predicted indifference and scant attention as Lincoln's portion, whenever he undertook to
entertain a New York audience: "All of which," contended Herndon, "simply shows how envious Stuart really
was of Lincoln's success and faith in himself."

That the Cooper Institute address made an early and
profound impression on the majority of the people of Lincoln's home town as well as elsewhere is proved by the
"Springfield Journal," which, in its issue of March 7, 1860,
publishes the address as it appeared in the New York papers. "We present herewith," says the "Journal" editori-
ally, "a very full and accurate report of Mr. Lincoln's
Cooper Institute speech; yet the tones, the gestures, the
kindly eye, and mirth-provoking look defy the reporter's

skill. . . . No man ever before made such an impression on his first appeal to a New York audience." In a later issue of the "Journal" attention is paid to the speeches made by Mr. Lincoln in New England, whither he had gone to visit his son Robert who was attending school at Exeter, New Hampshire. He spoke at numerous places in New Hampshire, Rhode Island, and Connecticut. "He indulges in no flowers of rhetoric, no eloquent passages," says the Manchester, New Hampshire "Mirror." "For the first half-hour, his opponents would agree with every word he uttered; and from that part he began to lead them off cunningly, little by little, till he seems to have gotten them all into his fold. He displays more shrewdness, more knowledge of the masses of mankind than any other public speaker we have had since Long Jim Wilson left for California." The "New York Tribune" on March 13th said: "Mr. Lincoln spoke on Friday at Norwich, Conn., and on Saturday at Bridgeport, whence he came by the night express to this city, attending the churches of Drs. Beecher and Chapin yesterday. He leaves this morning by way of the Erie Railroad, having spoken once in New England for every secular day since his address in this city two weeks ago. He has done a good work and made many friends during his visit."

The publication in an Ohio paper in November, 1858, of an editorial announcement favoring the nomination of Lincoln for President must have awakened similar utterances elsewhere, for no later than April, 1859, Lincoln in a letter to an Illinois friend, who had endorsed him for President, felt impelled to arrest the movement in his behalf, saying: "I must in candor say I do not think myself fit for the presidency. I certainly am flattered and gratified that some partial friends think of me in that connection; but I really think it is best for our cause that no concerted effort, such as you suggest, should be made."

Early in January, 1860, a long letter by a New York traveler appeared in the "Springfield Journal" in which the writer recorded his observations as he made his way over the country, claiming to have interviewed merchants, mechanics, and farmers everywhere, and instead of a pretended sentiment in Seward's behalf he reported a decided leaning toward Lincoln as the best and most available man for President. A few days later the "Central Illinois Gazette" came out in a ringing editorial endorsement of Lincoln. Meanwhile the Cooper Institute speech intervened, whereupon the "Jacksonville Journal," "Iroquois Republican," "Rock Island Gazette," "Menard Index," and other papers of like standard in Illinois joined the Lincoln column.

The first public or concerted action by the people of Springfield in support of Mr. Lincoln's presidential aspirations took place April 28, 1860. A few days earlier the Republican State Central Committee had issued a call for a State Convention to be held at Decatur May 9, 1860, signed by N. B. Judd, E. L. Baker, George T. Brown, Thomas J. Turner, W. T. Hopkins, N. C. Geer, J. Grimshaw, William H. Herndon, C. D. Hay, D. K. Green, D. L. Phillips, and Jesse W. Fell. The Republicans of Sangamon County promptly met in convention and selected the following delegates from Mr. Lincoln's home: Noah W. Matheney, William H. Herndon, John G. Nicolay, George R. Webber, and William Jayne. The following resolution was adopted:

"Resolved that our distinguished fellow-citizen, the tall pioneer of Sangamon County, Abraham Lincoln, is our first choice for President of the United States and that we deem ourselves honored to be permitted to testify our personal knowledge in every-day life as friends and neighbors, of his inestimable worth as a private citizen, his faithful and able discharge of every public trust committed to his care and the extraordinary natural gifts and brilliant attainments which have not only made his name a household word in the prairie state, but also made him the proud peer of the ablest jurists, the wisest statesmen and the most eloquent orators in the Union."

Scenes and events in Lincoln's life now began to unfold with surprising rapidity. In a few days followed the Decatur Convention made famous by John Hanks with his picturesque railsplitting interruption. Within a week the hosts had gathered at Chicago for the memorable tournament there. With the proceedings of the convention itself the world is familiar, and the varied and dramatic incidents have so vividly been portrayed by others I can hope to add but little to what has long since been recorded regarding it. Lincoln's attitude and connection therewith alone merit our attention.

The two men in that convention on whose counsel and judgment Lincoln probably placed the most implicit reliance were David Davis and Stephen T. Logan. The Illinois delegation, of course, were united and enthusiastic in their support. It was their plan to secure for him the votes of Indiana and Pennsylvania; and it has been asserted that the same was accomplished by David Davis on the promise of a cabinet portfolio for a man from each of those States; but whether true or not it developed that both States fell into line for Lincoln at the proper time.

The convention opened Wednesday, May 16, 1860. Lincoln was present at the Decatur Convention the previous week, but he refrained from going to Chicago. Instead he remained in Springfield going about his business as usual. It is a matter of history vouchsafed by Herndon, who was with the Springfield delegation gathered in Chicago, that Lincoln sent word to them by the hand of E. L. Baker, editor of the "Springfield Journal," directing Davis, and others in charge of his interests, to refrain from making any deals or agreements, as he was determined he would not be bound. Beyond this injunction there is no evidence that he communicated further with them or otherwise sought to restrict their action. Attention has been called to a letter, recently discovered, written by Mr. Lincoln a few days before the Chicago Convention, addressed to a delegate from Indiana, C. M. Allen, of Vincennes, asking him to await the arrival of David Davis and Jesse K. Dubois before deciding on any line of policy to be followed by him at the convention. A day later Lincoln wrote a letter to R. M. Corwine, saying: "I think the Illinois delegation will be unanimous for me at the start, and no other delegation will. A few individuals in other delegations would like to go for me at the start, but may be restrained by their colleagues. It is represented to me by men who ought to know that the whole of Indiana might *not be difficult to get*." And there are people who pretend to believe that Lincoln was a novice in political methods; that he sat still in his Springfield office, folded his hands, looked up at the ceiling, and, without manifestıng the least interest in the developments of his own cause, suffered things to drift along heedless of what might befall him!

The delegates-at-large from Illinois in the Chicago Convention were Norman B. Judd, of Chicago; Gustavus Koerner, of Belleville; David Davis, of Bloomington; and Orville H. Browning, of Quincy. The two delegates representing the Sixth District, which included Sangamon County — in which Lincoln lived — were Stephen T. Logan, of Springfield, and N. M. Knapp, of Winchester. The following letter was written by Knapp after he had reached Chicago. It was addressed to Lincoln and served to indicate how things appeared to his friends gathered at the convention and what they were planning to do in his behalf:

> TREMONT HOUSE — CHICAGO
> *Monday, May* 14, 1860
>
> DEAR SIR:
> Things are working; keep a good nerve — be not surprised at any result — but I tell you your chances are not the worst. We have got Seward in the attitude of the representative Republican of the East — you at the West. We are laboring to make you the second choice of all the delegations we can, where we can't make you first choice. We are dealing tenderly with the delegates taking them in detail and making no fuss. Be not too expectant, but rely upon our discretion. Again I say brace your nerves for any result.
> Truly your friend
> N. M. KNAPP

On Friday, May 18th — four days after the above letter was written — the nomination took place. Meanwhile we can well understand that if not a deeply engrossed man

Lincoln was certainly a very nervous and restless one. On a vacant lot south of the building which housed the office of the "Springfield Journal," John Carmody had leveled and smoothed the surface of the ground and maintained there a ball alley — a place where the lawyers sought amusement and exercise by playing at "fives" — a game in which the contestants would throw a ball against a brick wall and catch it when it rebounded, also known as hand-ball. The game was to keep the ball going. If the player failed to catch it on the rebound, he lost a point, and twenty-one points constituted the game. William Donnelly, a boy employed by Carmody, had charge of the alley, kept the floor in proper condition and collected the fees. Several years ago I visited Donnelly, then living in Springfield, and interviewed him regarding the enterprise. Lincoln, he said, was very fond of the game and was one of the most active and skillful players; his success being due to his agility and large hands, enabling him to catch the ball almost every time. Donnelly reported that during the week of the Chicago Convention Mr. Lincoln was about the place a good deal, indulging freely in the game.

In view of the numerous and varied accounts which have been written detailing Lincoln's activities during the week of the Chicago Convention, including descriptions of how and where he received the news of his nomination and his movements generally, the statement which follows is of undoubted interest and value. It is copied from the original notes of an interview with Mr. E. L. Baker, the editor of the "Springfield Journal," who accompanied the Springfield delegation to Chicago, and was put in writing by Mr. Herndon in July, 1865. Mr. Baker left Chicago before the convention was over, reaching Springfield early in the morning of the day the balloting took place:

"Baker, editor, said: 'Lincoln marked 3 passages in Mo. Democrat, directing me to show same to Davis and the others. I left Chicago on night train; arrived here (Springfield) in morning before balloting began. Met Lincoln and we went to ball alley to play at fives — alley was full — said it was pre-engaged; then went to excellent beer saloon near by to play game of billiards; table was full and we each drank a glass of beer; then went to Journal office expecting to hear result of ballot; waited awhile, but nothing came and finally we parted; I went to dinner. Logan had in his pocket letter of Lincoln authorizing withdrawal of name on conditions.' "

A further account of Lincoln's demeanor and bearing on the day of his nomination — a carefully worded and trustworthy version of the episode — has been prepared by the late Clinton L. Conkling, of Springfield. He and George M. Brinkerhoff, referred to in his statement, were in the company of Lincoln and heard him talk a few moments before the receipt of the telegram apprising him of his nomination. My acquaintance with the gentlemen, both of whom I had frequently visited at their respective abodes, convinced me they were in perfect accord in their recollection of the event. Mr. Conkling's account, as prepared by him to be read before the Illinois State Historical Society in 1909, is as follows:

"On Friday morning, May 18, 1860, the third day of the Chicago Convention, the delegates met at ten o'clock to ballot. James C. Conkling, of Springfield, who had been in Chicago several days, but was called back unexpectedly, arrived home early that morning. George M. Brinkerhoff of this city was reading law in Mr. Conkling's office which was then over Chatterton's jewelry store. About half-past eight Mr. Lincoln came into the office and asked Mr. Brinkerhoff where Mr. Conkling was, as he had just heard on the street that the latter had returned from Chicago. On being told that Mr. Conkling was not in, but would be in an hour, Mr. Lincoln left, saying he would soon return, as he was anxious to see Mr. Conkling. Presently Mr. Conkling came in and later Mr. Lincoln again called. There was an old settee by the front window on which were several buggy cushions. Mr. Lincoln stretched himself upon the settee, his head resting on a cushion and his feet over the end. For a long time they talked about the convention. Mr. Lincoln wanted to know what had been done, what Mr. Conkling had seen and learned, and what he believed would be the result. Mr. Conkling replied that Mr. Lincoln would be nominated that day; that after the conversations he had had and the information he had gathered, he was satisfied Seward could not be nominated, for he not only had enemies in other States than his own, but he had enemies at home; that, if Mr. Seward was not nominated on the first ballot, the Pennsylvania delegation and other delegations would immediately go to Mr. Lincoln and he would be nominated.

"Mr. Lincoln replied that he hardly thought this could be possible, and that in case Mr. Seward was not nominated on the first ballot it was his judgment that Mr. Chase, of Ohio, or Mr. Bates, of Missouri, would be the nominee. They both considered that Mr. Cameron, of Pennsylvania, stood no chance of nomination. Mr. Conkling in response said that he did not think it was possible to nominate any other one except Mr. Lincoln under the existing circumstances, because the pro-slavery part of the Republican Party then in the convention would not vote for Mr. Chase, who was considered an Abolitionist, and the Abolition part of the party then in the convention would not vote for Mr. Bates, because he was from a slave State; and that the only solution of the matter was the nomination of Mr. Lincoln. After discussing the situation at some length Mr. Lincoln arose and said: 'Well, Conkling, I believe I will go back to my office and practice law.' He then left the office.

"I was present during a part of this interview and depend largely for the details of this conversation upon what Mr. Conkling and Mr. Brinkerhoff have told me. In a very few moments after Mr. Lincoln left I learned of his nomination and rushed downstairs after him. I overtook him on the west side of the Public Square before any one else had told him, and to my cry, 'Mr. Lincoln, you're nominated,' he said, 'Well, Clinton, then we've got it'; and took my outstretched hand in both of his. Then the excited crowds surged around him and I dropped out of sight.

"In my possession are five original telegrams received by Mr. Lincoln on the day he was nominated. All are on the Illinois and Mississippi Telegraph Company forms. The first one sent was from the telegraph superintendent, Wilson, and shows signs of haste and bears no date. It reads:

To LINCOLN:
    You are nominated.
                    J. J. S. WILSON

"Mr. Pierce, the operator who received this message at Springfield, wrote from Young America, Illinois, under date of June 4, 1860, to Mr. Lincoln saying this was the first message for him announcing the nomination. A moment after this message was sent a messenger boy brought to the main office in Chicago a message addressed simply, 'Abe' and which read: 'We did it. Glory to God! Knapp.' The receiving clerk brought the message to Mr. E. D. L. Sweet, superintendent of the Western Division, calling his attention to the address and also to the expression, 'Glory to God.' Mr. Sweet directed that the words, 'Lincoln, Springfield,' be added and that the message be sent at once. The message was probably the first one to Mr. Lincoln from any person who was actively at work in his behalf in the convention and without doubt was from Mr. N. M. Knapp who wrote the letter of May 14th. The next two telegrams are from J. J. Richards, who was connected with the Great Western Railroad and resided at Naples which was the terminus of the road. The first one was as follows:

*May 18 1860*

By Telegraph from Chicago,
To Abraham Lincoln :
   You're nominated and elected.

            J. J. Richards

"The second read:
   You were nominated on the 3rd ballot.

            J. J. Richards

"Mr. J. J. S. Wilson followed his first message, probably within a few moments, by another which reads":

*May* 18 1860

By Telegraph from Chicago
To Hon. A. LINCOLN

Vote just announced. Whole No. 466. Necessary to choice 234. Lincoln 354. Votes not stated. On motion of Mr. Evarts of N.Y. the nomination was made unanimous amid intense enthusiasm.

J. J. S. WILSON

The only telegraph wires into Springfield in 1860 were owned and operated by the Illinois and Mississippi Telegraph Company, and were called the Caton lines, after Judge John D. Caton, of Ottawa, Illinois, the president of the company. The principal office of the company was in St. Louis. John James Speed Wilson was superintendent of the Eastern Division, with headquarters at Springfield, and E. D. L. Sweet, of the Western Division, with his office in Chicago. There was only one wire into the Wigwam — the building in which the convention was held in Chicago — and this was connected at the main office with the wire leading to the east. Mr. Wilson was in Chicago during the convention and divided his time between the main telegraph office at the southeast corner of Lake and Clark Streets and the Wigwam. It was before the day of the telephone, so that most of the personal messages from delegates to Illinois points — and that included those to Mr. Lincoln — were sent from the convention hall to the main office of the company by messenger boys.

For the first time in its history the city of Springfield had the honor of sheltering and numbering among its citizens a candidate for President of the United States; and judging by the activities of that period, as chronicled in the local papers, its people deeply appreciated the distinction.

"The news of Mr. Lincoln's nomination," says the "Journal" on Saturday, May 19th, "reached the city shortly after noon yesterday. Arrangements were at once made to fire a salute of one hundred guns and the different bells in the city were rung from five o'clock till sundown. Flags were flying from the State House; Republican Headquarters, and the JOURNAL office; and other evidences of joy were visible in various parts of the city. Many called on Mr. Lincoln at his home to congratulate him personally and a large and enthusiastic crowd assembled at the State House at eight in the evening where speeches were delivered by J. C. Conkling, George R. Webber, and others. An hour later the Young American Band started for the Lincoln residence. Arriving in front of the house the crowd made loud calls for Mr. Lincoln and they were soon gratified by seeing his tall form emerging from his doorway. When the cheering subsided Mr. Lincoln proceeded to make his first speech as a candidate for President."

Unfortunately for us no reporter was present to take down the speech and we must therefore content ourselves with the account of it as published in the local newspaper.

"For appropriateness the speech," observes the "Journal," "was never surpassed. Mr. Lincoln said he did not suppose the honor of such a visit was intended particularly for himself as a private citizen, but rather as the representative of a great party; and in reference to his position on the political questions of the day he referred his numerous and enthusiastic hearers to his previous public letters and speeches. The speech was a perfect model in its way, and the loud applause with which it was greeted shows that it struck the right place in the minds of his hearers. Just previous to the conclusion of his speech Mr. Lincoln said he would be glad to invite the whole crowd into his house if it were large enough to hold them (A voice: 'We will give you a larger house on the 4th of next March!'), but as it could not contain more than a fraction of those who were in front of it he would merely invite as many as could find room."

Meetings to ratify the Chicago nominations were held on the days following, not only in Springfield, but at other points in Sangamon County, where enthusiastic crowds gathered and listened to speeches by James H. Matheney, William H. Herndon, John H. Littlefield (a law student in Lincoln and Herndon's office), Shelby M. Cullom, William Jayne, and other local orators of like renown.

Two memorable and auspicious events in Lincoln's life took place on Friday. One was his marriage to Mary Todd, November 4, 1842; the other his nomination for President at Chicago, May 18, 1860. On the day following the last-named occurrence, which was Saturday, came the committee from the National Convention to notify Mr. Lincoln of his nomination. They reached Springfield at seven o'clock in the evening from Chicago on a special train of three cars, which, besides the members of the committee, contained numerous other delegates and many of Mr. Lincoln's personal friends. "Upon the arrival of the committee at the Chenery House," says the "Springfield Journal," "cheers were given by the crowd for Governor Morgan, of New York, Frank P. Blair, of Maryland, Governor Boutwell, of Massachusetts, and three cheers and a tiger for the Pennsylvania delegation. From the

272 THE REAL LINCOLN

hotel the delegation deployed off to the State House where a most enthusiastic Republican meeting, addressed by various distinguished speakers, was kept up to a late hour." The notification committee, meanwhile, after partaking of supper and bountiful refreshments at the hotel, proceeded to the residence of Lincoln. What took place there is so well known it need not be repeated here. An incident or two, however, has been preserved.

Among those who accompanied the delegation from Chicago was Ebenezer Peck, later Clerk of the Supreme Court of Illinois, who had once been a resident of Springfield, was a close friend of Lincoln, and therefore more or less familiar with the latter's social and domestic surroundings. On reaching the hotel Mr. Peck confided to the local people gathered there that, on account of the delay in the arrival of the train and the necessity of departing at an early hour, the committee desired that the least time possible be consumed by the notification ceremony at Lincoln's residence. To that end it was intimated that no ladies were to be invited and that even the presence of Mrs. Lincoln was not expected or, in fact, desired. Being acquainted with the mercurial disposition of Lincoln's wife, Peck called aside several Springfield people whom he knew and suggested that they notify Mrs. Lincoln of the committee's preference so that thus she would take the hint. But it happened that the Springfield people were also familiar with Mrs. Lincoln's peculiar temperament so that when appealed to by Peck they declined to intervene. Instead they admonished him: "Go tell the lady, yourself." Later, when the home on Eighth Street was reached and the committee filed gravely in, the first person they saw was Mrs. Lincoln dressed in her finest, bedecked with flowers, and graciously awaiting them in the parlor! Whether Mr. Peck had courage enough to deliver the message himself was never known.

A gentleman, who was living in Springfield when these lines were written, told me that he, among others, was consulted by Lincoln regarding the propriety of offering wine to the committee while they were at his house. At first it was deemed appropriate to comply with the custom then in vogue in welcoming and entertaining guests who ranked as high as the members of the notification committee; but later, after some reflection, Lincoln dissented, holding that, as he himself did not drink wine, it could with propriety be omitted in his own house. A few days after the departure of the committee Lincoln encountered the gentleman above mentioned — John W. Bunn — on the street. The latter asked him how his guests took to the cold water he had served to them at his house. "Greatly to my surprise," answered Lincoln, "they drank freely of it and I never knew the reason till one of them confided that they had just come from a sumptuous dinner at the hotel where they were given bountiful quantities of everything to drink but water, so that when they reached my house they were so dry, notwithstanding the refreshments at the hotel, even water was stimulant enough to satisfy their appetites."

In due time the campaign of 1860 was well under way With the dignity becoming his position Mr. Lincoln remained at home supervising his correspondence, receiving visitors, and, in general, managing his campaign. The leading incident — one of absorbing local interest — was the mammoth meeting at Springfield August 14th, which, in size and character, is graphically portrayed in the head-lines of the "Springfield Journal":

## A POLITICAL EARTHQUAKE !
## THE PRAIRIES ON FIRE FOR LINCOLN
## THE BIGGEST DEMONSTRATION
## EVER HELD IN THE WEST
## 75000 REPUBLICANS IN COUNCIL
## IMMENSE PROCESSION

*Speaking from Five Stands by Trumbull, Doolittle,*
*Kellogg, Palmer, Gillespie, etc.*
*Magnificent Torch Light Procession at Night.*
*Meeting at the Wigwam and Representatives Hall.*

This was not only Lincoln's first public appearance after the day of his nomination, but also, as described in the local papers, the greatest rally of the campaign. The meeting was at the State Fair Grounds. "The announce-ment that Mr. Lincoln had arrived on the ground," re-lates the "Journal," "was the signal for a display of wild enthusiasm the like of which was never before witnessed by an Illinois audience. There was a rush from every stand to-ward his carriage, which was immediately surrounded by his warm admirers and he was forced almost violently from his vehicle and carried upon the shoulders of the crowd to an impromptu stand where he was called upon for a speech. The huzzas and cheers which greeted him were continued nearly ten minutes without cessation, the uproar being so great he could not make himself heard. When order was partially restored he thanked his hearers in a brief speech and then descended from the platform. Meanwhile thousands pressed around to take him by the hand, but by an adroit movement he escaped on horseback while the crowd was besieging the carriage in which he was expected to return to the city."

Among other things the campaign was enlivened by a long letter published in the "Decatur Chronicle," written by Lincoln's kinsman John Hanks explaining why he had left the Democratic Party and was then warmly supporting the claims of his cousin Abraham Lincoln for President. No incident of the campaign made a deeper impression on Lincoln. Although John may not have written the letter exactly as printed in the newspaper, it does not follow that he neglected to dictate his ideas to another who possessed the requisite skill to put it into shape for publication. As it was the first and only endorsement of Lincoln's claims from any of his kindred, and as John Hanks was his favorite cousin (the only one, too, he honored with an invitation to his wedding), we can well understand that the latter with its plain logic and frank sentiments afforded Lincoln, as Herndon assured me, the deepest gratification. In view of the fact that Lincoln read the letter when published and was so deeply touched by his cousin's loyal and generous support, a reproduction of a portion of it in this connection may not be without more or less interest. After reciting that from boyhood he had been a supporter of the Democratic Party, Hanks insists that he is but repeating the tactics of Douglas in transferring his support to the Republican Party. Referring to Lincoln he says:

I have known him for more than thirty years. In boyhood days we've toiled together; many are the days we have lugged the heavy oar on the Ohio, the Illinois and the Mississippi Rivers together; many are the long cold days we have journeyed over the wild prairies and through the forest with gun and axe; and though it is now pleasant to refer to it well do I remember when we set out together in the cold winter to cut and maul rails on the Sangamon River in Macon County to enclose his father's little home and from day to day kept at work until the whole was finished and the homestead fenced in. We often swapped work in this way and yet, during the many years we were associated together as laborers sometimes flat-boating, sometimes hog driving, sometimes rail making and, too, when it was nearly impossible to get books he was a constant reader; I was a listener. He settled the disputes of all the young men in the neighborhood and his decisions were always abided by. I never knew a man more honest under all circumstances. Thus associated with Mr. Lincoln I learned to love him and when, in 1858, he was a candidate for the first time within my reach, against my feelings and, I may say, against my convictions my old party ties induced me to vote for Mr. Douglas. My Democratic friends all declared Lincoln was an Abolitionist. I heard him make a speech in Decatur just before the election and I could see nothing bad in it; but I was told by the party he was wrong and yet I did not see how he could be. They said I was a Democrat and must vote that way. My wife used to say to me that some day Abe would come out and be something great; I thought so too but I could not exactly see how a man in the lower walks of life, a day laborer and helplessly poor would ever stand much chance to rise very high in the world.

At last, one day at home, we heard that the Republican State Convention was to be held at Decatur and that they were going for Abe for President. As soon as I found this out I went into town and told a friend of Abe's that great and honest merit was at last to be rewarded in the person of my old friend Mr. Lincoln of the Republican Party. I thought of the hard and trying struggles of his early days and recollecting the rails we had made together thirty years ago made up my mind to present some of them to that convention as a testimonial of the beginning of one of the greatest living men of the age, believing they would speak more in his praise than any orator could, and honor true labor more than the praise of men or the resolutions of conventions. On our way to get the rails I told the friend of old Abe that if Abe should be nominated for President I would vote for him; everybody knows he has been and I rejoice that I live to give this testimony to his goodness and honesty, and hope I shall live to vote for him for President of the United States next November. Is there anything wrong in this? Who ought to refuse to vote for as good and as great a man as he is? I know that in voting for him I vote with the Republican Party and will be considered as adopting its principles. As I now understand him I see no good reason why I may not do so; our own party is divided and we have no Solomon to tell who shall take the child. Slavery has divided the Democratic Party and nobody can blame Republicanism for the destruction that came upon us at Charleston. Slavery has disunited us — has united the Republican Party, and if there is any good about the question they have it all and we have the trouble. If I understand Mr. Douglas now, he occupies a position on the question just as distasteful to the South as Mr. Lincoln does — with this clear difference; The South seems to understand Mr. Lincoln's position better than his and to respect it a great deal more; and I am convinced that if Mr. Douglas does not reflect the nigger he does the mulatto, and one brings just as much in Mobile as the other and stands as high in the market.

Many of my Democratic neighbors will say I have done wrong; but I know there are many who would do as I have done were it not that they do not feel willing to break away from party ties and encounter the talk of old friends. As long as I have old Abe to lead me I know that I shall never go very far from the right. Should he be elected President and find any trouble in steering his new boat he has only to remember how we used to get out of hard places by rowing straight ahead and never by making short turns. The tallest oaks in the forest have fallen by his giant arms; he still wields a tremendous maul; out of the largest timber he can make the smallest rails. I have seen him try a tough cut and fail once; in the second trial he never failed to use it up. Though not a very beautiful symbol of honesty I think the rail a fitting one and mean to present Abe with one of his own make should he be elected, in the city of

Washington on the day of inauguration to be kept in the White House during his administration.

JOHN HANKS

Illinois and especially Springfield was the storm center of the campaign. Hither came the celebrities from all directions so that the people were privileged to hear most of the great spell-binders of the day including Tom Corwin, Samuel Galloway, Galusha Grow, Carl Schurz, Robert C. Schenck, Leonard Swett, and others of like renown. Most of the meetings in Springfield were held in the Wigwam, a building erected for the purpose, and there Mr. Lincoln would generally be seen, occupying a seat on the platform, or sometimes walking beside the speaker in the parade as it marched down the street. Although a punctual and interested spectator at all the meetings, he invariably declined to make a speech.

There was also great activity among the local campaigners. Herndon was especially ubiquitous and energetic; so also were William Jayne, John H. Littlefield — a law student in Lincoln & Herndon's office — and the lamented Elmer Ellsworth. That Mr. Lincoln was himself not unmindful of their interest and zeal is demonstrated by the following message which he sent to Herndon who was billed to make a speech at Petersburg October 10th, just after the State election in Indiana and Pennsylvania:

SPRINGFIELD, ILLS., Oct. 10, 1860

DEAR WILLIAM:·

I cannot give you the details, but it is entirely certain that Pennsylvania and Indiana have gone Republican very largely. Pennsylvania 25,000 and Indiana 5,000 to 10,000. Ohio of course is safe.        Yours as ever

A. LINCOLN

This message in Lincoln's handwriting is still in existence having been presented by Herndon to a friend in Chicago who has preserved and allowed me to copy it. "I well re-member," related Herndon, "how, in the midst of my speech at Petersburg, a man hurriedly made his way through the crowd and thrust a message into my hand. I was more or less agitated, if not really alarmed, fearing it might contain sad or unwelcome news from my family; but great was my relief when I read it, which I did aloud. It was from Lincoln bidding me to be of good cheer, that Indiana, Pennsylvania, and Ohio had been swept by the Republicans. These were October States and this was the first gun of the campaign. The announcement created so much commotion, such a burst of enthusiasm, that the crowd in their excitement forgot they had a speaker. They ran from the hall and their cheers and yells were so vociferous I never succeeded in finishing my speech."

The incident is thus described in the "Axis," the Democratic organ published in Petersburg October 13, 1860:

Abraham Lincoln, of whom it has been stated by his private secretary that he was under obligations to his friends not to write or answer any interrogatories lest he should embarrass the canvass, being overjoyed at the intelligence from the late elections has violated the obligation imposed upon him. While Bill Herndon was delivering his tirade of abuse upon the Southerners and Southern institutions at the court-house in this place on Monday evening, he was stopped in the middle of his speech upon the arrival of a special messenger from Springfield (announced by the agent of the U. G. R. R.) bearing a note from the great Abraham himself, heralding a Republican victory of twenty thousand in Pennsylvania, twenty to twenty-five thousand in Ohio, and five to ten thousand in Indiana and closing as follows:
"I send this glorious news to my friends, greeting:
Your friend in haste
A. LINCOLN."

Upon this announcement his friends obeyed the summons by round after round of frantic shouts.

In an editorial bearing the headlines: "The Falsities and Fanaticism of Bill Herndon, the Law Partner and Confidant of Mr. Lincoln," the paper continues:

That the heresies and false dogmas of William H. Herndon are traceable to the law office of Mr. Lincoln himself is a sufficient reason why we feel called upon to expose them to the public in order that conservative men of the Republican Party may know whither we are drifting. It had for some time been previously announced that Mr. Herndon would address our citizens upon the political issues of the day and that this would be the ablest speech ever delivered in the town of Petersburg. Accordingly we were present Monday evening and have something to say of the result.

From the seeming insuperable mass of incongruous substances composing the speech of Mr. Herndon we are enabled to collate within the bounds of reasonableness a few of the points having a smattering of argument in them. We shall not attempt to follow him through the dark vaults of his truculent imagination nor to calm the fears of those who become frightened at the gentleman's ghost stories. Presuming upon the faith of our early fathers he has dared to resurrect them in the name of Abraham without offering the divine sacrifice that the people might have disclosed to them the hallowedness of the act.

The news of the Republican victory in the October States produced great enthusiasm especially in Lincoln's home town. A meeting was held at the Wigwam to which a long procession of Wide-Awakes and torchlight bearers made their way after marching over town. They stopped at Lincoln's residence. "Mr. Lincoln," so the "Journal" relates, "stood in his doorway surrounded by a large number of friends and bowed in silent acknowledgment of the deafening cheers, but declined to speak. But

Lyman Trumbull, who was conveniently at hand, made the speech for him, telling the crowd that they must excuse Mr. Lincoln as he was under engagement to address the people at a later date, March 4th, from the eastern portico of the Capitol of Washington."

# CHAPTER XIX

Lincoln the candidate for President — Meeting the expenses of the campaign — Judge Logan's plan — The ten friends of Lincoln who contributed — John W. Bunn's story of the fund — John G. Nicolay selected as Lincoln's secretary — Lincoln's attention to the details of the campaign — Meets with local committee — Recommends John Hay as assistant secretary — Interesting reminiscence of John W. Bunn — How Lincoln bore himself throughout the campaign — The election — Lincoln going to the polls — Assigned quarters for his office in the State House — His habits as President elect — Goes to Chicago to meet Hannibal Hamlin — Returns to Springfield — Visitors at his office and incidents of his stay there — Journeys to Charleston to see his stepmother — Account of his visit and interesting reminiscence by James A. Connolly — Returns to Springfield and begins preparations for the journey to Washington — Last visit to his law office — Final interview with Herndon.

INASMUCH as Abraham Lincoln was the first candidate for President that the city of Springfield had ever sheltered there were, therefore, no precedents, indicating the requirements of the occasion, to guide him or his friends. In a worldly sense Lincoln was of limited means, his accumulations after a quarter of a century at the bar never having exceeded ten thousand dollars. He was therefore ill constituted to bear, unaided, the burdensome expenses which a campaign for the presidential office necessarily entailed. That being the case I venture in this connection to give space to a reminiscence of Lincoln I heard in Springfield. It is so illuminative and affords such an insight into Lincoln's personal connection with the campaign of 1860, it cannot well be omitted. It is a recollection of the late John W. Bunn, who was a close friend of Lincoln and one of his political lieutenants in Springfield. The statement written and delivered to me by Mr. Bunn is as follows:

Shortly after Mr. Lincoln's nomination for President in May,

JOHN T. STUART

STEPHEN T. LOGAN

1860, Judge Stephen T. Logan, a warm friend and former law partner of Mr. Lincoln and one who had been active in his political interest, came to me at my brother Jacob Bunn's store, where I was then employed, and reminded me that Mr. Lincoln would necessarily receive a large amount of correspondence which should be attended to promptly and which would require clerical assistance; that prominent Republicans all over the country would be coming to Springfield to visit him; that the entertainment of these gentlemen would be an item of some consequence and that there would be various other expenses incident to the Springfield end of the campaign, all of which Mr. Lincoln, being a man of limited means, could ill afford to bear. Judge Logan then suggested that a fund for that purpose should be provided by Mr. Lincoln's personal friends in Springfield, at the same time handing me his check for five hundred dollars accompanied by a list of nine other friends of Mr. Lincoln including such men as Colonel John Williams, my brother Jacob Bunn, O. M. Hatch, Thomas Condell, and Robert Irwin, each one of whom, he was sure, would be glad to contribute five hundred dollars for a fund for this general purpose. He directed me to act as treasurer of the fund and I at once called on the gentlemen named, obtaining, as predicted, five hundred dollars from each one, thus accumulating the fund of five thousand dollars for the purposes indicated by Judge Logan.

Shortly after this John G. Nicolay, then a clerk in the office of O. M. Hatch, agreed, without compensation, to give such time as he could to attend to Mr. Lincoln's political correspondence. Mr. Hatch was then Secretary of State, and he and the clerks in his office arranged their duties so that Mr. Nicolay might have considerable time at his disposal in connection with Mr. Lincoln's correspondence. In the early part of August a great Republican rally, said to have been attended by seventy-five thousand people, was held at the State Fair Grounds in Springfield. The expenses attendant upon that mammoth gathering of the people consumed the unexpended portion of the five thousand dollars that had been raised. After the rally a meeting of the committee of gentlemen who had contributed the fund was held and each of the original subscribers put in an additional five hundred dollars. Meanwhile Mr. Lincoln's correspondence had so materially increased that Mr. Nicolay found it practically impossible for him to take care of it without assistance. At the meeting of the committee, referred to, the question of procuring an assistant for Nicolay was canvassed. The names of various persons were suggested, but none seemed to possess the peculiar qualifications deemed requisite for one who would necessarily have the responsible duties attending the disposal of Mr. Lincoln's weighty and oftentimes delicate correspondence. Finally Milton Hay suggested that his nephew John Hay, who was studying law in his office, had marked literary talent, decided tact, and was otherwise well equipped to fill the position and that, too, without expense to the committee. Moreover, he contended, it would be an excellent thing for young Hay in the way of practical experience. After due consideration the committee decided to make requisition on John Hay for his services and he immediately took his place beside Mr. Nicolay. The two worked together throughout the remainder of the campaign, disposing of Mr. Lincoln's correspondence which, especially after the election, and until the departure of Mr. Lincoln for Washington, in February, 1861, was very large and important.

Although more or less burdened by the weighty matters that necessarily demanded his attention as a candidate and later President elect, Lincoln in no respect overlooked the details of the campaign. Especially solicitous was he regarding local conditions, including campaign expenses. He relied on Mr. Bunn and repeatedly called on him and certain other discreet friends asking for reports of developments. He insisted that he should be told everything. Mr. Bunn, in his account of Lincoln's campaign expenses, says:

Shortly before he left Springfield, he called a meeting of the committee referred to above in order to close up the various unfinished matters connected with his end of the campaign. It developed that the fund was overdrawn about twenty-five hundred dollars. This I insisted on paying, as I had been responsible for incurring the deficit. At this meeting Mr. Lincoln said that he had been examining the laws of Congress with reference to Appropriations and found that, as President, he would have at his disposal for secretarial work only the sum of twenty-five hundred dollars per year, all of which amount, he judged, would be required for Mr. Nicolay; that he had found John Hay to be of great assistance and that he hoped after reaching Washington he might find some way of continuing the latter's connection with his personal work. Thereupon Milton Hay said that John Hay had greatly enjoyed working with Mr. Lincoln, and that he, Milton Hay, would provide for John's expenses for six months in Washington. Immediately thereafter Mr. Lincoln requested John Hay to accompany him to Washington in the capacity of Assistant Secretary in conjunction with Mr. Nicolay, which request was duly complied with. During the early years of the war John Hay returned to visit Springfield. He then told me that when Mr. Lincoln received his first month's salary as President he insisted on paying Hay a salary at the rate of three thousand dollars a year.

John W. Bunn, the author of the foregoing reminiscence, emigrated to Springfield from New Jersey about the time Mr. Lincoln was elected to Congress in 1847. His brother Jacob was the leading banker of Springfield and a client of Lincoln's, and he himself was one of the latter's protégés in the development of politics from 1850 to 1860. He and Lincoln were the closest of friends. Some of his recollections bring out characteristics of Lincoln that cannot fail to enlighten us.

In the year of 1857 [he related] Mr. Lincoln asked me one day if I did not wish to run for city treasurer of Springfield. The city was then almost hopelessly Democratic and the proposition rather startled me. He, however, gave me encouragement to believe that I could be elected if I would go about the matter in the right way. My brother, Jacob Bunn, who was present, said to him, "John will run if you want him to." The candidate of

the Democrats was Charles Ridgely. I confess I was pleased with
the idea, and when the Republican city convention met I was
an interested auditor of the proceedings. I expected to hear
my own virtues extolled in the lofty way common in such conventions. Lincoln told me nothing of his plans as to how the announcement of my candidacy would be made or in what manner I would be brought out. The convention was nearly over and
I began to think the matter of my nomination had been forgotten. In a city so Democratic as Springfield Republican nominations were regarded at best as rather formal and perfunctory
affairs. Near the close of the convention a young man — a lawyer who was an inmate of Lincoln's office — addressed the chairman and said he would like to make a nomination for the office
of city treasurer, but that, if the suggestion he should make did
not meet with the favor of every delegate present, he would
withdraw the name. He then put my name in nomination, but
again said: "If there is any delegate on this floor opposed to the
candidacy of Mr. Bunn I do not wish his name to be voted upon
or to go on the ticket." No one objected and I was nominated
by acclamation.

When I saw who was nominating me and knew that he was an
inmate of Mr. Lincoln's office, I, of course, knew very well that
he was acting under Mr. Lincoln's orders. The result of the election was that I was chosen for treasurer, and I may say I was
again chosen in 1858, in 1859, and in 1860. In all these campaigns I was, so to speak, under the political wing of Mr. Lincoln.

A day or two after the first nomination for city treasurer I was
going uptown and saw Mr. Lincoln ahead of me. He waited until
I caught up and said to me, "How are you running?" I told him
I did n't know how I was running. Then he said, "Have you
asked anybody to vote for you?" I said that I had not. "Well,"
said he, "if you don't think enough of your success to ask anybody to vote for you, it is probable they will not do it, and that
you will not be elected." I said to him, "Shall I ask Democrats
to vote for me?" He said, "Yes, ask everybody to vote for you."
Just then a well-known Democrat, named Ragsdale, was coming
up the sidewalk. Lincoln said, "Now, you drop back there and
ask Mr. Ragsdale to vote for you." I turned and fell in with Mr.
Ragsdale, told him of my candidacy, and said I hoped he would

support me. To my astonishment he promised me that he would. Mr. Lincoln walked slowly along and fell in with me again and inquired, "Well, what did Ragsdale say? Will he vote for you?" I answered, "Yes, he told me he would." "Well, then," said Lincoln, "you are sure of two votes at the election, mine and Ragsdale's." This was my first lesson in politics and I received it from a welcome source.

During the time between the election of Mr. Lincoln and his departure from Springfield for Washington he had his office in the old State House. I was, of course, deeply interested in the campaign being a member of a local committee which had charge of matters in Springfield and Sangamon County as well as treasurer of the same.

One day after the election had resulted successfully I went over to Mr. Lincoln's room in the State House, and as I passed up the stairway I met Salmon P. Chase, of Ohio, coming away. When I entered the room I said to Mr. Lincoln, rather abruptly, "You don't want to put that man in your Cabinet, I hope?" It was an impertinent remark on my part, but Mr. Lincoln received it kindly, and replied to me in a characteristic way, by saying, "Why do you say that?" "Because," I answered, "he thinks he is a great deal bigger than you are." "Well," inquired Lincoln, "do you know of any other men who think they are bigger than I am?" I replied, "I cannot say that I do, but why do you ask me that?" "Because," said Mr. Lincoln, "I want to put them all in my Cabinet."

On another occasion, after the campaign was over and I was again in Mr. Lincoln's office, mention was made of the interest and time I had given to the canvass locally. Lincoln asked me some questions which brought out the fact that I had spent a good deal of my own money in the canvass — a thousand dollars or more. Mr. Lincoln suggested that I was not able to lose that money. He spoke very seriously. I replied to him, "Yes, Mr. Lincoln, I am able to lose it because when you have reached Washington you are going to give me an office." The statement seemed to startle him and the look in his face grew very serious. He promptly denied that he had promised me any office whatever. "No, Mr. Lincoln," I replied, "you have not promised me anything, but you are going to give me an office just the same."

"What office do you think I am going to give you?" he asked. "The office of Pension Agent here in Illinois," I exclaimed. "During Isaac B. Curran's term as Pension Agent under Buchanan I have done all the work in the office in order to get the deposits in my brother's bank. The salary amounts to one thousand dollars, and when you go to Washington you are going to give me that office." To this he made no word of reply, and there was therefore no way of determining what effect my prediction made upon him. All I know is that three days after his inauguration as President, Caleb B. Smith, his Secretary of the Interior in Washington, sent to Springfield my commission as Pension Agent.

I do not believe that anything on earth could have exacted a promise from Mr. Lincoln to give me that office; nor do I think he would have bargained to give any man an administrative office before or after his election. It is probable that he selected the members of his Cabinet and that he had advised them of the fact before they were appointed, but outside of his Cabinet officers I do not believe he promised anybody an office before the day of his inauguration, and yet the incident I have above related shows that he was not by any means insensible to ordinary political considerations.

The presidential election of 1860 took place November 6th. "In the morning of that day," relates Herndon, "I dropped in at the office in the State House to see Mr. Lincoln and inquired how and when he expected to cast his vote. At first he questioned the propriety of his voting at all, but, on being reminded of his duty to his friends on the State ticket, he called for a ballot, cut off the names of the presidential electors, and started for the polls. On one side of him walked Ward H. Lamon, on the other side, Elmer Ellsworth, and I immediately in the rear. A goodly number had gathered at the polling-place, and there was more or less cheering when Lincoln appeared, but the crowd very gracefully gave way, many raising their hats, when he approached the ballot box and handed up his ticket. People forgot their political differences for the time, the Democrats vying with the Republicans in their endeavor to accord the first presidential candidate Springfield ever had proper deference and respect."

Aside from the fact that it resulted overwhelmingly in his favor, but little remains to be said regarding the election of Lincoln beyond what has already been recorded. A few days after the election the following announcement appeared in the "Springfield Journal":

"To-day and until further notice, Mr. Lincoln will see visitors at the Executive Chamber in the State House from 10 to 12 A.M. and from 3.30 to 5.30 P.M. each day."

His own residence being inadequate for the purpose he was now installed in the Governor's room in the State House, which was not used for official business during the period the Legislature was not in session, and here he greeted and received the procession of visitors who daily made their way to his office. "There was free access to him," relate Nicolay and Hay; "not even an usher stood at the door; any one might knock and enter. His immediate personal friends from Sangamon County and central Illinois availed themselves largely of the opportunity. With men who had known him in field and forest he talked over the incidents of their common pioneer experience with unaffected sympathy and interest as though he were yet the flatboatman, surveyor, or village lawyer of early days."

To be known as the President elect was a new experience for Lincoln, but its effect was not apparent, for it in no way wrought any change in his demeanor or attitude toward others. He was as unaffected, as thoughtful, and as easy of approach as ever. Two weeks after the election, accompanied by his wife, he journeyed to Chicago where he met Hannibal Hamlin, the Vice-President elect. After a visit of several days, which included a reception at the Tremont House, the two separated, Mr. Hamlin departing for Washington and the President elect returning to Springfield. It was the first time Lincoln had been away from his home since his nomination in May. At the reception a line of visitors for two and a half hours moved through the middle parlor of the hotel to the Dearborn Street front, shaking Lincoln's hand. At his right stood Mrs. Lincoln and next Mr. Hamlin. Being very tall, Lincoln had to stoop slightly when shaking hands with people of average height. When one tall man came along Lincoln raised his hand in astonishment and exclaimed: "Well, you're up some, too, are n't you?" The "Chicago Tribune" in its issue of November 27th reports that "Messrs. Lincoln and Hamlin on Sunday attended divine service in company with Congressman I. N. Arnold at St. James's Church on Cass Street, and in the afternoon they visited the North Market Mission where, after the usual services, the President elect delivered a short address which was received with much pleasure by the destitute children attending the Sabbath school."

In due time Lincoln was again in Springfield domiciled in the office assigned to him in the State House in which to receive and listen to the army of visitors destined to call on him before his departure for Washington. The procession was almost endless and from every part of the country. He denied himself to no one. "Among the visitors who called on Mr. Lincoln yesterday," reported the "Springfield Journal" early in January, 1861, "was an old gentleman dressed in plain homespun clothing who hailed from Mississippi. Mr. Lincoln talked freely with him, explaining that he, the President elect, entertained none but the kindliest feeling toward the people of the South and that he would protect the South in her just rights. The man went away delighted. After he had left Mr. Lincoln's office and stood outside the door, he remarked, while the tears stole down his furrowed cheeks: 'O if the people of the South could but hear what I have listened to, they would love instead of hating Mr. Lincoln. I will tell my friends at home, but,' he added sorrowfully, 'they will not believe me.' He repeated the wish that every man in the South could be personally acquainted with Mr. Lincoln."

A week after this incident one of the Springfield papers reports that "Mr. Lincoln was called upon to-day by an old man from Indiana named Jones for whom thirty years ago he worked as a common farm-hand at a dollar a day," referring to William Jones who kept the store at the village of Gentryville, where Mr. Lincoln spent his boyhood, and who later, as Colonel of the 53d Regiment, Indiana Volunteers, fell at the siege of Atlanta.

The following which appeared in the "Springfield Journal" serves to indicate that events in Mr. Lincoln's career as President elect were rapidly unfolding:

We had the pleasure yesterday of inspecting the magnificent suit of clothes which has been in course of preparation for Mr. Lincoln since his visit to Chicago. It is manufactured by merchant tailors in Chicago and consists of a dress coat, pants, vest, and cravat. The coat is of the best cloth that can be bought in the country and made up with a taste and in a style that cannot be bought in any country. The pants are of the best and finest black cassimere; the vest of the finest grandiere silk and lined with buff goods of the same kind. The whole was presented to Mr. Lincoln with the following inscription: "To Hon. Abraham Lincoln from A. D. Titsworth, Chicago, Ills." which is beautifully worked on the inside of the coat collar.

On January 8th Mr. Lincoln attended a joint meeting of both houses of the Illinois Legislature and witnessed the election of Lyman Trumbull to the United States Senate. His presence was the "signal for a demonstration of prolonged applause as he took his seat beside Judge Caton near the Speaker's desk."

That Mrs. Lincoln also was not without interest in the developments of the hour may be gleaned from this announcement which appeared in the "Cleveland Herald" January 10th: "Conductor Ames's train on the Cleveland and Toledo Railroad this morning brought in Mrs. Lincoln, wife of the President elect, accompanied by her brother-in-law, Mr. C. M. Smith, and Hon. Amos Tuck, of New Hampshire. They will proceed to New York by way of Buffalo and, after a few days' stay to make purchases for the White House, will go to Cambridge, Mass., to visit Mr. Lincoln's son who is at Harvard College. Pres. Gardiner tendered the courtesies of the road from Toledo to Cleveland and Supt. Nottingham set apart a special car to take the party to Buffalo."

The time for Lincoln's final departure from Springfield was now rapidly approaching, and although necessarily greatly preoccupied he was not so deeply engaged that he forgot the claims of those who had befriended him before he was either popular or famous. Accordingly, as soon as his wife returned from her Eastern trip, he tore himself away from the anxious crowd who had so sedulously followed his every movement and journeyed to Coles County, Illinois, to visit his aged stepmother, then living in the country a few miles from the town of Charleston. "He cannot hope to meet her again for several years," records the local paper, "and it is as characteristic of Mr. Lincoln triumphant as Mr. Lincoln defeated that he has always maintained the closest intimacy with all his kindred however humble their fortunes." While there he also paid a visit to the grave of his father. In the evening he rode back to Charleston in company with his aged relative, and, at the urgent request of the citizens, held an impromptu reception in one of the public halls. A large number of the people took advantage of the opportunity to shake him by the hand. Though called upon, Lincoln declined making any remarks shadowing forth his views of the present state of the country or the policy of the coming administration.

I knew and often talked with Augustus H. Chapman, whose wife was a daughter of Dennis Hanks, and who was Lincoln's companion when he drove from Charleston to see his stepmother. "During the ride," related Colonel Chapman, "Mr. Lincoln became more or less reminiscent, adverting frequently to family affairs. He spoke in the most affectionate way of his stepmother, characterizing her as the best friend he ever had. He alluded to the sad, if not pitiful condition of his father's family at the time of the marriage to his stepmother and described the wholesome change in the children due to her encouragement and advice. He also spoke of the campaign of 1860 and the loyal support of the Union men, dwelling especially on the eloquence and ability of Caleb B. Smith, of Indiana, who had, in his opinion, rendered him more effective service than any other public speaker."

This journey and visit by Lincoln to his stepmother has been so accurately and vividly recalled by the late James A. Connolly, a lawyer in Charleston at the time, that I feel I cannot consistently omit his account of the incident. It was carefully imparted to me one afternoon in his law office in Springfield, to which place Major Connolly had removed about ten years after the close of the Civil War. After describing how he emigrated from Ohio to Charleston, where he landed late in the fifties to begin the practice of law, he said:

"In the closing days of January, 1861, word came to Charleston that Mr. Lincoln was coming down from Springfield to pay a farewell visit to his aged stepmother at her home in the country. On hearing this I went down to the railroad station to witness his arrival, only to learn that he had failed to make connection with the regular passenger train at Mattoon and was therefore forced to come over from that place on the evening freight. We waited a long time and, when the train finally drew in and stopped, the locomotive was about opposite the station and the caboose, or car which carried the passengers, was some distance down the track. Presently, looking in that direction, we saw a tall man wearing a coat or shawl, descend from the steps of the car and patiently make his way through the long expanse of slush and ice beside the track as far as the station platform. I think he wore a plug hat. I remember I was surprised that a railroad company, with so distinguished a passenger aboard its train as the President elect of the United States, did not manifest interest enough in his dignity and comfort to deliver him at the station instead of dropping him off in the mud several hundred feet down the track. In addition to myself quite a crowd of natives were gathered on the platform to see him. I confess I was not favorably impressed. His awkward, if not ungainly figure and his appearance generally, failed to attract me, but this was doubtless due to the fact that I was a great admirer of Douglas whose cause I had earnestly supported. There were no formalities. Mr. Lincoln shook hands with a number of persons, whom he recognized or who greeted him, and in a few minutes left for the residence of a friend, where, it was understood, he was to spend the night. On the way uptown from the station I was joined by Colonel A. P. Dunbar, an old lawyer, who told me that he intended to call on Mr. Lincoln at the residence where the latter was expected to spend the night, and invited me to accompany him. I accepted the invitation and later we walked out to the house together. We timed our call so as to meet Mr. Lincoln after he had eaten his supper. On the way I remember Dunbar expressed a doubt as to how he should approach or address Mr. Lincoln. He told me they were old friends and associates at the bar, but now, since Mr. Lincoln had risen in life and was President elect, Dunbar felt that he must keep within the proprieties of the occasion. There was therefore some question in his mind as to his own manner and behavior. He dared not betray any familiarity in addressing him for fear of offending good taste, and yet there had always been the greatest freedom in their intercourse with each other. Finally he announced that his conduct would depend on Lincoln's attitude. 'If he is noticeably dignified and formal,' said Dunbar, 'I must act accordingly.'

"When we reached the house the family were still at the supper table, but Mr. Lincoln himself had withdrawn and was in the front room sitting before the fire. In response to our knock the door opened and who should step forward to greet us but Lincoln himself. Grasping Dunbar's outstretched palm with one hand and resting the other hand on his shoulder, he exclaimed in a burst of animation, 'Lord A'mighty, Aleck, how glad I am to see you!' That broke the spell; and if any stiffness or formality was intended it disappeared like magic. I was introduced and presently we were all sitting together and facing the fire. Lincoln did most of the talking. He was cheerful and communicative. After an exchange of ideas and recollections of the past with Dunbar, he was soon telling stories. Apparently there was a flood of them, one following another and each invariably funnier than its predecessor. It was a novel experience for me. I certainly never before heard anything like it. I shall never forget the one story which he had evidently reserved for the last, for he announced that it was the strangest and most amusing incident he had ever witnessed. I knew it would be interesting and was, therefore, all attention. It was about a girl whose duty it was to find and drive home the family cow. 'One day,' said Mr. Lincoln, 'she rode a horse bareback to the woods. On the way home the horse, frightened by a dog or something which darted from behind a bush, made a wild dash ahead, the girl still astride when suddenly —' at this point Mr. Lincoln halted a moment, for some one was knocking at the door. He stepped across the room and opened it, when lo, there stood the Presbyterian preacher, his wife, and two other ladies. Of course Mr. Lincoln had to suspend his narrative. Meanwhile other callers arrived and in a short time the house began to fill with them, whereupon Dunbar and I decided to withdraw. As we made our way downtown Dunbar, well knowing what an admirer of Douglas I was inquired: 'Now that you have seen and heard the long-legged individual whom our friend Douglas defeated for Senator, what do you think of him?' I had to confess that he was a marvel — a charming story-teller and in other repects one of the most remarkable men I ever listened to. 'But he was guilty of one thing I shall never cease to regret,' I said, 'What was it?' he asked. 'He failed to relate the closing chapter of that last story,' I answered."

Meanwhile owing to the approaching meeting of the Legislature of Illinois and the need by that body of the room in the State House which Lincoln for some months had occupied as an office, the latter deemed it proper to vacate the premises and secure quarters elsewhere. Accordingly he accepted the offer of Mr. Joel Johnson and took up his abode in the second story of a building owned by the latter opposite the Chenery House, the leading hotel in the town. We are therefore reminded in the "Springfield Journal," February 4th, that "The present week being the last that Mr. Lincoln remains in Springfield, and it being indispensable that he should have a portion of the time to himself, he will see visitors only at his office No. 4 Johnson Building from 3.30 to 5.00 P.M. each day"; and thither, until the time was ripe for the inaugural journey to Washington, trudged the long line of weary pilgrims anxious to congratulate or seek the favor of the President elect. It was during this period that Mr. Lincoln, betaking himself to an unfurnished room over his brother-in-law's store in Springfield, spent several days in the preparation of his Inaugural Address, the story of which is more minutely told in another chapter. But writing addresses and state papers was not the only thing that absorbed Mr. Lincoln's time, for one day early in February the local paper records that "Horace Greeley, returning from Jacksonville where he had lectured, had a three hours' interview with Mr. Lincoln and five Indianaians called to solicit a Cabinet position for the Hoosier State, three of them supporting the claims of Caleb Smith and two favoring Schuyler Colfax."

A day or two before his departure from Springfield in February, Lincoln climbed the unbanistered stairway leading to his law office on the west side of the Public Square for a final interview with Herndon. "I knew that Messrs. Lincoln and Herndon," is the testimony of Henry B. Rankin, a law student, "would prefer to talk alone, and so after Mr. Lincoln came in I left the office and sauntered below into Chatterton's jewelry store where I waited till they came down." For an account of what occurred or what was said when the two partners were alone we are indebted to Herndon.

"In the afternoon on one of his last days in Springfield," he relates, " Mr. Lincoln came down to our office to examine some papers and confer with me regarding the status of several lawsuits and certain other matters that concerned us both. Once or twice before he had intimated that he wanted to 'have a long talk' with me as he expressed it, but, until then, his visits to the office had been so brief and few in number the desired interview had not taken place. On this occasion we examined our books and arranged for the settlement of all pending and unfinished matters. Going over the record of our business he noted some cases in which he was especially interested and in others certain lines of procedure he thought I should follow. These things disposed of he crossed to the opposite side of the room and lay down on the old office sofa or lounge for a few minutes, his gaze fastened on a certain spot near the ceiling as if in a brown study. Presently he inquired: 'Billy' — he always called me by that name — 'how long have we been together?' 'Over sixteen years,' I answered. 'We've never had a cross word during all that time, have we?' to which I returned an emphatic 'No, indeed.' He began to hark back to the past, recalling the adventures of earlier days, and including the recital of more than one amusing incident. My memory was also stimulated, and although he did most of the talking he still afforded me ample opportunity to recall some of the things to which, otherwise, I would not have alluded. He was never more entertaining and cheerful. At the conclusion of our talk he arose, gathered a bundle of papers, and started to leave, meanwhile suggesting that our partnership should continue indefinitely. 'Give our clients to understand,' he said, 'that the election of a President makes no change in the firm of Lincoln & Herndon; for if I live I'm coming back in due time and then we'll resume practice as if nothing had ever happened.' He paused a moment as if to take a last look at the old quarters and then passed through the door into the narrow hallway. I accompanied him downstairs where we separated. He was never in the office again."

Herndon's account of this meeting with Lincoln is verified by H. B. Rankin, the law student mentioned above. He testifies as follows: "The evening I saw Messrs. Lincoln and Herndon come down the stairs from their office, Mr. Lincoln had just told Herndon that he expected to return to Springfield when his term of office had ended and resume with him their law practice the same as if nothing had happened. He further requested Herndon to let the office sign remain and conduct business in the firm's name until his return, all of which was complied with; for, until the day the bullet of the assassin Booth had done its gruesome and atrocious work, the little sign, 'Lincoln & Herndon, Attorneys at Law,' was still swinging on its rusty hinges at the foot of the stairway."

One incident attending this interview between Lincoln and Herndon, and which was communicated to me by the latter when I collaborated with him, has thus far not been told. Herndon, unfortunately, had a decided and well-developed weakness for liquor, a habit which not only militated against his success as a lawyer, but seriously impaired his usefulness in other respects. The appetite which manifested itself at an early day gradually increased, the so-called sprees occurring at more frequent intervals as the days rolled by. Herndon, in the account which he gave me of this period of his life, including the story of his deplorable and bibulous habits, seemed to be anxious to reveal all the facts. Apparently he withheld nothing. In some respects it was a painful recital, but, having told everything, he appeared to experience more or less relief, much after the manner of the man who, being closeted with one of his closest friends, makes a clean breast of his delinquency. He admitted that his conduct frequently was an embarrassment to Lincoln who was in every respect a total abstainer himself. "But although I have nothing to add in extenuation of my offense," he said, "I must insist that in his treatment of me Mr. Lincoln was the most generous, forbearing, and charitable man I ever knew. Often though I yielded to temptation he invariably refrained from joining in the popular denunciation which, though not unmerited, was so frequently heaped upon me. He never chided, never censured, never criticized my conduct — more than that, never, save on one occasion, alluded to it. That was the evening we were together in our office for the last time. It was near sunset. We had finished the details of our business and for a while were engaged in the exchange of reminiscences when suddenly, without rising from his seat, he blurted out: 'Billy, there's one thing I have, for some time, wanted you to tell me, but I reckon I ought to apologize for my nerve and curiosity in asking it even now. 'What is it?' I inquired. 'I want you to tell me,' he said, 'how many times you have been drunk.' It was, of course, a rather blunt inquiry, but unexpected though it was I realized that it came from an honest inquirer, one who had a right to the information, and I therefore answered it as promptly and definitely as the limited sources of knowledge at my command would warrant. Meanwhile I felt sure a lecture or moral admonition would follow and prepared myself accordingly, but much to my surprise nothing more was said by him on that subject. Instead he relieved my tension by describing the various efforts that had been made to induce him to drop me from the partnership and substitute certain others, whom he named, all of which was a surprise to me. He assured me that he invariably declined the intervention of others and admonished those who sought to displace me that, despite my shortcomings, he believed in me and therefore would not desert me."

# CHAPTER XX

Last social function at Lincoln's home — He receives threatening letters — Sends a friend to Washington to sound General Scott — General Thomas S. Mather returns with his report — Plans for Lincoln's journey to Washington as outlined in the local papers — Personnel of the party selected to accompany him — Leaving the Chenery House — His trunks — Departure from the railway station — Lincoln's farewell speech — Story of the two versions — His emotion when the train moved off.

THE social status of the Lincolns during their last days in Illinois is well indicated by the following letter of a correspondent of the "Missouri Democrat" written at Springfield February 7, 1861:

The first levee given by the President-elect took place last evening at his own residence in this city and it was a grand outpouring of citizens and strangers together with the members of the legislature. Your humble servant was invited to attend. Mr. Lincoln threw open his house for a general reception of all the people who felt disposed to give him and his lady a parting call. The levee lasted from seven to twelve o'clock in the evening and the house was thronged by thousands up to the latest hour. Mr. Lincoln received the guests as they entered and were made known. They then passed on and were introduced to Mrs. Lincoln, who stood near the center of the parlor, and who, I must say, acquitted herself most gracefully and admirably. She was dressed plainly but richly. She wore a beautiful full trail, white moire antique silk, with a small French lace collar. Her neck was ornamented with a string of pearls. Her head-dress was a simple and delicate vine arranged with much taste. She displayed but little jewelry and this was well and appropriately adjusted. She is a lady of fine figure and accomplished address and is well calculated to grace and to do honor at the White House.

She was on this occasion accompanied by four of her sisters — Mrs. W. S. Wallace, Mrs. C. M. Smith, of Springfield, Mrs. Charles Kellogg, of Cincinnati, and a Miss Todd, of Kentucky. They all appeared to be extremely happy and I hope there will be nothing thrown in their way to hinder them from experiencing in full all the pleasures which they now anticipate in coming events. I thought, when looking upon the lovely group of the Todd family, how proud old Kentucky would have felt if she could have been present to witness the position in which her son and daughters were placed.

T. W.

This was the last social function or gathering at Lincoln's home; for preparations even then were under way looking to his departure from Springfield.

Meanwhile, at this time and for a few weeks prior thereto Lincoln was in receipt of numerous notes and letters threatening his life in case he undertook the journey to Washington to be inaugurated. At first he paid no attention to them, but they so increased in violence and numbers that he finally concluded he could no longer ignore them. He, therefore, decided to send the late Thomas S. Mather, Adjutant-General of Illinois, to Washington commissioned to inquire into the military situation and especially to call on General Scott, apprise him of the threats the President elect had been receiving, and learn what, if any, precautions would be taken to protect the latter when he came to be inaugurated.

I knew General Mather well, and when I was in Springfield often heard him relate the incidents of his trip to Washington. The diary of Major E. D. Keyes, who was General Scott's military secretary, fixes January 29, 1861, as the date of his visit. He said that Lincoln more than all else seemed to be concerned regarding Scott's loyalty, anxious to learn if he was unreservedly for the Union — in short, if, in every emergency that might arise, he could be depended upon. "That," related General Mather, "seemed to be Lincoln's chief concern. Senator Seward, Mr. Washburn, and others had certified to General Scott's loyalty and high character, and the General himself had written to the President elect offering his services without reserve. 'But he is a Virginian,' explained Mr. Lincoln, 'and while I have no reason or evidence to warrant me in questioning him or his motives, still I shall feel better satisfied if you will visit him in my behalf. When you call insist on a personal interview and do not leave till you have seen and sounded him. Listen to and look him in the face. Note carefully what he says, and when you return with your report I shall probably be in a condition to determine about where he stands and what to expect of him.'"

General Mather further related that when he reached Washington General Scott was sick and confined to his bed so that he did not succeed in gaining access to him till two days later. He thus describes the interview: "Presently I was invited upstairs into the sick man's chamber. There propped up in bed by an embankment of pillows lay the hero of Lundy's Lane, wrinkled and pale. His hair and beard were disordered and his flesh lay in rolls across his warty face and neck. His breathing was labored and difficult. 'You may present my compliments to Mr. Lincoln when you reach Springfield,' he said in a wheezy voice, 'and tell him I shall expect him to come on to Washington as soon as he is ready. Say to him also that, when once here, I shall consider myself responsible for his safety. If necessary I'll plant cannon at both ends of Pennsylvania Avenue, and if any of the Maryland or Virginia gentlemen who have been so threatening and troublesome of late show their hands or even venture to raise a finger, I'll blow them to the infernal regions.' I shall never forget the scene nor how profoundly the old soldier seemed to be wrought up. His trembling frame betokened his unequivocal and righteous indignation at the perfidy of those of his countrymen who were so willing to destroy the Union which he had fought so long and ardently to maintain.

"In due time I reached Springfield and promptly made my report to Mr. Lincoln. He was anxious to hear it. Of General Scott's rigid determination and unswerving loyalty I assured him there was no question whatever; all of which seemed to be the most gratifying information. It allayed all doubt that may have found lodgment in his mind; for, thenceforward, the local situation in Washington gave him no further concern and he went ahead with his preparations for the inaugural journey."

The story of the departure from Springfield and the journey to Washington has in nowise been overlooked by Lincoln's numerous biographers, but it will not be considered a repetition, I hope, if I add a few things, gleaned from the local papers or from certain Springfield people whom I interviewed, and which have thus far not reached the public eye. It is recorded that he left Springfield Monday, February 11, 1861. The next day was his fifty-second birthday. Having shortly before leased his residence to Mr. L. Tilton, the president of the Great Western Railroad, he disposed of his furniture and removed with his family to the Chenery House, the leading hotel in the city where, for a few days, he occupied rooms on the second floor facing Fourth Street.

Robert Lincoln, the oldest son [reports the "Springfield Register"], came home from college to accompany the family to Washington. During Mr. Lincoln's sojourn at the hotel he had been visited by many men of prominence whom he had summoned for conferences on national affairs. The complete absence of ostentation and his physical self-reliance was illustrated on the morning of his departure when in the hotel office he roped his trunks with his own hands, took some of the hotel cards, on the back of which he wrote:

*A. Lincoln*
*White House*
*Washington, D.C. —*

and tacked them on the trunks, supplementing the act by writing his autograph on another card and giving it to the landlord's daughter. In due time the omnibus backed up in front of the hotel and he left for the depot.

The special train which is to bear Mr. Lincoln to Washington [is the comment of the "Springfield Journal" in its issue of February 11th] will start this morning at eight from the Great Western Railroad depot. It will be under charge of Mr. W. S. Wood from New York whose arrangements both for the comfort and the safety of the President elect are perfect and prove his managerial capacity to be of the highest order. The party numbers about fifteen persons besides special reporters for the leading newspapers. The train consists of one passenger and one baggage car drawn by a magnificent Rogers locomotive under the special direction of Messrs. Tilton and Bowen, the president and superintendent respectively of the road. Every precaution has been taken for the safety of the train. It will be flagged through — a pilot engine preceding — and under the direction of Mr. J. J. S. Wilson, Superintendent of the Telegraph, will be telegraphed from station to station and retelegraphed to headquarters as it passes. The speed will be about thirty miles per hour.

According to the original plans Mrs. Lincoln and the younger sons, William and Thomas or Tad, were to linger a few days in Springfield, or go to St. Louis for a brief stay and overtake the President elect at some point in the East, thus avoiding the slow and tedious journey through Indiana, Ohio, and New York. Her husband and eldest son Robert, then an undergraduate at Harvard, who had returned from the East a few days before, accordingly left Springfield in the morning without her; but, later in the day, she decided to leave for Indianapolis, nevertheless. She reached that place and rejoined her husband the next morning shortly before the special train departed thence for Cincinnati, her change of mind being due, it is said, to word from General Scott who thought Lincoln would be in less danger, if during his journey he was surrounded by his family. Regarding this change of programme I have been permitted to copy letters from two residents of Springfield each written the day after Lincoln's departure. In one the writer says:

Mrs. Lincoln was not to leave for some days after Mr. Lincoln's departure, but a dispatch from General Scott determined her to leave the evening of the same day. The General thought it would be safer for him to be surrounded by his family. Lockwood Todd was her escort.

In the other letter, after describing the scene at the railroad station when Lincoln made his farewell speech, the writer adds:

Mrs. Lincoln left here last evening to overtake her husband at Indianapolis at the suggestion of General Scott.

General Scott had detailed two army officers in the persons of Major David Hunter and Colonel E. V. Sumner to accompany Lincoln from Springfield to his destination. Sumner failed to report in time, but joined the special train at Indianapolis. These officers, along with Ward H. Lamon, of Danville, Illinois, who was an aide on the staff of Governor Yates, and Elmer Ellsworth, colonel of a Chicago Zouave regiment, constituted the military portion of the cortège. Dr. William S. Wallace, Mr. Lincoln's brother-in-law, was the physician. Besides those named, and the President elect and his son Robert, the following composed the party: John G. Nicolay and John Hay, secretaries, N. B. Judd, O. H. Browning, David Davis, Jesse K. Dubois, Ebenezer Peck, Robert Irwin, Edward L. Baker, and George C. Latham.

Long before the hour appointed for the departure of the special train provided for Mr. Lincoln and his suite [observes the "Springfield Journal" — February 12th] hundreds of his fellow citizens without distinction of party assembled at the station of the Great Western Railway yesterday to tender him their respects, grasp once more that honest hand and bid him God-speed on his eventful journey. A subdued and respectful demeanor characterized the vast assemblage. All seemed to feel that they were about to witness an event which, in its relations to the future, was of no ordinary interest.

Mr. Herndon was not at the railway station when Lincoln departed, but I have talked to others, including John G. Nicolay, John W. Bunn, and David Davis, who were there. Although early in the morning and the weather unpleasant, a goodly crowd had gathered.

Early Monday morning [relate Nicolay and Hay] found Mr. Lincoln, his family and suite at the dingy little railroad station with a throng of at least a thousand of his neighbors who had come to bid him good-bye. It was a stormy morning, which seemed to add gloom and depression to their spirits. The leave-taking presented a scene of subdued anxiety, almost of solemnity. Mr. Lincoln took a position in the waiting-room where his friends filed past him after merely pressing his hand in silent emotion.

At precisely five minutes before eight [says the "Springfield

Journal"] Mr. Lincoln, preceded by Mr. Wood of New York, slowly made his way from his room in the station, through the expectant masses which respectfully parted right and left at his approach, to the car provided for his ride. At each step of his progress friendly hands were extended for a last greeting. On reaching the platform of the car Mr. Lincoln turned toward the people, removed his hat, paused for several seconds till he could control his emotions and then slowly, impressively, and with profound emotion uttered the following words:

"Friends, no one who has never been placed in a like position can understand my feelings at this hour nor the oppressive sadness I feel at this parting. For more than a quarter of a century I have lived among you, and during all that time I have received nothing but kindness at your hands. Here I have lived from my youth till now I am an old man. Here the most sacred trusts of earth were assumed; here all my children were born; and here one of them lies buried. To you, dear friends, I owe all that I have, all that I am. All the strange checkered past seems to crowd now upon my mind. To-day I leave you; I go to assume a task more difficult than that which devolved upon General Washington. Unless the great God who assisted him shall be with and aid me, I must fail. But if the same omniscient mind and the same Almighty arm that directed and protected him shall guide and support me, I shall not fail; I shall succeed. Let us all pray that the God of our fathers may not forsake us now. To Him I commend you all — permit me to ask that with equal sincerity and faith you will all invoke His wisdom and guidance for me. With these few words I must leave you — for how long I know not. Friends, one and all, I must now bid you an affectionate farewell."

The half-finished ceremony was broken in upon [relate Nicolay and Hay] by the ringing bells and rushing train. The crowd closed about the railroad car into which the President-elect and his party made their way. Then came the central incident of the morning. The bell gave notice of the starting, but as the conductor paused with his hand uplifted to the bell-rope Mr. Lincoln appeared on the platform of the car and raised his hand to command attention. The bystanders bared their heads to the falling snowflakes and, standing thus, his neighbors heard his voice for the last time in the city of his home in a farewell address so chaste and pathetic that it reads as if he already felt the tragic shadow of forecasting fate:

"My friends: No one not in my situation can appreciate my feeling of sadness at this parting. To this place and the kindness of these people I owe everything. Here I have lived a quarter of a century and have passed from a young to an old man. Here my children have been born and buried. I now leave not knowing when or whether I may return, with a task before me greater than that which rested upon Washington. Without the assistance of that Divine Being who ever attended him, I cannot succeed. With that assistance, I cannot fail. Trusting in Him who can go with me and remain with you and be everywhere for good, let us confidently hope that all will yet be well. To his care commending you, as I hope in your prayers you will commend me, I bid you an affectionate farewell."

The speech of Lincoln on this occasion was published on the day of its delivery in the "Springfield Journal" and also in the "Chicago Tribune." Although both versions were substantially alike, there was just enough variation to occasion among those who are divided on the subject of Lincoln's belief in Christianity, his religious faith or lack of it, a difference of opinion as to what he actually said. Several years ago, when I visited John G. Nicolay at his home in Washington, the matter of Lincoln's farewell address at Springfield came up for discussion. Mr. Nicolay related that on the day before Lincoln departed he caused the newspaper correspondents gathered about the hotels to be notified that nothing warranting their attention would take place at the railroad station when he embarked on his journey; in other words, that speech-making, so far as he was concerned, would not begin till after he had left Springfield. But the next morning when he looked into the faces of the neighbors gathered about his car he forgot the assurances to the newspaper men made the night before and indulged in a brief but appropriate farewell speech. The moment the train steamed out of Springfield the newspaper men, one of them being the late Henry Villard, gathered about Lincoln and asked him to furnish them with a copy of his speech; reminding him that they were given no chance to take it down as delivered. He answered that his remarks were extempore and therefore not in manuscript form, but he assured them that he would write the speech in full. He therefore beckoned to Nicolay, who provided paper and pencil, and he proceeded to comply with the request. He penciled a few lines, then halted and turned the paper over to Nicolay, who began writing where he left off, Lincoln meanwhile dictating to him. Presently at his request Nicolay returned the paper to him and he resumed the writing himself, but erelong, due to nervousness or the motion of the train, he desisted a second time and again invoked the aid of Nicolay, who continued the task, all of which verifies the statement that the farewell address at Springfield published in the "Century Magazine" in connection with the Nicolay and Hay "Life of Lincoln," was correctly printed from the original manuscript, having been written immediately after the train started, partly by Lincoln's own hand and partly by that of his private secretary from his dictation. When I visited Mr. Nicolay he showed me not only this manuscript, but a number of others also in Lincoln's handwriting, explaining that before he left Springfield Lincoln was so solicitous and careful regarding his utterances *en route* to Washington that he prepared and wrote out in advance such speeches as he expected to make. The manuscripts were enclosed in separate envelopes and properly labeled. Knowing that I was a native of Indiana he withdrew from a package one envelope and turned it over to me to peruse. On it Lincoln had endorsed "For Indianapolis." It proved to be the manuscript of the speech intended for delivery to the Legislature of Indiana containing his definition of coercion and invasion, and a brief but ingenious dissertation on the sacredness of a State. I read it with the deepest interest.

As a rule Lincoln was well poised. He could not be called cold, but in the delivery of a speech or on public occasions he was dignified if not invariably serious; the result was that he never bubbled over — rarely ever wept or otherwise betrayed his emotion. That condition, however, did not prevail the morning he separated from his friends and neighbors in February, 1861, headed for Washington. On that occasion he was deeply moved. My authority for that statement comes from an intimate friend of Lincoln, James C. Conkling, a man in whom Lincoln reposed the fullest confidence and who stood within a few feet and immediately in front of him when he bade his neighbors farewell from the platform of his car. The testimony is in the handwriting of Mr. Conkling himself. Describing the incident, he says:

It was quite affecting. Many eyes were filled to overflowing as Mr. Lincoln uttered those few and simple words of farewell. His own breast heaved with emotion and he could scarcely command his feelings sufficiently to commence. There was scarcely a dry eye in all that vast crowd.

The following, which is the farewell incident as described in the "Springfield Journal," was the work of the editor Edward L. Baker:

It was a most impressive scene. We have known Mr. Lincoln for many years; we have heard him speak upon a hundred different occasions; but we never saw him so profoundly affected, nor did he ever utter an address which seemed to us so full of simple and touching eloquence, so exactly adapted to the occasion, so worthy of the man and the hour. Although it was raining fast when he began to speak, every hat was lifted and every head bent forward to catch the last words of the departing chief. When he said, with the earnestness of a sudden inspiration of feeling, that with God's help he should not fail, there was an uncontrollable burst of applause. At precisely eight o'clock city time the train moved off bearing our honored townsman, our noble chief, Abraham Lincoln, to the scenes of his future labors and, as we firmly believe, of his glorious triumph. God bless honest Abraham Lincoln!

In the closing days of January the following advertisement had appeared in the columns of the " Springfield Journal ":

### AT PRIVATE SALE

The furniture consisting of Parlor and Chamber Sets, Carpets, Sofas, Chairs, Wardrobes, Bureaus, Bedsteads, Stoves, China, Queensware, Glass etc. at the residence on the corner of Eighth and Jackson streets is offered at private sale without reserve. For particulars apply at the premises at once.

In the issue of March came this notice:

The notes and papers of Mr. Lincoln are left with Mr. Robert Irwin where persons interested can find them. If any of the accounts are left unpaid Mr. Irwin will pay them on being satisfied of their correctness.

A. LINCOLN

**THE END**

# Appendix 1
## Weik's Informants

## IDA M. ANDREWS TO WEIK, SPRINGFIELD, 23 AUGUST 1916[1]

Yours of Aug. 16 was forwarded to me at this place, the very location you enquire about. My father was pastor of the First M. E. Church in Springfield during the years 1860 and 1861.[2] He knew Lincoln, and he frequently attended my father's church. Of this time, my father has written in a little sketch I have as follows: "This period was conspicuous as the opening out of the 'Great Rebellion.' This was Pres. Lincoln's home and this (1860) the date of his first election. The overtowering excitements of the period centered very largely in this city (Springfield) and other matters (meaning outside of church affairs) held almost the entire attention of people."[3] I have heard both Father and Mother speak of incidents of this time and their acquaintance with Lincoln—but I do not recall anything that would be of any special interest to you. Father spoke with special interest, often, of the Douglass-Lincoln debates. — My uncle, Noah Matheny—with whose daughter I am now visiting—was very intimate with Lincoln. He was president of the First Nat. Bank—and was also clerk of Sangamon County for over thirty years.[4] I remember seeing a reproduction (small size) of Lincoln's marriage license in the Nicolai-Hay papers with my uncle's signature. My Aunt died last November and until a short time before her death had quite a number of letters written by Lincoln to Uncle Noah but as they were of purely personal and private nature she thought best to destroy them.[5] She had already cut off and given away several of the signatures. Lincoln was often here at her home and she knew him as a neighbor and friend. Of course, we, of this generation know the events only in the scrappy and happen-so way in which we have heard them. I just happened to have a little sketch with me that gave the date of Father's pastorate here.

I should like to add this also. I told you I would have printed and distributed the address of Dr. Bovard at De Pauw last summer. He said he would have the article prepared and I sent him a photograph which he requested. The photograph was returned and a very good print of it such as was intended to be used with the printed matter but that is the last I have heard of it. I suppose he has forgotten it, which is all right, but I wanted to explain why I had not come up with my part of the matter.

## IDA M. ANDREWS TO WEIK, INDIANAPOLIS, 8 JANUARY 1917[6]

I thank you for the interesting information concerning the store accounts of Mrs. Lincoln and that of my father made at the same time. It only makes me sorry that I did not gather more of this sort of information myself when I had so good an opportunity. Two years ago I could have referred you to my aunt, a woman almost ninety years of age, but with a wonderfully clear, strong mind, who knew the Lincoln family well, and I am sure could have told you much that would interest you. She died last spring. I think, perhaps, I told you that her husband was an intimate friend of Lincoln. She destroyed all of their correspondence a short time ago because it was of so personal a character that she felt it should not be given out as public matter. It seems to me they were all rather reticent on so interesting a subject. I gather from a few things said by my aunt and mother that neither one regarded Mrs. Lincoln very highly—that is her temper and disposition generally was not at all commendable.[7]

Thank you for the letter. I am much interested in the accounts.

## George Washington Brackenridge

### G. W. BRACKENRIDGE TO WEIK, SAN ANTONIO, TEXAS, 15 DECEMBER 1914[1]

In answer to yours of December 11th, [I] beg to say that I have no very distinct knowledge of the relation existing between my father, John A. Brackenridge, and Mr. Lincoln.[2] I only remember that I have heard my father speak of Mr. Lincoln, and also of his having taken considerable trouble to listen to speeches made in the Courts by my father. Indeed, in my childhood, the name of Abe Lincoln was very familiar and frequently heard in the conversation of the family.

My father was born in Washington, D.C., in 1800, the son of the Rev. John Brackenridge, Pastor of the First Presbyterian Church, and settled in Boonville, Ind., in 1826 or [1]827. He moved to Texas in 1853, and died in 1862.

## John W. Bunn

### INTERVIEW WITH JOHN W. BUNN, 15 OCTOBER 1914

John W. Bunn at Springfield told me:

In 1853[1]

An Englishman who posed as a nobleman had purchased some cattle or live stock below St Louis and succeeded in getting away without paying some debt and reached Springfield where he stopped en route to Bloomington. Meanwhile Jacob Bunn received a claim for $1000 to collect and for fear that he might press on to Bloomington while attempt to secure his extradition thro the Gov. was pending, he asked his brother and Lincoln to sit up all night in front of hotel where Englishman was lodging and stop him if he started out next morning. Meanwhile Englishman approached

Lincoln & John W. Bunn and offered to pay $1000 in money if claim was withdrawn or satisfied. Money was paid and Lincoln told Bunn not to bother about fee. Some time later he might demand fee. Long time afterward L. called on senior Bunn and demanded $100 for his fee. Bunn paid it and L. then took the money to sheriff's office where Dave Logan, Will I Ferguson and W H Herndon were under surveillance.[2] They had been drunk the night before and broke in the entire front of a saloon owned by Delos Brown making great destruction.[3] Both Logan and Ferguson were sons of wealthy parents and Lincoln tho poor could not deny their appeals for help.[4]

Lincoln had habit of rubbing his hands down front of trousers and [bending?] over when speaking. Rubbed trousers till slick etc

INTERVIEW WITH JOHN W. BUNN [15 OCTOBER 1914?][5]

Alex Lockridge present[6]

Says reason Lincoln appeared in so few suits in behalf of negroes was because he didn't want to be a party to a violation of the Fugitive Slave law. Said the way was to repeal the law. In more than one case he suggested and advised that a few dollars be paid to buy off those who were holding the Negro.[7]

A banker Geo Smith of Chicago had occasion to employ a lawyer in Springfield to collect a claim of over $500.[8] Jacob Bunn recommended Lincoln. The latter charged a fee of $25. Smith afterward told Bunn L. may not be the best but he was the cheapest lawyer he ever met.

Horological Cradle:

(Mt Pulaski inventor [Alexander Edmonds]) Lincoln had contrivance brought into Sup. Court and set to going. One of court asked how to stop it. "That's the one objection" said L. "when it gets going, its like some people doesn't know when to stop.[9]

Committee from Chicago Conv. reached Spfield in afternoon—about four o'clock. Local people had dinner at hotel for them. Geo Ashmun at head[10] – (Lincoln had asked Bunn whether he should serve wine. None was served at L's house but there was no lack of it at the hotel dinner.)[11]

Among those who accompanied the com from Chicago was Ebenezer Peck who formerly lived in Spfield.[12] The notification by committee took place in Mr Lincoln's house in evening—after dinner at hotel. Peck saw local people and stated that it was not expected that Mrs Lincoln should be present & she should be notified accordingly. "Go up & tell her yourself" said the local committee to Peck but he failed to do so and Mrs Lincoln in full evening, low-cut dress came sweeping into the room.[13]

Bunn also says:

He was executor of estate of John Irwin who owned the building on the west side of the square where Lincoln & Herndon had office; that for a long time he roomed on the third floor and had to pass the L & H office in going up & down stairs; that he frequently stopped in, seeing both Linc. & Hernd there etc.[14]

Was once walking with Lincoln who told Bunn that he had gained possession of farm [in] a law-suit and charged fee $200. Wondered if that was too much. – had thought about it during night. Just then we encountered Ben Edwards who was on other & losing side.[15] Lincoln asked E. what was his fee—$300 answered Edwards.

Going down street met Bunn. Lincoln told him he had gained possession of farm in suit and charged his client $200. Got to thinking a pretty stiff fee and asked Bunn what he thought about it. Just then they encountered Ben Edwards who was on the losing side. L. decided to ask Edwards what his fee was. "Three hundred dollars" was the answer.[16]

JOHN W. BUNN TO WEIK, SPRINGFIELD, 20 JULY 1916[17]

I acknowledge receipt of your letter of July 15th 1916, in which you inquired as to my recollection as to how John Hay came to be one of Mr. Lincoln's secretaries when the latter left Springfield in 1861, and in which you inquired in regard to several other matters.[18]

Shortly after Mr. Lincoln's nomination for President in May or June 1860 Judge Stephen T. Logan, a close friend and former law partner of Mr. Lincoln, and who had been active in Mr. Lincoln's political interests came to me at Jacob Bunn's store where I was then employed. Judge Logan stated that Mr. Lincoln would necessarily receive a large amount of correspondence which should be attended to promptly and which would require clerical assistance; that prominent Republicans all over the country would be coming to Springfield to visit Mr. Lincoln in Mr. Lincoln's interest and that the entertainment of these gentlemen would be a matter of some expense; that there would be various other expenses incident to the Springfield end of the Lincoln campaign; that a fund for that purpose should be provided by Mr. Lincoln's personal friends in Springfield.[19] He handed me a check for Five hundred dollars, and gave me a list of nine other friends of Mr. Lincoln's including Col. John Williams,[20] Jacob Bunn,[21] O. M. Hatch,[22] Thomas Condell,[23] Robert Irwin and others, and stated that each one of them would be glad to give a check for Five Hundred for a fund for this general purpose, and that I should act as Treasurer of the fund. I called upon these gentlemen and each gave their check for Five Hundred Dollars, thus raising a fund of Five Thousand Dollars for the purposes indicated by Judge Logan. Shortly after this Mr. John G. Nicolay, then a clerk in Mr. Hatch's office, agreed without compensation to give such time as he could to attend to Mr. Lincoln's political correspondence.[24] Mr. Hatch was then Secretary of State, and Mr. Hatch and the clerks in his office arranged their duties so that Mr. Nicolay might have a considerable time at his disposal in connection with Mr. Lincoln's correspondence. In the early part of August a great Republican rally, said to have been attended by seventy-five thousand people, was held at the Fair Grounds in Springfield. The expenses attendant upon this rally consumed the unexpended portion of the five thousand dollar fund. Shortly after this rally a meeting was held of a Committee of the gentlemen who had subscribed this fund and each of the original subscribers put in an additional five hundred dollars. At this time Mr. Lincoln's political correspondence had so increased that Mr. Nicolay found it impossible for him to take care of it without assistance. At a meeting of the Committee above referred to the question of procuring an assistant for Mr. Nicolay was canvassed. Various names were suggested but none of them seemed to possess the peculiar qualities which were thought necessary for one who would necessarily have the responsibility and duties connected with disposing of Mr. Lincoln's correspondence. Finally Mr. Milton Hay suggested that John Hay was studying law in his office; that he had great literary talent and great tact and that he would excellently fill the position and that without expense to the Committee; that moreover it would be an excellent thing for young Hay in the way of practical experience.[25] Under these circumstances John Hay immediately began work in connection with Mr. Nicolay. After the election and until he left Springfield in February 1861, Mr. Lincoln of course had a very large amount of correspondence and Mr. Nicolay and John Hay continued to assist him in disposing of this correspondence. Shortly before Mr. Lincoln left Springfield he called a meeting of the Committee above referred to to close up the various matters connected with that end of his campaign. The fund was overdrawn some Twenty Five Hundred Dollars, which I insisted upon paying, inasmuch as I had been responsible for incurring the deficit. At this meeting Mr. Lincoln said that he had been examining the Statutes and Appropriations and found that as President he would have at his disposal for secretarial work only the sum of Twenty-five hundred dollars per year and that he judged that all that sum would be required for Mr. Nicolay; that he had found John Hay to be a very great assistance and that he hoped after getting to Washington he might find some way of continuing John Hay's connection with his personal work. Thereupon Milton Hay said that John Hay had much enjoyed working with Mr. Lincoln and that he, Mr. Milton Hay, would provide for John Hay's expenses for six months in Washington. Immediately thereafter Mr. Lincoln requested John Hay to accompany him to Washington in the capacity of Assistant Secretary in connection with Mr. Nicolay, and John Hay so accompanied Mr. Lincoln to Washington. During the early years of the War John Hay returned to visit Springfield. He then told me that when Mr. Lincoln received his first month's salary he insisted on paying John Hay therefrom a salary at the rate of Three Thousand Dollars a year. My impression is that within two or three months after Mr. Lincoln's first inauguration John Hay was appointed by the Secretary of War as Military Secretary to Mr. Lincoln.[26] However the facts in this regard are doubtless matters of public record.[27]

I remember well the visit of General Robert C. Schenck and Don Piatt to Springfield.[28] General Schenck and Mr. Piatt were campaigning through Illinois and made speeches in Springfield one Saturday evening, probably in October 1860. They remained over Sunday in Springfield. Mr. Lincoln, Mr. Hatch, Mr. Dubois and possibly one or two others with myself spent a large part of Sunday afternoon in General Schenck's rooms at the Old Chenery House in Springfield. Nothing was said so far as I am aware during any of this time as to Mr. Piatt being appointed as one of Mr. Lincoln's secretaries. I am quite sure that the friends of Mr. Lincoln did not remonstrate with Mr. Lincoln over a proposed appointment of Mr. Piatt as one of Mr. Lincoln's secretaries. None of us knew that the appointment of Mr. Piatt as one of Mr. Lincoln's secretaries was being considered.

INTERVIEW WITH JOHN W. BUNN, 21 NOVEMBER 1916
AT I. R. DILLER'S OFFICE, SPRINGFIELD

John W Bunn

Says com. from Chic. convention arrived in afternoon – had dinner at Chenery House about six and had to ret[urn] to Chicago at ten in evening – therefore told local com that [they] could not be at L's much over hour & asked that [there] be no delay – no outsiders invited etc. – no ladies etc. – this would take time. Ebenezer Peck who came from Chicago & who once lived in Spgfld suggested to Spgfld committee that they tell Mrs L. not to be present. "Tell her yourself" said Spgfld people who were afraid to do so. But notwithstanding Mrs L all dressed up came sweeping into room low neck dress etc. with one of children

Bunn heard farewell speech at depot when left – first time he ever saw L deeply moved – tears ran down cheeks in waiting room when neighbors said good bye – about 1000 present – bad day raining etc.[29] demanded speech – but train made up – newspaper men & others in front – train started & went about half block when Tilton supt of road made train back up to depot & L made the speech.[30] Gen's Sumner & Hunter who had been sent out by Seward & Gen Scott demanded that Mr L. leave night before – slip away in dark & nobody would know – said Gen Scott had so ordered but Spfld people would not allow it to be done[31]

Wood act[in]g Gov. (Bissell died in office) lived at Quincy & gave his office in State house to L. but when Yates elected – legislature convened & L surrendered his office to Yates & took rooms in Johnson building.[32] Frank Blair & Gratz Brown of St Louis in town about once a week after L's election till he left[33] Bates there several times[34]

When Douglas made famous speech – key-note – in Spfield in 1854 someone in audience announced that Lincoln would reply in same place in a week. Next day L. asked Bunn what he thought of Douglas speech. "Hard to answer & hard to beat." Not so said L—would be easy. D made two statements or laid down 2 propositions that are untrue & cannot maintain a structure on such weak foundation.[35]

Said Douglas always insisted on having table on platform when he spoke – be behind & thus conceal his low stature. Bunn saw L. cast his ballot at court house in 1860 – tore off his name from top of ticket – No danger of any assault or insult to him on election day – Democrats thought too much of him – universally popular.

There were two clubs – Dems called Hickorys & Rep Wide awakes always had plenty about polls all day to prevent trouble

NOTES OF CONVERSATION WITH JOHN W. BUNN ON
MARCH THE 5TH 1918. CLINTON L. CONKLING.[36]

Jacob Bunn (born in 1814) was in 1840 a Clerk in the general store of McConnell & Van Sickle at Naples, Illinois.[37] In 1840 the great Whig Convention was held at Springfield for several days. Bunn wanted very much to attend the Convention, being a Whig. He could not get any conveyance or horse, so started to walk from Naples to Springfield. He reached Jacksonville late in the day after a tramp of twenty-five miles or more, and the first man he met there was Murray McConnell who lived in Jacksonville, and was one of his employers. McConnell asked him what he was doing there and he said to him that he wanted to go to the Convention at Springfield. McConnell said, "No, you won't go to the Convention at Springfield. You are working for McConnell & Van Sickle and you must go back to Naples. You are pretty tired and hungry. Come in with me and

Mrs. McConnell will give you something to eat and you can stay with us to-night and in the morning you can go back to Naples." Mrs. McConnell got him up one of the best suppers, Bunn said, he ever tasted. He said he never was so tired in his life. In the morning McConnell hitched up his horse and buggy and they got in and started. Bunn was so tired that after while he went to sleep and slept for an hour or more. He woke up and did not know the country and McConnell said nothing to him, nor did he say anything to McConnell, but they rode for a good while, until they came to a little town, passed through it, that was entirely unfamiliar to him, and along in the afternoon came into another little town and Bunn found out then that it was Berlin and that instead of being taken back to Naples he was on the road to Springfield. They reached Springfield in the evening and stopped at the old American House where McConnell got him a room and took care of him for several days.[38] Just before they came into Springfield they saw the tents and camps of those who had come to the Convention. At the end of the second or third day McConnell said to Bunn: "How would you like to go into business in Springfield?" and Bunn said he didn't know; but what was the matter with Naples. McConnell said, "We are in trouble at Naples." Bunn said, "I did not know that." McConnell said, "Van Sickle has bought about $50,000 worth of sugar and molasses at New Orleans and it is coming up. We will never be able to sell it at Naples. It is too small a place and we will have to make a branch store somewhere. Now, if you will go in with me we will open a store here in Springfield." So the firm was called McConnell, Bunn & Co., and they opened a store in a little two story brick building 20 x 60 ft on the southwest corner of Fifth and Adams at the southwest corner of the Square. They rented the store and in this building the firm of McConnell, Bunn & Co. continued as merchants until 1847. At that time, I (John W. Bunn) came west at my brother's request. McConnell said, "Now your brother is coming and you would like to have him go into partnership and I will sell out to you," which he did for $12,000. Just after that time Jacob Bunn bought the ground on the southeast corner of Adams and Fifth Streets just across the street east from the then store. On this he put up the four story brick building (within two or three years past changed to a three story building), which building J. Bunn, Grocer, occupied in 1848 and continued thereafter to occupy for many years. He had a very extensive trade with the farmers of Sangamon County who frequently asked him to take charge of their money and so gradually he commenced doing a little banking business, which increased until in 1858 he bought the 20 x 80 feet on the southwest corner of Fifth and Adams Street where McConnell Bunn & Co. had previously rented a store building and put up the building now occupied by the State Bank of Springfield. The south half of the building, or the second twenty feet belonged to George Woods and the building was erected jointly.[39] Afterwards Woods sold his half to J. Taylor Smith and J. Taylor Smith's devisees sold to the State National Bank, who thus became the owner of the forty feet.[40] After McConnell, Bunn & Co. removed in 1848 across the street, Hawley & Loose, Dry Goods, Boots Shoes, etc., occupied the little store on the southwest corner of Fifth and Adams Street until Bunn bought the place in 1858. Bunn's Banking business was carried on on this corner for some years thereafter.

Mr. Lincoln never was a depositor in the banking house of J. Bunn though he was for years attorney for J. Bunn Grocer and for him individually and may have advised him about various matters connected with the Bank although this is not probable because there were other attorneys who were depositors at that Bank.

The State of Illinois created the State Bank of Illinois and erected a very fine stone building on the south half of the north half of the block fronting on the east side of the Public Square. On a portion of the premises the present Springfield Marine Bank successor to Springfield Marine and Fire Ins. Co. is located. The old State Bank went out of existence and Commissioners were appointed to wind up its affairs and sell its property of which it held a great deal, having been compelled to take in very many pieces of real estate for bad loans which it had made. In 1851 these premises were sold by the Commissioners. Jacob Bunn, who afterwards became J. Bunn, Banker, John Williams, who during or after the Civil War formed the banking house of John Williams & Company which afterwards became the First National Bank of Springfield, Judge Stephen T. Logan and other well known men of the period in 1851 formed the Springfield Marine and Fire Insurance Company, modelled after a company, I believe, of the same name in Hartford, Connecticut. Judge Stephen T. Logan was the principal advisor as to the formation. Mr. Lincoln was consulted some but was not one of the incorporators. Most of the comparatively few attorneys in Springfield at that time became stockholders, but Mr. Lincoln was not one of them nor was William H. Herndon. Mr. Lincoln however was one of the group of men, so far as his associations were concerned, that formed the Bank and he became a depositor. The Bank has the old books now showing his account. His account was not an active account and perhaps one of the largest checks he ever drew was one for $200 dated in 1857 (July I think) payable to the order of Jacob Ruckel for the sum of $200, which check is now framed and hanging in my (John W. Bunn's) private office in the present Springfield Marine Bank.[41] In 1857 Mr. Lincoln went away on one of his trips to the various county seats on the circuit. During his absence Mrs. Lincoln caused the one and a half story house in which they were living to be made into a two story house, being the present house know as "Lincoln's residence" and which maintains to-day the appearance it had then.[42] Jacob Ruckel was an old citizen of Springfield and he painted and papered the house and this check was for that work. In this connection occurred the story that is told of Mr. Lincoln coming home and meeting his neighbor, Stout (of the firm of Lavely & Stout, Grocers)[43] a short distance from his house, but in full sight of it, and on which occasion Mr. Lincoln asked him if he knew where A. Lincoln lived. Mr. Stout said, "Yes, that is his house there", falling into Mr. Lincoln's humor. Mr. Lincoln said, "No, when I left here my house was a story and a half house but that is a fine two story house. That can't be mine." "Oh yes it is Mr. Lincoln" said Mr. Stout; "it has grown into a two story house during the two weeks you have been away."

UNDATED MEMO ON BACK OF TYPESCRIPT OF
HERNDON'S INTERVIEW WITH E. L. BAKER[44]

Bunn says when Presbyterians had meetings in forties and Logan, Stuart & others made speeches L. attended and listened but would not commit himself because he said he could not understand the question.

On way home from office would frequently stop at Bunns office in brothers store.

## Mrs. Arthur H. Carter

MRS. ARTHUR H. CARTER TO WEIK, HOLLY
HILL, FLORIDA, 18 NOVEMBER 1917[1]

Your letter with reference to my father [Gibson W. Harris] came a few days ago and I will do what I can to answer your questions.

My father was born in Albion, Illinois, Jan 21st 1828, and died in Holly Hill Fla. Dec 5th 1911.

He studied law under Mr Lincoln, for two years. I believe they were 1845 & 46.

He knew Mr. Herndon quite well and I think Mr H. was Mr. Lincolns partner then

I have a letter written by my father in May 1847 from Decatur Ill. where he speaks of his being at Court and that he has not made up his mind just where he will locate.

His father died that fall and being the oldest of nine boys, my father had to look after the business until younger brothers were able to do so.

He was married in 1850 and soon after moved to Cincinnati, where he went into business, remaining there until 1882 when he moved to Holly Hill.[2]

He was never in any other law office than Mr. Lincolns and I do not believe he ever practiced law.

My father was deeply fond of Mr. Lincoln and was always in close touch with him.

He wrote "Personal recollections of Mr Lincoln" published in the Womans Home Companion in Nov. 1903, running through four numbers.[3] You may be able to get a set. We have only one set left and do not feel we can part with it.

I was not born until July 1868 so while I have heard my father talk thousands of times of Mr Lincoln, some things are not real clear to me.

My father's name was William Gibson – he was always called Gibson, so wrote it G. W.

Hoping this will assist you in your research work. [P.S.] The law student of 1857 was certainly not my father.

### Augustus H. Chapman and Harriet Chapman

AUGUSTUS H. CHAPMAN AND HARRIET CHAPMAN, CHARLESTON,
ILLINOIS, 3 JANUARY 1896, INTERVIEW WITH WEIK[1]

Col. A. H. Chapman—A Lincoln and Dennis Hanks both gave Chapman this route they made from Indiana to Ills in 1830.[2] Gentryville to Jasper Dubois Co Ind – thence to Washington, Daviss Co – thence to Vincennes – across Wabash river – thence to Lawrenceville Ills – thence to Palestine Crawford Co – (At Palestine L & Hanks both said they found a large crowd drawn there by the land office) thence north to Darwin whence they left the Wab. river – thence [    ] through Rich Woods in Clark Co – thence to a point 6 mi West of Charleston called Dead Man's Grove – thence [ ] through Nelsonville in Moultrie Co to Decatur where they stopped[3] – (They may have left the Wab. river at Hutsonville. They went on what was known as the Springfield Trace.[4]

Mrs. Chapman: Says her grandmother (Sarah Bush Lincoln) told her the first printing press and the first Indians Abe ever saw were at Vincennes.

C. C. Coffin has picture of Maj. Chapman here when Lincoln stopped in 1860 when he visited his step mother Coffin lives in Brookline Mass.[5] Took Kodak of him.

Eli Wiley[6] –

Says local account of L. & D. debates – Charleston written by Edward S. Baker who moved to Tuscola & then to Oregon.[7]

### A. H. CHAPMAN

James Cunningham a wealthy man living near Mattoon purchased a pair of cream white horses which he used to have Mr. Lincoln and the party that rode with him from Mattoon in the morning of the debate with Douglas at Charleston.[8] The Democrats had also a fancy team which prompted Cunningham to outstrip them.

Reception for Lincoln was in City Hall or Opera House in 1858 – and in 1860 a reception was held at Col Thos A Marshall's house.[9] L. spent the night with Chapmans however.

Robert Matson's widow lived at Troy Tenn. and Col. C. saw her there during the war[10]

Mrs. Chapman also says that her grandmother [Sarah Bush Johnston Lincoln] told her that before her removal to Ills. she returned to her Kentucky home where some money was due her and with it bought side-saddles for herself and daughters—they rode on horseback a good portion of the way. The small children rode in the wagon.

After this interview with Col. Chapman and his wife his son Robert N. being present he took me outside of the house and standing with me on the portico told me that as I had once before asked the question by letter—and Mr Herndon also—he would state that Dennis Hanks told him Thomas Lincoln had been castrated. He had evaded and even denied the charge but now that he was growing old and liable to die he felt as if it would not be wrong to tell it. JWW.

### HARRIET CHAPMAN

#### HARRIET CHAPMAN, INTERVIEW WITH WEIK, CHARLESTON, ILLINOIS, 16 OCTOBER 1914[1]

Lived 18 mos at Lincoln home in Springfield. Mr Lincoln drove through with her from Charleston. Open top buggy and bay horse.[2] Mrs Lincoln and her sisters Mrs Wallace, Edwards & Smith proud Ky women.[3] One day Mrs L. tired of washing dishes said with sigh "What would my poor father say if he found me doing this kind of work"[4]

Says Douglas wanted to marry Mrs L. and finally after Mrs L. became sick and asked D. to release her from engagement.[5] Later Mr. L said he would have killed D. if he had not released Mary Todd.[6] One day Lincoln took Bob a baby down town. When he returned he told his wife he had met Douglas on the street. Mrs L. asked if D thought Bob was pretty and when Mr L. said he failed to notice or ask about Bob she became very indignant.[7]


## Robert N. Chapman

ROBERT N. CHAPMAN TO WEIK, CHARLESTON, ILLINOIS [22 JUNE 1896][1]

You never got this broken axle story from any of our family. We never heard it before and it is not true – The facts are as follows –

Mr Lincoln at the head of a procession was driven from Mattoon to Charleston in a carriage drawn by two cream colored horses purchased expressly for that purpose by James T Cunningham a wealthy Republican of this County who was a personal friend and admirer of Mr Lincoln. My Grand Father Dennis F. Hanks then owned a business house on the public square here and resided with his family in the second story rooms. When the carriage containing Mr Lincoln – at head of procession – arrived in middle of street in front of Grand Father Hanks – Mr Lincoln had the carriage stop and got out and went up stairs and greeted his old Step Mother with the others of the family present. Grand Mother Lincoln had been brought up from the farm on Goose Nest prairie where she was then staying, by her daughter Mrs Dennis F. Hanks – for the purpose of meeting her step son. Mr Lincoln visited his step mother that Evening at my Fathers house & public reception at City Hall that Evening—& he left on train late that night –

These are the facts—& you can shape them up –


## William Dodd Chenery

WILLIAM DODD CHENERY TO WEIK, 7 MARCH 1918[1]

This is written at my mother's request in answer to your letter of March 5 asking the loan of her copy of the picture of the Chenery House.[2] She instructs me to mail a copy to you with permission to keep it long enough to have the cut made therefrom after which time you may return it to her at the address below.

My mother and my aunt, Miss Susan Chenery, are the only members of that generation of the Chenery family now living. Both are at this time 78 years old and both were living in the hotel during the time Mr. Lincoln stopped there. My mother is still very active and is deeply interested in all current events and, most especially, in all that relates to the world war. She was the first secretary of the "Soldiers' Ladies Aid Society" of Springfield, organized at the period of the Civil War and that filled the place at that time now so wonderfully taken by the Red Cross. She is one of the only four surviving charter members of the Springfield branch.

On the morning of Mr. Lincoln's departure from Springfield he passed my mother on the stairs of the hotel as he descended to breakfast while she was ascending the stairs. It was before the days of elevators. He stopped to greet her and inquire for her health. His great affability was one of the traits that so endeared him to those who knew him well. It was customary for a group of men to sit on hotel office chairs under the trees in front of the hotel on pleasant summer evenings and chat. Mr. Lincoln and his partner, Mr. Herndon, were often there at such times. We still have a couple of the old oak chairs used then.

Enclosed with the hotel picture I will also send a picture of the home that has always been my mother's except at such times as the family lived in the hotel. It was built in 1840, the same year that my mother was born, and was honored on one occasion in 1857 by the presence of Mr. Lincoln, then a rising young lawyer, at a small social gathering. The house was then considered to be "away out in the country" but it is now almost within the shadow of the dome of the Illinois state capitol building, being four squares south west of the building. It was built from lumber largely cut on the ground. The sills are oak beams 18 inches square and 40 feet long and the framework is put together with wooden pins. The weather boards are walnut (now covered with concrete finish) and the interior is all old walnut dark with age. The laths are hickory turned by hand and as crooked as serpents. Carpenters have difficulty in making repairs or alterations because of the seasoned hard wood.[3]

My mother is known to the children near by as the "bird lady" because she feeds the birds all winter and keeps water for them in summer. The vines and most of the flowers in the picture were planted by her own hands and she still cares for them. She is standing in the picture and the writer is seated on the grass at her right.

Should the picture of either building be used kindly let us know where we may purchase a copy of the publication in which it appears.

## John Coburn

### John Coburn to Weik, Indianapolis, 14 April 1903[1]

Your letter just now came to hand. I am asked several questions as to occurrences forty years ago. I remember that Col Utley of the 22nd Wisconsin, in my brigade, had some trouble while in the fall of 1862 we were in Kentucky.[2]

His regiment was bran-new; not a month old; and going into Kentucky got into some complications about slaves. I almost forget the points; but recall the fact that Utley had some vague and wild notions as to the slave question. He was a good fellow and meant well; but had some uncertain notions as to the treatment of slaves, in Kentucky; which was a state that Mr Lincoln wanted to hold in the Union column. Somehow Utley thought that he was a crusader for the freedom of slaves and that it was a fine thing to get a Slave away from his master, in any way, shape, or form. So he put on airs about some fellow that had come into his camp. And in the end got into a scrape which involved him in a lawsuit about the value of a runaway negro slave. The result was, that he was sued in the United States court, in Kentucky, and a judgment was rendered against him for the value of the slave. And Congress passed an act to relieve him from the trouble.

It was a silly and needless thing on his part. But Uncle Sam paid Judge Robinson [George Robertson] for his Slave. Slavery then existed in Kentucky and he knew it, and he ought to have had sense enough to know that a Wisconsin Colonel could not issue an emancipation proclamation.

But he attempted to do it and when I was in congress I voted for an act relieving him from the payment of a judgment for the value of a Slave that he had prevented being returned to his master.[3]

It was a very silly performance on the part of Utley and did more harm than good. At the proper time Lincoln struck slavery down forever. Utley failed; not being authorized by law or the laws of war or any rule of our nation, to abolish slavery. A more ridiculous travesty was never played than this and while I do not know what the book says, I do know, that it was a farce as ridiculous as ever that was presented for exhibition. Not a member of Congress voted against the appropriation 'to pay poor old Utley for his losses by reason of the judgment, which was taken by default.

Col John P. Baird of the 85th Indiana was sued at the same time but defended his course in the U.S. Court and gained his case – Utley would not employ counsel; and the judgment went against him by default.

A nonsensical fiasco from start to finish.

JOHN COBURN TO WEIK, INDIANAPOLIS, 16 APRIL 1903[4]

I have not yet had an opportunity to look at Mr Coffin's book you referred to in your letter of the 14th.[5] So I can't say whether he fabricated words for me or not. But I will look over it someday. I very well remember that Judge Robinson who had been chief Justice of Kentucky came into our camp & called on Genl Baird who commanded our Division & myself who commanded a brigade and desired an order to obtain the slave who was in Utleys camp[6] We three went together and talked to Col Utley about it. Robinson claimed his slave – We told Utley that we were not there as an army to free slaves or to take them from their masters that they had a right to them as their property just exactly as they had to their horses and cattle, and that if this colored man was a slave of Robinson that he had a right to take him away, and that he, as Col. of the 22d Wisconsin, ought not to prevent it.

What Utley said I do not remember. He was a great dunderhead I do know; and so got into a scrape about the value of the negro which he refused to deliver to his master, for which the United States Court rendered judgment

N.B. I have just read Coffin's report or essay in Volume 8 Library of American Literature by Stedman & Hutchinson to which you refer. It is a work of fiction, Quixotic and nonsensical. The scene at Gilmore's Headquarters never occurred. I never reported to Gilmore that I remember of. Gen Absalom Baird was my Division Commander. He was an abolitionist as I remember. His wife was a niece of Gerrit Smith the greatest of all abolitionists. He Baird was a radical Republican.

As to Gilmore I had nothing to do with him. I did not report to him. Baird & myself and Judge Robinson the owner of the slave went to Utley and Baird who ranked me told Utley in plain terms that Judge Robinson's slave ought to be allowed to go with him, that the slaves in Kentucky were not emancipated then and that Robinson had a right to his property. I do not remember to have added a word to what Gen Baird said.

The article of Coffin is a silly fiction so far as I know all the way through. Utley was proposing to create a sensation and get a little cheap reputation among anti-slavery men. It was a farce and the Court rendered a judgment against him. The right of Judge Robinson to the slave was unquestionable at that time.

But not long after this the Emancipation proclamation came out and the institution of slavery tumbled to the gates of Hell where it belonged.

JOHN COBURN TO WEIK, INDIANAPOLIS, 12 MAY 1903[7]

I just now found your letter to which I gave two or three hasty answers, but never saw the letter till now, after the first day and now see that you spoke of calling on me on Sunday as your wife is here then.

Now if I had not lost your letter until today, when in making a general hunt for other papers, I found it, I would have invited you to call on me. Now nothing would please me more than for you to come and see me at my house. The number is 1518 Hendricks Street now called South New Jersey Street by a recent act of the City Council.

I have no scruples on the subject of Sunday visiting and will be very glad to see you any Sunday. Do come, by all means, & see me at home on Sunday.

Dont fail to do so. While my early training was as a Presbyterian I am no Puritan. My mother was a Methodist and I attended both churches.

I referred you to the book out of which you got some singularly distorted information about Col. Utley & a negro & Judge Robertson. The slender thread of facts was so loaded down with falsehoods that but for the names I could not have recognized myself as one of the actors or parties.

Mr Coffin shows himself to be unfit to write such stuff about myself when I lived so near him and was often in the town or city of his residence & he was there no doubt. I hope to meet him and have him explain a little.

## Jonathan N. Colby

### Jonathan N. Colby, undated memo[1]

Immig. to Ills in 1834 from N. Hampshire – was expecting letters – no one received over one – but he received 3 – was out west of Salem breaking prairie – tall man emerged from timber—& approached Colby saying "so many letters having come for you and supposing they were of importance I brought them out to you."

## Clinton L. Conkling

### Clinton L. Conkling to Weik, Springfield, 28 October 1916[1]

The photographer has made the prints and is sending the three to you to-day. He says he will make a picture of the settee and also send that to you. I trust that the points of view will be satisfactory to you.

I have no distinct recollection as to how or where I learned of Mr. Lincoln's nomination. All the positive recollection I have is that I heard the news and starting to find Mr. Lincoln, met him in the doorway of the General Store of N. W. Edwards & Co., which was then in the second building north of the office of James C. Conkling and was situated on the south side of the alley in the middle of the west side of the square.[2] There are two different accounts as to where the Telegraph Office was located in April 1860. One is that it was located in the rear of the office of James C. Conkling in the George W. Chatterton Building on the third twenty foot lot south of the alley on the west side of the square. Another account is that in April it was near the middle of the north side of the square, and shortly afterwards was removed to the second story back room of the George W. Chatterton Building on the west side. I recollect well when it was on the north side of the square and I also recollect when it was in the Chatterton Building, but I cannot say positively when the change was made nor can I say positively that it was there in April 1860. The best evidence that I can find would indicate that in April 1860 it was in the middle of the north side of the square. I do not wish to be understood as saying that the Telegraph Office was in the same building with Mr. James C. Conkling's office in 1860.

Mr. Lincoln's own statement as given to T. W. S. Kidd, former editor of the Sangamo Monitor, as printed in the Illinois State Register, February the 13th 1903, page 8, is better evidence of the facts than any statement I can make.[3]

I am sending you to-day a sketch of the life of Sen. Shelby M. Cullom and direct your attention particularly to the very exhaustive manner in which Mr. Converse has treated the matter.

CLINTON L. CONKLING TO WEIK, SPRINGFIELD, 17 FEBRUARY 1917[4]

Replying to yours of February the 11th will say that I have interviewed a member of the Logan-Hay family; a man of good, conservative judgment and well acquainted with the traditions of the Logan family. He says he never heard that Stephen T. Logan wanted to be one of the Supreme Judges of the United States, and thinks that such was not the case and is quite sure that no Springfield people went to Washington to urge Mr. Lincoln to make the appointment, and he believes that such was not the case, although individuals without authority may have suggested the matter as people will do who are seeking to intervene in other people's matters. I have consulted several persons who lived during that time, some of whom would individually have heard of it, and I find no such tradition known here. The gentleman referred to gave several reasons why he considered that it was unlikely that that should have been done. Among other things, he said that after Mr. Lincoln's nomination some of his friends, notably Judge Logan, and among others, Col. John Williams, James C. Conkling and others, raised a campaign fund of $5,000.00 for Mr. Lincoln, and the tradition is that it was distinctly understood at the time that those making the contribution were not, or were not to be, applicants for any positions within Mr. Lincoln's appointment.

I find no trace of any tradition that William H. Herndon applied specifically for appointment as United States Minster to Rome, but it is commonly understood here that Mr. Herndon was an applicant for most any large position that he would induce Mr. Lincoln to give to him.[5] I do not find anyone who knows that certain people from Springfield visited Washington in the interests of Mr. Herndon. The opinion seems to be that no persons from Springfield made such a visit. It was commonly said here, when Herndon's "Life of Lincoln" appeared, that he was now "getting back at" Mr. Lincoln for not having appointed him to some important diplomatic position or to some high office in the Government. Mr. Lincoln knew the capacities of his old acquaintance here perhaps as well as anybody. Those who knew Mr. Herndon could not consider him a proper person to act as United States Minister at Rome, either by education, training or disposition.

I have no knowledge whatever of any such facts as Mr. Henry C. Whitney seems to have told to you. I do not say that they did not exist, but I do say that persons here who would have known, say they have no knowledge of such facts having existed.

CLINTON L. CONKLING TO WEIK, SPRINGFIELD, 28 APRIL 1917[6]

I was pleased to receive yours of April the 22nd and to know of your conclusion as to the location of the telegraph office, in which conclusion I agree with you.[7]

I do not recollect Rev. Reuben Andrus, the Methodist minister you refer to, and who was in charge here in May 1860.[8] There is an attorney here by the name of Charles S. Andrus. I do not know whether he is a connection or not.

Since writing the above I have interviewed him and he has no knowledge of Rev. Reuben Andrus, or of any of his family that have ever lived in this section of the country.

If I can give further service, kindly command me.

CLINTON L. CONKLING TO WEIK, SPRINGFIELD, 13 NOVEMBER 1917[9]

Replying to yours of November the 8th I would say that I had an interview with Mr. John W. Bunn to-day about some of the facts concerning my father's connection with Mr. Lincoln.[10]

He told me the story of Judge Stephen T. Logan coming to him with a check for $500.00 after Mr. Lincoln had been nominated, and about the list of nine other men that was then made up, of whom James C. Conkling, my father was one,[11] and from whom $500 each were obtained, making a fund of $5,000 which was disbursed by Mr. John W. Bunn for whatever was thought necessary in the way of receiving prominent visitors, delegations or for expenses connected with the proper conduct of affairs relating to Mr. Lincoln in this community and incident to the position he occupied as candidate for the presidency. At a later time each one of these ten men contributed another $500. You doubtless have been told about Mr. Lincoln calling upon Mr. Bunn before going to Washington and desiring to pay sundry expenses which he understood Jacob Bunn, brother of John W. Bunn had incurred in connection with the matters above referred to. It appears that up to this time Mr. Lincoln did not know the amounts nor the donors of the above mentioned fund. He probably learned afterwards that Judge Stephen T. Logan and others had contributed to such a fund but it would seem that he never knew who the contributors were, nor the amount given except that Judge Stephen T. Logan and Jacob Bunn were among the number. At some other more favorable occasion (we were interrupted) I will endeavor to confirm the foregoing statements.

Did Mr. Bunn at any time tell you the incident about when he and some other young men requested Mr. Lincoln to deliver a Fourth of July oration in the early Forties and what his reply was in declining to deliver the address, and who he recommended, and why?

Kindly let me know if this meets your request.

CLINTON L. CONKLING TO WEIK, [SPRINGFIELD], 17 DECEMBER 1917[12]
I had hoped to have something for you before this in reply to yours of November the 15th.[13] As soon as I can get Mr. Bunn to tell me the story, the account of which you sent, I will let you know. I have heard Mr. Bunn tell this story several times some time ago, and I think you have it substantially correct. As you request, I send you Mr. Bunn's version of the story concerning Mr. Lincoln and my father and the Fourth of July address.

Vatchel Lindsay is a poet living here who has of late, attained some celebrity for his poems, concerning which there is some diversity of opinions. Mr. Lindsay is a young man, very pleasant in his manner and is a very excellent gentleman. He is somewhat visionary and idealistic. He never knew Mr. Herndon and I do not think he has any real conception of Mr. Herndon's book. I am satisfied that there is nothing in the book that would lead any artist to caricature Mr. Lincoln as has Mr. Barnard.[14] The statue that Mr. Barnard has created is that of a slouchy, stiff, wretchedly posed Southern Mountaineer. Mr. Lincoln was no such man. I contend that the statue does not suggest to the average man, and that is the one for whom such statues should be made, an ideal such as should be given. Personally, I am free to say that I class those who think so highly of this statue as a work of art, as being controlled by their friendly feelings for the sculptor more than by their genuine artistic judgments. However, these remarks concerning the statue are for you and to go no further.

Enclosure:

Memorandum dictated this 13th day of December 1917 by Clinton L. Conkling

In Judge Humphrey's Office in the Federal Building,[15] in his presence and in my presence, in a general conversation about Mr. Lincoln, Mr. John W. Bunn made the following statement: "After Mr. Lincoln went to Washington, he wrote no letters to Mr. Herndon nor to anyone else in Springfield except to Mr. James C. Conkling. I came to Springfield in 1847 when I was sixteen years old. The next year some of the young men, five of us, I do not recall all of their names now, but I was one and was the leader, wanted to get up a Fourth of July Celebration in Wrights Grove which was just West of the town about the intersection of Washington and Walnut Streets. We went to Mr. Lincoln's office and told him what we wanted and asked him to deliver a speech. He said to us: 'I cannot do it. You do not want me. You don't want to get either Logan (Judge Stephen T. Logan), Stuart (John T. Stuart), Edwards (B. S. Edwards) nor anyone else here except one man. He is the only man here who can make you the speech that you want. He is a college graduate and a man of literary attainments and can give you just the speech you want.' We asked him who the gentleman was, and he said 'James C. Conkling.' We then went to Mr. Conkling and asked him to deliver the speech, which he did, and which was just what we wanted."

In this same conversation at Judge Humphrey's office, William H. Herndon, Mr. Lincoln's law partner was spoken of. Mr. Bunn said:

"The partnership between Mr. Lincoln and Stephen T. Logan was dissolved because the partners did not agree on the fees to be charged and the manner of conducting the cases, etc. Mr. Logan was very keen after the money, and Mr. Lincoln didn't seem to care for money at all.

"The partnership between John T. Stuart and Mr. Lincoln was dissolved because of political differences and differences of opinion on the slavery question. Mr. Stuart was from Kentucky and was an old time Whig, but afterwards joined the Democratic party. He was pro-slavery in his leanings.

"The partnership between Mr. Lincoln and William H. Herndon

was one between two men of very radically different tastes, but was formed in the first instance, as a matter of kindness on Mr. Lincoln's part, to Mr. Herndon. Mr. Herndon belonged to a very radical pro-slavery Democratic family. His father sent him to Illinois College at Jacksonville, where he imbibed some of the anti-slavery principals held by the New England people who were in charge of that Institution. This fact greatly enraged his father, Archer G. Herndon, who took him away from College and practically turned him adrift. At this period, he was trying to make his own way, and Joshua Speed is said to have asked Mr. Lincoln to take Herndon into partnership with him. Mr. Lincoln did so out of sympathy for Herndon because of his straitened circumstances and the persecution which he was suffering at the hands of his family because of his anti-slavery views. Mr. Herndon occupied no social position in Springfield society such as Mr. Lincoln did. Dr. William Jayne used to say that Mrs. Lincoln would not have him in her house. Mr. Herndon's habits prior to 1860 were none of the best and not long after Mr. Lincoln went to Washington Mr. Herndon went there for the purpose of seeking some high diplomatic position (tradition says that he asked to be sent as Ambassador to the Court of St. James) and finally wanted some position of any kind just so it was a position. While there he went on a drunken spree. Through the 60's and in the 70's he was addicted to the excessive use of liquor."

Very shortly before Mr. Lincoln went to Washington, in February 1861, Mr. Bunn says he was present at an interview between Governor Richard Yates and Mr. Lincoln, in which Mr. Lincoln said substantially: "Governor Yates, I want you to give me something. I will give you a much better something than what I ask of you. Herndon wants some Government appointment. I can't give him any position. I want you to give him something here in Illinois." Governor Yates assented.

"Herndon was given, if I recollect, some position as Bank Examiner or Bank Commissioner, but just at this moment I don't recollect.[16]

"For some years before Mr. Lincoln was nominated for the Presidency, he attended to the legal business of J. Bunn Wholesale Grocers, in whose store I was at the time. It was my business to look after whatever law matters the firm had and in consequence I was frequently in Mr. Lincoln's office. I always transacted my business with Mr. Lincoln and not with Mr. Herndon. In the trial of any cases in which Jacob Bunn was concerned, Mr. Lincoln always conducted the case, while Mr. Herndon would sit by and hand him such papers as he might need from time to time. I never knew Mr. Herndon to try any of the Bunn matters.["]

CLINTON L. CONKLING TO WEIK, SPRINGFIELD, 22 JANUARY 1918[17]

George C. Latham is here.[18] He and I were old schoolmates together with Robert T. Lincoln. His recollection is very good as to details occurring about the times you ask about.[19] I will send for him or see him and write you the result.

CLINTON L. CONKLING TO WEIK, SPRINGFIELD, 23 JANUARY 1918[20]

I enclose you a statement made by Mr. George C. Latham of this city. I had it taken down in shorthand as he spoke it, changing it somewhat to keep it in consecutive order as much as possible as he stated it. If I have not covered all that you wanted to know, let me know. My recollection is that in Ward H. Lamon's "Life of Mr. Lincoln" he gives some of the particulars concerning this journey. Lamon was one of the party.[21] My impression is that he speaks of this incident, to-wit: Mrs. Lincoln not going with the party at first. It seems to me that she did not go upon the advice of various persons who thought that there might be trouble and she should not be involved. She wanted to go as I have been informed. I am not at all certain however of the foregoing statements, but you can verify them, I think, by looking in Lamon's book. For the details of the journey going East, I would suggest that you examine J. C. Powers' "Life of Lincoln" which gives many details of the journey, but more especially the details of the funeral cortege and burial ceremonies at Springfield.[22] Be sure and let me know whether Latham's statement is sufficient for your purpose. If not, I will try it again.

Recently one of the arms of the settee that you wanted photographed was broken and I am having a man mend it. As soon as this is done, I will have the picture made.

Enclosure:[23]

George C. Latham, living at No. 903 South Second Street, Springfield, says:

I was one of the party that on February 11, 1861 accompanied Mr. Lincoln to Harrisburg, Pennsylvania, at which place Mr. Lincoln left the party and hastened off to Washington with Col. Ward H. Lamon, and the party, of which I was one, followed on to Washington the next morning. Robert T. Lincoln and I, neither of us knew that Mr. Lincoln had gone ahead during the night to Washington, D. C. We only learned of it in the morning.

Robert T. Lincoln, son of Abraham Lincoln, was the only one of the latter's family who accompanied him on the above mentioned train from Springfield to Indianapolis. Mr. Lincoln and the party that left Springfield arrived at Indianapolis in the afternoon or evening and all went to the hotel. The next morning Mrs. Lincoln and the two boys, Tad and Willie (Thomas and William) joined Mr. Lincoln and went with him to Harrisburg. I don't know whether Mrs. Lincoln was at the Station, but I did not see her on the train before we left Springfield.

At Indianapolis Mrs. Lincoln and the two boys, Tad and Will, joined the party and accompanied Mr. Lincoln to Harrisburg. At Harrisburg, the whole party, including Mr. Lincoln, Mrs. Lincoln, Robert, Will, Tad and myself, went to the hotel, the name of which I have forgotten. Early in the morning I learned that Mr. Lincoln had, during the night, gone on to Washington, and I went in to Robert Lincoln's room and told him. I do not think that Mrs. Lincoln knew of his going, but I am not certain.[24] That next morning the whole party, except Mr. Lincoln who had gone ahead, continued the journey to Washington, where Mrs. Lincoln and the three sons joined Mr. Lincoln. Mrs. Lincoln and the three boys and myself went to the White House, where I stayed a week with them. I am not certain whether we stayed the first night at Willards Hotel in Washington, but I know we either went on the day of our arrival or the next day, to the White House. After spending a week with Robert in the White House, I came back to Springfield, Illinois.

The statement of the Indianapolis Journal for February 11, 1861—namely: "Mrs. Lincoln and her younger sons joined her husband in this City Tuesday morning, proceeding with him to Cincinnati. Had she been here Monday evening she would have been almost as much of a lion as old Abe, himself", is correct according to my recollection.

The train that left Springfield went to Indianapolis, and Mrs. Lincoln and her two sons joined the party there the next day, and from Indianapolis the whole party went to Cincinnati, thence to Columbus and various places on the way East to Albany, and thence down to New York City, Newark, New Jersey, and Philadelphia, and thence to Harrisburg, and there Mr. Lincoln left the party and went on to Washington and the rest of the suite, including Mrs. Lincoln and the two boys, Robert and myself, who had with the rest of the suite been taking the long journey all around, followed them to Washington.

Mrs. Lincoln and the two little boys joined Mr. Lincoln at Indianapolis and not at New York as the papers said she would.

I do not know why Mrs. Lincoln did not leave Springfield with her husband on the morning of February the 11th. I have never heard any reason given for her not doing so.

I think there was, among many other correspondents, one by the name of [Joseph] Howard [Jr.], who represented the New York Times. In the morning at Harrisburg, after Mr. Lincoln had left the night before, he said he must get up some sort of a story for his paper and he is the one who fabricated the Scotch cap story. Mr. Lincoln wore a slouch hat and not a Scotch cap, as I learned while staying in the family during the week I was in Washington. He wore a cloak, but it was the same one that he had worn from Springfield and was one that fastened in front near the neck like many that were worn at that time.

I never heard of Mrs. Lincoln going to St. Louis before reaching Indianapolis, on February the 12th.

CLINTON L. CONKLING TO WEIK, SPRINGFIELD, 31 JANUARY 1918[25]

My answer to yours of December the 14th has been long delayed. The occasion has been because I desired to get some information concerning your inquiries which I have been entirely unable as yet to get. I know nothing about the tradition that Mr. Lincoln was undecided whether to appoint David Davis or O. H. Browning to the Supreme Court in 1862.[26]

These two men were very different in most every way. It seems to be hardly fair to either one of them that they should be compared as to ability, either for the bench or in politics. They both were very able and strong men but their personal characteristics were very different. Each occupied his own position and each filled his own duties in an admirable way. David Davis was a much more rugged character and in practical and business matters was doubtless the superior of O. H. Browning. They were both men of sterling integrity, the former was more brusque and frequently reached a conclusion to do justice which was not according to the conventions of the day or of the bar. I do not say that this was a characteristic of him, but he at times did so. David Davis was more a man of the people and was not so much of a politician as was O. H. Browning. The former was a good lawyer and a good business man and not so much of a politician. The latter was a good lawyer and probably not a very successful business man, but was a most excellent politician. I use the word "politician" in its better sense. David Davis was not negligent in his personal appearance or dress. O. H. Browning always was immaculate in his dress, and while I was not acquainted with him, I have seen him frequently and remember well the frilled shirt bosom which he affected for many years. He was, as we say to-day, a "gentleman of the old school." David Davis acquired large wealth. I have been informed that O. H. Browning did not accumulate very much, but of this I have no knowledge. I do not think that one at this day can say that either one was the greater lawyer of the two or that either one was better equipped to be a Supreme Court Judge. David Davis acquitted himself well, and O. H. Browning would doubtless have done the same had he been appointed. Both were gentlemen. The former bluff, hearty and genuine. The latter, polite, gracious and fully as genuine.

I have done the best I can for you. Of course, I do not write this for publication but use the substance as you see fit but don't connect my name with it.

I hope you received the newspaper I sent you a few days ago containing some remarks made by Mr. Bunn.[27]

CLINTON L. CONKLING TO WEIK, [SPRINGFIELD], 6 MARCH 1918[28]

Replying to yours of March the 1st [I] would say that neither John W. Bunn nor William Ridgely, both of whom were well acquainted with George W. Chatterton for many years and knew a great deal about his business and what he did, have any recollection whatever of his having been appointed Indian Agent.[29] Personally, I never heard of it myself, although he might have been and I not have known about it. I knew him well and always knew him as a jeweler whose store was on the first floor of the building where my father had his office in 1860, of which I have told you before. Neither of these gentlemen ever heard that W. H. Herndon visited Mr. Lincoln late in 1861 in Washington on Chatterton's behalf, asking for the appointment of Chatterton as Indian agent. There was no relation by blood or marriage between Herndon and Chatterton. The gentlemen above named say that Herndon was a widower at that time and was anxious to marry a certain Miss Miles of Petersburg, Menard County, Illinois, about twenty miles northwest of here. They believe that he afterwards did marry her.[30] But neither of these gentlemen ever heard that Chatterton was in a position to help him in his suit or that he ever did.

I herewith enclose you certain memoranda made recently. There is much in it that is of no interest to you but is of some local interest here in matters not connected with Mr. Lincoln, but I send it as it is written.

The matter is not arranged as it should be but you can use it as it is only

I don't want my name to be associated with anything you may say in the matter.

Enclosure:

William Ridgely returned to Springfield from St. Louis about December the 1st 1860, having been in a Bank in St. Louis for several years. He recollects the fact that the Illinois & Mississippi Telegraph office was, sometime prior to 1860, on the north side of the Square. The first Telegraph office in Springfield was on the south side of the Square in the second story over the Hardware Store of E. B. Pease, now Number 506 East Adams Street, and now occupied by J. L. Hudson as a Hardware Store. Mr. Ridgely's recollection is that when he returned from St. Louis, the Illinois & Mississippi Telegraph Company's local office was situated in the second story back room over George W. Chatterton's Jewelry Store, and that James C. Conkling had his office in the front room. He knows positively that for a long time the Telegraph Company had its office in that room.

The Banking House of N. H. Ridgely & Co. was on the north side of the Chatterton Store. In 1864 N. H. Ridgely & Co. was succeeded by the Ridgely National Bank. There two Banking firms continued to occupy the building next north of Chatterton's store until a few years ago when the Ridgeley National Bank removed to its present location and the old building, together with the building next north, and adjoining the alley, and in 1860 occupied by N. W. Edwards & Co. as a General Store, was torn down, and what is known as the Reisch Building has been erected on the ground occupied by the two older buildings. The Chatterton Building is still standing. The upper part of the front is substantially the same as it was in 1860. The first floor front has been changed.

Mr. William Ridgely occupied various positions in the Banking House of N. H. Ridgely & Co. and then in its successor, The Ridgely National Bank, from December 1860 until the present time, he being now President of the Ridgely National Bank. The Banking Building belonged to his father and then became part of his father's estate; that is the Estate of N. H. Ridgely, deceased. On the West, or rear end of the Bank lot was a small two story brick building, which was put up by the Telegraph Office when it removed to the second story back room over Chatterton's Store. In this small brick building they had their batteries in numbers of large glass jars for producing the current used on their wires.

Mr. Ridgely recollects the fact that James C. Conkling had his office in the second story of the Chatterton Building and says that the third story in 1860 was occupied by a photographer, whose name at present he does not recollect. He cannot say just when the Telegraph office was moved from the north side of the Square to the west side, but his best recollection is that in December when he returned to Springfield from St. Louis, the office was in the Chatterton Building.

CLINTON L. CONKLING TO WEIK, SPRINGFIELD, 3 JULY 1918[31]

Enclosed please find a newspaper clipping containing the cut of the Chenery House and some historical data.[32] The vehicles and the front of the hotel are on the north side of Washington Street. The left hand side of the hotel as shown in the picture is on Fourth Street. The St. Nicholas Hotel is exactly one block north on the same side of Fourth Street but on the south side of Jefferson Street.[33] Immediately across Fourth Street west from the Chenery House stood from about 1855 to 1866 a row of three story store buildings facing south on the north side of Washington Street, the Chicago & Alton Passenger Station lying immediately west and in the same block. Over these stores which then ran back about 45 feet the owner, Joel Johnson, lived with his family in the Fall and Winter of 1860–61 (and both before and after). Mr. Lincoln, a very short time—only a few days or at most several weeks — removed from his own dwelling, he having rented it to Mr. Tilton of the Wabash Railroad, and took rooms in the Chenery House in the second story and facing Fourth Street, the windows of which are seen on the left of the picture with the shutters open. Joel Johnson and Mr. Lincoln had been friends and acquaintances for many years. Mr. Johnson remarked to his family that Mr. Lincoln now being without his office (the late Governor's rooms in the State House which he had had to give up on account of the convening of the Legislature and the necessity of the Governor occupying them himself) he thought he ought to ask him to occupy some of his rooms. So he tendered to Mr. Lincoln the use as a matter of courtesy of two rooms connected by folding doors in the second story of his building across the way from the Chenery House. Mr. Lincoln very gladly accepted the same and received his visitors there for about a week or ten days before he left in February for Washington. I enclose a pencil outline map showing the location of the several buildings referred to. In 1866 Joel Johnson added to his store buildings on the northwest corner of Fourth and Washington Streets, and transformed the whole into a Hotel and called the same the Revere House. It was not run as a hotel when Mr. Lincoln was there.

On the southeast corner of Fourth and Jefferson Streets, being on the same block as the Chenery House was located the St. Nicholas Hotel, which for very many years has been during the meetings of the Legislature here the Democratic headquarters, both for campaign purposes and general loafing activities. On this spot of ground Archer G. Herndon had his home for many years.[34] It was a one or one and one-half story wooden building facing north with a broad porch clear across the front of it—a gallery as it would be called in the south. Herndon probably sold this to a man by the name of Freeman who was a physician of some kind here.[35] On this Freeman built a three story [actually four story] brick building facing north on Washington Street, which was called subsequently or by him, the St. Nicholas Hotel. From him, John McCreery (father of the present owner) and _____ Sponsler bought the Hotel and added to it and they probably were running the Hotel in 1860–61.[36] It has always been a prominent hotel in Springfield since it first was built.

If the above is not sufficiently definite let me know. I am sending you a copy of the Centennial Edition of the Illinois State Register of June 23rd. I have not examined it but I take it that you will find some interesting data in it.

CLINTON L. CONKLING TO WEIK, SPRINGFIELD, 31 JULY 1918[37]

The Robert Irwin and the Benjamin F. Irwin about whom you ask are not in any way whatever related.[38]

Robert Irwin was born November the 7th 1808 in Monongahela, Penna. He came west when a young man and married in St. Louis, Mo. Clara C. Doyle, who was born in Philadelphia, Penna, March 9, 1815. He and his wife left St. Louis crossing the Mississippi River on the ice when it was in motion, jumping the open space between the ice and the shore. They came by stage, stopping two nights on the way and arrived in Springfield in January 1834. He had among other children, Robert T. Irwin who died many years ago. Robert Irwin formed a partnership with John Williams as dry-goods merchants soon after he came to Springfield. His brother, John, was admitted to the firm and later the Irwin brothers transacted the business alone, until Robert became connected with the Springfield Fire & Marine Insurance Co. which was in fact a Banking concern in Springfield. He was its Secretary and afterwards Cashier, in which position he continued until his death, March 8, 1865. If you will refer to the history of the Springfield Marine & Fire Insurance Co. (being a Banking concern) of which you have the data, I think you will find more details as to him. He was a warm personal friend of Abraham Lincoln, and together with Jacob and John Bunn were of much assistance to him. He was a very genial man and a good singer and formed one of a group of men who, during the campaign of 1860 took a large part in the local political meetings. He was full of humor and good will. I do not suppose that you care for any further particulars about him. As a boy I knew him well.

Now as to the other person of whom you inquire—Benjamin F. Irwin. His father, Samuel L. Irwin was born June 6, 1879 in Cabarras County, North Carolina. His wife's name was Rachel Hudson of Rockingham County, Virginia. They were married September 23, 1802. In the Fall of 1818 the family moved to Tennessee and from thence to Sangamon County, Illinois, arriving April 20, 1820 and first pitched their tents in the northeast part of what is now the town of Pleasant Plains. After a few months stay they moved a few miles further down Richland Creek where they remained on the farm until his death which occurred March 1, 1845, his widow dying July the 8th 1867, she dying on the same farm where they had lived since 1820. There were fifteen children born to them, of whom the one you inquire about, Benjamin F. Irwin, was born May 18, 1822 in Sangamon County, and was married October 11, 1844 to Jane Combs of Menard County Illinois. Mrs. Jane Irwin died March 7th 1848 and Benjamin F. Irwin was again married January 16th 1870 to Miss Mattie Huber of Florence Kansas. They continued to live at Pleasant Plains. Their son, Edward F. Irwin, is my partner in the law business. Benjamin F. Irwin died at Pleasant Plains, Illinois on January 31st 1902.

The home of Benjamin F. Irwin as a boy and man was about eleven or twelve miles from Old Salem and about thirteen miles from Springfield. The grinding of grain for the use of the Irwin family was done at Old Salem and the boys of this family were more or less frequent visitors there. Benjamin F. Irwin and his brothers in their early manhood hauled merchandise to Springfield, Illinois from Beardstown, Illinois, the river landing to which the goods were shipped form the East. He was intimately acquainted with all of the early settlers of the community and was acquainted with Mr. Lincoln as stated in the letter to which you refer, for twenty-five years prior to his death or from approximately the year 1840.

Mr. Irwin was, the greater part of his life, engaged in farming near Pleasant Plains, Illinois, but took a great interest in politics and did some political campaigning during the early days through central Illinois.

I do not know that he had any opportunity different from other con-temporaries of Mr. Lincoln of knowing Mr. Lincoln's religious views. In fact, in the article to which you refer he used the following language: "I do not personally claim to know anything about Lincoln's religious faith. Though personally acquainted with Lincoln for twenty-five years and often in his office I never heard him say a word on the subject of christianity or religious belief."

The article to which you refer was founded upon statements made by Menter Graham, an early-day schoolmaster, Thomas Mostiller, said to have been a physician, Isaac Cogdall, farmer, and Jonathan Harnett, business man at Pleasant Plains, and Mr. Manford, and Mr. Irwin's statement as to Mr. Lincoln's religious belief was based upon the statements made by men all of whom with the possible exception of Harnett, were more or less intimately associated with him.[39]

Had Mr. Lincoln been a pronounced and outspoken infidel there is no question but what that fact would have been well known to all of those associated with him, as infidelity was not considered any virtue in those days and a man holding infidel views was as publicly marked as a murderer. Mr. Irwin lived within two miles of Peter Cartwright, the Methodist evangelist who was in 1840 campaigning against Mr. Lincoln and was intimately associated and acquainted with Peter Cartwright.[40] Had Peter Cartwright known or believed the statements made in that campaign concerning Lincoln's infidelity, Mr. Irwin would have been thoroughly familiar with Cartwright's views on that question.

[P.S.] My partner gives me the facts about his father.


## James A. Connolly

### James A. Connolly to Weik, Springfield, 7 September 1909[1]

In reply to yours of the 28th ult Concerning Henry B Rankin, I have to say that he lives here, and has been a bedridden invalid for 20 years. He originally lived in the adjoining County of Menard, near the village of Athens.

In his youth he was an office boy in the office of Lincoln and Herndon, and slept in the office. He knew Lincoln as a boy may know a man. He is a man of independant means. He dislikes to say anything about Lincoln that might be quoted in public, and dont like to talk about him with strangers. He is engaged in no business, never goes out, and is but little known, indeed never has been much known in Springfield. He is a man of intelligence, and respectable Character.[2]

I shall be glad to meet you when you are here

### James A. Connolly to Weik, Springfield, 20 November 1911[3]

Since receiving yours of the 11th inst I have made such inquiries as I could from the few old persons here who would be likely to remember anything about your man Beverly Powell. Mr E H Thayer, p[a]st 96 years old, who is a merchant here now, and has been since the late 30s, remembers Powell as a clerk in the store of Speed & Bell.[4] He was a neat dresser, quite a popular fellow with the ladies, attended all the balls and parties, and he remembers one occasion when he and Powell got a team and carriage and went three miles in the country for two sisters whom they escorted to a ball and back home next morning after the ball. Mr Thayer says Powell went back to Kentucky, from whence he came. He probably returned there when the Speed & Bell [store] closed out here, for Speed then returned to Kentucky and likely Powell did too. Nobody else here remembers anything about him.[5] The memory of Mr Thayer is wonderful considering his great age, and everybody here goes to him for authentic information about very ancient Springfield matters.

I enclose three copies of my Peoria Lincoln address, as you request, and am pleased with your opinion of it.

P.S. Mr Thayer also says: "He was a handsome fellow, tall and straight."

JAMES A. CONNOLLY TO WEIK, SPRINGFIELD, 3 JANUARY [1914?][6]

Replying to yours of the 31st ult I have to say that I recieved a note from Mr Pillsbury a few days since in which he told me you had suggested to him that I would like to see it and, if that was so, he would send me a copy. I have not answered him yet but shall do so at once, and tell him I would like very much to see it.

Judge Zane was circuit judge in this circuit 12 years and was regarded as a very good judge.[7] He had been a practicing lawyer here many years before going on the bench. He was rather a chancery lawyer than a common law lawyer. He was not much of a jury lawyer, not an easy fluent talker, but was a quiet respectable character, much respected in the community. When his second term as circuit judge closed here he was appointed territorial judge in Utah, and when the Territory became a State he was elected judge of the Supreme Court of the State and, I think reelected at least once. While on the bench there he rendered some notable decisions on the polygamy matter that brought down on him the hostility of the Mormon church.

He was not regarded as a strong, forceful man. Intellectually he was about an average lawyer, reinforced, of course, by his judicial experience. He never returned to Springfield. I am not sure but what he is living in Utah yet, at Salt Lake City. He has a son, John, a practicing lawyer in Chicago, who is the author of a law book on "Banks and Banking". This son is a bright studious fellow. Judge Zane had no specially intimate acquaintance with Lincoln, simply knew him as scores of other young men of his time here knew him, and never thought of analyzing his mentality during his acquaintance here with him.[8]

INTERVIEW WITH MAJOR JAMES AUSTIN CONNOLLY,<br>SPRINGFIELD, 15 OCTOBER 1914[9]

Born in Ohio – studied law – was an ardent Douglas man and in 1859 set out for Mississippi to practice but after traveling through the south decided I had better return north – finally settled in the fall or winter of 59 in Charleston Ills. In Feby '61 I went down to the railway station to see Mr. Lincoln who was coming on the train from Springfield to visit his mother. When the train arrived the passenger car—it was a mixed train—stopped down the track a good piece and looking down we saw a tall man and several others step down from the car and wade thru the mud beside the track to the station platform. A number of persons were gathered there to see him. I was not favorably impressed, having been a great admirer of Douglas. L's awkward, if not ungainly figure and general make-up failed to attract me. He went with several men to the residence of a kinsman A H Chapman. About dark A. P. Dunbar an older lawyer invited me to accompany him to the Chapman home where he expected to call on Lincoln.[10] We thought we would arrive about the time Mr Lincoln had had his supper. On the way Dunbar expressed his doubt as to how he should address Mr Lincoln. They were old friends & associates but now since Mr L. was Pres elect D. dared not be familiar in addressing him for fear of bad taste. Finally he told his companion that it would depend on Mr L's conduct. If he was stiff formal & dignified D. must act accordingly. When they reached the house, the Chapman family & friends were still at the table eating & Lincoln was in the front room sitting in front of the fire. In answer to Dunbar's knock the door opened & Lincoln appeared. Almost instantly Lincoln grasped his hand and resting his other hand on D's shoulder exclaimed in a burst of animation "Lord A'mighty Aleck. How glad I am to see you." That completely broke the spell. Then I was introduced and we all three took chairs by the fire. Lincoln was unusually cheerful & jubilant and then commencement [commenced] a flow of stories one upon another all funny and entertaining. I never before in my life had heard anything like it. I shall never forget the last one. I cannot reproduce it but it related to a girl who used to milk the cow for Mr Lincoln. One day she rode the horse bare-back to the pasture – on the way home a dog or some like object frightened the horse and he shied etc. Just then some one knocked at the door and while still continuing the narrative he moved to the door—he had just about reached the nub or point of his story—and opened it when lo, there appeared the Presbyterian preacher with his wife & several other ladies. Of course, Mr L. had to change the subject and we never learned what happened to the girl when the horse shied at the dog. Presently other callers arrived & Mr. D & I left. Outside D. said ["]Now you have seen the man whom your friend Douglas defeated. What do you think of him?" I could not help responding "The most remarkable man I ever met."[11]

### George Perrin Davis

GEORGE PERRIN DAVIS, TO [WEIK?], N.P., N.D.[1]

The Eighth circuit, established in 1847, comprised 14 counties, extending on the north from Woodford to the Indiana state line, south as far as Shelby, and the western counties being Sangamon, Logan, and Tazewell. It had nearly 11,000 square miles, or nearly one-fifth of area of the state. A full account can be found in Mr. Prince's introductory [essay] in the third volume of the McLean County Historical society publications, which I advise you to read.[2]

There were no railroads for many years and but few bridges over the rivers. Courts were held in the various counties twice a year, lasting from two or three days to a week. After court had adjourned in one county the judge rode to the next county seat and was followed by the state's attorney, whose authority extended over the whole circuit, and by some of the lawyers to a few of the counties near their homes.

Mr. Lincoln rode the entire circuit to all the courts, which lasted about three months in the spring and three in the fall.

Most of the lawyers rode horseback. After a few years my father, who was the circuit judge, and Mr. Lincoln were able to afford a buggy. My father, who was a very heavy man, used two horses; Mr. Lincoln had a one-horse open buggy and drove his horse, "Old Buck," as I remember his name. In the fall of 1850, when I was eight years old, my mother went around the circuit with my father, and Mr. Lincoln took me in his buggy. I have a distinct recollection of the horse, the buggy and Mr. Lincoln, but nothing of what he said on that trip.

At Danville I saw Judge Oliver L. Davis and Mr. Constable, a lawyer, who wore a long frock coat.[3] I also saw my first coal fire, except in a forge, and amused myself with heating and bending the poker. Whether or not my mother whipped me afterwards I don't remember, but it was very likely, as it was the custom in those days. I recollect being at Paris and Shelbyville, where I saw Judge Anthony Thornton, a prominent lawyer of that part of the state.

At Springfield the state's attorney, Mr. Campbell, gave me some percussion caps, which were a new invention then; these I exploded on the buggy wheel and got some of the copper in my face.[4]

In June, 1856, I heard Mr. Lincoln speak one night from the balcony of the old Pike house, which was situated on the southeast corner of Center and Monroe Streets. I have heard him speak at many political meetings and several trials in court.

Mr. Lincoln was frequently at my father's house, and in 1858 for some time while he was writing some of his debates with Mr. Douglas. On one of his visits I had a new autograph book which he wrote in as follows: "My young friend George Perrin Davis has allowed me the honor of being the first to write his name in this book. Bloomington, Dec. 21, 1858. A. Lincoln."[5]

Mr. Lincoln was very tall, six feet four and one-half inches, as I measured him once, though he gives it himself in his autobiography, addressed to Mr. Jesse W. Fell, as six feet four inches nearly, but when he became much interested in his speech he looked as if he were eight feet high.[6]

He did not care much about dress, though he was always clean. I thought his clothes were too short for him, especially his coat.

For a necktie he wore an old-fashioned stiff stock which clasped around his neck. When he got interested in his speech he would take it off and unbutton his shirt and give room for his Adam's apple to play up and down. He had a clear voice, that could be heard a great distance, every word of a sentence equally clear, a great contrast to Mr Douglas, who failed sometimes to send every word to the same distance.

Mr Lincoln was clean-shaven until he was elected president. There is a very fair picture of him in the book referred to above.

Mr. Lincoln was liked by young and old because he liked both young and old.[7]

## Isaac R. Diller

### Isaac R. Diller, interview with Weik at Diller's
### office, Springfield, 21 November 1916[1]

I. R. Diller said Mrs L very hard to deal with. Said she often bought perfume at father's store & after opening would send back claiming it not good[2] — did not suit — but Roland Diller (father) would not take back and ordered clerks not to do so.[3]

Reason Lincoln so often spent spare time at Diller & Corneaus drug store was because his brother-in-law Dr Wallace was once a partner & for that reason Lincoln was there so often. Wallace partner 37 to 1849[4]

ISAAC R. DILLER TO WEIK, SPRINGFIELD, 29 NOVEMBER 1916[5]

Your favor of 26th inst duly received. I found the paper I spoke about and am sending it by mail today. I see it is getting rotten by standing but you will find the article I referred to on page 16 and the cut of picture on the front of Sec. 2. The ends that were out of the original wrapper collected some dust. I thought there might be some other articles you would be interested in. You may have one of these copies already. I will keep your letter and ask Mr [Josiah P.] Kent[6] the first time I see him about Maria Drake since her marriage if he can get any information about Wm Clarke.[7] I will mail your letter and the picture of the horse to Mr Kent with your stamped envelope and ask him to return the same to you and tell you anything he may know of the Clarke's also if he can identify anyone in the picture. All I know about it is that John Flynn,[8] told me a few years ago that he bought this horse from Mr Lincoln when he went to Washington and that they wanted to use him at the time of the funeral. Mr Flynn died only a few years ago. It may be that Mr Kent may know about the horse also. A few minutes ago Mr Wm Baker came in to see me as he had heard they were trying to locate the Lincoln trail through the town of Lincoln and he wanted to say that was not on his route.[9] You may have met him and there is an article in the paper I am sending from him. I hope you will hear soon from Mr Kent. When I can help any please call on me.

ISAAC R. DILLER TO WEIK, SPRINGFIELD, 21 JUNE 1921[10]

Your favor of 19th received yesterday but I did not get the fuller information until this morning. The facts Mr Pasfield gave were correct as far as they went. The mother of Walter Davis lived nearly back of us and I have known her as far back as I can remember but he died, as his daughter says, soon after Mr Lincoln went on to Washington, as she says the last person Mr Lincoln called on before leaving was her father and he promised to give him some foreign appointment in hopes of the change benefiting his health but he did not live to receive it.[11] He and his brother were in the Mexican War and his brother Tom was killed.[12] She said her father sold his house on Fifth Street to the Helmle's before moving to 5th and Cook Sts where he died. I saw George H. Helmle this morning and he says on the rear of the vacant lot next north was a small shop and it might have been in that he worked at his trade as cabinet maker.[13] W[h]ether that was the shop Mr Lincoln made the model in would be hard to verify but it seems probable.[14] Mr Helmle says his father bought the house in 1852.[15] The present number is 220 South Fifth St. Mrs Clara Davis Hoyt is the name of his daughter and she has a son in the office of the Probate Clerk who was named for his grandfather, Walter Davis Hoyt.[16] If you desire to communicate with Mrs Hoyt her address is #225 Milton Ave. We all miss Mr Conkling in many ways as he was one of Gods noblemen. I met Mr Pasfield on the street and showed him your letter and he was glad to have found the right Davis from the directory account. I wanted him to know how you appreciated his assistance. You need not apoligize for calling on me for any information I can give at any time as it is a pleasure to help even a little along this line.

## WILLIAM D. DONNELLY

### WILLIAM D. DONNELLY, UNDATED MEMO[1]

Wm D. Donnelly born Nov 1841

Kept ball alley – Lincoln plug hat narrow rim. Club of lawyers built alley. Hand ball alley. John Carmody irishman owned building across alley from Journal office – general store[2] – Ball players paid if lost 10¢ ea[ch] – if won Nothing – game was to keep ball going – if failed constituted a point – 21 points a game Hand ball was an Irish game – threw ball against wall & catch when rebounded – floor kept level Y scraped like a brick yard –[3]

### [ADJACENT MEMO]:

William Donnelly

J W Reynolds kept ball alley & chgd for it – called Hand Ball – lawyers often played[4] – L. had large hands & loved to play. Donnelly kept the alley Carmody owned the place

## DENNIS HANKS DOWLING

### DENNIS HANKS DOWLING TO WEIK,
### CHARLESTON, ILLINOIS, 5 MARCH 1915[1]

Mr Alex Briggs handed me your letter with the request that I look up the matter of Mr Lincoln's visit to Charleston in 1861[2] – In accordance with request I have interviewed several of our older citizens and particularly Mrs A H Chapman and my sister Mrs E H Clark both of whom were relatives of Mr Lincoln and were present at the reception and neither of whom have any recollection of meeting or seeing any [such] distinguished gentlemen of National Reputation or prominence as Mr Edward Bates, from the best information I can gather Mr Lincoln was accompanied by two correspondents of City papers and I have no doubt one of them was Mr Nicolay – Mr T A Marshall was not one of the party that left Springfield but was present when Mr Lincoln arrived in Charleston. A late dinner and reception was held at residence of Col Chapman and a later reception was held in Town Hall – after which Mr Lincoln passed the night at the residence of Col T A Marshall – Next Morning Col Chapman drove him down 6 miles in the Country to see his stepmother[3]

PS The Reporter of the State Register may have been right as to Mr Edward Bates leaving Springfield with the president and party[4] This could be explained as Mr Bates could have left the party at any change of cars

### DENNIS HANKS DOWLING TO WEIK,
### CHARLESTON, ILLINOIS, 28 MARCH 1915[5]

I have complied with your letter of request dated March 15th A D 1915.

I called on my Aunt Mrs A H Chapman and after an interview at some length I am sorry to inform you that I could gain no information as to the trip of the Lincoln family through Indiana after leaving Spencer County for Vincennes. Mrs Chapman was but a child five years of age and of course could not remember very much about the route.[6] However as to your other question Mrs Chapmans memory was quite clear – she informed me that she made the trip to Springfield Ill with Mr Lincoln about the year 1845 in single buggy with one horse the same rig used by Mr Lincoln when making the circuit while attending the courts in different parts of the state. The Route taken was what was called the Springfield trace (now called State Street in Charleston) thence westerly by dead man's grove about 7 or 8 miles West of Charleston – They started early in the morning and reached Springfield in the afternoon of the next day – They stoped one night on the way at the home of a friend of Mr Lincoln but Mrs Chapman does not remember the name of this friend.

She also stated that at that time she was making her home with her father and mother in Charleston when Mr Lincoln came for her—she did not state of any towns they passed through in making the trip but that the route was the one usually traveled and it was undoubtedly the Stage route.[7]

P.S. I am in receipt of the report of the board of trustees of the Ill His Library Investigation of the Lincoln way and of the final location of the route in Illinois – I am well pleased with the report for it confirms the statement of my mother who was one of the party and 9 years of age at that time and which was published in the Springfield News about twelve years ago—long time before the agitation of the Lincoln way[8] My Mother was quite positive as to the route, after leaving Palistine Ill they went North-

Westerly and direct to old Paradise or what was then called Wabash point about four miles south of Mattoon. The reason they went that way was because Mrs Hannah Radley an own sister of Sarah Bush Lincoln (her name was Hannah Bush before she married Ichabod Radley) was living at paradise and it would be unreasonable to suppose that Mrs Lincoln and party would not call on her sister in going to and returning from Decatur as the route was almost in direct line[9]

### Elizabeth Edwards

#### EDWARDS ELIZABETH, UNDATED INTERVIEW WITH WEIK[1]

Mrs Edwards says

Mrs L loved fine clothes and was so close or economical at the kitchen that she might have money for luxuries. Had servants only when company came. She had high temper and after her outburst normally was penitent. If she punished children would seek to make amends by presents and affectionate treatment. Was economical even requiring Robert to wash dishes etc.

### Annie M. Fleury

#### ANNIE M. FLEURY TO WEIK, SPRINGFIELD, 29 APRIL 1918[1]

Your letter received which I will try to answer to the best of my ability with the proviso that my name will not be mentioned. I remember very well my father going to Washington to get an appointment for Mr Charles W Chatterton as Indian agent but could not say that Mr Chatterton went with him as I do not know. My fathers wife (my Step Mother) and Mrs Chatterton were Sisters the daughters of Major Miles of Petersburg: my father also got Major Miles appointed Post-Master.[2] Mr Chatterton and wife died very near together leaving two daughters one of which died very young, and the other is a widow living in Petersburg she is Mrs Julia Levering she has two sons Mrs Chatterton I think is buried in Petersburg. I have a faint recollection that Mr C. was killed out there in some way I could not tell you this for the truth as I was married soon after my father and moved to Bloomington Ill so was not thrown much with my Step-Mothers people. There are still several [friends?] of the Miles in Petersburg. I hope this will do you some good it is a long time since I have had these things brought to mind and when one gets as old as I am they forget. I have been out to see the Monument and am very much pleased with it it is beautiful, wish I could thank every one that gave to it. I wish you every Success.

## Frederick Dent Grant

### FREDERICK DENT GRANT TO WEIK,
### GOVERNORS ISLAND, NEW YORK, 2 FEBRUARY 1911[1]

In reply to your letter of the 31st of January inclosing a letter of introduction from General Jesse M. Lee, I write to say that the reason my father and mother declined the invitation of President and Mrs. Lincoln to attend the performances at Ford's Theatre on the evening of April 14, 1865, was the intense desire of both my father and mother to go to our home at Burlington, N. J. and see their children, from whom they had been separated for several months.

As to the statement in the papers that morning that my parents would attend the theatre party, it was undoubtedly due to the press having been furnished with the list of guests who would be invited, as is customary, and the natural inference that the invitation would be accepted. However, when my father received the invitation, sometime in the forenoon of that day, all his arrangements had been made to leave Washington, and he begged the President to excuse him from his theatre party.[2]

## Charles H. Gray

### CHARLES H. GRAY, UNDATED INTERVIEW WITH WEIK[1]

Father [Isaac H. Gray] owned American House in Springfield[2]

Saw Lincoln playing ball when news of nomination [was brought to him]

## B. A. Harvey

### B. A. HARVEY TO WEIK, MT. CARMEL, ILLINOIS, 19 JANUARY 1914[1]

The letter, herewith handed to me for reply has been held for some days, that I might better obtain information. But, I have been thus far, unable to ascertain more than as follows.

Judge E. B. Green informs me, that Mrs Hay, of Carmi, Illinois, a very old woman, and still living told him, that in the year 1840, she accompanied her father and Abraham Lincoln to Mt. Carmel Ill; that they drove through from Carmi in a buggy, and that Lincoln made a speech in front of the Old Market House, which then stood in the streets at the crossing of Third and Market Streets in Mr. Carmel, and this was in the year eighteen forty.[2]

Mr Thomas McGregor of this city, informs me that one Kaleb Lingenfelter, now deceased, had often remarked to him and others, that he,

Lingenfelter, had heard Abraham Lincoln make a speech in Mr. Carmel, and while not certain as to date, fixes it at about 1858.

I have lived here all my life, and was eight years of age in 1858, and would certainly know, had Lincoln made a speech here in 1858, and I have been unable to find any one to verify the above statements, or that Lincoln was ever in Mt. Carmel.

### Robert Roberts Hitt

ROBERT ROBERTS HITT TO WEIK, WASHINGTON, 30 MARCH 1895[1]

You are correct in supposing, as you do in yours of the 25th, that I took down the Lincoln-Douglas debates of 1858 for the "Press and Tribune;" and James B. Sheridan reported those of Judge Douglas for the "Times."[2] Mr. Sheridan was, I believe, a Philadelphian in origin; was in Washington a good deal at the opening of the war; was afterward a paymaster, which gave him the rank of major; subsequent to the war was a stenographer and lawyer in New York, and some years later became judge of the Surrogate's Court. I have not heard of him for a good many years. I have no picture of the time of which you speak, but I send you one taken a few years ago, which I suppose is fair as such things go.

### Clara Davis Hoyt

MRS CLARA DAVIS HOYT TO WEIK, SPRINGFIELD, 10 SEPTEMBER 1921[1]

Your letter of June 22nd received & I am just answering it. In answer to your questions regarding my father Walter Davis, I will say, my father was a cabinet maker & he had a shop at #220 South 5th Street. He was born Feb 5th 1817 in Richmond Virginia, & died Jan 6th 1861 in Springfield Ills.[2] This is all I am able to inform you about at present should I glean anything more I will be glad to inform you concerning same. Mr Lincoln & my father were very close friends, & my father was the last person that he called on before his leave for Washington the first time at his residence on South 5th & Cook Street, one block south of the governors mansion, at 5th & Edwards.[3]

### Ephraim Fletcher Ingals

EPHRAIM FLETCHER INGALS TO WEIK, CHICAGO, 28 FEBRUARY 1894[1]

The error to which I alluded in Herndons Lincoln is on page 115 & 116 Vol I[2] – The story as always narrated in our family was as follows. Dr

Charles Chandler lived many years on Sangamon Bottom twenty miles above Beardstown, where Chandlerville now is.[3] He was a physician of wide reputation, of remarkable energy, & the most wealthy man in that section. My brother Henry L. Ingals,[4] who was Chandlers brother & [in] law lived on his farm that adjoined Chandlers.[5] He was in every respect quite the reverse of Dr. Chandler—poor & easy going. He settled there in 1832 & Mr. Lincoln surveyed his land. A [section of] forty acres of land near their farms was coveted by both Chandler & Ingalls. My brother did not spell his name as you may notice I do mine. Both set out for Springfield—forty miles away—at near the same time. Chandler had talked of buying a horse about half the distance to Springfield, when he reached this place he told the man he would take the horse at his price, mounted him & pushed on for Springfield. When he reached the city the land office was not open. He was too impulsive to wait & had too much business to afford to do so, & leaving $50 with an agent with instructions to buy the land when the office was open he set out for home. On his way he soon met my brother plodding along towards Springfield & he asked him if he was going to enter that land. My brother said "*no*" & they parted. When the office was opened he was there. Fifty dollars was the minimum price for forty acres, but it was offered at public sale & my brother bid an advance. The agent had neither authority or money to pay more & of course it was struck off to my brother. Chandler was a passionate man & was very angry. When he met my brother, he said, why did you lie to me about that land. My brother said I did not lie to you. Chandler said You told me you were not going to buy it. I know it, said my brother, but you had no business to ask me such a question. My brothers reply very much pleased the family, & I for one justified him for making it. A Mr. Clark—his Christian name I have now forgotten—told me he loaned Mr. Lincoln money to buy a suit of clothing when he first went to the legislature & that he took his compass as security.[6] The biography says the loan was from some other person.[7] I am sure Mr. Lincoln had nothing to do about the land purchase. I saw this account in a newspaper many years ago & sent it to my brother Henry L in Minnesota, where he then lived. I did not know it was in the biography until my late reading. The anecdotes I have not time to write, but will try & send to you when I have more leisure. Should you be in Chicago I shall be pleased to see you if you can find leisure to call

UNDATED MEMO ON STATIONERY OF EPHRAIM INGALS[8]

Chicago Ills. – friend took him down to Ill Cen RR. & introduced him to colored porter on sleeping car saying "I brought my friend Lincoln down to you to ride with you, as he is a friend of your people & would make you free if he could." Later this friend saw the porter who told him L. called for a darning needle, saying these pillows are so small and my ears so large I fear I might need a needle to pick one out of the other.

### MOORE, UNDATED MEMO ON STATIONERY OF
### EPHRAIM INGALS, M.D., OF CHICAGO[9]

Moore – no legs – girl falling down & showing short legs at N B Judd's residence[10] – reminded of man Moore – at Springfield whose legs were so short when he walked in snow the seat of his trousers wiped up his foot-prints.[11]

### UNDATED MEMO ON STATIONERY OF EPHRAIM INGALS[12]

E. B. Stiles—Dixon Ill.

Day S. C. seceded, S. called at L's office in Springfield. Stiles announced to L. who was sitting on chair made of rails supposed to have been split by Lincoln given by a friend with names of states carved on rounds of chair – story of girl in Indiana – who one [day?] asked of her fam – [deliver?] to young man – who to overcome her by argument appealed [to] her sense of justice [she?] allowed other persons. "What man" She answered "Why John –" was the response. "No" she retorted "he didn't do it; he only thought he did."

## WILLIAM JAYNE

### WILLIAM JAYNE TO WEIK, SPRINGFIELD, 26 DECEMBER 1895[1]

I am in receipt of your letter of Dec 23rd. Neither your letter or Mr Lincolns to Judd, states just what W. H Herndon is alledged to have said about N B Judd.[2] It is difficult for me to tell what he may have said to me concerning Judd, which he Judd complained of. But I can likely explain the nature of the complaint.

N B Judd Leonard Sweet & Richard Yates were all candidates for Governor.[3] Dubois[4] & Butler[5] were respectively candidates for renomination for Auditor & Treasurer. They desired the aid of Judd in Cook & other northern counties, where Judd's influence was very strong & consequently Dubois & Butler favored Judd as the candidate for Governor. Lincoln I have no doubt was in favor of Judds nomination, yet I would say with his discretion & good common sense I would say that he Lincoln was not very loud or boisterous about his preference. The other candidates for Governor were also good republicans & friends of Mr Lincoln. W H Herndon was in favor of Yates for governor, but as a partner of Mr Lincoln he was not very noisy about it. Mr Judd was over sensitive about any preference shown to either Yates or Swett. I was equally favorable to Yates & Butler, so that I was willing that Judd should have some votes in State Convention from Sangamon, if thereby Butler was benefited by Judds friends in the north. Our county gave Yates 10 votes & Judd 5 votes of course for Treasurer Butler had our entire vote, 15

I was a delegate, I believe Herndon was also Mr Herndon had the same right to favor Yates, which Lincoln had to favor Judd. Yates was raised in our county—he then lived in Jacksonville in the adjoining county of Morgan I shall be pleased to see you & give you any information I can about W H Herndon. He was a marked man of profound convictions, he was intense & radical on the slavery question—if not more advanced, he was more pronounced in his views than Mr Lincoln at an early day

WILLIAM JAYNE TO WEIK, SPRINGFIELD, 13 NOVEMBER 1907[6]
I am in receipt of your letter of the 12th & note your enquiry about General Adams & [Erskine?] Douglas.

I have no knowledge of [Erskine?] Douglas—if he ever lived here—he left no trace as a lawyer—for I personally knew ever[y] lawyer who lived here between 1830 & 1850.

James Adams came to Springfield from New York in 1821. He was elected Justice of [the] Peace in 1823 or 1824 & successively reelected for some years.

He was elected Probate Judge early in the thirties & continued in office up to his death in 1843. He was not regarded highly as a lawyer, but was thought well of generally – had strong enemies & strong friends – had a bitter controversy with Lincoln – was charged by Lincoln with forgery of a deed.[7] He has a grandson living here now—a man sixty years of age—a good citizen & he has a son in the Navy

WILLIAM JAYNE TO WEIK, SPRINGFIELD, 31 AUGUST 1908[8]
I am in receipt of your letter of the 28th.

I have no idea of what Mr Lincoln refered to in his letter to Judd.

I have no recollection of anything Mr Herndon could have said to me about Judd.

It might have been to Judd choice for President between Seward & Lincoln.

Might have been to Lincoln choice for nomination for Governor. In 1860, Judd, Swett & Yates were all candidates for republican nomination for Governor. Lincoln may have proposed Judd. But if he did, he was not active in his support, so far as I know. As he was a close friend of each of the candidates, it is likely he said little about the nomination of either one. Herndon was for Yates, as our county was. Elliott Herndon was a brother of William H.[9] He was a good lawyer, had no children. Elliott was as pro Slavery in his views, as William was a radical republican.

Elliott did not estimate Lincoln as a great lawyer. Never thought as high of him as others members of our city bar, intellectually or legally.

I should be pleased to see you any time & talk with you about Lincoln & the politics of 50 years ago

## EDWARD S. JOHNSON

### EDWARD S. JOHNSON TO WEIK, SPRINGFIELD, 9 JANUARY 1914[1]

Your letter came yesterday. Glad to hear from you and to learn that we may look for you in Springfield in the near future. How fast the years are passing. Thirty years must have elapsed since your first visit to our City when a member of Major [Gelliock's?] party and in the government service. I remember it was quite a large party and I often think of the members composing that company of pension examiners.

Erastus Wright spoken of in your letter I knew well. He was a customer of mine when engaged in the lumber and coal business in the 60's and 70's.[2] I think it was in 71 that the old gentleman committed suicide by placing his head upon the rail of the Alton track quite near the grain elevator and just west one block of the Revere. A few minutes before he came into my office and settled a coal bill. It was at my father's tavern that Herndon speaks of, the old City Hotel and afterward the Chenery House. My father sold to Mr Chenery in 1856.[3] The location of this hotel was on 4th and Washington, opposite the Revere your home while in S. Hotels in those days though named were styled or called taverns by many of our people. My father having sold to Mr Chenery in 1856, the incident referred to by Mr Herndon must have occurred prior to that date. Yes Wright was a cold, selfish man. He was a widower for many years but married again in the 60's. He was unhappy in this marriage and I believe for some time previous to his death had separated from his wife and had been living or making his home with his son-in-law, R. Johnston.[4] I think this wife must have been 30 years younger than Mr. W.[5] The *new* hotel Mr Herndon mentioned must have been none other but the Chenery House my father's old (City) hotel. The only hotels at that time were the American, Chenery, and the Globe. The American was conducted by Mr Chenery prior to his taking charge of our (City) hotel. Isaac H. Gray was the proprietor of the Globe but was named the National during his management.

When you come to town you will find me here at the tomb of Lincoln, where I have been for the past 18 years. My predecessor, Jno Carroll Power was custodian for 20 years.[6] The present new administration does not, I believe, look upon this position as a political place and on that account I do not expect to be disturbed.[7]

I thank you ever so much for your good wishes and for you and yours for the New Year I hope you will have plenteous prosperity and good health.

### EDWARD S. JOHNSON TO WEIK, SPRINGFIELD, 19 OCTOBER 1916[8]

Yesterday I omitted to tell you the Revere House was a business block at the time Mr Lincoln occupied the rooms as shown in the picture inclosed herewith. It had a frontage on Washington Street of nearly 100 feet and depth on Fourth Street of only 45 feet. In 1866 my father, Joel Johnson, built an addition on the north side fronting on 4th St and the whole property was converted into a hotel and named the Revere House upon my suggestion.

You, no doubt, will remember the rooms used as parlors when you were a guest a good many years ago. They were the rooms occupied by Mr Lincoln for Reception rooms just prior to his departure for Washington. Our little family occupied all of the 2d floor and the building was known as Johnson's Building or Block before it became a hotel, in 1866.

### JOSIAH P. KENT

#### JOSIAH P. KENT, INTERVIEW WITH WEIK AT I. R. DILLER'S
#### OFFICE, SPRINGFIELD, 21 NOVEMBER 1916[1]

Lived next to Lincoln – boys would hide and with a long lath when lying on bank of earth through a crack knock off hats of passers by. Late one evening saw plug hat but could not tell whose – knocked it off – proved to be Lincolns who stopped picked it up and gave boys mild reproof – saying next man might not let them off so well.

While Rob[er]t at college slept in R's room – tended to horse and drove Mrs L in carriage – One day Kent wanted to borrow horse & carriage [to] go driving. Asked Mr. L. who said 2 things he would not loan—wife & carriage—Lincoln Dubois along – Lincoln told Kent could have horse & harness – got spring wagon – Willie Lincoln along[2] – horse ran away – dumped boys out scratched Willie Lincoln up – Irishman who caught asked Kent if Abe L. was on his way to brewery – as horse ran in that direction

Harrison Gourley[3] – Bob L. took Ls carriage to country against orders of L – Kent was with them—broke down in buggy – took to blacksmith who [would?] & [boys?] painted black & Bob threw dust on [paint] to make look old so that A. L. would not notice & never heard anything from it

Mariah Drake who afterward married Wm Clark conductor on Wabash RR. was servant of Mrs Lincoln

Kent often hauled Mrs L. in carriage while making calls. Mrs L. was turbulent – loud – always yelling at children – could hear her blocks away & furious temper – put on plenty style but stingy & short in dealing with people

Mrs L made Myers who sold ice mad – charged that he was swindling her in weight – Myers got mad – cursed – and vowed she should never get ice again – Refused to come in her part of town – Myers cursed her like a man. Mrs L offered K. 25 ct if he would see Myers & try to induce him to make up with Mrs L and buy ice – succeeded. Mr L also offered K another 25 ct for driving Mrs L around in carriage – Circus coming. Mrs had not paid. Kent told Lincoln Dubois & latter said why not dun the old man.[4] – One day followed L & Dubois said now ask him. K. mustered up courage and asked L. who paid 50 ct and 25 ct extra for interest, but when K. reached home his mother made him take money back & give to Mrs L. Latter said she had given money to Bob but when K. told her Bob had not paid she became angry and shouted "Dont you tell me Bob didnt pay you["] – but K still insists Bob never paid

House immediately north of L. occupied by the Allsops.[5] Ed. Alsopp chum of Robert killed during war at Murfreesboro.[6] Younger brother named Henry[7]

JOSIAH P. KENT TO WEIK, ILLIOPOLIS, ILLINOIS, 3 DECEMBER 1916[8]

I am in receipt of note & enclosed letter from Mr Diller in which some enquiries are made regarding the Lincoln folks. Mr Diller refered your letter to me.

I cannot recognize any one of the persons in the picture. (The print is very indistinct.

The Horse that I cared for and drove many times during the years 1858– 59 & 60 and the only horse Lincoln owned then was a bright Bay, about sixteen one half hands and was called Tom. *Not Bob.* I don't believe – Mr Lincoln used Tom to ride. In 1856 Lincoln owned another horse. He was also a bay, but somewhat smaller than Tom and was an aged horse at that time.

I don't know what became of the Clarks – soon after the war they left Springfield. In 1878 I met Wm. Clark in Springfield. He was then under the influence of liquor and I did not learn of the whereabouts of his wife who was Maria Drake and worked for Mrs Lincoln during the time I lived there.[9]

I have not seen or heard from Mr or Mrs Clark since that time.

Sorry I cannot give you more aid

JOSIAH P. KENT TO WEIK, ILLIOPOLIS, ILLINOIS, 28 MARCH 1917[10]

Yours of the 27th before me. I am pleased to hear from you, and would inform you that I live in the above named town, at present & would be pleased to meet you at your convenience, here at any afternoon you may designate (I am sometime at the farm during the morning.)

Since meeting you I have tried to trace Mrs. Wm Clark (Maria Drake) but without avail. Time and circumstances seems to have completely obliterated all knowledge of the whereabouts of those people.

Clark was a Sober Steady man up to the time He left the G.W.R.R. and was a conductor of a freight train. He married Miss Drake 1860 or 1861. Mrs Lincoln seemed much concerned to loose Her as a servant and I remember Mrs. Lincoln asking me about Clark.

Clark was a rather frail man physicaly.

I last met him during the Murphy Temperance crusade of 1878 He was intoxicated then and showed strong marks of dissipation.

## GEORGE C. LATHAM

### STATEMENT OF GEORGE C. LATHAM, 24 JANUARY 1918[1]

On arriving in Washington, D. C., I went to the Willard House and stayed there, and after the Inauguration I went to the White House and spent a week there. Mr. Buchanan was still at the White House when we arrived in Washington, so for that reason we could not go there until after the Inauguration. I do not know where the balance of the party who went to Washington, stayed.

One newspaper clipping which I have said that Mrs. Lincoln was to join Mr. Lincoln and party at Indianapolis the next morning and that she was coming from the west. Another paper said she was going to come from St. Louis and join Mr. Lincoln and party at Indianapolis. I am rather of the opinion that she did go to St. Louis, probably to do some shopping, and from there went to Indianapolis. Of this however, I am not certain.

Mrs. Grimsley, a cousin of the Lincolns, whom they called "Cousin Lizzie" was also at the White House while I was there.[2] When she got there I do not know, but I know she was there during my visit.

## John M. Lockwood

JOHN M. LOCKWOOD TO WEIK, MOUNT VERNON, INDIANA, 4 JANUARY 1896[1]

I have your favor of December 31st 1895    Contents noted, you ask me to write to you a statement about A. Lincoln in an early day having come to Princeton to get some wool carded.[2] In the month of August 1827 about 1 oclock P.M a tall beardless long legged Boy dressed in a suit of Jeans which looked to be about two thirds worn out, pants, if ever they were of full length he had out grown them a wool hat and coarse country shoes as he laid down his sack of wool I walked forward and spoke to him he said I want this wool carded    I told him this is like going to the Mill    People take turns,    where are you from    Spencer County.    As you are from a distance I will card your wool directly    how long will I have to wait    two hours    stepping to the desk I asked him what is your name    he said A. Lincoln    making the letter A    a stop then    how do you spell Lincoln he spelled Lincoln    will you pay for the carding in money or take toll out his reply was take toll out    This long legged quick speaking beardless country Boy then went out, walking east, in the middle of the street    we had no side walks then    One of the handsomest girls in Princeton Age 17 or 18 after shopping was returning home west    as she passed A Lincoln she spoke a pleasant evening to him. A little further on he met a Farmer and asked him do you know that young Lady    yes her name is Evans    No wonder Lincoln's heart when pitty pat    In about two hours he returned his wool was carded into rolls and pinned up with thorns leaving two ends of the sheet sticking out    he had 18 Lbs of wool    I tolled it 3 Lbs    the rate for carding was 1/6th or 6 1/4 cents per Lb    he said good evening picked up his bundle and carried it out layed it on the top of a rail fence got on his Horse rode up to the bundle took it on behind him and rode off.    Time passed on as no News Papers were then Published in Gibson Posey Vanderburg Warrick or Spencer County I lost sight of the Boy A. Lincoln for 33 years.    some enterprising men had commenced publishing weekly papers, two in Evansville William Town a Whig in the month of April 1834 published a small weekly paper named Evansville Journal & General advertizer in 6 months after this a Mr Rhodes & Pond Published a Democrat Weekly Paper These papers gave us the news    As I had lost trace of the long legged Boy from August 1827 to 1860 a period of 33 years, the above named papers stated that his residence was in Illinois and that he was a Candidate for President of these United States    This was 33 years after his trip to Princeton    I was much surprised that the 6 foot country Boy that had out grown his Pants wanted to be President    I decided quickly if living he was certain to get my vote    The newspapers reported that he was

making stump speaches through the State one to be made at Mt Carmel
or near the Wabash in Ill. Many of the Citizens of Princeton went to the
speaking    among the croud that went was Dr. Lewis[3]    The immense
croud was well pleased    After the speaking Abe Lincoln as he was then
called was introduced to all of the leading men and said to Doctor Lewis
where are you from    Princeton Indiana    Oh said Abe that reminds me
of my first Love    I took a sack of wool in my Boyhood days to the Evans
carding machine to be carded    as I had to wait for the work to be done up I
walked up the Street & passed a Miss Evans the most beautiful young Lady I
ever saw and for two years scarcely a day passed that she was out of my mind
I had determined to return to Princeton and get an introduction to my first
love. Sad to relate some little bird about 6 months after this whispered in
his Ear that she was married to Silas Stephens and moved to Evansville[4]
Doctor Lewis returned from the speaking told his wife and others what Mr
Lincoln had said about his first Love[5]    she said it was Melissa her older
Sister for she was caled the Handsomest girl in town    James Evans had
but the two daughters[6]    Melisa had departed this life before the Doctor
ever saw her    as he was delighted to think his Wifes Sister was the one
tha[t] Lincoln fell in love with I dare not whisper in his ear that it was her
Cousin Julia Evans Daughter of General Evans[7]    one more item about
the Lincoln Family may be of interest    in the Spring of 1831 I took a flat
boat load of ear corn out of Patoka River down to Vicksburg hired Peter
Hanks to stear the boat[8]    he lived west of Princeton    he told me that
Tom Lincoln married his sister Nancy Hanks.[9] He said I hear they have a
smart boy caled Abe    I have not seen them for over 15 years when I return
I will make them a visit    Peter was about 38 years old Height five feet 9
inches weight one hundred and eighty lbs, Black eyes dark hair and thin
beard

The pionear Parents and Children emegrating to southern Indiana from
1816 to 1830

There is so much sameness in Pionear life that my age is about all that
may be of interest    I was born in Westchester County New York on
Sunday the twenty fourth of April 1809. Early in the spring of 1818 Thre[e]
Familys left New York going West in Wagons to Pitsburg purchased a Flat
boat and floted down the Ohio river to Evansville    they did not se[e] or
here of a Steam boat from Pitsburg to Evansville From there to Princeton
Ind[i]ana in wagons arrived in the Month of July. That more and time
pas[s]ed on getting older I learned to be a wool carder in James Evans
carding Machine at Princeton    Hoping that in the ending of time all of

the Sons and Daughters of Adam may hav[e] a Home in Paradice for ever
and ever[10]


## W. E. LOOMIS

### W. E. LOOMIS TO WEIK, SPRINGFIELD, 8 MAY 1912[1]

Dr. J[ayne] declares that there were three groomsmen and a like number
of bridesmaids at the Lincoln wedding but he don't remember the name
of the clerk etc who was one of said groomsmen [Beverly Powell]; but says
that he was a very fine looking young man.[2] Wish that you would write me
the name of said clerk as I have not been able to find your letter that had
it in – as I remember.

### W. E. LOOMIS TO WEIK, SPRINGFIELD, 10 OCTOBER 1912[3]

In reply to your two letters I have to say that John W Bunn was away from
the city so much & often that I did not get to see him until recently and he
said that Mr Lincoln had gotten up the Peoples Convention in 1857 to defeat
the democrats here.[4] That Lincoln was to make the nomination speech of
Mr Bunn as candidate for city treasurer and while Mr Bunn was waiting
anxiously & wondering why Mr Lincoln did not put in his appearance a
young attorney from Mr Lincolns office arose in the convention and placed
Mr Bunn in nomination[5] But Mr Bunn said he did not know said attorney
or his name that he soon after left here for the southern U.S So you see I
was lost to know what to do until some 10 days ago I met Dr Jayne and
he did not know said attorney but that some of Mr Lincoln office fellows
boarded among the Enoses so I began a search among them and succeeded
day before yesterday in learning that the attorneys name was W. Gibson
Harris and that he went from here & located in Cincinnati Ohio where
Mr Lincoln visited him but Harris soon lost his health and moved to and
became a resident of Holly Hill Florida where he died in December 1911
leaving a daughter there by the name of Mrs M. H. Carter. But I have had
the worst time in finding the date of death of Jacob Bunn. I called upon
John W Bunn 3 times and Jacob Bunns son in the bank here 5 times and
once or twice as I met him on the street to receive the word that they had
forgotten the date but would let me know the next day. I stopped John
W. Bunn on the street this morning and went to see the son at the bank
to be put off as usual I went to the court house and examined the estate
records to find that no administration had been had there I examined a
county history of our leading citizens and nothing of him. About half an
hour ago I found Jacob Bunn at the watch factory and he was not certain,

but would ascertain and phone me right away; which he has and gives me the date as October 17, 1897. Miss Susan Enos has a group containing a picture of said W. Gibson Harris James H. Matheney Zimri Enos and one of the famous Backer boys.[6] All young men then. I am glad to finally serve you as aforesaid. Try me again etc

## Hugh McLellan

Your letter to my father, Charles W. McLellan, concerning the banking habits of Mr. Lincoln, was received by him shortly before his death.[2] I was with him at the time, and although he was too ill to write himself, he dictated to me the following, which, with other notes which he intended to incorporate into his reply to your letter, I made a memorandum of.

Father dictated: "As I remember it was quite the custom of Mr. Lincoln to come to the Ridgely Bank to get checks cashed; but I should judge that if he had any regular Bank (account) it would have been with the Springfield Marine & Fire Insurance Company, because Mr. Robert Irwin, who was the Secretary of the Bank (banking department) was his most particular friend.[3] Mr. Lincoln at one time remarked, after he was president, that he [']would cut off his right hand if Robert Irwin asked him to do it.[']" (Said on the occasion of the appointment of George Dennison to Naval Office of New York, which was made at the request of Mr. Irwin.)[4]

Father also told me to write you that he was in Springfield from May 28, 1856 to October 10, 1860. Also that the banking institutions at that time were:

Springfield Marine & Fire Insurance Co.
Jacob Bunn.
N. H. Ridgely & Co. Later became the Ridgely National Bank.
John Williams & Co., who besides being a general goods merchant
     kept the cash accounts of many of the large farmers around; after
     the war formed into the First National Bank.

In 1860, James Campbell (formerly of Ridgely's) was agent for the Old State Bank of Illinois, and probably had a desk in Ridgely's bank.

In connection with the Dennison appointment, Father thought it might interest you to know that the "old friend who has served me all my life, and who has never before received or asked anything in return" mentioned in Mr. Lincoln's letter to Sec. Chase, May 18, 1861, was Robt. Irwin.

I am glad to add that Father was much interested in learning, through the article you kindly sent him, that finally the grave of Mr. Herndon is appropriately marked.

As I shared with Father his devotion to Lincoln and his zeal in the collecting of Lincolniana, the many happy hours we spent together over his collection are very precious memories to me. He left, in his diaries and letters, and in a manuscript book of recollections, much that may prove to be of historic value and interest.

I find from this book that Father arrived in Springfield, Ill., on May 28, 1856 to take the position of book-keeper in the store of Charles R. Hurst at a salary of $500 a year.[5] In the following September he accepted an offer of $600 a year from John Williams & Co. (mentioned above) and in the beginning of 1857 he went with N. H. Ridgely & Co. bankers with whom he remained until he left Springfield for Mobile, Ala. in September 1860.

I trust that the above notes will be of use to you, and beg that you will pardon this long delay in replying to your letter, in the writing of which I have been often interrupted, but my time has been so fully occupied that I am just beginning to fulfill duties long over-due. Father was ill from the 10th of January to the 11th of March, when he was taken from us; during all this time I was constantly with him.

## HENRY A. MELVIN

### HENRY A. MELVIN TO WEIK, SAN FRANCISCO, 1 NOVEMBER 1915[1]

In reply to yours of October 25th, let me assure you that the notes of Mr. Lincoln's lecture on "Discoveries and Inventions" published recently by my friend John Howell are genuine. The manuscript has been in the possession of our family since the year 1865. My father gave it to me just before his death in 1898.[2] Attached to it is my father's account of the manner in which he obtained it.[3] This is published by Mr. Howell. In it he described an occasion, just after Mr. Lincoln's election, when they met one evening at Dr. Todd's home. Mr. Lincoln on this occasion left with Mrs. Grimsley a valise containing some of his manuscripts. He called this his "literary bureau" and told Mrs. Grimsley that if he ever returned to Springfield he would claim it but if not she might make such disposition of the papers as seemed best to her. Shortly after the President's death, she gave my father a bundle supposed to be the manuscript of one lecture on "Discoveries and Inventions". In reality it contained notes of two lectures on the same subject.[4] One of these manuscripts some years later went into the collection of Mr. Gunther,[5] the other has remained in my father's and my own possession. It was never published until 1909 when I allowed the late Charles S. Aiken to print the text in *Sunset Magazine*.[6]

Doubtless my father was the former citizen of Springfield to whom Mr. Herndon referred.

We have other prized memorials of the great President. My sister Mrs. Dewing of Oakland has an autograph written for my mother, I think in the year 1864.[7] My brother James B. Melvin has a chess table which belonged to Mr. Lincoln and a document signed by him less than a month before his death.[8] Mr. Lincoln and my father used to play chess on this table and after it had been moved to my father's office, he and Col. U. S. Grant (then recruiting regiments at Springfield) used it for the same purpose. Mrs. Charles S. Melvin of Oakland, widow of another of my brothers, possesses a "whatnot" which was Lincoln's and the bill of sale of certain furniture purchased by my father from him after his election.[9] I have a big wardrobe that used to be in Mr. Lincoln's bedroom in Springfield. It is too massive for modern rooms so I have loaned it to the Municipal Museum in Oakland, the city in which Dr. Melvin passed the last twenty years of his useful and honored life.

## JOHN G. NICOLAY

### JOHN G. NICOLAY TO WEIK,
### WASHINGTON, 25 NOVEMBER 1894[1]

Yours of November 19th is received.[2] I have not read either of the books you mention: but of course there will be no end to the extravagant stories invented and repeated about Mr Lincoln.

I never knew of his attending a *séance* of Spiritualists at the White House or elsewhere, and if he ever did so it was out of mere curiosity, and as a matter of pastime, just as you or I would do. That he was in any sense a so-called "Spiritualist" seems to me almost too absurd to need contradiction.

## S. G. PADDOCK

### S. G. PADDOCK TO WEIK, PRINCETON,
### ILLINOIS, 6 MAY 1914[1]

Replying to your favor of 3d I shall have to explore in the long unused closets of my brain for the material anent the meeting of July 4 1856.

I was present, in fact was one of the committee managing it.

It was a sure enough political gathering, the opening signal gun for the Fremont Campaign.

I shall have to take a little or perhaps much time to revive the recollections needed, but I will do my best and as soon as possible for my 86+ years to get into good order.

So before many days I will try to tell you what I know of it.

S. G. PADDOCK TO WEIK, PRINCETON,
ILLINOIS, 16 MAY 1914[2]

I enclose herewith my attempt to revive the recollections you ask for.

In thinking of Lincoln it has been exceedingly hard to separate in my mind the man of 1856 from he who later became canonized in the hearts of our people yes of the world.

I have tried to tell how it was in 1856 and with what success I am doubtful.

I was then a youngster of 26 years and had no more premonition of what was going [to happen] than even older men had, but the stamp was made in me and perhaps because I was so young enabled me to tell how things worked better than I could have done if I had been older.

Such as it is you are welcome to it.

GEORGE PASFIELD

GEORGE PASFIELD TO WEIK, SPRINGFIELD, 13 NOVEMBER 1914[1]

Please pardon my delay in answering your letter of the second. I have learned from a number of sources that the sister of Mrs May who was at the Lincoln wedding was Anne Rodney.[2] All informants do not agree that she stood with Mrs Lincoln as a bridesmaid. At any rate she was a very close friend and was prominent at the wedding. Mr. May was married twice, the second wife being a Cline, but all are agreed that Rodney is the name you are looking for.[3]

I have been trying to arouse interest in various quarters in the commemorative tablets that you suggest. Your idea is well received and I think will have result before long but not from the present city government. These things come slowly unless one does them themselves. I hope to give you some definite assurance of success before long and will be glad if I can give you any information or be of assistance at any time.

EDWARD LILLIE PIERCE

EDWARD LILLIE PIERCE, UNDATED MEMO[1]

Mr George H Monroe, a young man living in Dedham in 1848, wrote out forty years later his recollections of Mr Lincoln's visit to that town.[2] Mr

Monroe has a vivid and retentive memory, and has since been identified with the public life and journalism of Massachusetts.

## Hiram Rutherford

### HIRAM RUTHERFORD, INTERVIEW WITH WEIK, OAKLAND, ILLINOIS, [3?] APRIL 1892[1]

Dr Hiram Rutherford came to Ills. in 1840. Knew Lincoln in 1841 – met him on circuit in Taylorville Ills first time. In fall of 1847 negroes (Anthony Bryant) (was free)[2] his wife & 4 children came down from Black Grove to Oakland (then Independence) and sought refuge at home of Gideon M. Ashmore.[3] Anth B. had consulted with his Methodist brethren who kept their hands off – declined to assist him – Rev Watson said he would pray for them – was politician & dared not interfere – After coming to Ashmore's house Rutherford consulted with him & backed him up. "We engaged Mr. Ficklin before anything came up."[4] First tried before three Justices of the Peace – Wm Gilmore (pro-slavery), John M. Eastern (pro-slavery) and then Charles Scranton (anti-slavery) afterwards hung himself with rope of court house bell in Charleston.[5] They decided they had no jurisdiction over freedom of negroes but found them in foreign state without letters of freedom. The Black Law made fine of $500 for harboring negroes – Then Sheriff made notice of sale. Then Matson owner of negroes brought suit against Ashmore, Rutherford, for $2500 (being $500 for wife & same for each of children).[6] Tried before Judges Wilson & Treat.[7] Rutherford further says: "I went to Lincoln and asked him to rep me in suit but he declined on ground that he had been spoken to by Gen Matson but not retained. L. said he wanted to see the man who had spoken to him & if he didn't make any arrangements with him he would rep. Rutherford. Then I said "my money is as good as any one's else" but I left his room at the hotel determined to find another lawyer. Everybody had advised me to hire Lincoln as he had good reputation. I was a little hasty. Two hours later he sent me ans[wer] that he would represent me, but I declined to have him although I hadn't got any one else. Later I hired Charles Constable & Ashmore hired Ficklin.[8] Constable & Ficklin had no sentiment—simply a professional matter. Trial before Magistrates lasted two days & before court one afternoon.

Sim Wilmouth died about 2 years ago – was in Charleston at time but not a party to it.

After trial in winter 1847 – Bryant and family sold out – people in Oakland helped them & sent them to Liberia. wagoned to Quincy Ills

– thence went by river to New Orleans – Dr Rutherford wrote out full accounts of this matter in *Oakland Herald* in 1874 – paper afterward moved to Charleston still *Herald* – [W. M.] McConnell pres editor.[9] Subscription collected by people at Oakland to send negroes to Liberia. Ashmore accompanied them to Miss river at Quincy. Stopped at Springfield & Jacksonville & money collected there. Anthony Bryant negro born free – could spell his way through the Bible & Dr R. once saw him reading that book at Gen Matsons house. Matson was polite man & introduced Dr R to Bryant.

SEPARATE, UNDATED SHEET:

Dr. R. born Harrisburg Pa. 79 yrs old.

The plan was to wait till Magistrates decided that Matson was to have possession of negroes in which case negroes were to be driven to the Ohio river. Joe Dean had horses & wagon and Rutherford saw rope D. was to use in tying slaves [wagon was?] hitched to fence.[10] Rutherford & his crowd had men detailed to pursue & overtake them on the road if they endeavored to escape.[11]

## Rev. Mr. W. F. F. Smith

### REV. MR. W. F. F. SMITH, INTERVIEW WITH WEIK,
### GREENCASTLE, INDIANA, 25 MARCH 1896[1]

Robert Wood 1 mi S.W. Gentryville. Father [William Wood] had roan steer and A. L. another like it.[2] L. proposed to trade another steer for RW's fathers roan steer so that A. L. would have match. Took the steer home but next day strayed back to Wood's. A.L. came down and got it. A second & third time steer escaped. When third time came L. went down to Woods with a cudgel and told W. he intended to ride the animal home. Latter was in barn yard – high rail fence almost circular in shape. L. slyly flung his hand across steers should[er] quickly mounted back – using cudgel on either side of head to guide & to keep steer away from the fence. Animal went around the place three or four times in a dead run. R.W. stood at gate ready to swing it open at signal from L. Finally with a yell & bound they came. R.W. opened gate & they went tearing through, sailed out through the woods & over the hill. R. W. at his fathers instance had to follow & see that L. was not hurt. At a cleared place in the hill R Ws father said he saw them bounding along. Finally animal became exhausted & reached home safely with L. on his back

JUDGE ANTHONY THORNTON

NOTES OF AN INTERVIEW WITH JUDGE ANTHONY
THORNTON, SHELBYVILLE, ILLINOIS, 18 JUNE 1895[1]

Anthony Thornton born – Bourbon Co Ky Nov 9 1814 – admitted to bar Spfield – with David Davis 1836 – Sup. Judge Ill. 70 to 74 – travelled circuit with Lincoln over 10 years. Visited Shelby Coles, Edgar, *Fayette*, *Effingham, Bond, Montgomery*, Christian, Macon & Piatt. L. not in counties underlined. L & Linder both great story-tellers[2] – often sat up till 2 A M spinning yarns

2

Remembers [Hiram] Rutherford [      ] – Says [lwer?] St John was arrested at Charleston for sheltering negroes at time – Dont think L. [naturally?] had much humor in him – but cultivated habit. Told story well & improved on stories he told.

In coming from Taylorsville & 12 miles for Shelbyville – L. stopped with old story teller – Ben Hunter – over night & gathered up stories while other lawyers in party went ahead. The next

3

L. decidedly melancholy when not engaged—& T. thought L. told stories to whistle off melancholy – In June 56. after having been a Whig all my life I joined Dem. L. & I debated here in Shelbyville. I gave him opening speech as courtesy but he consumed 3 hours & tired the crowd out for me.

Peter Cartwright said of L. (who stooped his head and his knees projected also his feet) that if you let a broadax fall in front of him it would cut him in three places head – knees & feet.

4

L. saw his wife dancing at ball one evening in Sp. & remarked to a friend who asked what he was thinking about "I was just thinking if Mary had a baby with one leg as short as hers and the other as long as mine what a deuce of a child he would be"

L. seemed to love to parade his honesty. In one case when I was associated with him in Macon Co when a witness halted in his testimony & seemed reluctant L. jumped up & cried out to the court "If the witness doesn't answer the questions I shall withdraw from the case." This was foolish & unprofessional

In South when S. W. Moulton born in Wenham Mass. was prosecuting where it was shown that man had skinned hog & cut ears off.[3] It was also shown that work was done on Sunday whereat Moulton began berating man. L. replied that the rebuke came with bad grace from M as in his country they used to whip the cider or wine barrels for working on Sunday & fined a man for kissing his wife on that day. Mr. Thornton has heard Peter Van Bergen state that he has heard Mrs. L. yelling & screaming at L. as if in hysterics.[4]

L. generally wore plug hat – always broken in middle—& always filled up with papers – sometimes three times weight – buggy broken

5

Buggy was rickety & ramshackle – once between Taylorville & Decatur – tires came off and the other boys helped to tie on with hickory bark.


## Lyman Beecher Todd

LYMAN BEECHER TODD TO WEIK, LEXINGTON, KENTUCKY, 17 APRIL 1895[1]

I regret not being able to furnish information you wish.[2] Concerning Mr Lincoln's letters regarding his wife'[s] interest in slaves inherited, I never heard. My Uncle, R. S. Todd died June 1849 without a will.[3] I then [17?] yrs old was very intimate with his family. His widow was Admx and in Report of Sale recorded in our County Clerk [     ]—Dec 10 1849—no record of sale of slaves. If such letters were written, his Daughter Mrs. Chas H Kellog, Eden Park Terrace Cincy Ohio, who was 31 years old when her father died,[4] or Mrs Benj H Helm of Elizabethtown Ky, who was 23 years old[5] – his only surviving children would likely remember hearing their mother speak of them. I knew Mr Lincoln, saw him in Washington in 1861—he commissioned me P.M. here—1861–1869. I was present at his death bed, and assisted at the Post-Mortem, and saw him laid in tomb at Springfield. *The best and greatest American.* He made one visit here to Mr Clay of which I have a carefully prepared paper—also of his *last* hours and *Post Mortem* never published. Could I further serve you, I gladly will.

P.S. Mrs Frances Todd Wallace a venerable lady – only surviving sister of Mrs Lincoln – at Springfield Ills – Possibly may have heard of such letters having been written.


## Gilbert A. Tracy

GILBERT A. TRACY TO WEIK, PUTNAM, CONNECTICUT, 14 MARCH 1914[1]

Your favor of the 8th is duly at hand. In reply I would state that Mrs. Teillard née Lamon has one or more copies of Marshal Lamon's letter to Gen. Gridley;[2] I have a copy, the Library of Congress has one, and there was one sold in the auction room in New York a year ago this present month.

The main point of interest in the letter centers in Horace White. He, M. Halstead and Horace Greeley gave no end of trouble to President Lincoln by their severe and unrelenting criticism thus manufacturing sentiment adverse to the administration and the welfare of the country.[3] I [apprehend?] the files of the Chicago Tribune from '61-'65 would be immensely interesting reading. When Mr White turned his shaft or point of criticism on Lamon, he struck back for he was in a position to know much of the doings of the time. He was devoted and faithful in his duties, alert and vigilant of the safety of Mr. Lincoln's person and there was no power potent enough to remove him from his position, although it was strenuously tried to be accomplished. Col. McClure was a close observer of the two men—Lincoln and Lamon—and he said the love and friendship between the two men were beautiful to see.[4]

With the bitter abuse, severe censure and infamous calumny of the three editors named, I almost wonder how they escaped imprisonment in Ft Lafayette and their newspapers suppressed. I have a copy of a letter written by Mr Halstead to Secretary Chase that is simply scandalous – written in 1863 or 4. It shows the folly, conceit and indiscretion of the times – and such men were loudest in their fulsome eulogies after the assassination.

Now, about Mrs Teillard, I have not heard from her in many weeks, or since I returned her MSS. two months or more ago. She, with her husband Prof. Teillard has been very busy in a literary way in revising a French translation of an American book and of course has not written me as often as was her wont, and I can only give you my impression of her courtesy in extending it to the loan of her manuscript. I think that she would not only deny you the privilege, but all who might ask her. – The way I gained the privilege was this wise: At the time of sale of his Lincolniana to [Geo. D. Lewis?] of N. J. in which was included a typewritten copy of the biography (easily read) I expressed my regrets that the good fortune of reading it was forever denied me not knowing that a manuscript copy existed at his home in West Va. Last summer on a visit to her home where a goodly lot of her father's books and papers are stored she found the original draft or manuscript in sheets, tho' much of it bound and sent it me for perusal at my leisure.—

I do not know but I committed a breach of confidence in mentioning it, consequently I am a little delicate about the matter myself.

I have not made any definite plans about a trip to the Southwest. Winter weather still holds its grip on us, though it is March! Snow is on the hilltops, in the valleys and by the roadside – mercury standing at 12° above zero only this morning.

I shall go sometime when the way seems clear and shall certainly "swing around" through Greencastle and pay my respects to the co-author of Herndon's Lincoln; [but?] give you an account of the matter—it is rather a long story and too much to crowd into a letter. I suppose I am really the one responsible for the second edition of Lamon's Recollections – vide preface.[5]

The letters of Mrs. Lincoln which you assisted Mr Nicolay in securing from a colored woman might have been those Mrs. Elizabeth Keckley published in her book in 1868 severing and destroying the friendship of the Lincoln family, I conjecture.[6] In my reading and investigation, I have run on to three separate parcels or paquets of letters: Mrs. Keckley's, those found fifteen years or more ago in a secret drawer while a[n] old desk was being sold at auction in N. J. addressed to Mr Norman Bentley a friend of the Lincolns,[7] and a lot sold in the auction rooms of [Marvin Clayton Sales Co. and Hudson Bay?] some of these letters sold as high as $70.00 each. All these letters—60 or more in the several lots—are very much of the same tenor. The only charitable way in looking at Mrs. Lincoln is to consider her insane, or unbalanced mentally, caused through her greedy, spiteful and vindictive spirit which Robert so largely inherited. I could tell you quite a lot of things if we ever meet.

Mrs. Teillard has a card written in John Hay's handwriting which reads something like this: Col. Lamon, I. O. U. $200.00 signed John Hay. This obligation was never cancelled; John forgot it. He married rich and forgot he ever borrowed. Again: a man and his wife by the name of Watt were steward and stewardess in the White House under Pres. Lincoln's administration.[8] They knew much of Mrs. Lincoln and when Robert became Sec of War, he found a place in Europe to send both out of the way from gossips. Marshall Lamon spent dollars out of his own private purse to suppress White House scandals: an instance: two weeks after Mr. Lincoln's death, Mrs. Lincoln sold a dozen of her husband's shirts for $84.00! and signed a receipt for the money.[9] Marshal Lamon dispatched a messenger to overtake the purchaser as soon as he learned of the transaction and by all means, bring back the shirts at whatever cost. – Mrs. Teillard is a refined, cultivated woman and has felt the wrong and abuse heaped upon her noble father and when she heard of the Herndon letters published in Mr Newton's book—"Lincoln and Herndon"[—]it gave her heart a fresh wound and could hardly credit it from Mr. Herndon—the friendship between him and her father had been so strong and true. It is possible she would place her manuscript volume for your perusal; but it is the original draft mostly in Marshal Lamon's handwriting and not in consecutive order or arranged for the printer. Mrs. Teillard sold the larger share of her Lincoln material including a typewritten copy of this second volume some time since, but still holds all copyrights over all.

It is my intention and wish to make another pilgrimage to Hodgenville, Ky and go thence back to Louisville directly to Greencastle to make you a brief visit of a few hours and thence to Springfield, Ill. but at my age life is not certain.

I have written in great haste and [disconcertedly?] and must have permitted errors to creep in which please excuse for my hand is out of joint.

## Lyman Trumbull

### lyman trumbull to weik, chicago, 17 april 1895[1]

In reply to yours of April 1st, I can only give my present recollection. I always understood that Mrs. Francis was instrumental in bringing about the reconciliation between Mr. Lincoln and Mary Todd, by bringing them together at her house without either knowing that the other was to be there;[2] but never understood that the Shields duel had any thing to do with hastening the marriage. It is my impression that Miss Todd and Miss Jayne had something to do in writing the poetry published in the Illinois Journal, at which Gen'l. Shields took offense, but I cannot give you particulars.[3]

## Horace White

### horace white to weik, palisades, new jersey, 26 august 1908[1]

Yours of Aug 23d is received.

Dr C. H. Ray was the Chief editor of the Chicago Tribune in 1858 & remained such until 1862 or 1863 when he sold his interest in the paper.[2] Medill succeeded him as chief editor, but remained such only till the beginning of 1865, when he retired voluntarily & was succeeded by myself.[3] I held the position till the autumn of 1874 when I retired voluntarily & sold the larger part of my stock in the company to Medill. He then became the Chief editor again & remained such until his death.

N. B. Judd, C. H. Ray & Ebenezer Peck were chosen as the executive committee of the Repub. State Committee of Illinois by the State Convention in 1856 & I think that they were chosen for four years. I do not think that Medill was the Secretary of the State Committee at any time. I think that Jesse W. Fell was the first Secretary & that I was the second. I held the position in the Campaign of 1860.

Medill was an important member of the Tribune Co in 1858, but he concerned himself more with the business department at that time than with the editorial work. He always did more or less writing for the paper & was the Washington correspondent during the winter of 1860–1.

What Medill told you about his talk with Lincoln at Dixon, in reference to the forthcoming debate at Freeport, is undoubtedly true.[4] It corresponds with all that I know touching the preliminaries of the Freeport meeting, although I was not present at the Dixon Conference. I saw Medill at the Freeport debate & we came away together feeling rather blue, because both of us believed that Douglas's reply would enable him to win the election.

HORACE WHITE TO WEIK, NEW YORK, 23 AUGUST 1909[5]

Yours of 20th is rec'd.

John Wentworth was always a candidate for anything within his reach, but he knew that the Senatorship was not within his reach.[6] The Democrats, however, affirmed that if the Rep's should carry the Legislature they would elect Wentworth. To offset that kind of talk was one of the reasons why the Convention nominated Lincoln. That is the explanation of the words which you quote from Lincoln's letter to Trumbull of June 23, 1858.

I received the enclosed letter a few days ago from Joseph Newton of Cedar Rapids, Iowa. I replied to him that the letters from Herndon to Trumbull were all in the Library of Congress, open to the inspection of everybody; that I did not have any of them but that you had copies of all of them, & that you could give him more of the kind of information he wants than all other persons taken together. Perhaps you will not thank me for putting him on your track!

HORACE WHITE TO WEIK, NEW YORK, 2 JANUARY 1911[7]

Mr. Robert Lincoln writes me that he was at the Alton joint debate, Oct. 15, 1858, & that his mother was *not there*. At all events that is his belief. He remembers seeing me & Robert Hitt on the platform. Thinks that if his mother had been there he should have known the fact & remembered it. Says that his mother was not in the habit of attending political meetings.

As regards Koerner's statement that Mr & Mrs. Lincoln came down together from Springfield to Alton,[8] there is abundant evidence in the newspapers to the effect that Lincoln came by steamboat from Quincy to Alton, arriving at the latter place about four o'clock A.M. Oct. 15.

HORACE WHITE TO WEIK, NEW YORK, 24 FEBRUARY 1913[9]

Yours of the 22d is received. In reply to your inquiry I will give you my recollection of the conversation I had with Leonard Swett, in the year 1872.

He came into the office of the Chicago Tribune, of which I was then the editor & said that he & David Davis had had a severe struggle with Ward Lamon in reference to a chapter in the Life of Lincoln which he (Lamon) had been writing for a Boston publisher. The book was nearly ready for publication & Lamon had submitted the page proofs to Swett & Davis for their criticism. They found in it a chapter showing or arguing that Lincoln was not the son of Thomas Lincoln, his reputed father, but of some other man. In short that, although born in wedlock, he was really illegitimate. They (S & D) were horrified. The[y] got Lamon into a room, locked the door & kept him there nearly a whole afternoon, trying to force him to take that chapter out of the book, & they succeeded after great difficulty. Swett did not tell me what proofs L. advanced to support his statement but he said that they were *prima facie* strong.

This is my recollection of the story, but of course allowance must be made for the lapse of years & the faultiness of the human memory.

The late Wm H. Lambert of Phila. had in his collection of Lincolniana a letter from Henry C. Whitney on the suppressed chapter of Lamon's book, differing somewhat from the foregoing narrative as related to me by Swett.[10] Maj. Lambert once showed Whitney's letter to me.

The letter from Herndon in which he says that Lamon was no solid firm friend of Lincoln during the latter part of his Administration was written to me & is printed in Newton's book "Lincoln and Herndon," pages 307–8. You are right in saying that Lincoln would have been better off without his friendship. The House Committee on Government Contracts brought the lash down heavily on Lamon once. This was at the beginning of the war, however.

### HORACE WHITE TO WEIK, NEW YORK, 5 OCTOBER 1913[11]

Your letter of Sept. 27 was extremely gratifying to me by reason of your approval of my Life of Lyman Trumbull.[12] You are a student & an authority on the history of those times, and you are a man who weighs his words. Hence my appreciation of your flattering estimate of my work. I was engaged five years in writing it & searching authorities, etc.

You ask how I obtained the letter of Sam C. Parks on the subject of T's first election as Senator. You have forgotten your own generosity. You gave it to me & authorized me to make such use of it as I might choose. It is most valuable for the saying of Lincoln, which Parks quotes, that the election of Trumbull at that time was the best thing that could have happened.[13] I did not think so at the time when it happened but I do think so now.

In the early part of 1858 the Democrats in Illinois were peddling a story to the effect that if the Republicans should carry the next Legislature they would elect John Wentworth Senator. No doubt Wentworth was a candidate for the place, but without the smallest chance of being elected. When the Rep. State Convention was held a resolution was adopted to nominate Lincoln for Senator in order to put an end to the talk about Wentworth, & it had that effect.

I thank you cordially for your invitation to visit you again at Greencastle. I should love to do so, but the flight of years (I am now in my 80th) forbids me to do much visiting. I am not without hope, however, that we may meet again & that I may again see the son & daughter whom I so pleasantly remember.

### HORACE WHITE TO WEIK, NEW YORK, 10 DECEMBER 1913[14]

Yours of the 6th is received. The enclosures which you send me from your diary of former years are very interesting. I beg that you will send me more of the same sort, if you find any relating to Lincoln & Trumbull & their intimates.

The laws that Trumbull referred to, as passed by Congress for the freedom of slaves before Lincoln issued his proclamation, were the two so-called confiscation acts referred to in my Life of Trumbull on pages 168 & 176. The former was passed at the July session of Congress in 1861 & the latter was reported by Trumbull from the Judiciary Committee on the 5th of Dec. 1861, & was passed during that session. It is summarized in my book.[15]

The fact that Charley Wilson unexpectedly nominated Lincoln for Senator at the Springfield Convention, 1858, had escaped my mind, although I was present, sitting on the platform. I have no doubt that what Nicolay said to you about it was true. Charley Wilson was the chief owner and director of the Chicago *Journal*.[16] He hated John Wentworth & he made the motion in order to checkmate W's chances of worming himself in as a candidate for the Senatorship. He (Wilson) did a good thing & it is the only good thing he ever did, in the way of politics, that I can now recall.

That remark made by Lincoln to C. H. Moore about Douglas's facility for lying had a modicum of fact to rest upon.[17] I could give an instance from my own recollection if it were worth while, but Douglas's services in the last year of his life were such that I don't want to remember anything of detriment to his fame.

### HORACE WHITE TO WEIK, NEW YORK, 14 DECEMBER 1913[18]

Yours of the 12th is received. The fact that I had in mind when I spoke of Douglas's unveracity in stump speaking was a statement which he made at the Ottawa joint debate Aug 21, 1858, in which he said that Lincoln as a young man "could ruin more liquor than all of the boys of the town together." This was said in order to draw L. into a personal controversy. Everybody who knew L. knew that he never used liquor or tobacco at all. He said to me once that he had never taken a drink of any alcoholic beverage in the past twenty years. That he should have been a drunkard before 1838 is impossible. Not only was Douglas's statement essentially false as to Lincoln but it would have been a true description of himself (D) at the time of the Ottawa debate. The fact was that D. was at that very time drinking himself to death—an end which he reached three years later. The pen of the historian has not touched upon that fact as yet.

I have no doubt whatever that D. made that false statement about L. in order to get a denial from him that he was a drinking man, in which event he would have enlarged upon it & given particulars which he could easily have invented & would have assured L. that he did not wish to injure him, etc, etc, leading off the debate into a personal quagmire as was his habit, when he was getting the worst of it. But Lincoln was too smart. He never noticed the charge at all. So Douglas never repeated it.

The statement that I refer to is on page 281 of vol I of Nicolay & Hay's collection of Lincoln's Complete Works.

As all I have said in this letter is matter already public to readers of the joint debates, you need not regard it as confidential.

### HORACE WHITE TO WEIK, NEW YORK, 26 JANUARY 1914[19]

I have read the Lamon-Robert Lincoln correspondence that you sent to me.[20] The first paragraph that you have blue-penciled is easily explained. Leonard Swett must have been the person who read the proof sheets of the Lamon biography of Abraham Lincoln & advised Lamon to omit the indicated paragraph. Swett told me, at the time of the occurrence, that he & Judge Davis were asked by Lamon to read certain proof sheets of the book, & to their horror they found matter therein purporting to show that Lincoln was of illegitimate birth. Swett said that he & Davis got Lamon into a private room & labored with him half a day to get the matter stricken out; that L. was very obstinate, contended that it was no discredit to Lincoln but rather creditable than otherwise, since he had risen so high from such a lowly origin, etc, etc; but finally they did succeed in getting the worst part of the matter stricken out. My recollection is that Swett told me this on the very day that he & Davis had the interview with Lamon. At all events it was at very nearly the same time. . . .

I have got a kink in my head to the effect that the quarrel between Lamon

& Chauncey Black had its beginning in the exclusion from the book of this matter about Lincoln's birth. Black considered the excluded matter true & extremely valuable in the way of advertising.

Your letters are always full of interest to me, because they betoken searching intelligence & thoughtfulness. There was a certain degree of moral obtuseness in Abraham Lincoln that the public do not recognize, & will refuse to believe, in the present generation. The most glaring instance of this obtuseness was his appointment of Simon Cameron to a place in his Cabinet, knowing what manner of man he was. I have presented the facts in my Life of Trumbull, because Trumbull was the most active opponent of Cameron at the time when L. was choosing his Cabinet.[22]

There is another fact in this connection which somebody else will bring out in the course of historical criticism. That is that after Cameron came back from Russia Lincoln was just as friendly to him as though nothing had ever happened to force him out of the Cabinet. He appointed him Minister to Russia with all his imperfections on his head & he received him back in the same way &, if I recollect rightly, employed him in running political errands just prior to the National Republican Convention of 1864. That I call moral obtuseness, of the same kind as his intimacy with Lamon, Delahay,[23] etc. Lamon at one time conceived the idea of being a Brigadier General. In order to gain a standing for that elevation he went West in the beginning of 1862 (as I recollect) & ordered two regiments of soldiers to be sent to the Potomac to be a part of "Lamon's Brigade." In the haste & general mix-up of the period the commanders of these regiments assumed, from L's intimacy with Lincoln, that he had authority to give these orders & they accordingly moved their troops as L. directed, at a cost of more than $50,000. But he (L) had no authority whatever. The House Committee on Gov't Contracts discovered these facts & made a scathing report on them, said that the money was wasted or worse than wasted because the troops were at the wrong place when wanted for service, etc. etc. Senator Grimes of Iowa exposed this fraud in a speech in open Senate early in 1862.[24] If I had access to a file of the Cong. Globe I could easily find it, but I think you can find it if you care to see it. The point in the case is that Lincoln never took any notice of this glaring infraction of law & morals. His obtuseness on this occasion was the cause of the coolness that existed between Grimes & Lincoln during all the remainder of L's life. There is an entry in John Hay's diary which refers to this coolness & expresses Lincoln's surprise that Grimes had fallen away from him.[25] He could not imagine why this was so. Lamon remained Marshal of the Dist. of Columbia all the same.

All of these things will filter through the fabric of history in due time, but I do not feel inclined to assemble them. I should be accused of attacking the memory of Lincoln. Some people have said that my Life of Trumbull disparages Lincoln, & also that Trumbull himself disparages Lincoln in the estimate of L. which I have printed in the last chapter of the book.[26] All that need be said in reply is that the muse of History will take care of that.

HORACE WHITE TO WEIK, NEW YORK, 14 SEPTEMBER 1914[27]

I have your letters of the 10th & the 12th, both of which interest me greatly. I will first answer your direct questions.

I received the letter in which you renewed your suggestion that I should write something for publication, now or in the future, about Lincoln's moral obtuseness as manifested in his association with & tolerance of low & dishonest characters like Simon Cameron, Ward Lamon & M. W. Delahay. This list of names might be lengthened to include William H. Seward & Thurlow Weed;[28] altho' the word "low" might not be applicable to them, the word dishonest would be. That Thurlow Weed was a grafter & that Seward aided & abetted him, but did not share the proceeds, must have been known to Lincoln. Gideon Welles makes this plain, in more than one instance.[29] Nevertheless I do not feel inclined to go out of my way to pick flaws in Lincoln's record. I have set forth my opinion of his conduct in con[n]ection with Cameron because that was an essential fact in the Life of Trumbull. I have also, for the same reason, exposed Thurlow Weed's [graftiness?] in connection with Cameron's tool, Alexander Cummings.[30]

Now in regard to French's statue of Lincoln: I have never seen that statue, nor did I ever see Lincoln in the attitude which that statue represents.[31] I never saw him standing with his head dropped or his hands clasped. I did see him more than once standing with his hand clasping the lapel of his coat. That was not an unusual attitude for him, at the beginning of a speech.

Richard Watson Gilder once told me that in St Gaudens' original figure, in clay, of the statue now at Lincoln Park, Chicago, the head was erect, but that he (Gilder) suggested a change to give it a more thoughtful attitude – he did not say what kind of a change.[32] He said that St Gaudens agreed with him that that would be a betterment of the work & that he thereupon posed the head downward as we see it in the statue. I think myself that the figure is more impressive in that way, but I do not recognize it as Lincoln's way. I agree with Henry C. Whitney's observation as quoted by you.

HORACE WHITE TO WEIK, NEW YORK, 3 FEBRUARY 1915[33]

I have not seen in the Journal of the Illinois State Historical Society your paper on "An unpublished Chapter in the Early History of Chicago."[34] I received a copy of that Journal yesterday, but it bore the date April, 1914.

I happened to open Herndon-Weik's Lincoln 2d edition a day or two ago & my eye fell upon these words in my introduction (p. xxii):

"Mr. Lincoln never gave his assent so far as my knowledge goes to any plan or project for getting votes that would not have borne the full light of day. At the same time he had no objection to the getting of votes by the pledge of offices, nor was he too particular what kind of men got the offices. His preference always was for good men; but he could not resist pressure where persons were concerned even though his conscience told him that he was doing wrong."

Does not that last sentence embrace the idea that you wanted me to convey, about L's moral obtuseness?

Nicolay & Hay do not make any allusion to the rascalities of Simon Cameron. They give an entirely false account of the reasons for his expulsion from Lincoln's Cabinet. You will find the real reasons in my Life of Lyman Trumbull, Chapter XI. You will find in this chapter quotations from speeches of Dawes & others in the Congressional *Globe* & references to the report of the House Committee on Government Contracts, of the most damning kind. In the *Globe* you will also find the resolution passed by the House censuring Cameron for putting money in the hands of Alex. Cummings for the purchase of army supplies.

It was impossible for Lincoln to retain Cameron after the House had censured him. He could not have carried on the Government with such burden & blot. Yet L. whitewashed him by giving him the Russian mission & after he came back Lincoln made him his friend & confidential agent in politics as described by A. K. McClure in his book entitled "Lincoln & Men of War Times," p. 166. I remember well how Lincoln fell, in the estimation [of] the best men in Congress, in consequence of his association with C. after the latter came back from Russia.[35]

HORACE WHITE TO WEIK, NEW YORK, 12 JUNE 1916[36]

Yours of the 9th is gladly welcomed. I shall procure the House Doc. 1056 as soon as possible. I never heard before of Greeley's ambition to be a member of Lincoln's second Cabinet.[37]

I have read the greater part of Mr. Richards' "Abraham Lincoln – Lawyer-Statesman," & have formed a favorable opinion of it.[38] I have not read

Henry B. Rankin's "Personal Recollections of Lincoln," nor did I ever hear of him in connection with Lincoln. If you will give me the name of the publisher I will procure a copy of it.[39]

I regret that I am not able to travel so far as Indiana. Therefore I must deny myself the privilege & pleasure of accepting your invitation to attend the Sarah Lincoln dedication at Gentryville.


## JAMES H. WILSON

JAMES H. WILSON TO WEIK, WILMINGTON, DELAWARE, 14 DECEMBER 1913[1]

Of course the story of what Lincoln said to Russell Jones, is true.[2] Jones told it to me himself, and we laughed and spoke about it frequently to the day of his death which took place a few years ago in Chicago. He was originally from Galena, & became Grant's minister at Brussels, where I visited him several times. I knew him intimately from 1863. He was a very intelligent, studious and worthy man, cautious, prudent and wise, and the Soul of honor and truthfulness. He was Grant's Trustee in certain business matters & knew a great deal about him.[3] I also knew Genl. Thos. Mather well.[4] He visited us frequently in the Army, and although far from a military genius and somewhat of a Miss Nancy, he was always welcome, and as Grant was for a while a clerk with Mather as A. G. of Illinois, it is fair to assume that any story of Mather's in reference to Grant's appointment to the Colonelcy of the 21st Ills. is reasonably true. As a matter of fact, Grant as a graduate of West Point and an ex captain of the regular Army, was the *only* man connected with the state Govt. and especially its A. G. O. who knew anything about military administration and the U. S. supply departments. He knew Army Regulations and forms and upon whom to make requisitions for military supplies. He was therefore useful to Gov. Yates & could teach, and doubtless did teach, others how to get what was needed from the War Department, while organizing troops.

But the Col. of the 21st Illinois was not so far as I ever heard before, a drunkard – simply a country preacher who knew nothing about command-ing a regiment though he had served as Chaplain of an Illinois regiment in the Mexican War.[5]

Chas. A Dana and I published a Life of Grant in *1868 which I wrote* (Gurdon Bill & Co Hartford Conn)[6]

You might find a second hand copy in some old book store. It was widely distributed prior to his first election as President.

Did you get a copy of "The Southernor" from Appleton's six or 8 months ago?[7] It contained a story of Lincoln's sending for McClellan just before the Battle of Gettysburg, and asking him "to save the Union." I wanted to know if there was any truth in the story?

How are you getting on with "Lincoln and His Ancestry["]?

## Louis H. Zumbrook

STATEMENT BY LOUIS H. ZUMBROOK, SPRINGFIELD, 5 DECEMBER 1916[1]

I am seventy-six years of age. I came to Springfield, Illinois in 1853. In February 1861 I was working for Dr. William Jayne. One evening during that month he said to me, "Louie, if you go down to the Great Western Depot tomorrow morning you can see Mr. Lincoln leave for Washington." The next morning I went to the Great Western Passenger Depot, which was then situated on the southwest corner of Tenth and Monroe Streets. The north end fronted on Monroe Street and the side on Tenth Street, and was used as a Passenger Depot, and the south end as a Freight Depot. The whole of it is now used, with some changes, as a Freight Depot of the Wabash Railroad. At that time the main track of the Great Western Road ran north and south through Tenth Street as it does now. There were some side tracks south of the Depot. The office and lumber yard of George L. Huntington was at that time on the northwest corner of the two streets.[2] On the east side of Huntington's Lumber Yard and between it and the main track there was a stub side track which came in from the north and ran south along the west side of the main track and along the east side of the lumber yard until it came to a stop about ten feet north of the north line of Monroe Street. This stub side track did not at that time cross the street.

I got there between six and seven o'clock in the morning. When I got there, the train on which Mr. Lincoln left was standing on the stub side track just north of Monroe Street. The party was on board. It was a chilly morning and a drizzling rain was falling. I was there some minutes, perhaps ten minutes, before Mr. Lincoln spoke. He came out on to the rear platform about ten feet from the sidewalk and talked to the crowd, which numbered perhaps between one and two hundred. There were not very many. I heard his address from beginning to end. After he had finished, the train moved north on the stub side track and thence on to the main track and then disappeared without stopping. Before Mr. Lincoln commenced to talk I was talking with people in the crowd and I was told by them that the train was first on the main track, but that they had switched it on to the stub side track so he could speak to the people as they stood on Monroe Street, and without their standing on the main track, because some thought it would be safer. I did not see the train go up the main track and then come back. When I first saw it, it was standing on the stub side track.

APPENDIX 2

"A Hard-hearted Conscious Liar and an Oily Hypocrite":
Henry B. Rankin's Reliability as a Lincoln Informant

Henry B. Rankin, who alleged that he was a student in the Lincoln-Herndon law offices from December 1856 to February 1861, wrote two controversial books about the sixteenth president—*Personal Recollections of Abraham Lincoln* (1916) and *Intimate Character Sketches of Abraham Lincoln* (1924)—in which he asserted that his relations with Lincoln were close:

• "In the eventful political years following the Fremont-Buchanan campaign of 1856, I entered the law office of Lincoln and Herndon as a law-student. I retained this connection until Lincoln's election to the Presidency and his departure for Washington in February, 1861."
• "as I look back over daily intimacies with this law firm from 1856 to 1861"
• "I never had any hesitancy, while a student in his office, about going to Lincoln with a question regarding a point of law or the minutest details of papers I was expected to prepare. He never dismissed me with impatience. If he knew the answer to my question he stated it, or told me where to find it."
• "In the years when I was intimate with the daily life at the Lincoln and Herndon office, I learned to know and respect the peculiarity of Lincoln's moods."[1]

Born in 1837 near the village of Athens in Sangamon County (in the area that later became Menard County) to the farmer Amberry A. Rankin and his wife (née Arminda Rogers), Rankin was educated at the North Sangamon Academy in Indian Point by private tutors. For *Who's Who* Rankin stated that he was a student in the law office of Lincoln and Herndon from December 1856 to February 1861 but "Abandoned law on account of Civil War and engaged in farming, banking and investing." He also listed his occupations as "Editorial writer and press corresp[ondent]."[2] He served as vice president of the First National Bank of Petersburg for many years and ran his own insurance company.[3] In 1915 Ida Tarbell reported that in the mid-1870s, "he came home from business one night and was stricken with an illness [myalgia] which has never left him. He has lived in one room suffering the most intolerable torment a great deal of the time through all these years."[4] Rankin resided in Jacksonville, Illinois, from 1891 to 1905, when he moved to Springfield, where he spent the rest of his long life.

Among some Springfield residents, Rankin enjoyed the unsavory reputation as a "loan-shark and merciless forecloser of mortgages." Shortly before Rankin died a Lincoln biographer visiting the Illinois capital "was told that a widow to whom he [Rankin] had shown no mercy cursed him with 'the widow's curse' and this was believed to be the occasion of his paralysis." With the help of his son Rankin continued as a banker and was "known as [a] skinflint and loansharp" who was held "in very little respect by those whose memory is longest."[5]

In 1994 Merrill Peterson described Rankin's *Personal Recollections* as a "truly important volume of reminiscences."[6] Emanuel Hertz declared in 1930 that "Rankin contributed a great deal of valuable Lincoln material which fills many a hiatus in the life of Lincoln. His writings are valuable and display a fine loyalty to his great chief."[7] Ida M. Tarbell wrote a favorable introduction to *Intimate Character Sketches of Lincoln* and praised its author for having "an unusual personality and an amazing will. He is one of the most ethereal creatures I ever saw and yet intensely practical."[8] In 1924 she described him as a man of "a cheerful and courageous spirit" who "accepted his physical handicap and has led a life not only of remarkable business activity— he has multiplied his estate by five and given a college education to his three children—but more important, of amazingly beautiful intellectual and spiritual quality."[9] The Springfield book and manuscript dealer Harry E. Barker said that "he knew Rankin intimately, read the manuscript of Rankin's first book before it was published, and that nothing can swerve him from his faith in Rankin."[10] M. L. Houser, an amateur Lincoln scholar, reported that other Springfield residents, including Georgia L. Osborn of the Illinois State Historical Library, "believe Rankin was absolutely reliable."[11]

Many other Illinoisians disagreed. An Athens merchant, Charles Salzenstein, who knew Rankin, said that he "was never in Lincoln's office."[12] In the mid-1920s Albert J. Beveridge, a Lincoln scholar and former senator from Indiana, visited Springfield and shared his findings with a fellow biographer: "As to old Rankin: He has caused me no end of trouble. I was inclined to take him seriously, but, in the end, found that he is utterly untrustworthy. Those in Springfield who ought to know and who do [know] him and who are helping me no end, told me to be very careful about him. They said that he never was in Lincoln's office but a short time; he never practiced law, but began immediately to make money, at which he succeeded; and that, moreover, he knew very little about Lincoln."[13] To another Lincoln author Beveridge observed in 1925, "all that Rankin says was written nearly 70 years after the events he pretends to remember. Still worse, during long years while the row was going on about Herndon's lectures, etc. Rankin kept his mouth shut. Nobody heard a word out of him. Then suddenly, fifteen or twenty years ago he breaks out as a Lincoln oracle."[14]

Beveridge was reluctant to commit to paper all he had heard about Rankin. To Lincoln Dubois he confided, "the best lawyers in Springfield who are *ardent* Lincoln men, tell me to be careful about Rankin. They say that he never practiced any law and, instead, devoted himself to money-making, in which art he was unusually successful—and they say a lot of other things."[15]

In a similar vein he told Weik that in Springfield he had "found out a good deal about Rankin—not only from the adherents of Mrs. Lincoln but also from the other side; and all say the same thing. . . . I shall not pay the slightest attention to his two books which, from the data I have gathered at Springfield about him, I consider to be wholly without merit. When I see you I will be glad to tell you what they say about him in Springfield."[16]

In 1924 Weik called Rankin "the latest luminary in Illinois on Lincoln" and expressed astonishment that "during my four years stay in Springfield [1882–86] I never saw or heard of him. Herndon never mentioned him and now years after Herndon has gone as well as [James] Matheny, [John M.] Palmer and others of like standing Rankin springs up with a store of so-called 'Personal Recollections' that for almost forty years he seems to have refrained from giving to the world."[17] (Rankin claimed that he wrote to Herndon "often and quite fully from time to time, at his request, concerning the general outlines to be adopted in his life of Lincoln." No such letters are known to have survived, though their purported recipient meticulously saved his correspondence about Lincoln.)[18]

Beveridge did not include an analysis of Rankin's credibility in his monumental *Abraham Lincoln, 1809–1858*, published posthumously in 1928. Two years later, however, William E. Barton shared his misgivings about Rankin with the public in *Abraham Lincoln and Walt Whitman*: "So far as is known, he [Rankin] never claimed to have been a student in the Lincoln and Herndon office until most of the men were dead who could have contradicted him. When he put forth the claim, at first with a discreet vagueness as to the precise time which the apprenticeship covered, most of the men who could have contradicted him kept silent in public. What they said in private need not here be repeated." With some delicacy Barton concluded that "Rankin, in common with many other old men, mixed his memories with his imagination."[19]

Privately Barton was less delicate, referring to Rankin as "a hard-hearted conscious liar and an oily hypocrite." After interviewing several Spring-fielders (including Rankin), Barton observed: "No one who is in position to judge of the facts believes him. When Weik was in Springfield Herndon sent him to every blacksmith, hack-driver, etc who had known Lincoln and never mentioned Rankin as having been a student in the office. Nor did any one else. In all the controversies following Herndon's book no word from Rankin."[20] In a memo dated Springfield, 5 February 1926, Barton said that the head librarian at the Illinois State Historical Library, Jessie Palmer Weber, and her assistant, Georgia L. Osborne, "told me—I think as from Mr. Rankin—that when the latter sent his book to Robert T. Lincoln, Mr. Lincoln returned it *unopened*. I asked 'What do you think of Mr Rankin as historian?'

"Mrs. Weber said 'He confuses his memories and imagination. Any child of 7 in 1860 could well have had memories of Lincoln. It was a town of 10,000 – he knew and noticed children. Mr. Rankin lived in the country . . . . He could have known Lincoln & Herndon.'

" 'As intimately as he professes?'

" 'Most of the older people in Springfield when confronted by Mr. Rankin's books merely shrugged a little and said nothing—Mr. [Clinton L.] Conkling, for instance.'

" 'Do you know of *anyone* in Springfield who belongs to the older or the critical group who credit Mr. Rankin's memoirs?'

" 'I am afraid not. Yet, he is a good man, and what he professes to remember, he thinks he remembers.' This accords with much that I had heard previously from many people—Weik, H. W. Masters—Conkling and others—and is why I do not credit his memoirs."[21]

In 1929 Paul M. Angle, the young secretary of the Abraham Lincoln Association who that very year had exposed Lincoln forgeries published by credulous editors at the *Atlantic Monthly*, expressed similar doubts about Rankin's credibility. With Charles T. White, a journalist examining Lincoln and prohibition, Angle shared the findings of his research into Rankin's activities between 1856 and 1860: "While Mr. Rankin is generally accepted as a credible witness, some of us have very little faith in what he has to say. . . . It is unequivocally stated in Petersburg, near which Mr. Rankin's home was located, that during those four years he was working on his father's farm." In the 29 February 1856 issue of the *Illinois State Journal*, Angle discovered an announcement of a meeting, signed by Rankin, who identified himself as a resident of Petersburg. In vain Angle searched the 1855 and 1858 Springfield directories for Rankin's name. In the hundreds of Lincoln legal documents examined by Angle, Rankin's name never once appeared. Nor did it appear in any of the political news of Springfield published by the local newspapers. In addition to that, Angle noted that Rankin had pirated material from other books, including Weik's *Real Lincoln*.[22] Angle told Barton that *Intimate Character Sketches of Lincoln* "contains not only plagiarism, but with the added detriment of claiming as his own the experiences & the very language which he purloins." When asked if any Springfielders "competent to judge" took Rankin seriously, Angle "thought not."[23] Along with Jacob C. Thompson, the assistant superintendent of public instruction in Springfield, Angle considered Rankin "a fraud."[24] Angle hesitated to make public his criticism of Rankin in part because Rankin's son was a prominent Springfield banker.[25]

In 1930 Angle modified his assessment of Rankin. "I have been disregarding his writings entirely," he told Barton, "largely on the ground that there was no evidence that he was in Springfield between 1856 and 1860, and considerable that he was elsewhere during most of this period. I find, however, that strictly speaking he never claimed to have been a student in the office, and that the family story is that he studied at Athens, visiting the office periodically." This seemed "reasonable" to Angle, who was "willing to be convinced." In short, he "substituted a doubt for a certainty."[26] This turnabout is puzzling, for Rankin *did* state explicitly that he had been a student in the Lincoln-Herndon law office enjoying daily contact with those two attorneys.

Earlier in 1930 M. L. Houser summarized the family story to which Angle referred: "Clayton Barber, Rankin's son-in-law, has the impression that Rankin studied with Lincoln & Herndon, but did most of his studying at home in Menard County, with occasional visits at the office to discuss and review the matters covered by his studies. This impression he gained by his talks with Rankin. Mrs. [Mollie Herndon] Ralston and Mrs. [Annie M.] Fleury, Herndon's daughters, say that Mr. Rankin was not a law student, but that he often came to the law office to secure books and talk over what he had read; that he spent much time there; that he sometimes walked all the way from Athens to secure or return books; that he was very fond of the partners, particularly Herndon, and they of him. I do not believe that Mr. Rankin, in his books at least, claimed more than that he was intimately acquainted with Lincoln and Herndon over a period of years, and that he spent considerable time in their office."[27] Houser is wrong; Rankin in *Intimate Character Sketches of Lincoln* quite definitely stated that he was a law student in the Lincoln-Herndon office and saw the partners daily. Rankin made the same assertion in his autobiographical sketch for *Who's Who*.

In 1934 William H. Townsend, a lawyer-historian in Kentucky, joined the chorus of Rankin skeptics with the publication of *Lincoln and Liquor*, in which the author cast serious doubt on Rankin's various statements about Lincoln and prohibition.[28] Rankin had vouched for the accuracy of the highly unreliable James B. Merwin, who claimed that Lincoln wrote an Illinois prohibition statute and campaigned for that cause. Sarcastically Townsend observed that "there may be some who attach derogatory significance to the fact that Rankin, after the elapse of sixty-four years, in private correspondence, readily identified Lincoln as a prohibitionist, and finally as the author of the Illinois law, but omitted to do so on the two occasions when he had an opportunity to reveal this important information publicly [that is, in his books]."[29]

In 1949 Marion Bonzi, assistant editor of *The Collected Works of Abraham Lincoln*, told her future husband, the able Lincoln scholar Harry E. Pratt, "I quite agree that it has not been established by any reliable source that Rankin was a law student in the Lincoln-Herndon office (I know I have worked on that). . . . We do know that he exaggerated aplenty."[30] A year earlier William H. Herndon's biographer, David Donald, pointed out that Rankin was a "notoriously inaccurate writer" who had made a false assertion about Herndon's youth.[31] Rankin also alleged incorrectly that Herndon was addicted to drugs and that he abused alcohol in his later years.[32]

A decade later John J. Duff, an authority on Lincoln's legal career, stated that "Most Lincoln scholars view Rankin's claim to inclusion in the not-too-select group of Lincoln law students as being of dubious authenticity. . . . Rankin speaks of 'papers I was expected to prepare.' Though the files of all the counties in which Lincoln & Herndon practiced have been combed for evidence of Lincoln's cases, not a single document in Rankin's handwriting has ever turned up." Although it was possible "that Rankin may have served in the Lincoln & Herndon office," Duff concluded, nevertheless, that "historical opinion has tended toward the conclusion that Barton's strong case in opposition remains unimpaired, and that the heavy burden of proof resting on Hertz has never been sustained."[33] Since Duff's time, his conclusion has been strengthened by the findings of the Lincoln Legal Papers staff, who have unearthed far more documents shedding light on Lincoln's career at the bar than Duff and others consulted. In those voluminous papers there is no mention of Rankin.

Other grounds for skepticism exist. Rankin's name does not appear in the hundreds of reminiscences about Lincoln in Springfield and New Salem that William Herndon and Jesse Weik collected, nor in the large Robert Todd Lincoln Collection of Abraham Lincoln Papers at the Library of Congress, nor in Herndon's many letters discussing Lincoln.

As Paul M. Angle had surmised, Rankin did not live in Springfield between 1856 and 1861. In October 1857 Rankin—supposedly living in Springfield—contributed an essay to a newspaper giving his address as Athens.[34] The 1860 census lists Henry Rankin as a farm laborer in Menard County.[35] In 1856 he wrote to Senator Lyman Trumbull from Athens.[36] In 1859 he corresponded from the same place with Congressman Elihu B. Washburne.[37] In February 1861 Rankin appealed to Washburne for copies of speeches:

> Will you be so kind as to send me such Republican speeches as you have on hand. I see we have a battle still to fight & I want to gather up such material as I can & again reenter the field. I was the first Republican in Menard & if needs be, sir, I shall stand on the original Fremont & Chicago Platforms to the bitter end—if needs be solitary & alone in Menard. We are about to reorganise the Wide Awake & Rep. Clubs.
>
> I desire a thorough supply of the best speeches. Friend Lovejoy has sent me Oregon, Ind. Wis. Ill, & R.I. speeches but I have none yet from any New England, Ohio or N. Y. members.
>
> Even at this late hour of the Session I hope, *most sincerely*, that I may have the favor of receiving some speeches from you who have in the previous sessions been so thoughtful to my requests.[38]

If Rankin had actually been working in the Lincoln-Herndon law office in February 1861, as he claimed, he probably would have found it unnecessary to appeal to Washburne for such documents, which would surely have been available to the president-elect.

Rankin stated that John E. Denny, a carpenter, worked as a law student in the Lincoln-Herndon office. No contemporary evidence supports that assertion.[39] The Rankin papers at the Illinois State Historical Library contain no documents from the period 1856–61 indicating that Rankin worked with Lincoln and Herndon. Hence it is no wonder that, as Don E. Fehrenbacher and Virginia Fehrenbacher noted in 1996, most scholars regard Rankin's books as "unreliable."[40]

Clearly Rankin is not a trustworthy source, and historians should stop consulting his memoirs for information about Lincoln's time in Springfield.[41] In fairness it should be acknowledged that Rankin performed a useful service in helping to preserve and mark Springfield sites associated with Lincoln.[42]

# Notes

EDITOR'S INTRODUCTION

1. Review by Isabel Paterson, *New York Tribune*, 29 October 1922, section 5, p. 9.

2. Townsend to Weik, Lexington, Kentucky, 23 October 1922, Weik Papers, Illinois State Historical Library, Springfield.

3. Albert J. Beveridge, "Lincoln as His Partner Knew Him," *Literary Digest International Book Review* 1 (September 1923): 33–35, 51. Herndon's biographer, David Donald, felt differently about Weik. In 1948 Donald told an editor of Lincoln's writings: "I don't know why I get so angry about Weik, but there is a quality of shadiness about everything the man ever did—in sharp contrast to Herndon's bluntness and forthrightness." David Donald to Marion Bonzi, New York, 13 May 1948, Small Collection no. 1633 (Weik), Manuscripts Division, Illinois State Historical Library, Springfield.

4. Beveridge to Weik, Indianapolis, 22 December 1922, Weik Papers.

5. *New York Times*, 17 December 1922, section 3, p. 10.

6. *Outlook* 136 (27 February 1924): 358–59.

7. *New York Call*, 29 November 1922, 10.

8. D. C. S. in the *New York World*, 5 November 1922 (copy), Herndon-Weik Papers, Manuscript Division, Library of Congress.

9. *Boston Transcript*, 30 December 1922, book section, 3.

10. *Springfield Republican* (Massachusetts), 7 January 1923, 7A.

11. *The Bookman* 56 (February 1923): 771.

12. *American Review of Reviews* 67 (February 1923): 220.

13. Douglas L. Wilson and Rodney O. Davis, eds., *Herndon's Informants: Letters, Interviews, and Statements about Abraham Lincoln* (Urbana: University of Illinois Press, 1998), xxiii.

14. Douglas L. Wilson, *Honor's Voice: The Transformation of Abraham Lincoln* (New York: Alfred A. Knopf, 1998), 14, 51, 234.

15. Jesse W. Weik, *The Real Lincoln: A Portrait* (Boston: Houghton Mifflin, 1922), 197.

16. Weik's quotes from Herndon's letters can be checked against the originals at the Library of Congress, which are available on microfilm. Emanuel Hertz published many of those letters in *The Hidden Lincoln: From the Papers and*

*Letters of William H. Herndon* (New York: Viking, 1938), but his transcriptions are unreliable. Douglas Wilson and Rodney Davis are preparing a new edition of that valuable correspondence. Weik's long quotations from Jonathan Birch should be compared with his article based on Birch's testimony, "A Law Student's Recollection of Abraham Lincoln," *Outlook* (11 February 1911): 311–14.

17. Cullom Davis et al., eds., *The Law Practice of Abraham Lincoln: Complete Documentary Edition* (DVD-ROM publication; Urbana: University of Illinois Press, 2000).

18. David Donald, *Lincoln's Herndon* (New York: Alfred A. Knopf, 1948), 181n.

19. Weik, *Real Lincoln*, 129.

20. Paul M. Angle, *A Shelf of Lincoln Books* (New Brunswick NJ: Rutgers University Press, 1946), 105.

21. In 1875 Weik began a three-year pursuit of law studies in the office of Thomas Hanna and then began practicing law in 1878. Much of his legal work consisted of prosecuting pension claims before the Interior Department. Weik to the Secretary of the Interior, Greencastle IN, 5 July 1882; Thomas Hanna to W. W. Dudley, Greencastle, 24 June 1881; Weik to Chester Allen Arthur, Washington [July 1882]; records of the Interior Department, Appointments Division, Applications and Appointments 1882, Record Group 48, box 75, entry 27, National Archives Building, College Park MD.

22. John G. Dunbar to Benjamin Harrison, Greencastle, 22 July 1882; John Coburn to James A. Garfield, Indianapolis, 17 February 1881; John Clark Ridpath to James A. Garfield, Greencastle, 21 February 1881; A. J. Hays to Harrison, Sullivan IN, 21 July 1882; Michael A. Gilmet to W. W. Dudley, Greencastle, 28 May 1882; S. D. Coffey to Benjamin Harrison, Brazil IN, 3 July 1882; W. R. Holloway to James A. Garfield, Indianapolis, 17 February 1881; "Applications and Appointments," Interior Department records of 1882.

Weik was a dyed-in-the-wool regular Republican who abhorred party dissidents. In 1913 he told Horace White: "In my political faith and creed I was brought up under the teachings of the old Radical school. My views were rigid as well as ultra. I was taught to avoid such men as [Carl] Schurz, [Lyman] Trumbull and [Charles Francis] Adams as one would the plague. These men failed in their loyalty to Grant; therefore they were not only false but hare-brained reformers, kickers and sore-heads unfit for association with patriots and honest men." Weik to White, Greencastle, 27 September 1913, Horace White Papers, Illinois State Historical Library, Springfield.

23. Weik to Albert J. Beveridge, Greencastle, 13 May 1923, Albert J. Beveridge Papers, Manuscript Division, Library of Congress; obituary in the Greencastle *Daily Banner*, 18 August 1930; Mary Hays Weik, "My Father and Lincoln" ("written for Glenn Tucker in Sept. [19]68"), photocopy of a typescript, Herndon-Weik Papers, box 36; Glenn Tucker, "Lincoln's Jesse W. Weik," *Lincoln Herald* 77 (1975): 3–15, 72–86; Jesse W. Weik, *Weik's History of Putnam County, Indiana* (Indianapolis: B. F. Bowen, 1910), 704–6.

24. Mary Hays Weik, "My Father and Lincoln," 2.

25. *Ridpath's History of the World, Being an Account of the Ethnic Origin, Primitive Estate, Early Migrations, Social Conditions and Present Promise of the Principal Families of Men* 4 vols. (New York: Merrill & Baker, 1897).

26. Tucker, "Lincoln's Weik," 8.

27. Weik to Horace White, Greencastle, 11 March 1914, White Papers.

28. Herndon to Weik, Springfield, 8 October 1881, Herndon-Weik Papers; Donald, *Lincoln's Herndon*, 296–97.

29. Donald, *Lincoln's Herndon*, 313–14.

30. Herndon to Weik, Chicago, 24 December 1886, Herndon-Weik Papers.

31. Tucker, "Lincoln's Weik," 9–10.

32. Weik's role in the composition of the book is discussed in Donald, *Lincoln's Herndon*, 366–67.

33. Mary Hays Weik, "My Father and Lincoln," 3.

34. See the appendix to this volume, " 'A Hard-hearted Conscious Liar and an Oily Hypocrite': Henry B. Rankin's Reliability as a Lincoln Informant."

35. Brochures about these lectures, with press notices and endorsements, can be found in box 36 of the Herndon-Weik Papers; they also are enclosed in Weik to John G. Nicolay, Greencastle, 19 November 1894, John G. Nicolay Papers, Manuscript Division, Library of Congress.

36. Weik to A. E. Malsbury, Greencastle, 11 December 1899, copy, Herndon-Weik Papers.

37. Weik, *Real Lincoln*, vii–ix.

38. In 1923 Beveridge told Weik: "I am depending on this [use of the Herndon-Weik archive] in view of our conversation some years ago when you layed before me your project for writing the new book 'The Real Lincoln,' and asked me to get H. M. Co. to publish it." Beveridge to Weik, 10 January 1923, copy, Beveridge Papers. In 1915 Weik told Horace White: "Before I die I intend to furnish the world with what I believe to be the portrait of *The Real Lincoln*." Greencastle, 5 January 1915, White Papers. The previous year Weik had referred to "the volume which I intend to write after a while on *The Real Lincoln*." Weik to Horace White, Greencastle, 30 September 1914, White Papers.

39. Weik did little interviewing in the early twentieth century. In 1914 he told Horace White that he had recently visited Springfield for the first time in over a decade. "But few of Lincoln's contemporaries are yet living but I managed nevertheless to glean some items." Weik to White, Greencastle, 15 November 1914, White Papers.

40. Wilson and Davis, *Herndon's Informants*, xix.

41. Those magazine articles include "Some Traces of Lincoln's Eloquence," *Harper's Weekly* 40 (15 February 1896): 158–59; "Lincoln and the Matson Negroes: A Vista into the Fugitive-Slave Days," *Arena* 17 (April 1897): 752–58; "A New Story of Lincoln's Assassination: An Unpublished Record of an Eye-Witness," *Century Magazine* 85 (February 1913): 559–62; "Side-Lights on Lincoln: His Campaign Scrap-Book," *Century Magazine* 81 (February 1911): 589–91; "Side-Lights on Lincoln: How Lincoln Was Convinced of General Scott's Loyalty," *Century Magazine* 81 (February 1911): 593–94; "Lincoln as a Lawyer, with an Account of His First Case," *Century Magazine* 68 (June 1904): 279–89; "Lincoln's Vote for Vice-President in the Philadelphia Convention of 1856," *Century Magazine* 76 (June 1908): 186–89; "Lincoln's Gettysburg Address," *Outlook* (12 July 1913), 572–74; "Personal Recollections," *Outlook* (13 February 1909), 345–48; "A Law Student's Recollection of Abraham Lincoln," *Outlook* (11 February 1911), 311–14.

42. Weik to Horace White, Greencastle, 2 June 1907, White Papers. He reported to White in 1908 that in "order to earn a little ready money I'm doing a bit of hackwork these dog days. Some time ago I contracted with a Chicago publisher to write what he has entitled a *History of the Republican National Convention of 1908*. It is a work which is mainly a collection of biographical sketches and portraits of the delegates with just enough historical matter to give it the appearance of having been 'hand-made.'" Weik to White, Greencastle, 26 July 1908, White Papers.

43. Weik to Horace White, Greencastle, 6 December 1913, White Papers; Charles M. Thompson, *The Lincoln Way* (Springfield: Illinois State Journal, 1913); Charles M. Thompson, *Investigation of the Lincoln Way* (Springfield: Illinois State Historical Library, 1915).

44. Beveridge, "Lincoln as His Partner Knew Him," 33–34.

45. Mary Hays Weik, "My Father and Lincoln," 3–4.

46. Tucker, "Lincoln's Weik," 85.

47. Tucker, "Lincoln's Weik," 7.


### IDA M. ANDREWS

1. Weik Papers. The 1880 Census lists an Ida M. Andrews living in Chicago.

2. James Leaton, pastor of the Methodist Church in Springfield (1858–59), lived with his family at Fifth and Monroe Streets, five blocks from the Lincolns' house. He wrote *History of Methodism in Illinois, from 1793 to 1832* (Cincinnati: Walden and Stowe, 1883).

3. Leaton wrote a report titled "Springfield Sta. 1858–59," which contains the following reminiscence about Lincoln:

During the closing months of my term public feeling was much excited on the presidential contest. Mr. Lincoln being then a resident of Springfield, and Mr. Douglas having been a resident formerly, and well known to most of the people. Aware of the injury to the cause of Christ resulting from great political excitement, and knowing that Springfield would be the very fountainhead of it, I took occasion at one of our prayer meetings to caution the members against yielding to improper excitement, stating that whilst I would have every one go to the polls and exercise his right as an American citizen according to his judgement and conscience, no one could take an active part in partisan politics without endangering his soul. And I determined myself that I would not attend a convention or listen to a speech during the campaign. The very next day after the prayer meeting I received a letter from a man in Minnesota, addressed to the Pastor of the Methodist Church in Springfield, enquiring about the Moral Character of Hon. Abraham Lincoln. I saw at once that any reply would be used for electioneering purposes, and whilst I could not tell to which of the parties the enquirer belonged, I felt satisfied that he merely wished to make me a tool for his own purposes. A stamp was enclosed for a reply. Whilst I was reflecting in the post office on the kind of answer I should give him, Mr. Lincoln himself came in, and on the spur of the moment I handed the letter to him, remarking that I had just received the letter, and as it concerned him I wished to know what reply to make. He glanced over it, and with one of his loud laughs replied, "I shall have to decline expressing an opinion on the subject." I accordingly wrote to the enquirer that having learned a distinct public rumor in regard to the character and conduct of our great man, I had submitted the letter to Mr. Lincoln himself who declined expressing an opinion on the subject.

I am grateful to William Hosking, historical council chair of the First United Methodist Church of Springfield, for providing me a transcript of Leaton's reminiscences, which repose in the church's archives in Springfield.

4. Noah W. Matheny (b. 1815), like his father, Charles R. Matheny, served as Clerk of the Sangamon County Commissioners Court (1837–73).

5. Elizabeth J. Stamper (1825–1916), daughter of the Rev. Dr. Jonathan Stamper of the Methodist Church, married Noah Matheny in 1843; they had four children.

6. Weik Papers.

7. Mrs. Andrews's sister, Mrs. Hillary A. Gobin (née Clara Leaton), heard her mother say that the Lincolns "were very unhappy in their domestic life" and that Mary Lincoln "was seen frequently to drive him from the house with a broomstick." Mrs. Hillary A. Gobin to Albert J. Beveridge, South Bend, Indiana, 17 May 1923, Beveridge Papers, Library of Congress. Her husband taught Greek at Indiana Asbury University. On Mrs. Lincoln's temper, see Michael Burlingame, *The Inner World of Abraham Lincoln* (Urbana: University of Illinois Press, 1994), 270–79.

### GEORGE WASHINGTON BRACKENRIDGE

1. Weik Papers. A wealthy philanthropist, Brackenridge (1832–1920) founded the San Antonio National Bank, which he headed from 1866 to 1912. During the Civil War Lincoln sent him to Mexico to assure the rebel leader Benito Juarez that the United States would abide by the Monroe Doctrine and respect Mexican sovereignty once the French were expelled from that land.

2. Cf. Weik, *Real Lincoln*, 131, and Wilson and Davis, *Herndon's Informants*, 354. John A. Brackenridge was an attorney in Boonville, Indiana, when Lincoln was growing up near there. He was, according to Francis Marion Van Natter, renowned on both sides of the Ohio River "for his eloquent pleading. Admitted to practice law *ex gratia* in the Third Circuit Court at Indianapolis, this aristocratic Kentuckian had formed a partnership with C. Fletcher." Francis Marion Van Natter, *Lincoln's Boyhood: A Chronicle of His Indiana Years* (Washington: Public Affairs Press, 1963), 93. He apparently thought little of the future president. After listening to Brackenridge at a trial where he was serving as the prosecuting attorney, young Lincoln reportedly approached and tried to congratulate him; Brackenridge refused to shake the hand proffered by "the Shabby boy." S. T. Johnson, interview with Herndon, Indiana, 14 September 1865, Wilson and Davis, *Herndon's Informants*, 115. Lincoln, "humiliated, shamefacedly left the court room." William L. Barker, talk given to Loyal Legion at Indianapolis, 12 February 1929 (copy), Francis Marion Van Natter Papers, Vincennes University. During the Civil War Lincoln allegedly said to Brackenridge, "it was the best speech that up to that time I had ever heard; if I could as I then thought, make as good a speech as that, my soul would be satisfied." It has been suggested that Lincoln often visited Brackenridge's home to read volumes in his extensive library, but no reliable evidence supports that

speculation. Louis A. Warren, *Lincoln's Youth: Indiana Years, Seven to Twenty-one, 1816–1830* (New York: Appleton, Century, Crofts, 1959), 198–99.

## JOHN W. BUNN

1. Herndon-Weik Papers. In 1847 the New Jersey–born philanthropic merchant banker John W. Bunn (1831–1920), brother of Jacob Bunn, settled in Springfield, where he served as the Springfield city treasurer and was an active member of the Springfield Republican Club in the 1850s. J. McCan Davis described him as someone who "knows many things about Lincoln. . . . He was a young man at the time of Lincoln's election as president and had not attained a place of prominence in politics. He was, however, quite familiar with much that happened on the 'inside' here in Springfield at that time. . . . Mr. Bunn is well known to be averse to publicity and for that reason interviewers have been able to get very little from him." Davis to Ida M. Tarbell, Springfield, 16 May 1906, Ida M. Tarbell Papers, Allegheny College, Meadeville PA.

2. David Logan, son of Lincoln's second law partner, Stephen T. Logan, was an alcoholic. William I. Ferguson was a Springfield attorney who, in company with David Logan and Edward D. Baker, moved to California, where he was killed in a duel. William H. Herndon (1818–91) was Lincoln's biographer and third law partner (1844–61).

3. Delos Brown appears in the 1830 census of Sangamon County. In 1853 he killed John Glasscock.

4. Cf. Weik, *Real Lincoln*, 203–5. Jacob Bunn allegedly told this story at greater length to Amberry Rankin. Henry B. Rankin, *Intimate Character Sketches of Abraham Lincoln* (Philadelphia: Lippincott, 1924), 64–66.

5. Weik Papers. The date is not entirely clear. Someone has penciled in a date within brackets (15 Oct. 1914) but the document itself is on stationery of The New Leland Hotel, Springfield, and dated Oct. 1916, with the day of the month unclear—it could be 21 or 4.

6. In 1879 Alexander H. Lockridge married Laura Pickrell in Sangamon County.

7. Cf. Weik, *Real Lincoln*, 197–98.

8. In 1839 George Smith (1809–99) founded the first banking house in Chicago, George Smith & Co. He lived in Chicago from 1833 to 1856, at which time he returned to his native Scotland.

9. Cf. Weik, *Real Lincoln*, 159.

10. Congressman George Ashmun (1804–70) of Springfield, Massachusetts, represented his district in the U.S. House (1845–51) and served as chairman of the 1860 Republican National Convention in Chicago.

11. Cf. Weik, *Real Lincoln*, 273.

12. Attorney Ebenezer Peck of Chicago, a Democratic member of the Illinois State Legislature, introduced the idea of a convention system during a special session in Vandalia in 1835–36. Peck became chief clerk of the Illinois State Supreme Court (1841–45). With his son he established a Chicago newspaper, the *Democratic Argus*. In protest against the Kansas-Nebraska Act of 1854 he broke with Douglas and became a leading Republican political strategist and organizer. Lincoln appointed him to a seat on the U.S. Court of Claims.

13. Cf. Weik, *Real Lincoln*, 272–73.

14. For more on John Irwin see the statement by Clinton L. Conkling, infra.

15. Benjamin Stephenson Edwards (1818–87), the youngest son of governor Ninian Edwards, studied law with Stephen T. Logan, and was the law partner first of Edward D. Baker, then of John Todd Stuart. Usher Linder called him "one of the vainest men I ever knew, having inherited it from his father." Usher F. Linder, *Reminiscences of the Early Bench and Bar of Illinois* (Chicago: Chicago Legal News, 1879), 350.

16. Cf. Weik, *Real Lincoln*, 164–65.

17. Herndon-Weik Papers.

18. John Hay (1838–1905) served as Lincoln's private secretary (1861–65).

19. Stephen Trigg Logan (1800–1880), Lincoln's second law partner (1841–44), was exceptionally prosperous.

20. A native of Kentucky and a leading merchant banker of Springfield, John Williams (b. 1808) was active in building railroads, packing pork, carding wool, underwriting insurance, and promoting public utilities, as well as in merchandising. In 1824 he arrived in Springfield where forty years later he founded the First National Bank of that town. During the Civil War he served as commissary general of Illinois. Lincoln appointed him disbursing agent of the federal government for funds to build a courthouse and post office in Springfield. See Robert E. Coleberd Jr., "John Williams: A Merchant Banker in Springfield, Illinois," *Agricultural History* 42 (July 1968): 259–65.

21. The merchant Jacob Bunn (1814–1907) was the director of the bank known as Springfield Marine & Fire Insurance Company.

22. Ozias Mather Hatch (1814–93) was Lincoln's neighbor in Springfield and political ally. He served as Illinois's secretary of state.

23. Born in Ireland in 1808, the merchant Thomas Condell became president of the bank known as the Springfield Marine & Fire Insurance Company.

24. German-born John G. Nicolay (1832–1901) was Lincoln's principal private secretary (1860–65).

25. Milton Hay allegedly said, "Well, I've got a nephew who will never be a lawyer. He may be a poet some day, and he can at least write good English. He can be your secretary." "John W. Bunn," unsigned article, *Journal of the Illinois State Historical Society* 13 (July 1920): 277.

26. Hay was hired by the Interior Department and detailed to work at the White House.

27. Cf. Weik, *Real Lincoln*, 282–85.

28. Republican Congressman Robert Cumming Schenck (1809–90) of Dayton, Ohio, represented his district in the U.S. House (1843–51, 1863–71) and served as a general in the Civil War. Donn Piatt (1819–91) was a lawyer and journalist from Ohio.

29. Herndon-Weik Papers. Cf. Weik, *Real Lincoln*, 311–14.

30. Lucian Tilton, president of Great Western Railroad, rented the Lincoln home from 1861 to 1869, when he and his family moved to Chicago.

31. General E. V. Sumner (1797–1863) was a corps commander during the Civil War. David Hunter (1802–86) was a West Point graduate who became a controversial Union general during the Civil War. William Henry Seward (1801–

72) served as secretary of state under Lincoln and Johnson (1861–69). Winfield Scott (1786–1866) was general in chief of the U.S. Army (1841–61).

32. William Henry Bissell (1811–60) served as governor of Illinois (1857–60). John Wood (1798–1880) of Quincy was elected lieutenant governor in 1856; he became governor on the death of Bissell in 1860. In 1831 Kentucky-born attorney Richard Yates (1815–73) settled in Jacksonville, Illinois, where he attended Illinois College. He represented his district in the U.S. House (1851–55), and served both as governor of Illinois (1861–65) and as U.S. senator from Illinois (1865–71.) Johnson's building was owned by Joel Johnson.

33. Francis P. Blair Jr. (1821–75) helped lead the antislavery forces in Missouri. The Radical Republican Benjamin Gratz Brown (1826–85) was a U.S. senator from Missouri (1863–67).

34. Edward Bates (1793–1869) of Missouri served as Lincoln's attorney general (1861–64).

35. Bunn told this story to Jacob C. Thompson, who reported his words thus: "When Mr Lincoln told Mr John W. Bunn, he intended to answer Douglas, Mr Bunn replied: 'Why, Mr Lincoln, that will be pretty hard to do, won't it?' 'No, it won't; Douglas lied; he lied 3 times and I'll prove it!' (Statement of Bunn to writer)." Thompson added that "when Mr Bunn reduced his interview with Mr Lincoln to writing, he substituted the word 'misstatement' for 'lie.' But Mr Bunn told me more than once that Mr Lincoln used the word 'lie' on this occasion." Thompson to Albert J. Beveridge, Springfield, 15 February 1927, Beveridge Papers.

36. Herndon-Weik Papers.

37. A long-time friend and patron of Stephen A. Douglas, Murray McConnell (1798–1869) of Jacksonville was a wealthy landowner. He won election to the Illinois House of Representatives in 1832 and to the state senate in 1846. He became the fifth auditor of the U.S. Treasury in 1855.

38. When it opened in 1838 the American House was Springfield's largest hotel.

39. George Woods was the proprietor of a clothing store, Woods & Henkle, situated on the public square in Springfield.

40. J. Taylor Smith (b. 1825) was a merchant in Springfield (1844–74).

41. Cf. Weik, *Real Lincoln*, 214. A native of New York, Jacob Ruckel (b. 1815) settled in Springfield in 1837 and worked as a cabinetmaker, upholsterer, and merchant.

42. In 1856 Mary Lincoln had the upstairs of the house converted into a full second story. Wayne C. Temple, *By Square and Compasses: The Building of Lincoln's Home and Its Saga* (Bloomington IL: Ashlar Press, 1984), 41–54. This alteration was undertaken while Lincoln was on the circuit. When he returned he pretended not to recognize his domicile. The neighbors, anxious to see how Lincoln would react, observed his conduct with amusement. Mary Lincoln, however, was not amused. "Come in, you old fool," she ordered. "Don't you know your own house when you see it?" Reminiscences of Mrs. John S. Bradford, recorded in Eugenia Jones Hunt, "When Mrs. Abe Called Lincoln 'You Old Fool,'" *Chicago Tribune*, 8 February 1931. Mrs. Hunt, whose father was Albert Jones, a friend and colleague of Lincoln at the bar, commented: "Mrs. Lincoln, we knew, was cultured and used choice diction." See also Eugenia Jones Hunt, *My Personal Recollections of Abraham Lincoln and Mary Todd Lincoln*, ed. Helen A. Moser (Peoria IL: Helen A. Moser,

1966), 26. Some residents of Springfield were puzzled by this remodeling job. Mrs. John Todd Stuart told her daughter, "Lincoln has commenced raising his back building two stories high. I think they will have room enough before they are done, particularly as Mary seldom ever uses what she has." Mrs. John Todd Stuart to her daughter Bettie, [Springfield], 3 April [1856], Stuart-Hay Family Papers, Illinois State Historical Library, Springfield. In fact, the expansion added so much extra space that the Lincolns took in a boarder. The boarder, who slept at the Lincoln home but took his meals elsewhere, was Stephen Smith, brother of Clark M. Smith (husband of Mary's sister Ann). Temple, *By Square and Compasses*, 65.

43. Ebenezer Stout was a partner of William Lavely's in the grocery business (1847–49). In the 1860 census he appears as a fifty-year-old merchant born in New Jersey and residing in McLean County.

44. Weik Papers.

## Mrs. Arthur H. Carter

1. Weik Papers.

2. Harris married Ann Henshaw (1830–1907).

3. Cf. Weik, *Real Lincoln*, 106–8.

## Augustus H. Chapman and Harriet Chapman

1. Weik Papers. Augustus H. Chapman (1822–98) served as a Union officer in the Civil War and as an agent to a Montana Indian tribe after the war. He married Harriet Hanks, daughter of Lincoln's second cousin, Dennis Hanks, and Lincoln's stepsister, Sarah Elizabeth Johnston Hanks. Cf. Weik, *Real Lincoln*, 293.

2. Dennis Hanks (1799–1892), second cousin of Lincoln, lived in the Lincoln cabin from 1817 to 1821, when he married Lincoln's stepsister, Sarah Elizabeth Johnston. In 1830 Hanks and his family migrated to Illinois from Indiana with Thomas Lincoln's family.

3. The town in Moultrie County was called Nelson, not Nelsonville.

4. In 1913 Weik provided a slightly different version of this interview to C. M. Thompson, the chief investigator of the Illinois commission investigating the Lincoln way. Enclosure in Weik to Thompson, 28 November 1913 (copy), Herndon-Weik Papers, box 36.

5. During the Civil War the journalist-historian Charles Carleton Coffin (1823–96) was an army correspondent for the Boston *Journal*, using the nom de plume "Carleton." He wrote *Abraham Lincoln* (New York: Harper and Brothers, 1893).

6. Eli Wiley (b. 1823?) was a plasterer and a justice of the peace in Coles County who wrote an account of Lincoln's 1861 visit to Charleston. Unidentified newspaper clipping, dated 8 February 1888 [perhaps taken from the Charleston *Courier*], quoted in Charles H. Coleman, *Abraham Lincoln and Coles County, Illinois* (New Brunswick NJ: Scarecrow Press, 1955), 198–99.

7. The 1860 census identifies Edward S. Baker, age forty-one, as a plow manufacturer living in Charleston Township.

8. In 1830 Kentucky-born James T. Cunningham (1802–63) settled in Coles County, where he won election to the state legislature in 1834, 1837, 1838, and 1840. According to Cunningham's grandson, the horses were "Claybanks," the "best in

the county." Interview with James T. Cunningham by Charles H. Coleman, 7 January 1950, in Coleman, *Lincoln and Coles County*, 175n.

9. In 1839 Kentucky-born Thomas A. Marshall (1817–73) settled in Coles County, where he practiced law and entered politics, becoming a state senator and member of the state constitutional convention in 1847. In 1863 Lincoln appointed him superintendent of Indian Affairs in Utah; the following year the president named him postmaster at Vicksburg, Mississippi.

10. Robert Matson owned slaves in Kentucky, whom he brought to Illinois to work, occasioning a lawsuit in which Lincoln represented Matson. In the 1850 census for Fulton County, Kentucky, Matson is listed as a fifty-four-year-old farmer with real estate worth $3,500. In 1848 he married Mary Ann Corbin in Illinois. Her age is given as thirty-two in the 1850 census of Fulton County, Kentucky.

### Harriet Chapman

1. Weik Papers. Harriet Hanks Chapman (1826–1915), daughter of Lincoln's second cousin Dennis Hanks and Lincoln's stepsister, Sarah Elizabeth Johnston Hanks, lived in Charleston near Lincoln's stepmother, Sarah Bush Johnston Lincoln.

2. Cf. Weik, *Real Lincoln*, 53–54.

3. Frances Todd married Dr. William S. Wallace, a Springfield physician and druggist. Elizabeth Todd married Ninian Edwards, son of the governor of Illinois. Ann Todd married Clark M. Smith, a merchant in Springfield.

4. In 1857 Mrs. Lincoln complained to one of her half-sisters that when she saw in New York Harbor large passenger steamers ready to sail for Europe, "I felt in my heart, inclined to sigh, that poverty was my portion, how I long to go to Europe." She added significantly that "I often laugh & tell Mr. L[incoln] that I am determined my next Husband *shall be rich.*" Mary Lincoln to Emilie Todd Helm, Springfield, 20 September [1857], *Mary Todd Lincoln: Her Life and Letters*, Justin G. Turner and Linda Levitt Turner, eds. (New York: Alfred A. Knopf, 1972), 50.

5. Mary Todd Lincoln told a somewhat similar story to Elizabeth Keckley, her closest friend at the White House. Elizabeth Keckley, *Behind the Scenes, or, Thirty Years a Slave and Four Years in the White House* (New York: Carleton, 1868), 229–30.

6. No evidence supports this highly improbable allegation.

7. In an earlier interview with Mrs. Chapman, Weik took the following notes: "Mrs L. was engaged to Sen Douglas but she broke off engagement—she became sick—Douglas did not want to release her but her bro in law Dr Wallace who was treating her told Douglas he must give her up. Ms L. told Ms C. that she was engaged to D.

"Story of leaving out her cousin dau of Dr. Todd when inviting guests to a party because cousin had intimated that Robert L. who was baby was a sweet child but not good looking." Weik's interview with Harriet Chapman, Charleston [1886–87], Wilson and Davis, *Herndon's Informants*, 646.

### Robert N. Chapman

1. Weik Papers. Robert N. Chapman, son of Harriet Hanks Chapman and A. H. Chapman, served as postmaster of Charleston.

## WILLIAM DODD CHENERY

1. Herndon-Weik Papers. William Dodd Chenery (b. 1845) married Laura Putnam (b. 1843).

2. Chenery's mother was Eleanor Hallihan Chenery.

3. In 1855 John W. Chenery (1826–1903), manager of the American House Hotel, bought the City Hotel on West Washington Street and made several improvements to the 130-room hostelry. In 1852 his father, Massachusetts-born William Dodd Chenery (1796–1873), settled in Springfield, where he took over the management of the American House. Previously he had run a hotel in Jacksonville. On 15 December 1917 William Dodd Chenery gave the following statement to Clinton L. Conkling:

> The following story is told in our family concerning Mr. Lincoln –
>
> Some two weeks prior to his leaving for Washington in February 1861, he rented his dwelling house on the corner of Eighth and Jackson Streets to Mr. Tilton, then connected with the Wabash Railroad. Mr. Lincoln and family then took rooms in the hotel known at that time as "The Chenery House" kept by my grandfather, W. D. Chenery, assisted by his sons, of whom John W. Chenery, my father, was one. Just before Mr. Lincoln left for Washington, and probably the day before his leaving the Wabash Station in this city where he delivered his farewell address to his friends and neighbors of Springfield, his trunks were placed in the office where he himself "corded" them, that is, tied them around with ropes. After he had finished this himself, he took some of the hotel cards and wrote on the back of them, "A. Lincoln, White House, Washington, D. C." and himself tacked them on his trunks. While he was writing these, my aunt, Miss Fanny Chenery, said to him she would like to have his autograph, and on the back of one of the hotel cards he wrote his name and handed it to her. This card is now one of the cherished possessions of the family. I have a picture of the old Chenery House showing the windows of the rooms occupied by Mr. Lincoln and family, and in front is standing the "bus" which belonged to the hotel, and in all probability the same vehicle that took Mr. Lincoln and family to the station on that rainy morning in February when he left Springfield for the last time.

Clinton L. Conkling Papers, Illinois State Historical Library, Springfield.

## JOHN COBURN

1. Weik Papers. John Coburn (1825–1908) of Indianapolis served as colonel of the Thirty-third Indiana Volunteers.

2. In 1844 Massachusetts-born William L. Utley (1814–87) settled in Wisconsin, where he served as a state assemblyman (1851–52) and state senator (1861–62). After the war he edited newspapers in Racine.

3. In November 1862 George Robertson (1790–1874) of Lexington, Kentucky, demanded that Utley turn over one of his slaves who had somehow managed to reach Utley's camp. When Utley refused, Robertson sued him. Utley then appealed to Lincoln. The case was dropped, but after the war Robertson renewed his suit and won a judgment against Utley for $934.46, a sum that Congress on 14 February 1873 voted to pay Utley to reimburse him. Roy P. Basler, " 'Beef! Beef! Beef!': Lincoln

and Judge Robertson," *Abraham Lincoln Quarterly* 6 (September 1951): 400–407. See also J. Winston Coleman Jr., "Lincoln and 'Old Buster,'" *Lincoln Herald* 46 (Feb. 1944): 3–9. Robertson served as chief justice of the Kentucky Supreme Court (1829–43) and represented his district in the U.S. House (1817–21).

4. Weik Papers.

5. Charles Carleton Coffin, "An American Colonel," in Edmund Clarence Stedman and Ellen Mackay Hutchinson, eds., *A Library of American Literature from the Earliest Settlement to the Present Time* 10 vols. (New York: Charles L. Webster, 1889), 8:162–68.

6. During the Civil War Gen. Absalom Baird (1824–1905) served as a division commander under William S. Rosecrans, George H. Thomas, and William T. Sherman.

7. Weik Papers.

## Jonathan N. Colby

1. Weik Papers. This is written on the stationery of Ephraim Ingals. In 1837 Jonathan Colby (b. 1808), who owned a 460-acre farm near Petersburg, married Lydia Ingalls (1809–58) of Pomfret, Connecticut. In 1852 he ran for sheriff of Menard County. In the 1860 census his worth is listed at $20,000.

## Clinton L. Conkling

1. Conkling Papers. Clinton Levering Conkling (b. 1843), son of James C. Conkling and Mercy Levering Conkling, was a good friend of Robert Todd Lincoln. A prominent corporation lawyer, he participated in many civic enterprises, serving as president of the Board of Education and for a long while as the secretary of the Lincoln National Monument Association. He was an avid student of Springfield's history, contributing several articles to *The History of Sangamon County*, part of Newton Bateman and Paul Selby, eds., *Historical Encyclopedia of Illinois and History of Sangamon County* 3 vols. (Chicago: Munsell, 1912).

2. See Clinton L. Conkling, "How Mr. Lincoln Received the News of His First Nomination," *Transactions of the Illinois State Historical Society* 14 (1909): 63–66.

George M. Brinkerhoff Sr. gave the following account of how the news of Lincoln's nomination in 1860 was received in Springfield:

> On the morning of the day on which Mr. Lincoln was nominated for President in 1860 I was in Mr. James C. Conkling's office reading law. Somewhere between 8:00 and 8:30 Mr. Lincoln came into the office and asked me where Mr. Conkling was. I told him that he was in Chicago at the convention. Mr. Lincoln replied that he had been told on the street just before coming upstairs to the office, that Mr. Conkling was here; that he had returned from Chicago that morning. I told him that if he had so returned I had not seen him nor did I know anything about it as Mr. Conkling said when he went away that he would be away until the convention was closed. And I also told Mr. Lincoln that if Mr. Conkling was home that he would not be at the office for half an hour or an hour, as he did not come to the office until about 9:00 o'clock when he was in the city.
>
> Mr. Lincoln then said he would go out on the street and come back as he was anxious to see Mr. Conkling. He left the office and very shortly Mr.

Conkling came into his office and I told him of Mr. Lincoln's having been there and of our conversation and Mr. Conkling said to me that he had come home unexpectedly; that he thought after looking the situation over that he had done everything he could at that time, so he came home.

I told Mr. Conkling that Mr. Lincoln would be back in a short time as he was very anxious to see him. I should think that inside of 15 or 20 minutes Mr. Lincoln came back and he immediately engaged in conversation with Mr. Conkling concerning the convention; what had been done there and what he had seen and learned and what he believed would be the result of the convention. Mr. Conkling replied to him that he would be nominated that day. He said that after the conversations he had had and the information he had gathered up in regard to Mr. Seward's candidacy he was satisfied that Mr. Seward could not be nominated; he not only had enemies in other states but he had them in his own state; that if Mr. Seward was not nominated on the first ballot he was satisfied that the Pennsylvania delegation and other delegations would immediately go to Mr. Lincoln and he would be nominated. Mr. Lincoln replied that he hardly thought that could be possible, and he said to Mr. Conkling that in case Mr. Seward was not nominated on the first ballot that it was his judgment that Judge Chase of Ohio or Gen. Bates of Missouri would be. They both considered that Mr. Cameron of Pennsylvania stood no chance of nomination. Mr. Conkling replied to Mr. Lincoln in response to that statement that he did not think it was possible to nominate any other one except Mr. Lincoln under those conditions because the pro-slavery part of the Republican party then in convention would not vote for Judge Chase who was considered an abolitionist and the abolitionist part of the republican party would not vote for Gen. Bates because he was from a Slave State and that the only solution of the matter was the nomination of Mr. Lincoln.

Mr. Lincoln and Mr. Conkling continued the conversation for quite a while and in a short time I was compelled to leave the office and go to the Illinois State University where I was then acting as a teacher and I knew nothing more of the matter until about noon when I learned that Mr. Lincoln was nominated.

I was reading law during this time with Mr. Conkling and had been doing so for some time before. Mr. Conkling's office was then in the room over the Chatterton Jewelry Store which is the store now occupied by Newman on the West Side of the Square and the Illinois & Mississippi Telegraph Office was in the same building. (My recollection is that it was on the third story.) I knew the General Agent, Col. John J. S. Wilson who was then and for many years an intimate friend of mine, and my recollection is that I used to go up there to see him"

In the east end of the office under the window there was an old settee on which we had two or three pillows, (buggy cushions) and Mr. Lincoln during the conversation with Mr. Conkling took up a position on that settee and stretched himself out and laid down and when I went away he was lying there and talking to Mr. Conkling.

I learned during the day that after I had left the office Mr. Lincoln also left the office and went out on the street and Mr. Clinton Conkling who was a boy then, came into the office and in some way or other learned of the news of Mr. Lincoln's nomination and took the word that came from the telegraph office out and found Mr. Lincoln on the street and told him of it and as I understand it he was the first one to give Mr. Lincoln the news of his nomination to him.

Years after all this happened Mr. James C. Conkling and myself have gone over this matter and in substance we have agreed that this was what happened that day.

I was a member of the hand ball club that played ball south of Carmody's store and north of the Logan Store. The key was hung in Carmody's store where we could get it. Maj. Arny Robinson kept the grounds being custodian.

On the morning of the day Mr. Lincoln was nominated he was there for a while. He was a member of the club and paid his dues just like the rest of us. But my understanding then and now is that he did not receive the word of his nomination. I was told at the time that he received the news on the street from Clinton L. Conkling.

Conkling Papers. Cf. Weik, *Real Lincoln*, 265–67.

In 1859 Pennsylvania-born George Madoc Brinkerhoff Sr. (1839–1928), freshly graduated from Gettysburg College, settled in Springfield, where he taught math at Illinois State University. Subsequently he served as city comptroller, chief clerk in the state auditor's office, and secretary of the Springfield Iron Company. He also was active in banking and real estate ventures on the location of the telegraph office. See note 7 in this section.

3. T. W. S. Kidd was the court crier in Springfield.
4. Weik Papers.
5. See Donald, *Lincoln's Herndon*, 153–56.
6. Weik Papers.
7. Weik had written to Conkling, saying:

I am convinced now that the telegraph office in Springfield, when Mr Lincoln was nominated in May 1860, was in the third story of the Chatterton building on the west side of the Public Square. The directories at first misled me. Thus, in endeavoring to determine who was the Methodist preacher in Springfield in the summer and fall of 1860, I learned from the directory that it was Rev James Leaton, but the fact is Leaton's term ended in 1859 and Rev. Reuben Andrus was in charge when Mr Lincoln was nominated in May 1860. Apparently the material for the directory of 1860 was collated and possibly in type before the beginning of that year. This will explain the confusion as to the location of the telegraph office.

By the way did you ever know the Rev. Reuben Andrus the Methodist preacher alluded to above? He was the president of Asbury (now DePauw Univ.) when I graduated in 1875. His acquaintance with Lincoln was brief but he knew Richard Yates well and often talked to him about us in chapel [rather, to us about him]. The daughter of James Leaton, his predecessor, lives here now.

Weik to Conking, Greencastle, 22 April 1917, Conkling Papers.

8. Reuben Andrus was a Methodist leader who headed the Illinois Conference Female College in Bloomington in 1853. Two years earlier he was on the faculty at Illinois Wesleyan College. In 1857 he was appointed to lead the church in Quincy, Illinois.

9. Herndon-Weik Papers.

10. Weik had written to Conkling, saying:

As you doubtless are aware I am endeavoring to winnow together a few items regarding the career of Mr. Lincoln which have been glossed over and, in some cases, entirely overlooked by his numerous biographers. Apparently some of these facts (such, for instance, as how and where he actually received the first news of his nomination etc.) are of little importance but you and I know that in time the world will want to know the minutest detail. To that extent I have been slowly and carefully trying to put into shape for preservation certain items and incidents so that posterity when it comes to study Mr. Lincoln, may have all the facts. This will account for my persistence and the liberty I take in applying to you and the few remaining friends of Mr Lincoln for information.

One favor I ask is that you learn from Mr. John W. Bunn whether Mr. Lincoln knew about the fund which was being collected in Springfield in the summer and fall of 1860 to pay for the expense of entertaining visitors etc. Mr. Bunn was very kind to me and told the whole story, who the contributors were and the total of the collection but I failed to learn whether the fund was raised with Mr. Lincoln's knowledge or not. Mr. Bunn is an old man and very cautious to strangers so that I fancied he might not care to tell me more than he has. You know him well and I am sure he will withhold nothing from you.

Later in the season I'm coming over to Springfield but in view of Mr. Bunn's advanced years I am afraid to postpone interviewing him much longer. If, therefore, you will be good enough to see him I shall be deeply obliged.

I thank you for your letter and the enclosed newspaper clippings as to the Barnard statue of Lincoln. The people of Springfield with striking unanimity seem to oppose it but many of the artists and certain persons who are noteworthy as authorities on Lincoln (Ida Tarbell and others) are proportionately firm in pinning their faith to it. It is an unfortunate controversy.

Weik to Conkling, Greencastle, 8 November 1917, Conkling Papers.

11. James Cook Conkling (1816–99) was a friend and political ally of Lincoln. In the 1830s he settled in Springfield, where he was elected mayor in 1844.

12. Copy, Conkling Papers.

13. Weik wrote to Conkling, saying:

Your letter detailing what you learned from Mr. Bunn has been received and I thank you for it. I hope you will continue to pump Mr Bunn about Mr. Lincoln till you have exhausted the reservoir of information he has. You realize, of course, he is an old man and may be with us for a short time only. By all means let me have the story of the Fourth of July address to which you refer in the closing paragraph of your letter; also anything else that may occur to you. Mr. Bunn probably can recall additional items if you will prod him and keep him on the subject. Don't omit anything—however trivial or conventional it may be—if only it relates to Lincoln. I'm sure I am already deeply in your debt for your kindly intercession this far.

P.S. Who is Vachel Lindsay? I noticed that he was the only person interviewed by your local newspaper that had a good thing to say about or in favor of the Barnard statue of Lincoln. I notice also that you who oppose the Barnard statue do so on the ground that it is not a good likeness of Lincoln whereas its advocates—mainly those artistically inclined—including Theo Roosevelt—contend that it is the best expression thus far of Lincoln's nobility and spirituality. The endorsement of such men as [MacManus?] and John S. Sargent is not without significant weight—but the dispute has gone so far already I doubt if it will ever be settled.

Weik to Conkling, Greencastle, 15 November 1917, Conkling Papers.

14. George Grey Grub Barnard (b. 1863) created bronze statues of Lincoln in Cincinnati, Louisville, and Manchester, England. The one in Cincinnati was especially controversial.

15. In 1897 J. Otis Humphrey (1850–1918) was appointed judge of the U.S. Court for the Southern District of Illinois. In 1909 he helped found the Lincoln Centennial Association and served as its president (1909–18).

16. In February 1857 Republican governor William Bissell appointed Herndon one of the three state bank commissioners. After his election as president but before he left for Washington, Lincoln urged governor-elect Richard Yates to reappoint Herndon to that post. Donald, *Lincoln's Herndon*, 146.

17. Weik Papers.

18. George C. Latham (1842–1921), a classmate and close friend of Robert Todd Lincoln at Phillips Exeter Academy, was in business with his father-in-law, John W. Priest. Latham accompanied Robert and his father on the train trip from Springfield to Washington in February 1861.

19. Weik wrote to Conkling, saying:

I have never yet met Mr. George C. Latham of your city but the next time I visit Springfield I want to see him. Meanwhile if you know the gentleman and you find it agreeable I wish you would interview him briefly regarding an incident which took place at the time of Mr. Lincoln's departure for Washington in February 1861. The Springfield papers, and likewise the Chicago papers, of Feby 10th (the day before the departure of the special train from Springfield) announce that Mrs Lincoln would depart for St Louis and join the special train at Indianapolis or some point further east. She would be accompanied by her two sons Tad and Willie but Robert would go on to Indianapolis with his father.

I have taken the pains to consult the files of the Indiana papers of that period and I find this in the Indps *Journal* Fri Feby 11: "Mrs Lincoln and her two younger sons joined her husband in this city Tuesday morning and proceeded with him to Cincinnati. Had she been here Monday evening she would have been almost as much of a lion as old Abe himself." The *Courier* of LaFayette Ind. thru which place the Presidential train passed just after noon of the day of departure in its issue printed that evening says: "There were no ladies in the party, Mrs. Lincoln having determined to defer her departure for Washington until some time next week so as to join her husband in New York and accompany him thence to Washington." In another place in the same issue I find this item:

"Mr Lincoln is in excellent health and spirits. His family (Mrs Lincoln and two little boys) join him tonight in Indianapolis. Mrs Lincoln had planned to meet the party in New York but prefers to accompany her husband now."

In its issue Feb 11 (printed before the special train left Springfield) the Springfield Daily Journal says: "Mrs. Lincoln with her children and domestics will not leave for Washington until Thursday and will overtake Mr. Lincoln at New York."

In the Spfield Journal Feby 12 the correspondent Henry Villard who accompanied the Pres-elect on his journey telegraphs from Tolono Ills saying:

"Just before leaving Springfield, Mrs Lincoln determined to join the party with her two sons at Indianapolis after visiting St Louis."

If Mr. Latham recalls the details of the trip what is his recollection of this matter? Surely if Mrs Lincoln left Springfield the day or even two days before the Pres-elect departed on the special train she could hardly have gone to St Louis and visited any one there and then overtaken her husband in Indianapolis within twenty-four hours after the latter set out from Springfield. Besides a gentleman who lived in our town and whose word I would be willing to take any time told me a few months before his death, eight years ago, that he rode from LaFayette to Indianapolis on the morning of the day following Feby 11th (when Mr. Lincoln passed through) and that Mrs Lincoln and her two boys were on the same train en route to join Mr. Lincoln at Indianapolis.

If therefore Mrs L did reach Indps as detailed above why did she not travel with her husband in the first place? What was the matter? If Mr. Latham or any one else tells you anything about the affair pray assure them in my name that if they so desire their names will not be used if the incident should ever be published.

Weik to Conkling, Greencastle, 18 January 1918, Conkling Papers.

20. Weik Papers.

21. Virginia-born Ward Hill Lamon (1828–93) practiced law in Danville, Illinois. A close friend of Lincoln, he acted as an unofficial presidential bodyguard during the Civil War. His official post at the time was marshal of the District of Columbia.

22. John Carroll Power, *Abraham Lincoln* (Springfield IL: E. A. Wilson, 1875).

23. Herndon-Weik Papers. Weik wrote "Jan 23 1918" on this document.

24. While en route to Washington Mary Lincoln threw a tantrum in Harrisburg, Pennsylvania, where the president-elect learned that assassins might attempt his life in Baltimore. Hurried changes were made in Lincoln's route and schedule; lest spies discover the revised plans, the strictest secrecy was enjoined on all who knew

about it. One of those who helped revise the schedule, Alexander K. McClure, later described how Mary Lincoln failed to cooperate: "To our utter surprise Mrs. Lincoln became very unmanageable. She suspected that some movement was going on and insisted that if Mr. Lincoln's route was changed she must accompany him, and spoke publicly about it in disregard of the earnest appeals to her for silence. Prompt action was required in such an emergency, and several of us simply hustled her into her room with Colonel [E. V.] Sumner and Norman Judd, chairman of the Lincoln campaign in Illinois[,] and locked the door on the outside. The men with her explained what was to be done and forced her to silence as she could not get out of the door." McClure "thought Mrs. Lincoln was simply a helpless fool and was so disgusted with her conduct that evening" that he "never spoke to her afterwards." A. K. McClure to an unidentified correspondent, n.p., 9 May 1907, in Emanuel Hertz, *Abraham Lincoln: A New Portrait* 2 vols. (New York: Liveright, 1931), 249–51.

25. Weik Papers, copy.

26. In 1862 Lincoln appointed his old friend, judge David Davis (1815–86) of Bloomington, Illinois, to the U.S. Supreme Court. Orville Hickman Browning (1806–81) first met Lincoln in the mid-1830s, and from that time until 1865, as Browning said, "our relations were very intimate: I think more so than is usual. Our friendship was close, warm, and, I believe, sincere. I know mine for him was, and I never had reason to distrust his for me. Our relations, to my knowledge, were never interrupted for a moment." Browning to Isaac N. Arnold, Quincy, Illinois, 25 November 1872, Isaac N. Arnold Papers, Chicago Historical Society. One historian maintained that Browning "was Lincoln's life-long associate in law and politics, his cherished adviser and his intimate friend—hardly anyone [was] closer to him." Harlan Hoyt Horner, "Lincoln Rebukes a Senator," *Journal of the Illinois State Historical Society* 44 (1951): 116. Browning served in the Illinois State Senate for four years (1836–40), while Lincoln sat in the Illinois State House of Representatives. They lodged at the same house and spent much time together. From July 1861 to January 1863 Browning was a U.S. senator and he visited the White House almost every day while Congress was in session. Maurice Baxter, *Orville Hickman Browning: Lincoln's Friend and Critic* (Bloomington: Indiana University Press, 1957); Theodore Calvin Pease, in *The Diary of Orville Hickman Browning* 2 vols., Theodore Pease and James G. Randall, eds. (Springfield: Illinois State Historical Library, 1925, 1933), xi–xxxii. Browning was critical of Lincoln in 1864, when he told a friend: "I am personally attached to the President, and have faithfully tried to uphold him, and make him respectable; tho' I never have been able to persuade myself that he was big enough for his position. Still, I thought he might get through, as many a boy has got through college, without disgrace, and without knowledge, but I fear he is a failure." Browning to [Edgar] Cowan, Quincy, 6 September 1864 photostatic copy, James G. Randall Papers, Manuscript Division, Library of Congress.

27. Weik replied to this letter on February 2, saying:

Your letter relating to the David Davis–O H. Browning matter received. Thanks. Unfortunately the paper alluded to by you and containing something by our venerable friend John W. Bunn has thus far not reached me. As I value highly every thing that emanates from Mr. Bunn I will appreciate it profoundly if you will send me another copy of the paper; and if it is not accessible kindly tell me the name and date so that I may try to procure a copy myself.

Among other things I want to learn something about Mr Lincoln's habits and connection with the business world in Springfield. Where did he do his banking and who and how many were the bankers? Did he and Herndon deposit with a bank and if so who was the banker? Who were the bankers in Spfield from 1850 to 1860? Is any bank in existence now that was in business prior to 1860? Was either Lincoln's, Herndon's or Lincoln's & Herndon's account worth running after? What was its probable value or extent? I presume our friend Bunn would be a competent witness on that point but unless you could get the information from him I fancy it would be idle for me to ask him. Can't you see him for me?

I have been permitted to see and copy the books of two stores in Springfield—or rather that part which relates to Mr. Lincoln—so that I can determine the character and extent of his household expenditures and I have concluded that his wife's purchases (and I understand she ran the establishment) were extremely economical. He never allowed his accounts to remain unpaid very long and he himself always paid cash when he bought any thing. His income must have been small for Gov. Pennypacker of Penn. who came into possession of one of his account books let me see it (Lincoln & Herndon's book) and out of almost 200 separate entries covering a period of about 4 years only one account equalled $100. How, therefore, could he afford to send his son to Harvard College or even to a preparatory school in New England with such a meagre income?

Conkling Papers.

28. Copy, Conkling Papers.

29. George W. Chatterton was a prominent jeweler in Springfield. On 1 March Weik wrote to Conkling from Greencastle, saying:

I want to learn a little about Geo. W. Chatterton of Springfield. Mr Herndon once told me that he visited Mr Lincoln late in 1861 in Washington on Mr. Chatterton's behalf; that Lincoln accompanied him to the office of Wm. P. Dole Com. of Indian Affairs and asked the latter to appoint Chatterton Indian Agent which was promptly done. What is your understanding? Also what relation either by blood or marriage existed between Herndon or Chatterton? I have heard (I cannot remember the source of my information) that Herndon was a widower at the time and anxious to gain the favor of a certain lady whom he wanted to marry; that Chatterton was in a position to help him and that in return for his aid in gaining the lady's hand Herndon secured his appointment. What are the facts?

On 9 April 1918 Weik wrote to Conkling from Greencastle, saying:

You will recall that I asked you once about G. W. Chatterton and if you knew that he had once been appointed Indian Agent by Lincoln at the instance of Herndon and you answered you knew nothing about the incident. Since then I have had the records of the Indian Office at Washington examined and learn that there is no record there of Geo. W. Chatterton but that it is shown that *Charles W. Chatterton* of Ills. was "appointed by Pres Lincoln on March 10 1862 Indian Agent for the Cherokee Indian Nation for a term of four years."

This materially corroborates Herndon who says he visited Lincoln in the winter of 61–62 and urged the appointment of Chatterton. If you are unable to recall or locate Charles W. Chatterton perhaps Mr. Bunn or some other old resident can. I understand Geo. W. Chatterton has a daughter still living in Springfield. If I knew her name or address I would write her myself. Meanwhile I would be glad to have a line from you.

After leaving Springfield, when I saw you a few days ago, I went on to Bloomington where David Davis II showed me his grandfathers letters. I didn't have time to examine them all but I read enough to convince me that there was great merit in the contention of Leonard Swett, that Lincoln was not willing to make David Davis U.S. Supreme Judge until assured by Swett that Davis's appointment would also cancel or satisfy the claims of Swett.

30. Herndon's first wife died in August 1861; eleven months later he wed Anna Miles, a beautiful woman eighteen years his junior. Anna's sister, Elizabeth, had wed Charles W. Chatterton.

Weik told the story of Herndon's courtship to a journalist:

During the long months I was engaged with Mr. Herndon in preparing the life of Lincoln, which bears his name, he told me many stories regarding the great emancipator which have not been printed; among others how he, Herndon won his present wife through the kindly help of Lincoln. In the city of Springfield, the home of both Lincoln and Herndon, there lived a most estimable young lady, proud, beautiful and imperious, whose intellectual and physical graces captured the susceptible heart of Lincoln's old law partner, himself a grim and gruff widower, not particularly attractive to a woman with an eye for beauty and youth. Herndon laid violent siege to the hand of this lady, but she would have nothing to do with him, and the old widower was compelled to resort to stratagem, in order to capture the object of his mature affection, and this is the scheme he worked, as told by himself. The young lady lived with her brother-in-law, a smart and ambitious jeweler, by the name of Charles W. Chatterton, and it was through him and Lincoln that Herndon finally obtained the hand of the lady now his wife. Knowing that Chatterton was anxious to make money fast, and become a rich man, Herndon called him into his office one night . . . and asked him if he didn't want a good paying position, where he would have a chance, under the government, to make money easily and rapidly. Of course Chatterton did. It was the opportunity he had long sought. Herndon then went on to explain what the young jeweler already knew, that he was in love with his pretty sister-in-law, Hannah [Anna], and that he was determined to have her for his wife if such a thing was within the range of the possibilities; and then disclosed his plan, which was that Chatterton and his wife should do all in their power to bring about the desired result, in return for which Herndon was to obtain from Lincoln such a position as might be decided upon. He explained to Chatterton, however, that the place sought for should be something within reason and suited to his capacities. This struck the jeweler as a good scheme, and he willingly gave Herndon his promise that he and his wife would leave nothing undone that would aid in the slightest in convincing Hannah [Anna] that her duty laid in the direction of accepting the old lawyer as a suitor for her hand. This sort of campaign was kept up for several weeks, in fact, several months, but at last the lady surrendered and gave up the unequal contest, and agreed to become the wife of Lincoln's old law partner.

As soon as this was settled Chatterton demanded the promised office, and suggested that he and Herndon go on to Washington at once and secure the fat plum. To this Herndon would not consent. He did not want Chatterton with him when he went to the President with his story and unique request. He told Chatterton that there was no question but what Lincoln would give him anything he might ask for, but that he would go alone to the Capital and lay the whole affair before his true and tried friend; and off he started on his mission of love.

Arriving in Washington Herndon, of course, had no trouble in gaining an audience with his old partner. To the President he told the whole story, which his Excellency enjoyed immensely. He was well acquainted with all the parties, and the matter appeared wonderfully funny to him, but he was only too glad to assist in the conspiracy.

"Now, said Lincoln, after the whole matter had been talked over, what does Charley want?"

"He wants an Indian agency," answered Herndon.

"He shall have it," replied the great-hearted magistrate, "and I will see that he gets his commission this very day; so come along." And together Lincoln and Herndon posted off to the Commissioner of Indian Affairs, then the Hon. W. P. Dole, formerly of Paris, Ill. Here Lincoln told a good story and then Herndon made his request for an Indian agency for Herndon's prospective brother-in-law.

It did not take very long to find one of Buchanan's appointees who could be spared from the service, and "in an amazingly short time," to quote Herndon's exact words, the commission for Chatterton was in his pocket, and he and Lincoln were on their way back to the White House, where Herndon dined that day, and the same evening took the train for Springfield with the precious document.

Shortly afterward Herndon and the young lady were married, and have lived happily ever since, she bearing him two children, now the joy and pride of his old age. Young Chatterton made his Indian agency pay after the manner of all his predecessors and successors, and became a wealthy man. Whether Herndon's wife was ever made acquainted with the part Lincoln's administration took in her matrimonial affairs I was not informed, but I presume the old man told her all about it, or he never would have given me the story. And so they were married.

"Lincoln in a New Role. How He is Alleged to Have Helped His Law Partner to a Young Wife," unidentified clipping, sometime not long before 1891, Weik scrapbook, Lincoln Museum, Fort Wayne IN. Cf. Herndon's memo, "Lincoln's 'Ingratitude,'" Herndon-Weik Papers.

31. Herndon-Weik Papers.

32. Conkling is responding to Weik's letter of 20 June, written at Greencastle:

I am a little confused as to the matter of the history of the hotel situation in Springfield in Jany & Feby 1861 and hope you can properly enlighten me. It is understood that late in January or early in February (probably the latter) Mr Lincoln and his wife, having practically surrendered their house, were boarding for a few days at the Chenery House and that it was from the latter hostelry that Mr. L. took his departure when he drove to the Gr[ea]t Western station the morning he set out on the special train for Washington. The Chenery House, judging from the personal items in the local papers relating to the arrival and departure of distinguished people who came to call on Mr Lincoln must have been the leading hotel and yet in several instances I have noticed references to the St. Nicholas Hotel.

For instance, one item in the Chicago Tribune written by its Springfield correspondent Jan 14 mentions the presentation of a gold-headed cane to Mr Lincoln by a returned Californian and says that the presentation took place "in the business office of the St Nicholas Hotel" and elsewhere I find other references to the latter concern. When did it begin to do business and what was its location with reference to the Chenery? You doubtless recollect it well.

Conkling Papers.

33. For more on the St. Nicholas see the pamphlet by Wayne C. Temple, *Abraham Lincoln and Others at the St. Nicholas* (Springfield: St. Nicholas Corporation, 1968).

34. Archer Gray Herndon (1795–1867), Springfield tavern owner, was the father of Lincoln's law partner and biographer, William H. Herndon.

35. New Hampshire native John D. Freeman (1810–80) was a physician and real estate developer who built the St. Nicholas in 1856–57. He left Springfield for Carbondale in 1867.

36. Pennsylvania native James W. Sponsler (b. 1830?), a restaurateur from Decatur, acquired the hotel in 1860. Born in Rochester, New York, the merchant John McCreery (1832–1903) settled in Springfield in 1857 and bought the hotel seven years later. He served as mayor of Springfield for several terms. McCreery ran the hotel until his death, when his son John Hubbel McCreery took over its management.

37. Weik Papers.

38. Weik wrote to Conkling from Greencastle, saying:

Please tell me a little about Robert and Ben F. Irwin. What was the relationship and what was the business or calling of each? I understand Robert was a banker and a very close friend of Lincoln. All I have been able to learn about Benjamin F. is that he wrote and published a spirited, if not spicy, letter in the Springfield Journal in the seventies in which he took issue with Herndon as to Lincoln's religious belief. Was he older than Robert? What kind of a man was he and what opportunities for knowing about Lincoln's religious views did he have over that possessed by other contemporaries of Lincoln? Mr. Chas. W. McClellan who recently died in Champlain N. Y. and who claims to have been a clerk in the Ridgely bank in Springfield from 56 to '60 reports that Lincoln once exclaimed that he "would cut off his right hand if Robert Irwin asked it of him." P.S. Among some papers turned over to me by Mr. Herndon I have learned that the slanderous language which was the basis of the suit by Archer G. Herndon vs Reuben Radford was the charge that Herndon was "a dirty murderer." In an affidavit executed by the deft, Radford, the latter contends he will be able to prove by the testimony of William L. May that Herndon admitted to the latter that he shot a fellow soldier named [Cherry?] after dark one night as he lay under a tree. They were both soldiers in the War of 1812.

Weik to Conkling, Greencastle, 17 July 1918, Conkling Papers.

39. Irwin's long letter to the *Illinois State Journal*, dated Pleasant Plains, 20 April 1874, appeared in the newspaper's issue of 16 May 1874. Kentucky-born William Mentor Graham (1800–1886) helped Lincoln study grammar at New Salem. Thomas Mostiller's age is given in the 1840 Sangamon County census as between thirty and forty. His letter to Irwin about Lincoln's religion was titled and dated Pleasant Plans, 28 April 1874. Mentor Graham's letter to Irwin is dated Petersburg, 17 March 1874. Isaac Cogdal's is dated 10 April 1874. Jonathan Harnett claimed to have visited Lincoln at his office at Springfield in 1858. Erasmus Manford (1815–84) of Chicago wrote about Lincoln's religion in his book *Twenty-five Years in the West* (Chicago: E. Manford, 1867). He also wrote *An Oral Debate on the Coming of the Son of Man, Endless Punishment, and Universal Salvation* (Indianapolis: Indiana State Journal, 1848).

40. Kentucky-born Peter Cartwright (1785–1872) was a celebrated circuit rider who unsuccessfully opposed Lincoln in his race for a seat in the U.S. House in 1846. Toward the end of the campaign Cartwright spread rumors that Lincoln was an infidel.

## JAMES A. CONNOLLY

1. Weik Papers. In 1861 the New-Jersey-born and Ohio-based Maj. James Austin Connolly (1843–1914) settled in Charleston, Illinois, where he became a lawyer and won election to the U.S. House of Representatives (1894, 1896). In the Civil War he rose from the rank of private to lieutenant colonel in the 123rd Illinois Infantry. After his service in Congress he moved to Springfield, where he continued to practice law.

2. For more on Rankin see the appendix to this volume, "'A Hard-hearted

Conscious Liar and an Oily Hypocrite': Henry B. Rankin's Reliability as a Lincoln Informant."

3. Weik Papers.

4. Edward H. Thayer was a prominent merchant in Springfield.

5. Cf. Weik, *Real Lincoln*, 59.

6. Weik Papers.

7. In 1861 Charles S. Zane (1831–1915) replaced Lincoln as Herndon's law partner in Springfield.

8. Zane's reminiscences of Lincoln can be found in "Lincoln As I Knew Him," *Sunset Magazine* (October 1912): 430–38.

9. Weik Papers.

10. In 1831 Kentucky-born Alexander P. Dunbar (b. 1810) settled in Charleston, Illinois, where he became the first lawyer to practice in Coles County. In 1836, 1837, and 1844 he won election to the state legislature, where he met and befriended Lincoln. An old line Whig, Dunbar joined the Republican party in 1856 and stumped for Republican presidential candidates regularly.

11. Cf. Weik, *Real Lincoln*, 294–97.

## GEORGE PERRIN DAVIS

1. Copy, Herndon-Weik Papers. George Perrin Davis (1842–1917) of Bloomington, Illinois, son of Lincoln's close friend David Davis, was trained as a lawyer but spent most of his professional career as a stock raiser and farmer on his father's extensive land holdings. He served as president of the McLean County Historical Society and was a founder of the Illinois State Historical Society.

2. Ezra M. Prince, ed., *Transactions of the McLean County Historical Society, Bloomington, Illinois: Meeting of May 29, 1900, Commemorative of the Convention of May 29, 1856, That Organized the Republican Parity in the State of Illinois* vol. 3 (Bloomington: Pantagraph, 1900), 14–23.

3. Oliver Lowndes Davis (1819–92) won election to the seventh circuit court in 1861 and held that post until 1866. From 1873 to 1879 he served as judge of the fifteenth judicial circuit. He eventually became a justice of the state supreme court. Originally a Democrat, he switched to the Republican Party in 1856 and four years later was a delegate to the Chicago Convention which nominated Lincoln for president. Maryland-born Charles H. Constable lived in Mt. Carmel, Illinois.

4. In 1838 New-Jersey-born David B. Campbell settled in Springfield, where he served as prosecutor (1848–56). In 1842 he was elected mayor of Springfield. In 1846 he was attorney general of Illinois. Campbell was noted for his prankish sense of humor.

5. Roy P. Basler et al., eds., *Collected Works of Abraham Lincoln* 8 vols. (New Brunswick NJ: Rutgers University Press, 1953–55), 3:347.

6. Lincoln's autobiography written for Jesse W. Fell, enclosed in Lincoln to Fell, 20 December 1859, Basler et al., *Collected Works*, 3:511–12.

7. Cf. Weik, *Real Lincoln*, 191–92.

## ISAAC R. DILLER

1. Weik Papers. A graduate of the Philadelphia College of Pharmacy, Isaac Roland Diller (b. 1854) worked in the drugstore which his father, Roland W.

Diller, founded. He served as clerk of the Illinois House of Representatives (1850–53), postmaster of Springfield (1853–57), consul at Bremen (1857–61), and consul at Florence (1886–90). In 1907 he switched fields and devoted himself to the real estate business.

2. Cf. *Real Lincoln*, 93–94.

3. In 1844 Pennsylvania-born Roland Weaver Diller (1822–1905) settled in Springfield, where he worked as a printer and surveyor. In 1849 he joined Charles S. Corneau in establishing a drugstore, which he ran for half a century.

4. Dr. William S. Wallace, a physician and druggist in Springfield and husband of Mary Todd Lincoln's sister Ann, won appointment as a paymaster in the Civil War.

5. Weik Papers.

6. See the entry for Josiah Kent elsewhere in this volume.

7. According to the 1860 Springfield City Directory, William Clarke was the baggage master for the Great Western Rail Road Company. (See also the testimony of Josiah P. Kent in this volume.) That directory contains no entry for Maria Drake, though it does list Miss Mary M. Drake boarding at William C. Greenwood's.

8. "John Flynn, of the Court House, . . . served a term of years with Mr. Edwards." *Illinois State Journal* (Springfield), 20 July 1882, p. 6, c. 3. In the 1860 Sangamon County census John Flynn is listed as a twenty-six-year-old Irish-born drayman.

9. The gentleman referred to was perhaps William G. Baker (b. 1878), who owned a plumbing business in Springfield, his native town.

10. Weik Papers.

11. Davis was born in 1817 and died in 1861. See the statement by his daughter, Clara Davis Hoyt, elsewhere in this volume. In 1849 Lincoln helped him win appointment as receiver in the Springfield land office. His mother, Maria Mumford Davis (1797–1889), was described by one historian as a "dynamic matriarch." Wayne C. Temple, *Lincoln's Connections with the Illinois & Michigan Canal, His Return from Congress in '48, and His Invention* (Springfield: Illinois Bell, 1986), 55.

12. Lt. Thomas Davis, an attorney in civilian life, was killed at the battle of Cerro Gordo in 1847. Walter Davis was a sergeant in the Fourth Illinois Volunteers, commanded by Lincoln's friend Edward D. Baker.

13. The architect George H. Helmle (b. 1853) of Springfield was elected town clerk (1874, 1875) and assessor (1876).

14. It was. See Temple, *Lincoln's Connections with Canal*, 54–72.

15. William Helmle, father of George H. Helmle, was a stonemason who carved the tops of the pillars in the hall of the Illinois House of Representatives.

16. See the letter by Clara Hoyt elsewhere in this volume.

## WILLIAM D. DONNELLY

1. Weik Papers.

2. John Carmody's establishment is listed in the 1860 Springfield City Directory as a "Saloon & Grocery" on the east side of Sixth Street between Washington and Jefferson Streets. In 1851 Carmody opened a night school in Springfield. Eight years later he ran for alderman; that same year he extinguished a fire in the nearby office of the *Illinois State Journal*. See Carmody's reminiscences in Walter B. Stevens, *A*

*Reporter's Lincoln*, Michael Burlingame, ed. (Lincoln: University of Nebraska Press, 1998), 140–41.

3. Cf. Weik, *Real Lincoln*, 264.

4. In 1859 J. W. Reynolds was tried for public drunkenness. *Illinois State Journal* (Springfield), 17 December 1859. In the 1850 Sangamon County census, a James Reynolds, age twenty-three, is identified as a laborer born in Kentucky. A Joseph Reynolds bought land in Sangamon County in 1848.

## DENNIS HANKS DOWLING

1. Weik Papers. Dennis Hanks Dowling, son of Thomas S. Dowling and Dennis Hanks's daughter, Sarah Jane Dowling, was employed at the statehouse in Springfield.

2. In the Civil War Alexander Briggs served in Company D of the 116th Illinois Infantry.

3. The fullest account of Lincoln's visit to Charleston in 1861 is Coleman, *Lincoln and Coles County*, 191–210.

4. The reporter was wrong.

5. Weik Papers.

6. Harriet Hanks Chapman said that the Lincoln party in 1830 traveled from Indiana to Illinois in "three covered wagons, two drawn by oxen, and one by horses, and two saddle horses." Affidavit dated Charleston, Illinois, 2 November 1912, in Charles M. Thompson, *The Lincoln Way* (Springfield: Illinois State Journal, 1913), 18. For detailed accounts of that journey see *ibid.* and *The Lincoln Memorial Way Through Indiana* (Indianapolis: State of Indiana, 1932). For a detailed account of the Lincolns' travels through Coles County in 1830 see Coleman, *Lincoln and Coles County*, 8–18.

7. Cf. Weik, *Real Lincoln*, 53–54.

8. A copy of Sarah Jane Dowling's article in the *Springfield News* (undated) is enclosed in Jessie Palmer Weber to Charles M. Thompson, 13 December 1912, appendix D in Thompson, *Lincoln Way*. See also *Bloomington (Illinois) Bulletin*, 31 January 1909.

9. Sarah Bush Lincoln's sister Hannah (listed as age forty-eight in the 1850 census) and her husband, Ichabod Radley, had a daughter named Hannah, who wed a Maryland-born farmer, John Sawyer (1788–1861). In the 1850 census they are listed as residents of the Wabash precinct in Coles County. "Lincoln Unwritten History," address by Clarence W. Bell in Mattoon, Illinois, 11 February 1931, *Lerna (Illinois) Eagle*, 27 February 1931; Dennis Hanks Dowling to Charles M. Thompson, 1 January 1913, in Thompson, *Lincoln Way*, 39; J. K. Rardin, editor, communication dated 10 September 1912, *Charleston (Illinois) Daily News*, 12 September 1912, in Thompson, *Lincoln Way*, 64–65; William F. Cavins, "The Lincoln Family – Neighbors of Our Fathers," pamphlet (Mattoon IL: Mattoon 80th Anniversary Lincoln Day Committee, 1934), 3; Coleman, *Lincoln and Coles County*, 2–3, 22. In 1828 the Radleys left Elizabethtown, Kentucky, for Paradise, Illinois, where John Sawyer had settled two years earlier. Clarence W. Bell's testimony, 18 September 1930, in "Proceedings of Hearing Held before the Special Committee Appointed to Recommend the Proper Routing of the Proposed Lincoln National Memorial

Highway," typescript, pp. 21–40, Abraham Lincoln Association reference files, folder "Lincoln Memorial Highway," Illinois State Historical Library, Springfield. John Sawyer was "the best friend that Thos. Lincoln ever had, both in Kentucky and Illinois." Clarence Bell's talk of 18 September 1930, "New Lincoln History," *Lerna (Illinois) Eagle*, 7 November 1930. See also Carmen Weir, "The 'Lost' Lincolns," *Illinois Magazine* supplement to the *Decatur (Illinois) Herald and Review*, 11 February 1934.

### ELIZABETH EDWARDS

1. Undated memo by Weik on back of a typed copy of William H. Herndon's interview with E. L. Baker, Herndon-Weik Papers. Elizabeth Todd Edwards (1813–88), Mary Todd Lincoln's oldest sister, married Ninian Edwards, son of the governor of Illinois, and became a prominent hostess in Springfield.

### ANNIE M. FLEURY

1. Herndon-Weik Papers. Annie M. Fleury (b. 1843) was the daughter of William H. Herndon and his first wife, Mary Maxcy Herndon.

2. In 1816 Maryland-born George Uriah Miles (1796–1882) migrated to Illinois, where he moved about for many years. In 1836 he settled in Menard County.

### FREDERICK DENT GRANT

1. Herndon-Weik Papers. Frederick Dent Grant (b. 1850), son of U. S. Grant, was attending school in Burlington, New Jersey, at the time of Lincoln's assassination. He later graduated from West Point and served in the army until 1881, when he resigned to enter business. He served as U.S. minister to Austria (1888–93).

2. The main reason why the Grants did not accompany the Lincolns to Ford's Theater was because the general and his wife could not abide the First Lady. On April 13 she had asked General Grant to escort her to view the illuminated capital buildings. At the urging of the president he accepted, and as the two entered their coach the huge crowd gathered at the White House lustily cried out "Grant" nine times, "whereupon Mrs. L[incoln] was disturbed, & directed the driver to let her out." But when the crowd then cheered for Lincoln, she gave orders to proceed. This "was repeated at different stages of the drive" whenever the crowd learned the identity of the coach's occupants. Evidently Mary Lincoln found it unsettling that Grant should be cheered first. The following day, when invited by the president to attend the production of "Our American Cousin" at Ford's Theater, the general declined lest he endure Mary Lincoln's displeasure yet again. Grant related this story to his cabinet more than four years after the assassination. Hamilton Fish, diary, 12 November 1869, Hamilton Fish Papers, Manuscript Division, Library of Congress. Mrs. Grant told Fish "that she objected strenuously to accompanying Mrs. Lincoln."

### CHARLES H. GRAY

1. Weik Papers.

2. Rhode Island native Isaac H. Gray (b. 1815) was a merchant and gold prospector before turning hotelier in the early 1850s. He moved to Springfield

in 1853 and purchased the American House. In 1855 he dissolved his partnership with Hiram C. Walker. The following year he formed a partnership with Nicholas Ridgely, which was dissolved three years later. In March 1860 he bought a hotel in Bloomington. He was an old line Whig before becoming a Republican.

### B. A. Harvey

1. Weik Papers. B. A. Harvey was an attorney in Mt. Carmel.

2. For more on Lincoln's trip from Carmi and Mt. Carmel on 1–3 September 1840, see George W. Smith, *When Lincoln Came to Egypt* (Herrin IL: Trovillion, 1940), 60–62.

### Robert Roberts Hitt

1. Herndon-Weik Papers. Congressman Robert Roberts Hitt (1834–1906) of Freeport, Illinois, represented his district from 1882 until his death. His valuable reminiscences of the 1858 debates can be found in Stevens, *A Reporter's Lincoln*, ed. Burlingame, 66–90.

2. James B. Sheridan was a skilled shorthand reporter for the *Philadelphia Press*, whose editor, John W. Forney, vigorously supported Douglas in his quarrel with President Buchanan in 1857 and 1858. Forney sent Sheridan west to help Douglas win reelection in 1858. Sheridan was assisted in his reporting by Henry Binmore.

### Clara Davis Hoyt

1. Weik Papers. Born in Springfield in 1854 to Walter Davis and Emeline Planck Davis, Clara Davis married New York–born James Hoyt in 1875.

2. Around 1836 Walter Davis settled in Springfield, where he became a partner of Jackson A. Hough. He was an active Whig, serving on the Sangamon County Whig Committee and joining the Zachary Taylor Club. In 1856 he was an alternate delegate to the Know-Nothing convention. For more information about Walter Davis see the testimony of Isaac R. Diller elsewhere in this volume.

3. Cf. Weik, *Real Lincoln*, 242.

### Ephraim Fletcher Ingals

1. Herndon-Weik Papers. Ephraim Ingals (1823–1900), a professor at Rush Medical College in Chicago and a generous patron of that institution, was born in Pomfret, Connecticut, the youngest of nine children.

2. Ingals here alludes to a letter he had written to Weik's publisher, saying: "I have just read with much interest the life of Lincoln by Herndon & Weik. My brother settled on the Sangamon River in 1832 & Mr. Lincoln surveyed his land for him. Members of my family lived near New Salem while Mr. Lincoln was there. I have some anecdotes of him that cannot be known to many. As to one circumstance that Mr. Herndon narrates I am sure he is quite in error, for my brother was one of the actors & it was familiar to us as a family tradition. If you will forward this to Mr. Weik—whose address I do not know—he can communicate with me if he desires to do so." Ephraim Fletcher Ingals to D. Appleton and Company, Chicago, 15 February 1894, Herndon-Weik Papers.

3. In 1832 Dr. Charles Chandler (1806–79) moved from his native Connecticut to Illinois, where he founded the village of Chandlerville, halfway between Beardstown and New Salem along the Springfield Road.

4. In 1832 Connecticut-born Henry Laurens Ingalls (1804–76) settled with his wife, the former Lavinia Child of Woodstock, Connecticut, and his younger siblings Charles Francis, Ephraim, Deborah, and Lydia in Illinois, where he lived for seventeen years until health problems led him to move to California. Returning to Illinois in 1853, he established a farm in Branch and ran a popular hotel. Mary F. C. Dixon, "The Coming of the Ingalls Family to Illinois in 1834," *Journal of the Illinois State Historical Society* 18 (July 1925): 416–21.

5. Dr. Chandler married Clarissa Child, sister of Henry Ingalls's wife.

6. The Clark referred to was perhaps Philip Clark (1812?–97), who served in Jacob Ebey's company during the Black Hawk War. He lived in Neal's Grove near Rochester, in the vicinity of Springfield. Reminiscences of O. C. Stafford, unidentified clipping, George Pasfield Scrapbook, p. 205, Illinois State Historical Library, Springfield. After unsuccessfully running for delegate to the 1847 Illinois State Constitutional Convention, Clark went to California briefly during the 1849 gold rush.

7. Coleman Smoot asserted that he had lent the money to Lincoln. Smoot to William H. Herndon, Petersburg, Illinois, 7 May 1866, Wilson and Davis, *Herndon's Informants*, 254.

8. Weik Papers.

9. Weik Papers.

10. Norman B. Judd (1815–78) was a Chicago lawyer and Republican political leader who played a key role in helping Lincoln win the 1860 presidential nomination.

11. Weik Papers. During the Civil War Lincoln allegedly said, "That reminds me of a short-legged man in a big overcoat, the tail of which was so long it wiped out his footprints in the snow." David Homer Bates, *Lincoln Stories, Told by Him in the Military Office in the War Department during the Civil War* (New York: Rudge, 1926), 24.

12. Weik Papers. In 1840 Pennsylvania-born Elias B. Stiles settled in Dixon, Illinois, where he, John V. Eustace, and L. W. Atherton edited the *Advertiser* (1858–59). He is identified in the 1850 census as a thirty-year-old broker.

## WILLIAM JAYNE

1. Herndon-Weik Papers. The Lincolns' family physician, Dr. William Jayne (1826–1916), was the brother of Mary Lincoln's good friend Julia Jayne Trumbull. In 1859 he was elected mayor of Springfield, and two years later Lincoln appointed him the first governor of the Dakota Territory. He returned from Dakota to Springfield in 1864.

2. Herndon accused Judd, then chairman of the Republican state committee, of improperly using party funds to promote his own candidacy. Donald, *Lincoln's Herndon*, 135.

3. Maine native Leonard Swett (1825–89) settled in Bloomington, Illinois, where he practiced law and became a prominent Republican, working hard to promote Lincoln's career. At the 1860 Chicago convention he was instrumental in helping secure the nomination for his Springfield friend. That same year he contended for the gubernatorial nomination himself, but when his chances faded he threw his support to Richard Yates, who eventually won the nomination and the election.

4. Jesse K. Dubois (1811–76) served with Lincoln in the Illinois legislature, was a neighbor of Lincoln in Springfield, won election as Illinois state auditor in 1856 and 1860, and worked hard for Lincoln's nomination and election in 1860.

5. William Butler (b. 1797), clerk of the Sangamon County Circuit Court, befriended Lincoln when he served in the state legislature. In 1856 and 1860 he won election as Illinois state treasurer. Lincoln boarded with Butler for free from 1837 to 1842.

6. Herndon-Weik Papers.

7. For more on Adams see Kent L. Walgren, "James Adams, Early Springfield Mormon and Freemason," *Journal of the Illinois State Historical Society* 75 (1982): 121–36.

8. Herndon-Weik Papers.

9. Attorney Elliott Bohannon Herndon (b. 1820) edited the pro-Buchanan newspaper, the *Illinois State Democrat* (1857–60), that attacked the "heresies" of Stephen A. Douglas. Elliott Herndon was city attorney of Springfield (1854–55), Sangamon County Attorney (1856), and U.S. District Attorney for the Southern District of Illinois. During the Civil War he was a leader of the antiwar Order of American Knights. His unflattering assessment of Lincoln can be found in Wilson and Davis, *Herndon's Informants*, 459–60.

## Edward S. Johnson

1. Herndon-Weik Papers. Maj. Edward S. Johnson (1843–1921) served throughout the Civil War in the Seventh Illinois Volunteers. After the war he managed a lumberyard and hotels in Springfield and Chicago. In 1895 he became custodian of the National Lincoln Monument (better known as the Lincoln tomb), in which capacity he wrote the pamphlet "Abraham Lincoln and His Last Resting Place" (Springfield: State Journal, 1903?).

2. In 1821 Massachusetts-born Erastus Wright (1779–1870) settled in Springfield, where he taught school, served as the school commissioner of Sangamon County, became a wealthy land dealer, and achieved renown as an ardent abolitionist.

3. In 1833 Joel Johnson (b. 1806) settled in Springfield, where he at first established a shoe and boot business. In 1835 he opened the City Hotel and remained in the hotel business for forty-one years.

4. In 1851 Nova Scotia–born Robert P. Johnston (b. 1828) settled in Springfield, where he married Maria Jane Wright five years later.

5. In 1868 Erastus Wright married Lucy F. Johnson Carpenter, widow of Thomas Carpenter.

6. In the 1860s Kentucky-born John Carroll Power (1819–94) of Springfield turned from farming to literary endeavors, writing for magazines and publishing several books, including a biography of Lincoln (1875) and a history of the early settlers of Sangamon County (1876). In 1874 he became custodian of the newly completed National Lincoln Monument.

7. In 1895 the state of Illinois took control of the National Lincoln Monument from the private association that had been running it. The custodian, instead of relying for an income on the twenty-five-cent admission fee, became a state employee.

8. Herndon-Weik Papers.

## JOSIAH P. KENT

1. Herndon-Weik Papers. Born in Springfield in 1847, Josiah P. Kent worked for railroads before becoming a prosperous stock-breeder and farmer in Illiopolis.

2. William Wallace Lincoln (1850–62), Lincoln's third son, was his favorite child.

3. No Harrison Gourley is listed in the 1860 Springfield City Directory, though it does contain an entry for W. Harry Gourley, a law student.

4. Lincoln Dubois was the son of Lincoln's good friend Jesse K. Dubois.

5. The jeweler Thomas Alsop and his wife Jane Hopkins Alsop, who conducted a millinery store, lived on the south side of Adams Street between Sixth and Seventh Streets. In 1855 Thomas teamed up with Horace Hickox to run a mill in Springfield. Thomas is identified in the 1860 census as a forty-four-year-old watchmaker born in Pennsylvania.

6. Edwin Alsop was a salesman working with Yates & Smith, a dry goods store located on the public square. He is identified in the 1860 census as an eighteen-year-old born in Pennsylvania.

7. Cf. Weik, *Real Lincoln*, 122–26.

8. Herndon-Weik Papers.

9. In Sangamon County in 1862 a Maria Drake married one William H. Center, according to marriage records in the Illinois State Archives.

10. Herndon-Weik Papers.

## GEORGE C. LATHAM

1. Herndon-Weik Papers.

2. Mrs. Harrison J. Grimsley (née Elizabeth Todd Brown, 1825–95), a cousin of Mary Lincoln, stayed in the White House for six months after the inauguration. She later wrote memoirs about her 1861 sojourn in Washington. Grimsley, "Six Months in the White House," *Journal of the Illinois State Historical Society* 19 (October 1926–January 1927): 43–73.

## JOHN M. LOCKWOOD

1. Herndon-Weik Papers. Lockwood (b. 1809) was president of the First National Bank of Mt. Vernon, Indiana. Weik published a highly embellished version of this story. See *Lincoln Lore* no. 1193 (18 February 1952).

2. Princeton is twenty-seven miles north of Evansville, Indiana.

3. The Pennsylvania-born physician Andrew Lewis, whose age is given in the 1850 census as thirty-seven, served as county clerk.

4. In 1829 Silas Stephens married Juliene Evans in Vandenberg County, where Evansville is located.

5. Elinor A. Lewis is described in the 1850 census as a twenty-seven-year-old native of Indiana.

6. James Evans (d. 1832) operated a wool-carding machine in Princeton from 1818 to 1832 and worked a large farm southwest of the town, where he served as justice of the peace. He was a nephew of Gen. Robert M. Evans.

7. In 1805 Virginia-born Gen. Robert M. Evans (1783–1844) settled near Princeton, Indiana, where he joined Gen. William Henry Harrison's army and fought at the battle of Tippecanoe. Evans was elected clerk of the county and was appointed county agent.

8. Peter Hanks's age is given in the 1840 census of Gibson County as between forty and fifty.

9. Lincoln's mother, Nancy Hanks Lincoln, had no brother named Peter.

10. In the Weik Papers at the Illinois State Historical Library in Springfield are typescripts of letters (perhaps originals, though neither contains a signature) from "Hastings" to Mr. J. A. Stuart of Indianapolis:

Princeton, Indiana, 25 January 1909:

> With reference to the visit of Abraham Lincoln to this city I have gathered the following from stories told by old inhabitants.
>
> Lincoln made the trip on horse back from Gentryville, Spencer county, in about the year 1828, and he was then about nineteen years of age. He brought a bunch of wool carded at the Evans carding mill. Owing to the great distance from his Spencer county home he was obliged to remain here over night and he is said to have been given lodging with James Evans, proprietor of the carding mill. That evening he met Miss Malissa Evans, James Evans' daughter with whom he fell in love at first sight. Lincoln at that time was tall and awkward and the impression he made on the beautiful young woman does not appear to have been very lasting. With Lincoln, however, it was different as he spoke of her many times after that meeting and when citizens from this section visited Washington, D.C., several years later when Lincoln was president he asked concerning Miss Evans.
>
> John M. Lockwood was a young man about Lincoln's age and was employed at the carding mill when Lincoln came here. Lockwood was bound out to Mr. Evans to learn the trade, and after completing it went into business for himself and years later, after removing to Mt. Vernon, Ind., he became wealthy and was president of the Mt. Vernon bank.
>
> Miss Evans was a sister of Mrs. Andrew Lewis, one of the early settlers of Princeton. A few years after Lincoln's visit she married Robert Ing and removed to Illinois, where she died several years later, no children being born to the union. The nephews of Miss Evans are Will H. and Rankin E. Lewis, of Indianapolis, and James and Andrew Lewis, of this city, sons of Dr. and Mrs. Andrew Lewis.
>
> Another incident in connection with Lincoln's visit here is told by Andrew Lewis. Princeton was only a struggling little village of perhaps two or three hundred inhabitants and among the business men was Robert Stockwell, who owned a general merchandise store on what is now the southwest corner of the public square. There was a big gilt sign hanging out in front of this store and this attracted Lincoln's eye because it was the first sign of the kind he had ever seen, and he never forgot it. Years later when he was elected president he was on his way from Illinois to Washington a committee of citizens from Lafayette, Ind., met him at the state line and accompanied him through the state. In the delegation was Robert Stockwell.
>
> "Stockwell — Stockwell," said Lincoln when introduced to him. "Let me see, I remember of having seen that name before. It was in Princeton, Ind., on a gilt sign hanging in front of a store."
>
> Mr. Stockwell informed him that he was formerly the owner of that sign

and he congratulated Lincoln on his excellent memory. "I remember that incident," Lincoln explained, "because it was the first gilt sign I had ever seen."

Mr Stuart — Will have you a picture of the old carding mill by Wednesday night or Thursday morning.

"Hastings" to Mr. J. A. Stuart, Princeton, Indiana, 26 January 1909:

Find enclosed picture of old carding mill which Abraham Linocoln visited in about the year 1828. Old residents do not remember when the mill was built, but it is known to have been standing a few years prior to Lincoln's visit. It was probably erected in about 1820, by James Evans, one of the early settlers of Gibson county. It stood near the site of the new Lowell school building, between West and Hall streets. It was torn down about eighteen years ago and on the lot where it once stood new residences have sprung up.

The mill was one of the first of its kind erected in this part of the state and people came here within a radius of forty miles bringing wool to have it carded. Lincoln came on horse back fifty miles to this mill. Some say he made the trip several times, while others maintain it was the old grist mill that stood a short distance south of town that he frequently visited. It was such a common thing for people to come forty or fifty miles to mill in those day[s] that Lincoln's coming here from Gentryville—a mere country boy from a cross-roads town—made little impression at the time.

## W. E. LOOMIS

1. Weik Papers. Webner E. Loomis was a lawyer in Springfield.

2. Beverly Powell, according to William Jayne, clerked in a dry goods store, "was very popular, and was regarded as the best dressed man in Springfield." Jacob C. Thompson to Albert J. Beveridge, Springfield, 23 May 1925, Beveridge Papers. His age is listed in the Sangamon County census for 1840 as between twenty and thirty.

3. Weik Papers.

4. The "People's meeting" nominated Bunn for treasurer on 31 March 1857. The convention was held in Representatives Hall to nominate city officers. Bunn was nominated by acclamation for city treasurer. The only real contest was for mayor, in which William Jayne lost out to Josiah Francis. *Illinois State Journal* (Springfield), 2 April 1857.

5. When Bunn was running for city treasurer he reportedly "came out of a restaurant one day and met Lincoln with another man. Bunn stopped to talk to the other man, explaining that he was running for the office and would like some support. Lincoln spoke up with— 'Well, you've got two votes right here, his and mine.'" "John W. Bunn," unsigned article, *Journal of the Illinois State Historical Society* 13 (July 1920): 275.

6. Susan Enos (b. 1829) lived in Springfield with her mother. Zimri A. Enos (b. 1821) of Springfield served as Surveyor of Sangamon County for four years and as an alderman of the city for three terms. Attorney James Matheny (1818–90) of Springfield served as groomsman at Lincoln's wedding and became a county judge.

## HUGH McLELLAN

1. Herndon-Weik Papers. Hugh McLellan was a partner in the New York architectural firm of Dillon, McLellan, and Beadel.

2. Massachusetts-born Charles W. McLellan (1836–1918), a veteran of the Confederate army, was one of the so-called "big five" Lincoln collectors of the early twentieth century. His impressive collection of Lincoln memorabilia was bought by John D. Rockefeller Jr., who donated it to his alma mater, Brown University.

3. In 1834 Robert Irwin (1808–65) moved from St. Louis to Springfield, where he became a successful merchant and banker. See Clinton L. Conkling's description of him elsewhere in this volume.

4. Lincoln reluctantly appointed New York attorney George Denison to accommodate Irwin. See Lincoln to Irwin, Washington, 20 March 1861, in Basler et al., *Collected Works*, 4:296.

5. In 1834 Philadelphia-born Charles R. Hurst (1811–81) settled in Springfield, where he worked at Joshua Speed's store for several years. Eventually he bought it and ran it until 1877.

## HENRY A. MELVIN

1. Weik Papers. Henry Alexander Melvin (1865–1920) was appointed a justice of the California Supreme Court in 1908.

2. Henry Melvin's father was Samuel Houston Melvin (1829–98), a prosperous Springfield druggist who supplied Lincoln with laxatives. In 1865 Melvin received from Elizabeth Grimsley the manuscript of Lincoln's lecture on "Discoveries and Inventions," the first part of which he sold to Charles Gunther; he kept the second part.

3. See Samuel H. Melvin to William H. Herndon, East Oakland, California, 16 June 1888, Wilson and Davis, *Herndon's Informants*, 657.

4. In fact there was only one lecture consisting of two parts. See Wayne C. Temple, "Lincoln the Lecturer," *Lincoln Herald* 102 (fall 1999): 94–110.

5. German-born Charles F. Gunther (1837–1920) of Chicago was a wealthy candy manufacturer who collected Lincolniana.

6. "Discoveries and Inventions: A Hitherto Unpublished Lecture by Abraham Lincoln," *Sunset: The Magazine of the Pacific and of All the Far West* (May 1909): 463–74. Charles Sedgwick Aiken edited *Sunset Magazine*. Cf. Weik, *Real Lincoln*, 245–50.

7. The reminiscences of Mary Todd Melvin Dewing (b. 1861) concerning the Lincolns can be found in the *Christian Science Monitor*, 12 February 1935.

8. James Breed Melvin was born about 1856.

9. Charles Stuart Melvin was born about 1857.

## JOHN G. NICOLAY

1. Herndon-Weik Papers. German-born John G. Nicolay (1832–1901) was Lincoln's principal personal secretary (1861–65).

2. Weik wrote to Nicolay, saying:

I have just finished reading two books relating to Mr. Lincoln's religious notions. You have doubtless read them both. One is by J. E. Remsburg:

"Was Lincoln a Christian;" the other by Nettie Coleman Maynard: "Was Lincoln a Spiritualist." I know something about the former but I never heard of the Spiritualist work.

At your leisure please tell me what you know about the latter. Did Mr. Lincoln ever attend a *séance* or have one held at the White House? The writer of the book tells some more or less wonderful things and I have been wondering whether the so-called interviews with and calls on Mr. Lincoln and his expressions regarding Spiritualism are apocryphal. I shall be glad to hear from you on the subject.

Weik to Nicolay, Greencastle, 19 November 1894, Nicolay Papers.

### S. G. Paddock

1. Weik Papers. In 1853 New-York-born Stephen Gorham Paddock (b. 1828) settled in Bureau County, Illinois, where he was elected sheriff (1854) and County Clerk (1857, 1861, 1877, 1882). In 1867 he was appointed clerk of the Illinois House of Representatives. He became a Republican activist in 1854 and took part in election campaigns regularly thereafter.

2. Weik Papers.

### George Pasfield

1. Weik Papers. George Pasfield III (b. 1831), though trained as a physician, never practiced medicine; instead he engaged in real estate speculation and general trading.

2. Delaware-born Ann Rodney (d. 1888) was the sister-in-law of Congressman William L. May and the granddaughter of Caesar Rodney, a signer of the Declaration of Independence. In 1843 she married Col. W. H. W. Cushman of Ottawa, Illinois. *Ottawa (Illinois) Free Trader*, 6 October 1888; *Ottawa (Illinois) Republican Times*, 2 February 1957. William L. May of Springfield (1783?-1849) represented his district in the U.S. House (1834–39).

3. Cf. Weik, *Real Lincoln*, 59.

### Edward Lillie Pierce

1. Herndon-Weik Papers. Edward Lillie Pierce (1829–97), a Massachusetts lawyer, wrote among other works a four-volume biography of Charles Sumner.

2. Letter by "Templeton" [George Harris Monroe], Boston Highlands, 22 April 1885, *Boston Herald*, 26 April 1885. In the 1860 census Monroe is listed as a thirty-three-year-old editor born in Massachusetts.

### Hiram Rutherford

1. Weik Papers. Hiram John Rutherford (b. 1815) moved from his native Pennsylvania to East Oakland, Coles County, Illinois, where he practiced medicine and held several public posts, including school treasurer and county supervisor.

2. Anthony Bryant was a free black and "a licensed exhorter in the Methodist church" of Illinois. D. T. McIntyre, "Matson Slave Trial," *Oakland (Illinois) Herald*, 17 July 1896.

3. A native of Tennessee, Gideon Mathew Ashmore owned a tavern-hotel in Oakland. He was, according to D. T. McIntyre, "a wide-awake business man, and

nothing pleased him so well as a stiff legal fight, and in these contests he never knew when he was whipped, and like the bull dog, he never let go." He left to his children a legacy of "his hate and detestation of the institution of slavery." As a devout Presbyterian he also "hated the Methodists most cordially." D. T. McIntyre, "Matson Slave Trial," *Oakland (Illinois) Herald*, 17 July 1896.

4. Democrat Orlando Bell Ficklin (1808–86) of Charleston represented his district in the U.S. House (1843–49, 1851–53).

5. John M. Eastin is listed in the 1850 census as a forty-eight-year-old trader from Kentucky with $4,000 worth of real estate. He was reputedly "a pro-slavery man" but also "a conservative man and careful in making his decisions." D. T. McIntyre, "Matson Slave Trial," *Oakland (Illinois) Herald*, 17 July 1896.

6. Robert Matson "had represented Bourbon county, Kentucky, in the State Senate and was a thoroughbred Kentuckian of wealth and prominence." "A Story of Long Ago," *Mattoon (Illinois) Sunday Sun*, 24 August 1884.

7. William Wilson was chief justice of the Illinois Supreme Court. Samuel Treat (1815–1902) served as judge of the Illinois Supreme Court (1841–55) and as judge of the U.S. Court for the Southern District of Illinois (1855–87).

8. Charles Constable, who later became a circuit court judge in Coles County, was "the best educated lawyer at the bar, the only one who had ever attended a law school." D. T. McIntyre, "Matson Slave Trial," *Oakland (Illinois) Herald*, 17 July 1896.

9. Rutherford said that his story "occupied three or four issues of the Herald." Rutherford to Ivan Sumerlin, Oakland, 21 August 1884, *Mattoon (Illinois) Sunday Sun*, 24 August 1884.

10. In the 1850 census Joseph Dean is identified as a fifty-four-year-old farmer born in Kentucky. He was Matson's friend.

11. Cf. Weik, "Lincoln and the Matson Negroes: A Vista into the Fugitive-Slave Days," *Arena* 17 (April 1897): 752–58, which contains long quotes from Rutherford, evidently based on this interview. Rutherford was also interviewed by D. T. McIntyre. McIntyre, "Matson Slave Trial," *Oakland (Illinois) Herald*, 17 July 1896.

## REV. MR. W. F. F. SMITH

1. Weik Papers.

2. Maryland native William Wood (1784–1867) migrated to Kentucky and then to Indiana, where he established a farm close to that of the Lincoln family.

## JUDGE ANTHONY THORNTON

1. Weik Papers. Anthony Thornton (1814–1904) of Shelbyville served as a judge on the Illinois Supreme Court (1870–73) and as a congressman (1865–67).

2. Attorney Usher F. Linder (1809–76) was born in Kentucky near Lincoln's birthplace. The two men served together in the Illinois legislature.

3. Samuel W. Moulton of Shelbyville, Illinois, was a leading Democrat.

4. Peter Van Bergen was a noted horseman and a moneylender in Springfield. For more on Mary Lincoln's hysteria see Burlingame, *Inner World of Lincoln*, 293–96.

## LYMAN BEECHER TODD

1. Herndon-Weik Papers. Lincoln named Dr. Lyman Beecher Todd, a cousin of Mrs. Lincoln, postmaster at Lexington, Kentucky.

2. Weik wrote to Todd, saying:

I am engaged in preparing for the American Press Association a series of articles pertaining to the life of Abraham Lincoln and am in quest of certain information to be had at Lexington. I wrote to my friend Capt J. R. [Howard?] late postmaster but he answered that he was absent in Danville most of the week and referred me to you.

I learned some time ago from what I consider reliable authority that among other things inherited by Mr. Lincoln's wife from the estate of her father the late Hon R. S. Todd who died in 1848 or '49 were some slaves; and that Mr. Lincoln wrote several letters to the executor or administrator of the estate in connection therewith. What I should like to have is copies of those letters and if not on file with the papers in the estate in the records of the probate court, I should like to know what those papers show as to whether any such slaves were so inherited. No doubt the papers are still on file. Is it too much to ask you to call on the clerk of the proper court and ascertain if the information can be obtained? In any event can the officer named not tell me what the amount of property bequeathed to Mrs. Lincoln was valued at and of what it consisted. At this distance I can obtain the facts in no other way and I shall be under lasting obligations for your kindly intercession.

Weik to Todd, Greencastle, 16 April 1895, Herndon-Weik Papers.

3. Robert Smith Todd was the father of sixteen children, among them Mary Todd Lincoln.

4. Mary Lincoln's half sister, Margaret Todd, married Charles H. Kellogg.

5. Emilie Todd (1836–1930), half sister of Mary Todd Lincoln, married a fellow Kentuckian, Ben Hardin Helm, who became a general in the Confederate army.

## GILBERT A. TRACY

1. Herndon-Weik Papers. A Connecticut farmer, Gilbert Avery Tracy (b. 1835) compiled *Uncollected Letters of Abraham Lincoln* (Boston: Houghton Mifflin, 1917). While a clerk in the War Department (1863–68) he often observed Lincoln.

2. Dorothy Lamon Teillard edited her father's book, *Recollections of Abraham Lincoln, 1847–1865* (Chicago: McClurg, 1895). The letter referred to, Lamon to Asahel Gridley, n.p., (May 1866), was published in pamphlet form with the title "Ward H. Lamon and the Chicago Tribune" (no publisher, place of publication, or date indicated).

3. Murat Halstead (1829–1908) was a reporter for the *Cincinnati Commercial*.

4. Alexander Kelly McClure (1828–1909), an influential Pennsylvania journalist, wrote *Abraham Lincoln and Men of War-Times* (Philadelphia: Times, 1892).

5. In the preface to the second edition, published in 1911, Dorothy Lamon Teillard wrote in explanation of her decision to issue a new version of the 1895 volume: "I have been influenced also by a friend who is a great Lincoln scholar and who, impressed with the injustice done my father, has urged me for several years to reissue the book of 'Recollections,' add a sketch of his life and publish letters that

show his standing during Lincoln's administration." Ward Hill Lamon, *Recollections of Abraham Lincoln*, Dorothy Teillard, ed. (Washington: privately published, 1911), xxviii.

6. Elizabeth Keckley (1818?-1907), Mary Lincoln's confidante, wrote *Behind the Scenes, or Thirty Years a Slave, and Four Years in the White House* (New York: Carleton, 1868).

7. Norman S. Bentley, a prosperous New York businessman, helped raise funds for Mrs. Lincoln soon after the Civil War. Mrs. Lincoln's letters to him have not surfaced. It is possible that they were bought up at Robert Lincoln's request and destroyed.

8. Scottish-born John Watt and his wife, Jane Masters Watt, worked at the White House and were involved in numerous corrupt schemes. See Michael Burlingame, "Mary Todd Lincoln's Unethical Conduct as First Lady," in *At Lincoln's Side: John Hay's Civil War Correspondence and Selected Writings*, Michael Burlingame, ed. (Carbondale: Southern Illinois University Press, 2000), 186–98.

9. This is evidently a reference to a receipt for $84.00 given by Mrs. Lincoln to John Hammack, a Washington restaurateur with a shady reputation. In Mrs. Lincoln's handwriting, a letter dated May 1865 written on White House stationery says "Received of John D. Hammack Eighty four dollars for Sundry &c in full payment. Mrs. Lincoln." Ward Hill Lamon Papers, Huntington Library, San Marino, California.

## LYMAN TRUMBULL

1. Herndon-Weik Papers. Lyman Trumbull (1815–96) was a U.S. senator from Illinois (1855–73).

2. Mrs. Simeon Francis, wife of the editor of the *Illinois State Journal*, was probably less influential in bringing about the reconciliation of Lincoln and Mary Todd than were John J. Hardin and his wife. See Douglas L. Wilson, *Honor's Voice: The Transformation of Abraham Lincoln* (New York: Alfred A. Knopf, 1998), 283.

3. In 1842 James Shields (1806–79), then state auditor of Illinois, challenged Lincoln to a duel because he felt insulted by a pseudonymous newspaper satire written by Lincoln. The duel was called off at the last moment through the intervention of friends. Julia Jayne, a good friend of Mary Todd, wed Lyman Trumbull.

## HORACE WHITE

1. Herndon-Weik Papers. Horace White (1834–1916) wrote for the *Chicago Tribune*, covering the 1858 Lincoln-Douglas debates and Lincoln's presidency. For the 1892 version of Herndon and Weik's biography of Lincoln, White contributed a chapter on the 1858 debates.

2. New York native Charles Henry Ray (1821–70) settled in Illinois in the 1840s. He became acquainted with Lincoln in 1845. After editing the *Galena Jeffersonian*, he bought a part interest in the *Chicago Press & Tribune* in 1855 and eventually became its editor in chief. He helped found the Republican party in Illinois.

3. A native of Canada, Joseph Meharry Medill (1823–99) moved to Ohio, where he helped found the Republican Party. In 1855 he bought an interest in the *Chicago Press & Tribune*.

4. See Wilson and Davis, *Herndon's Informants*, 723–24.

5. Herndon-Weik Papers.

6. "Long John" Wentworth (1815–88) edited the *Chicago Democrat*, represented his district in the U.S. House (1843–51, 1853–55, 1865–67), and won election as mayor of Chicago (1857, 1860).

7. Herndon-Weik Papers.

8. Thomas J. McCormack, ed., *Memoirs of Gustave Koerner, 1809–1896*, 2 vols. (Cedar Rapids IA: Torch Press, 1909), 2:66–67.

9. Herndon-Weik Papers.

10. After serving as a major in the Civil War and winning a Congressional Medal of Honor, William Harrison Lambert (1842–1912) entered the insurance business and became a bibliophile, amassing large collections of Lincoln and Thackery items.

11. Herndon-Weik Papers.

12. Horace White, *The Life of Lyman Trumbull* (Boston: Houghton Mifflin, 1913).

13. Parks, statement for William H. Herndon, [1866], Wilson and Davis, *Herndon's Informants*, 537–38.

14. Herndon-Weik Papers.

15. White, *Life of Trumbull*, 165–77.

16. In 1861 Lincoln named Charles Lush Wilson, editor of the *Chicago Daily Journal*, first secretary of the legation in London.

17. The first attorney to establish a practice in DeWitt County, Clifton H. Moore (1817–1901) collaborated with David Davis in highly successful land speculations. The only political post he held was as a delegate to the 1870 Illinois Constitutional Convention. According to Moore, Lincoln said: "Douglas will tell a lie to ten thousand people one day, even though he knows he may have to deny it to five thousand the next." Weik, *Real Lincoln*, 231.

18. Herndon-Weik Papers.

19. Copy, Weik Papers.

20. In 1883 when Robert Todd Lincoln blocked the appointment of Lamon as postmaster at Denver, Lamon wrote him an abusive letter, to which Lincoln responded tartly.

21. Herndon-Weik Papers.

22. White, *Life of Trumbull*, 142–48.

23. Mark W. Delahay was a Kansas journalist whom Lincoln appointed surveyor general of Kansas (1861) and judge of the U.S. District Court in Kansas (1863). See Weik, *Real Lincoln*, 221–26.

24. James W. Grimes (1816–72) was a Republican senator from Iowa (1859–69).

25. Lincoln said, "my greatest disappointment of all has been with Grimes. Before I came here, I certainly expected to rely upon Grimes more than any other one man in the Senate. I like him very much. He is a great strong fellow. He is a valuable friend, a dangerous enemy. He carries too many guns [to] not be respected in any point of view. But he got wrong against me, I do not clearly know how, and has always been cool and almost hostile to me." Michael Burlingame and John R. Turner Ettlinger, eds., *Inside Lincoln's White House: The Complete Civil War Diary*

*of John Hay* (Carbondale: Southern Illinois University Press, 1997), 245 (entry for 8 November 1864).

26. Trumbull said, "A more ardent seeker after office never existed. From the time when, at the age of twenty-three, he announced himself a candidate for the legislature . . . till his death, he was almost constantly either in office, or struggling to obtain one." Trumbull to his son Walter, n.p., n.d., in White, *Life of Trumbull,* 429.

27. Herndon-Weik Papers.

28. Thurlow Weed (1797–1882) edited the *Albany (New York) Evening Journal* and was a close advisor to William Henry Seward.

29. The Connecticut journalist Gideon Welles (1802–78) served as secretary of the navy (1861–69).

30. In 1861 Pennsylvania-born Alexander Cummings (1810–79) was Simon Cameron's special purchasing agent, a post in which he demonstrated little competence or integrity. He served as a colonel of the Nineteenth Pennsylvania Volunteers and later as Superintendent of Troops of African Descent in Arkansas. After the war he became Territorial Governor of Colorado (1865–67).

31. In 1912 the sculptor Daniel Chester French (1850–1931) created a statue of Lincoln for the Nebraska State Capitol grounds. Later he sculpted the statue of Lincoln for the Lincoln Memorial in Washington DC.

32. The poet and essayist Richard Watson Gilder (1844–1909) edited *Century Magazine.* Augustus St. Gaudens (1848–1907) created the statue of Lincoln in Chicago's Lincoln Park.

33. Herndon-Weik Papers.

34. *Journal of the Illinois State Historical Society* 7 (January 1915): 329–48.

35. Cf. Weik, *Real Lincoln,* 216, 226–28, 231–35.

36. Herndon-Weik Papers.

37. Horace Greeley (1811–72) edited the *New York Tribune.*

38. John T. Richards, *Abraham Lincoln: The Lawyer-Statesman* (Boston: Houghton Mifflin, 1916).

39. Henry B. Rankin, *Personal Recollections of Abraham Lincoln* (New York: G. P. Putnam's, 1916). See the appendix on Rankin in this volume.

JAMES H. WILSON

1. Herndon-Weik Papers. A noted cavalry leader in the Civil War, Gen. James Harrison Wilson (1837–1925) also served on U.S. Grant's staff (1862–64).

2. Wilson told the following story:

Amongst the most sagacious and prudent of General Grant's friends was J. Russel[l] Jones, Esq., formerly of Galena, at that time United States Marshal for the northern district of Illinois, and also a warm and trusted friend of the President. Mr. Jones, feeling a deep interest in General Grant, and having many friends and neighbors under his command, had joined the army at Vicksburg and was there on the day of its final triumph. Lincoln, hearing this, and knowing his intimacy with Grant, sent for him, shortly after his return to Chicago, to come to Washington. Mr. Jones started immediately and traveled night and day. On his arrival at the railway station at Washington he was met by the President's servants and carriage, taken directly to the White House, and at once shown into the President's room. After a hurried but cordial greeting the President led the way to the library, closed the doors, and when he was sure that they were entirely alone addressed him as follows:

"I have sent for you, Mr. Jones, to know if that man Grant wants to be President."

Mr. Jones, although somewhat astonished at the question and the circumstances under which it was asked, replied at once:

"No, Mr. President."

"Are you sure?" queried the latter.

"Yes," said Mr. Jones, "perfectly sure; I have just come from Vicksburg; I have seen General Grant frequently and talked fully and freely with him, about that and every other question, and I know he has no political aspirations whatever, and certainly none for the Presidency. His only desire is to see you reelected, and to do what he can under your orders to put down the rebellion and restore peace to the country."

"Ah, Mr. Jones," said Lincoln, "you have lifted a great weight off my mind, and done me an immense amount of good, for I tell you, my friend, no man knows how deeply that presidential grub gnaws till he has had it himself."

James Harrison Wilson, "Reminiscences of General Grant," *Century Magazine* 30 (October 1885): 954. Jones was the U.S. marshal for the northern district of Illinois.

3. In 1869 Grant named James Russell Jones as minister resident to Belgium. Six years later the president named him collector of customs at Chicago.

4. Thomas Scott Mather (1829–90) served as adjutant general of Illinois (1858–61) and during the Civil War was colonel of the Second Illinois Light Artillery and chief of staff to Gen. John A. McClernand. He was brevetted a brigadier general in September 1865.

5. John Washington S. Alexander, who served as a lieutenant in the Mexican War in company F of the Fourth Illinois Infantry, led the Twenty-first Illinois Infantry after Grant was promoted. In 1857 he ran for clerk of Edgar County. He was killed at the battle of Chickamauga in 1863.

6. *The Life of Ulysses S. Grant, General of the Armies of the United States* (Springfield MA: Gurdon Bill, 1868). The journalist Charles A. Dana served as assistant secretary of war (1864–65) and spent much time at Grant's headquarters.

7. Thomas Dixon's novel *The Southerner: A Romance of the Real Lincoln* was published in New York by Appleton's in 1913.

## Louis H. Zumbrook

1. Statement enclosed in Clinton L. Conkling to Weik, [Springfield], 6 December 1916, Conkling Papers. Conkling reported that he had held two interviews with Zumbrook who, he said, "is in every way entitled to belief in the statements that he makes. He is in the very best of health and vigor and is one of those men who remember small circumstances of years ago remarkably well. He is now in active business in his own hardware store and attends to sales daily himself." In

1852 Louis H. Zumbrook (b. 1842) settled in Springfield, where he eventually ran a hardware store with his son, Charles W. Zumbrook.

2. George L. Huntington, a lumber dealer and insurance agent, served as mayor of Springfield (1861–62).

### APPENDIX 2: RANKIN'S RELIABILITY

1. Henry B. Rankin, *Intimate Character Sketches of Abraham Lincoln* (Philadelphia: Lippincott, 1924), 21, 60, 59, 145; Henry B. Rankin, *Personal Recollections of Abraham Lincoln* (New York: G. P. Putnam's Sons, 1916), 138.

2. *Who Was Who in America, 1897–1942* (Chicago: Marquis, 1943), 1010.

3. Obituaries in the *Illinois State Journal* (Springfield) and the *Illinois State Register* (Springfield), 15 August 1927; 1910 U.S. census, Sangamon County, Springfield, E.D. 134, sheet 11B, lines 97–100.

4. Ida Tarbell to Mitchell Kinnerley, n.p., 24 November 1915 (copy), Tarbell Papers.

5. Memorandum dated Springfield, 25 January 1927, titled "Henry B. Rankin and the Widow's Curse, Jacob Thompson and Mrs. McPherson," William E. Barton Papers, University of Chicago.

6. Merrill Peterson, *Lincoln in American Memory* (New York: Oxford University Press, 1994), 221.

7. Emanuel Hertz, "Abraham Lincoln: His Law Partners, Clerks and Office Boys" (pamphlet, 1930), 20. When asked about William E. Barton's skepticism concerning Rankin's trustworthiness, Hertz responded: "I disagree entirely with Barton's doubts and condemnation of Rankin, and I think Rankin has done excellent work, and I take his word for it." Hertz to Paul Angle, 10 April 1933 (copy), John J. Duff Papers, Illinois State Historical Library, Springfield.

8. Ida Tarbell to Mitchell Kinnerley, n.p., 24 November 1915 (copy), Tarbell Papers.

9. Ida M. Tarbell, *In the Footsteps of the Lincolns* (New York: Harper & Brothers, 1924), 213.

10. M. L. Houser to William E. Barton, Peoria, Illinois, 15 January 1930, Barton Papers.

11. M. L. Houser to William E. Barton, Peoria, Illinois, 15 January 1930, Barton Papers. William E. Barton, one of the most outspoken of Rankin's critics, demurred, saying: "I knew Mr. Rankin very well. I knew the opinions of the persons you name when I wrote [my criticism of Rankin in] 'Lincoln and Whitman.' I do not think you quote Miss Osborne quite correctly, but I do not wish her to be asked any questions. I know what her predecessor Mrs. Weber thought." Barton to Houser, Nashville, Tennessee, 17 January 1930 (copy), Barton Papers.

12. Undated memo, Harry E. Pratt Papers, University of Illinois, Urbana.

13. Beveridge to Nathaniel Wright Stephenson, Beverly Farms, Massachusetts, 18 December 1925 (copy), Beveridge Papers.

14. Beveridge to Frank H. Hodder, Beverly Farms, Massachusetts, 15 December 1925 (copy), Beveridge Papers.

15. Beveridge to Lincoln Dubois, n.p., 13 February 1926 (copy), Beveridge Papers.

16. Beveridge to Weik, Indianapolis, 20 December 1924, Weik Papers.

17. Weik to Beveridge, New Rochelle NY, 12 July 1924, Beveridge Papers.

18. Rankin, *Personal Recollections of Lincoln*, 88–95. Rankin here reproduces a letter he alleges that he wrote to Herndon in 1866, but one which is not extant in the Herndon-Weik Papers.

19. William E. Barton, *Abraham Lincoln and Walt Whitman* (Indianapolis: Bobbs-Merrill, 1928), 93, 94.

20. Memorandum dated Springfield, 25 January 1927, titled "Henry B. Rankin and the Widow's Curse, Jacob Thompson and Mrs. McPherson," Barton Papers. In 1922 Barton told a correspondent: "You ask me a rather embarrassing question when you inquire about Mr. Rankin. He is a personal friend of mine. I go to see him every time I am in Springfield. If I were speaking to you here in my study, I should say that the Abraham Lincoln whom Mr. Rankin remembers is not precisely the Abraham Lincoln whom he knew. He did know Abraham Lincoln as a boy might know a man, but the Lincoln of whom he now talks is that Lincoln plus a great deal more he has read and thought since." Barton to a Dr. Cameron, n.p., 7 February 1922 (copy), Barton Papers. Barton's notes of an interview with Rankin on 9 March 1920 are preserved as well.

21. Barton Papers.

22. Angle to White, [Springfield], 5 December 1929 (copy), Paul M. Angle Papers, Chicago Historical Society. Rankin is self-identified as a resident of Athens and editor of a literary journal there in the *Illinois State Journal* (Springfield), 29 February 1856. An example of plagiarism that Angle cited is striking. In *Intimate Character Sketches of Lincoln*, Rankin when describing the February 6, 1861, reception at the Lincoln home clearly pirated the February 7 dispatch to the *Missouri Democrat* quoted at length in Weik's *Real Lincoln*, 303.

23. Barton memo dated Springfield, 5 February 1926, Barton Papers.

24. Undated memo, Pratt Papers. This memo, presumably written by Pratt, goes on: "To [Harry] Lytle, Rankin said he could write as well with his toes as well as his hands [M. L.] Houser says story is O.K. [Harry] Lytle & [James W.] Bollinger suspect him." See also Jacob C. Thompson to Albert J. Beveridge, Springfield, 2 January 1925, Beveridge Papers. Thompson's voluminous correspondence with Beveridge indicates that he was unusually knowledgeable about Lincoln's years in Springfield.

25. Angle to C. T. White, [Springfield], 21 December 1929 (copy), Angle Papers. Albert H. Rankin was vice president of the First National Bank of Springfield.

26. Angle to William E. Barton, Springfield, 6 May 1930, Barton Papers.

27. Houser to William E. Barton, Peoria, Illinois, 15 January 1930, Barton Papers.

28. William H. Townsend, *Lincoln and Liquor* (New York: Press of the Pioneers, 1934), 79–85.

29. Townsend, *Lincoln and Liquor*, 84–85.

30. Bonzi to Pratt, Springfield, 10 December 1949, Pratt Papers.

31. Donald, *Lincoln's Herndon*, 12.

32. Donald, *Lincoln's Herndon*, 291; Benjamin P. Thomas, *Portrait for Posterity: Lincoln and His Biographers* (New Brunswick NJ: Rutgers University Press, 1947), 213n.

33. John J. Duff, *A. Lincoln, Prairie Lawyer* (New York: Rinehart, 1960), 290–92.

34. *Illinois State Journal* (Springfield), 30 October 1857.

35. 1860 Federal census, Menard County.

36. Rankin to Trumbull, Athens, 21 July 1856, Lyman Trumbull Papers, Manuscript Division, Library of Congress.

37. Rankin wrote to Washburne, saying:

What shall I do? We are "blessed" with another democrat representative in the Central district or rather a "northern man of southern proclivities." Documents I can't expect from them or if they come they are like Swift's dreams – "of the doubtful sort[.]" So I will claim you as my representative, & I desire a few favors even though I am [beyond] your district. Please send me occasionaly such documents as you can & place me among the list that will recieve garden vegetable seeds or rare specimen[s] of flower seeds or bulbs. There is to be a "battle to be fought" here on the election of Harris's successor for the last term. We are called upon to be men then—all together & in earnest.

Rankin to Washburne, Athens, 14 January 1859, Elihu B. Washburne Papers, Manuscript Division, Library of Congress.

38. Rankin to Washburne, Athens, 25 February 1861, Washburne Papers.

39. Rankin wrote to Edward L. Denny stating that "he remembered my father [John E. Denny] as a law student in the firm of Lincoln & Herndon in Springfield about 1858." Clipping marked "Indianapolis Star, 8 Feb. 1929," Lincoln Museum, Fort Wayne. Denny, according to his son, was twenty-three years old in 1856, when he delivered a talk to the Philomathean Club of Springfield. In the 1850 Sangamon County census he is identified as a seventeen-year-old carpenter born in Illinois; in the 1860 Sangamon County census he does not appear.

40. Don E. Fehrenbacher and Virginia Fehrenbacher, eds., *Recollected Words of Abraham Lincoln* (Stanford: Stanford University Press, 1996), 374.

41. Those volumes may be used, with caution, for some data about Lincoln's years in New Salem, near which Rankin's parents lived. Rankin's father served as sheriff of Menard County, and his mother's family knew Lincoln during his New Salem days.

42. Peterson, *Lincoln in American Memory*, 265.

# Index

*Abraham Lincoln: A History* (Nicolay and Hay), xxix, 33, 221, 289, 309–11
*Abraham Lincoln and Walt Whitman* (Barton), 393
*Abraham Lincoln: Lawyer-Statesman* (Richards), 385
*Abraham Lincoln, 1809–1858* (Beveridge), 393
Adams, James, 360
Aiken, Charles S., 370
Alexander, John Washington S., 386, 439
Alsop, Edwin, 363, 429
Alsop, Henry, 363
Alsop, Thomas, 363, 429
Alton IL, debate at, 379
American House, 324, 361, 406
Andrews, Ida M., 317–18
Andrus, Charles S., 335
Andrus, Reuben, 335, 412, 413
Angle, Paul M.: on H. B. Rankin, 394–96; on R. T. Lincoln, xxii
Ashmore, Gideon, 372, 433–34
Ashmun, George, 319, 404

Bagley vs. Vanmeter, 160
Bailey vs. Cromwell, 146, 197
Baird, Absalom, 331–32, 410
Baird, John P., 331
Baird, Mrs. Absalom, 332
Baker, Edward D., 120

Baker, Edward L., 264–65, 314
Baker, Edward S., 328, 407
Baker, William G., 352, 423
banks, in Springfield, 325, 343, 368
Barber, Clayton, 395
Barker, Harry E., 392
Barnard, George G. G., 336, 413, 414
Barrett, Joseph H., 18
Barton, William E., 28; on H. B. Rankin, 393–94, 396, 440–41
Bates, Edward, 353, 354, 406, 411
Bentley, Norman, 377, 436
Beveridge, Albert J., xxv; on *Real Lincoln*, xix–xx; on H. B. Rankin, 392–93
Binmore, Henry, 426
Birch, Jonathan, 132–34, 199–201, 400
Bissell, William H., 323, 406, 414
Black, Chauncey, 7, 383
Black laws of Illinois, 372
Blair, Francis P., Jr., 323, 406
Bloomington Convention (1856), 253–57
Bollinger, James W., 441
Bonzi, Marion, 396
Bovard, Dr., 317
Brackenridge, George W., 318
Brackenridge, John, 318
Brackenridge, John A., 131, 318, 403
Bradford, John S., 99–100
Brayman, Moses, 152

Briggs, Alex, 353, 424

Brinkerhoff, George, 265, 410–11

Brown, Benjamin Gratz, 323, 406

Brown, Delos, 319, 404

Browne, Thomas C., 63

Brownfield, George, 31

Browning, Orville H., 341–42, 416

Bryant, Anthony, 372, 373, 433

Bunn, Jacob, 345, 368, 405; career of, 323–25; death of, 367; and Lincoln, 203–5, 283, 318–30, 336; and M. McConnell, 323–24; store of, 320

Bunn, John W., 203–5, 342, 345, 404, 431; candidacy of, for office, 367; reminiscences of Lincoln by, 159, 165, 273, 282–88, 309, 318–26, 335–39, 413

Butler, Evan, 70

Butler, William, 135, 359, 360, 428

Cameron, Simon, xxi, 384, 411; appointment of, to cabinet, 383; rascalities of, 385

Campbell, David B., 351, 422

Campbell, James, 368

Canton, Edgar, 197

Carman vs. Glasscock, 146–47

Carmody, John, 264, 353, 412, 423–24

Carter, Mrs. Arthur H., 326–27, 367

Cartwright, Peter, 347, 421

Castle, Edward, 219

Chandler, Charles, 358, 426

Chapman, Augustus H., 293, 349, 354, 407; on Lincoln, 327–28

Chapman, Harriet Hanks, 353, 408, 424; reminiscences of, 53–55, 327–29, 354

Chapman, Robert N., 328, 329, 408

Charleston IL, debate in, 233–35, 328

Charnwood, Lord, xix

Chase, Salmon P., 287, 411

Chatterton, Charles W., 355, 418

Chatterton, Elizabeth Miles, 355, 418

Chatterton, George W., 342, 417–18

Chatterton's Jewelry Store, 343–44, 411, 412

Chenery, Eleanor H., 329, 330

Chenery, Fanny, 409

Chenery, John W., 361, 409

Chenery, Susan, 329

Chenery, William Dodd, 329–30, 408, 409

Chenery House, 322, 329–30, 344–45, 361, 409, 420

Chicago, Lincoln's visit to, 290

Chicago and Alton train station (Springfield), 344

Chicago Convention (1860), 261–68, 319, 411

*Chicago Journal*, 381

*Chicago Tribune*, 378–79

Chiniquiy, Charles, 161–62

City Hotel (Springfield), 361

Clark, Mrs. E. H., 353

Clark, Philip, 427

Clarke, William, 352, 363–64, 423

Clay, Henry, 10–11, 375; Lincoln's eulogy of, 245

Coburn, John, 330–33, 409

Coffin, Charles C., 327, 331–33, 407

Cogdal, Isaac, 347

Colby, Jonathan, 333, 410

Colfax, Schuyler, 298

Combs, Jane, 346

Condell, Thomas, 283, 320, 405

Confiscation acts, 381

Conkling, Clinton L., 269, 333–47, 353, 394, 410

Conkling, James C., 313, 334, 335, 410, 411, 413; Lincoln on, 337; office of, 333, 334, 343–44

Connolly, James A., 294–97, 347–50, 421

Constable, Charles, 350, 372, 422, 434

Cook, Sherwin Lawrence, xx–xxi

Cooper Institute speech, 257–59

Creal, Richard A., 19–20

Cullom, Shelby M., 334

Cummings, Alexander, 384, 438

Cunningham, James T., 328, 329, 407

Dana, Charles A., 386

Davis, David, xxi, 217, 374, 416, 437; acquisitiveness of, 141; character and personality of, 341–42; at Chicago Convention (1860), 261–62; on judicial circuit, 350; on Lincoln, 65, 76, 81, 90, 126–27, 211, 244, 309; and W. H. Lamon, 380, 382

Davis, David II, 418

Davis, George Perrin, 189–92, 350, 422

Davis, Maria Mumford, 423

Davis, Oliver L., 350, 422

Davis, Rodney O., xxi

Davis, Sarah Walker, 350

Davis, Tom, 352

Davis, Walter, 242, 352, 357, 423, 426

Dawes, H. L., 385

Dawson vs. Ennis, 158

Dean, Joe, 373, 434

debates. See Lincoln-Douglas Debates

Delahay, Mark W., xxi, 221–26, 383, 384, 437

Denison, George, 368, 432

Denny, John E., 397

Depauw University, xxii

Dewing, Mary Todd Melvin, 370, 432

Dickey, John, 61

Diller, Isaac R., 351–53, 363, 422–23

Diller, Roland W., 351, 422–23

Diller and Corneau Drug Store, 351

divorce cases, Lincoln and, 148–51

Dixon, Thomas, 439

Dole, William P., 419

Donald, David, 396, 399

Donnelly, William D., 264, 353

Donnonue, Dillard, 235–36

Dorman vs. Lane, 167–68

Douglas, Adele Cutts, 235–36

Douglas, Stephen A.: in campaign of 1854, 231, 323; debates with Lincoln, 200–201, 229–36, 328; dishonesty of, 381–82; drinking habits of, 236, 383; height of, 323; Lincoln on, 229–31, 406; and Mary

Todd Lincoln, 328–29, 408; mendacity of, 231–33, 323; voice of, 351

Dowling, Dennis Hanks, 353–54, 424

Dowling, Sarah Jane, 424

Doyle, Clara C., 345

Drake, Maria, 126, 352, 363, 364

Dresser, Charles, 59

Dubois, Jesse K., 322, 359, 427–28

Dubois, Lincoln, 362, 362, 393, 429

Duff, John J., 396

Dunbar, Alexander P., 295, 349, 422

Duncan, John, 15

Dungey vs. Spencer, 162–64

Eastin, John M., 372, 434

Eddy, Franklin M., 167–68

Edmonds, Alexander, 157–58, 319

Edwards, Benjamin S., 165, 320, 337, 405

Edwards, Elizabeth Todd, 61, 328, 355, 425; and story of defaulting bridegroom, 63

Edwards, Ninian W., 58, 63, 333, 343, 408

"Effie Afton" case. See Rock Island Bridge suit

Eighth judicial circuit (Illinois), 145, 188–89, 350; Lincoln's practice on, 90

Ellsworth, Elmer, 228, 278, 309

Emancipation proclamation, xxix, 332

Enloe, Abraham, 31–32

Enos, Susan, 368

Enos, Zimri, 368, 431

Euclid, 239

Evans, James, 366, 429, 430, 431

Evans, Juliene, 365, 429

Evans, Melissa, 366, 430

Evans, Robert, 366, 429

Fehrenbacher, Don E., 397

Fehrenbacher, Virginia, 397

Fell, Jesse W., 21, 35, 131, 378

Ferguson, Will I., 319, 404

Ficklin, Orlando B., 233–34, 362, 434

First National Bank of Springfield, 325, 368

Fiske, John, 238

Fleury, Annie, 355, 395, 425
Floyd, George P., 143
Flynn, John, 352, 423
Forney, John W., 426
Francis, Mrs. Simeon, 60, 63–64, 378, 436
Freeman, John D., 345, 420
Freeport IL, debate at, 379
Freese, Jacob, 132
Fremont campaign (1856), 370–71
French, Daniel Chester, 384, 438
Fugitive slave cases, 195–98

Gilder, Richard Watson, 384, 438
Gillmore, Quincy A., 332
Gilmore, William, 372
Globe tavern, 63, 361
Gobin, Clara Leaton, 403
Gollaher, Austin, 14, 17–18
Gourley, Harrison, 362, 429
Gourley, James, 119–22
Graham, William Mentor, 347, 421
Grant, Frederick Dent, 356, 425
Grant, Julia Dent, 356, 425
Grant, U. S., 356, 370; and J. R. Jones,
    386, 438; and M. T. Lincoln, 425
Gray, Charles H., 356–57
Gray, Isaac H., 356, 361, 425–26
Great Western depot (Springfield), 387
Greeley, Horace, 298, 376, 385, 438
Green, E. B., 356
Green vs. Green, 148
Gridley, Asahel, 375
Grimes, James, 220, 383–84, 437
Grimsley, Elizabeth Todd, 246, 364, 369,
    429
Grubb vs. Fink, 156
Gunther, Charles F., 32–33, 369, 432

Hall, Levi, 40, 41
Halstead, Murat, 376, 435
Hanks, Dennis, 38–41, 48, 327, 328, 329,
    407; description of, 39; on Hanks fam-
    ily, 42–45; interviewed, 25; and Lincoln,

26; reliability of, 26, 38–39; reminis-
    cences of, 27, 41–45
Hanks, Harriet. See Chapman, Harriet
    Hanks
Hanks, John, 39, 41, 45, 47, 58; on Al-
    abama, 275–78; and Decatur conven-
    tion, 261; reliability of, 26, 38–39; remi-
    niscences of, 45–46
Hanks, Lucy, 37, 38, 40–42
Hanks, Peter, 366
Hanks, Sarah Elizabeth Johnston, 329
Hanna, Thomas, 400
Harnett, Jonathan, 347, 421
Harris, Gibson W. See Harris, William
    Gibson
Harris vs. Great Western Railway Co.,
    156–57
Harris, Jasper, 156
Harris, William Gibson, 106, 108, 326–27,
    367, 368
Harvey, B. A., 356, 426
Hatch, Ozias M., 283, 320, 321, 322, 405
Hawley and Loose store (Springfield), 325
Hawthorne vs. Woolridge, 134–38
Hay, John, 140, 218, 284, 320–22, 377, 383,
    405
Hay, Milton, 70, 284, 321, 322, 405; on
    Mary Lincoln, 90–91
Haycraft, Presley, 15
Helm, Emilie Todd, 375
Helm, John B., xxii, 15
Helmle, George H., 352, 423
Helmle, William, 423
Herndon, Anna Miles, 342, 355, 418, 419
Herndon, Archer G., 338, 420, 421, 428
Herndon, Elliott B., 361, 428
Herndon, William H., xxiii, xxiv, 404; an-
    tislavery views of, 195, 360; as bank ex-
    aminer, 338; banking habits of, 212–14;
    biography of Lincoln by, xxiv, xxv, xxvi,
    xxix, 7, 13–14, 335, 357, 394; character of,
    3–4; at Chenery House, 330; courtship
    of, 418–20; and C. W. Chatterton, 342;

family of, 338; grave of, 355, 369; and
G. W. Harris, 326; H. C. Whitney on,
2–3; H. White on, 1–2; as lecturer, 110–
11, 113–18, 249–50, 256; letters of, 227,
379; and Lincoln, xxix, 3–4, 76, 81–
85, 100–102, 105, 110–18, 128, 139–40,
155, 206–8, 240, 255, 288, 299, 301; and
Lincoln's ancestry, 29–30, 37, 40–45;
and liquor, 300–301, 319, 338, 396; and
M. T. Lincoln, 338; and N. B. Judd, 359;
partnership of, with Lincoln, 139, 144,
298–302, 337–38; and patronage, 334–
35, 338; potential of, as diplomat, 335;
researches of, 13–14, 33–34; resentment
of, of Lincoln, 335; and R. Yates, 360–
61; speeches by, 278, 280; and Weik, xxv,
4–5
*Herndon's Informants* (Wilson and Davis),
xxi, xxii
Hertz, Emanuel, 392, 396, 399–400, 440
Hesler, Alexander, xxix
*Hidden Lincoln* (Hertz), 399–400
Hill Frederick T., 178
Hildreth vs. Turner. *See* Horological Cra-
dle case
Hillis, Lois E., 76–80
Hitchcock, Caroline, 39–40
Hitt, Robert Roberts, 179, 357, 379, 426
Horological cradle case, 157–59, 242, 319
Houghton Mifflin, xxv
House Committee on Government Con-
tracts, 383, 385
Houser, M. L., 392, 395, 441
Howard, Joseph, 341
Howell, John, 369
Hoyt, Clara Davis, 352–53, 357, 426
Hoyt, Walter Davis, 353
Huber, Mattie, 346
Hudson, J. L., 343
Humphrey, J. Otis, 337, 414
Hunter, Ben, 374
Hunter, David, 220, 323, 405
Huntington, George L., 387, 440

Hurd vs. Rock Island Bridge Co. *See* Rock
Island Bridge suit
Hurst, Charles R., 369, 432

Illinois and Mississippi Telegraph Office,
343
Illinois Central Railroad, 152–54
Indiana and Illinois Lincoln Route Com-
missions, 47, 49. *See also* Lincoln Way
Indiana Asbury University, xxii
Ingalls, Henry L., 358, 427
Ingalls, John J., 223
Ingals, Ephraim F., 357–58, 426
*Intimate Character Sketches of Abraham
Lincoln* (Rankin), 391, 392, 395
Irwin, Benjamin F., 345–46, 420–21
Irwin, Edward F., 346
Irwin, John, 320
Irwin, Robert, 283, 314, 345–46, 368, 420–
21, 432
Irwin, Samuel, 346

Jayne, Julia, 59, 378
Jayne, William, 59, 243, 278, 338, 359–61,
367, 387, 427
Johnson, Edward S., 361–62, 428
Johnson, Joel, 344, 361, 362, 428
Johnson's Building, 323, 362
Johnston, John D., 50, 161
Johnston, Robert P., 428
Johnston, Sarah Elizabeth, 407
Johnston, Thomas L. D., 50–53
Jones, J. Russell, 386, 438, 439
Jones, William, 291
Joy, James F., 152
Judd, Mrs. Norman B., 75
Judd, Norman B., 73, 359–60, 378, 416,
427

Karsner, David, xx
Keckley, Elizabeth, 377, 408, 436
Kellogg, Margaret Todd, 375
Kent, Josiah P., 122–26, 352, 362–64, 429

Kentucky, xxiv, 13–20, 331–33
Keyes, E. D., 304
Kidd, T. W. S., 334, 412
Knapp, N. M., 263, 268

Lambert, William H., 380, 437
"Lamon's Brigade," 383
Lamon, Ward Hill, xxi, 217–21, 384, 415;
  biography of Lincoln by, 7, 63, 68, 339,
  376–78, 380, 382–83; and Chauncey
  Black, 383; criticism of, by Congress,
  380; as general, 383; and John Hay, 377;
  letter by, to Asahel Gridley, 375–76; and
  L. Swett, 376; as marshal of Washington
  DC, 220, 384; *Recollections of Abraham
  Lincoln*, 377; and R. T. Lincoln, 382,
  437; and train journey to Washington
  (1861), 308, 339
Lane, James, 223
Latham, George C., 339–41, 364, 414, 415
Lavely, William, 326, 407
Leaton, James, 317, 402, 412
Lewis, Andrew, 366, 429, 430
Lewis, Elinor A., 366, 429, 430
Levering, Julia, 355
*Library of American Literature* (Stedman
  and Hutchinson), 332
*Life of Lyman Trumbull* (White), 380, 381
*Life of U. S. Grant* (Wilson and Dana), 386
Lilienthal, David, xx
Lincoln, Abraham: absence of, from home,
  90, 122–23; acquisitiveness, lack of, 91;
  affability of, 330; ambition of, 49–50,
  438, 439; ancestry of, 28–33, 36–38, 387;
  animals, solicitude for, 69; and Anthony
  Thornton, 374; and A. P. Dunbar, 349–
  50; appearance of, 107, 110–15, 120, 191–
  93, 199–200, 351, 365, 374; arithmetic
  book of, xxiii; autobiographies by, 21,
  34–35, 131, 252; and banks in Springfield,
  212–14, 325, 368; and blacks, 358; as bor-
  rower, 358; boyhood in Kentucky and
  Indiana, 13–27, 130–31, 291; buggy of,

375; and cabinet, 383; campaign funds of
  (1860), 320–22, 334–36; and campaign
  of 1856, 351; and campaign of 1860, 273–
  89; and Charles W. Chatterton, 418–
  20; and Chenery House, 329–30, 344,
  362, 409; and chess, 102–3, 107, 370; on
  Chicago Convention, 411; churchgoing habits of, 108; on circuit, 350; and
  Congress, 385; as conversationalist, 74–
  76; Cooper Institute speech of, 257–59;
  correspondence of, 321; courtship of,
  56–64; digestion of, 112; dignity of, 104,
  273, 313; domesticity, lack of, 100–101;
  eating habits of, 111, 190; education of,
  21–24, 144; emotionalism of, 322; and
  Euclid, 239; on failure, 239; farewell
  address of, 309–14, 322, 387–88; finances
  of, 417; and fugitive slaves, 319; gossip, aversion to, 70; and gubernatorial
  campaign (1860), 360; handwriting
  of, 144; and Harriet Hanks Chapman,
  354; hat of, 124, 375; height of, 120, 351;
  and Henry Clay, 375; honesty of, 374;
  horses of, 121, 123, 350, 363; house of,
  120–21, 319, 325–26, 406–7; humor of,
  359, 374; inaugural address of (1861),
  5; and H. Ingals, 358; intellect of, 110,
  115–18, 128–29, 140, 237–38; and Jacob
  Bunn, 318–19; and James Adams, 360;
  and James Grimes, 383–84, 437; and
  James Leaton, 402–3; on J. C. Conkling, 337; and John A. Brackenridge,
  318; and John Hay, 320–22; and John
  W. Bunn, 367; and Joel Johnson, 344;
  and J. Russell Jones, 438–39; law office
  of, 4–5, 7–9, 104, 106–7; as a lawyer,
  xxv, xxx, 127–205, 319, 325, 337–39, 350,
  361, 374–75; as lecturer, 243–49, 369–
  70; legal draftsmanship of, 144, 170–76;
  legal fees of, 141–43, 151–56, 160, 163–65,
  168, 203–5, 212–14, 319, 320; legitimacy
  of, 30–32, 380; leisure pursuits of, 24–
  25, 75–76, 85–86, 206–9; letters by, 222,

379; and liquor, 382; loan policy of, 125, 362; "Lost Speech" of (1856), 255–57; and Lyman Trumbull, 381; mannerisms of, 319; married life of, 89–108, 119–26, 326, 363, 378; in Massachusetts (1848), 371; melancholy of, 28, 57, 111–13, 374; and money, 337; moods of, 105, 199; moral obtuseness of, 384, 385; on move from Indiana to Illinois, 21, 327; and Mt. Carmel (IL), 357; musical taste of, 85–86; nomination of, for president (1860), 259–71, 333, 410–11; nomination of, for senator (1858), 379; and Norman B. Judd, 73–75; notification of, of nomination (1860), 265–73, 319, 322, 356, 410–11; and O. H. Browning, 416; orthography of, 144–45; as a parent, 101–3; patent of, 241–42; and patronage, 385, 418–20; popularity of, 323, 330, 351; as postmaster, 333; prankishness of, 209–11; as president-elect, 289–314; and prohibition, 396; proposals of marriage made by, 56, 66–67; pun by, 164; reading of, 23–24, 104–6, 120, 130, 239–40; relations with children, 124–25, 362; relationship with father, 50; religious views of, 326, 346–47, 432–33; reputation of, as a lawyer, 127–29, 194–95; reserve of, 104–5, 241; retirement of, from politics (1849–54), 251–52; and Robert Stockwell, 430–31; and S. A. Douglas, 200–201, 230–36, 252, 323, 328–29, 357, 379, 382, 406; and Sarah Bush Lincoln, 349; sartorial indifference of, 199–200, 351; scrapbook of, 9–12; secretiveness of, 241; self-confidence of, 241; self-reliance of, 241; and Simon Cameron, 226, 383, 385; and slavery, xxii, 200–201, 360; sociability of, 66, 198–99; spelling of, 144; and spiritualism, 370, 433; statues of, 336, 384, 413, 414; and steer, 373; as story-teller, 66, 104–5, 120, 207–8, 221, 349–50, 359,

374; Supreme Court appointments of, 418; as surveyor, 358; tomb of, 362; train journey of, to Washington (1861), 339–41, 414–15; unhappiness of, 90–91, 121–22, 403; and U. S. Grant, 356, 439; and vice-presidential nomination (1856), 209–11; in Vincennes IN, 327; visit of, to Charleston IL, 353–54; visits of, to Kentucky, 13; voice of, 351; wedding of, 58–62; and W. H. Herndon, 216–17, 319, 338; wife-beaters, detestation for, 70–71; and women, 69–85

Lincoln, Mary Todd, xxii, 51, 216, 356, 374; abrasiveness of, 351, 363; abuse by, of Lincoln, 403; acquisitiveness of, 91, 94; ambition of, 94–95; attainments of, 96–97, 108; bridesmaids of, 371; chauffeur of, 363, 363; character of, 97; churchgoing habits of, 108; disposition of, 318, 351; domesticity of, 328; dress of, 273, 319, 322, 355; fearfulness of, 108, 121; frugality of, 94, 355; fury of, 121–22, 126; half-sisters of, 375; house improvements made by, 320; hysteria of, 375; indignation of, 329; inheritance of, 375; insanity of, 377; letters by, 377; and Lincoln, 378, 379, 406; and merchants, difficulties with, 123, 351, 363; as a mother, 363; neighbors on, 119–26, 318; "poverty" of, 408; pretensions of, 407; pride of, 328; punitiveness of, 355; sells Lincoln's shirts, 377; servants of, difficulty with, 101, 364; shopping trip of, 292; shrill voice of, 102, 126, 209; sisters of, 303, 328; slave states, desire to reside in, 99; spitefulness of, 377; and Springfield, 319, 322; stinginess of, 123, 363; store accounts of, 92–93, 317; tantrums of, 415–16; temper of, 121–22, 209, 318, 355, 363, 375, 403; and tradesmen, 93–95; and train journey to Washington (1861), 339–41, 364, 414–16; turbulence of, 121–22, 363; unpopularity of, 351; and U. S.

Lincoln, Mary Todd (*continued*)
Grant, 425; vindictiveness of, 377; and
W. H. Herndon, 94–98, 338

Lincoln, Nancy Hanks, 39–40, 43, 366;
character and personality of, 46; death
of, 20, 45; Lincoln on, 38; wedding of,
33

Lincoln, Robert Todd, 339, 362, 363, 394;
as a baby, 329; domestic duties of, 355;
at Phillips Exeter Academy, 414; reminiscences of, 379; resemblance of, to his
mother, 377; as secretary of war, 377; on
train journey to Washington (1861), 309,
340–41, 414; and W. H. Lamon, 382, 437

Lincoln, Sarah, 33–34

Lincoln, Sarah Bush Johnston, 22–23, 327,
328, 329, 355; visited by Lincoln, 50, 349

Lincoln, Thomas (Tad), 101, 307, 340, 414

Lincoln, Thomas (father of Abraham),
20, 50, 328, 366, 380, 425; character of,
49; migratory spirit of, 47–48; relations
with Abraham, 50–51, 160–61; wedding
of, 33

Lincoln, William (Willie), 101, 307, 340,
362, 414, 429

Lincoln and Herndon (firm), xxv, 320

*Lincoln and Herndon* (Newton), 377, 380

*Lincoln and Liquor* (Townsend), 395–96

*Lincoln and Men of War Times* (McClure),
385

Lincoln-Douglas Debates (1858), 200–201,
229–36, 328

Lincoln Way, 354. *See also* Indiana and
Illinois Lincoln Route Commissions

Linder, Usher F., 160, 374, 405, 434

Linder vs. Fleenor, 165–67

Lindsay, Vachel, 414

Lingenfelter, Kaleb, 356

Littlefield, John H., 278

Lockridge, Alexander H., 319, 404

Lockwood, John M., 365–67, 429, 430

Logan, David, 319, 404

Logan, Stephen T., 196, 405; acquisitiveness of, 141; appointment of, by Lincoln
to government post, 139; and banks, 325;
at Chicago Convention (1860), 261; and
Lincoln's 1860 campaign fund, 139, 320–
21, 335–36; and money, 337; partnership
with Lincoln, 135, 337; and religion, 326;
and U.S. Supreme Court, 334

Logan-Hay family, 334

Logan vs. Chinn, 195–96

Loomis, Webner E., 367–68, 431

Lytle, Harry, 441

Manford, Erasmus, 347, 421

Marshall, Samuel D., 167–68

Marshall, Thomas A., 328, 354, 408

Masters, Hardin W., 394

Matheny, Charles, 201–2

Matheny, Elizabeth Stamper, 317, 318

Matheny, James H., 70–71, 368, 431; on
Lincoln's domestic unhappiness, 90, 91;
on Lincoln's wedding, 59–62; on Mary
Lincoln, 98

Matheny, Noah, 317, 318, 403

Mather, Thomas, 304–6, 386, 439

Matson, Mrs. Robert, 328

Matson, Robert, 372, 373, 408, 434

Matson slave case, 372–73

May, William L., 59, 371, 421, 433

Maynard, Nettie Coleman, 433

McClellan, George B., 387

McClure, Alexander K., 376, 385, 435; on
Mary Lincoln, 416

McConnell, Bunn & Co., 324, 325

McConnell, Mrs. Murray, 324

McConnell, Murray, 323–24, 406

McConnell, William M., 373

McCormick vs. Manny, 187

McCreery, John, 345, 420

McGregor, Thomas, 356

McKibben vs. Hart, 160–61

McLean, John, 187

McLean County tax case, 151–55

McLellan, Charles W., 368, 369, 421, 432
McLellan, Hugh, 368–69, 432
Medill, Joseph, xxix, 378–79, 436
Melvin, Henry A., 369–70, 432
Melvin, James B., 245, 370, 432
Melvin, Mrs. Charles S., 370
Melvin, Samuel H., 369, 432
Merwin, James B., 396
Miles, George U., 355, 425
Miller vs. Miller, 149–51
minstrel shows, Lincoln's fondness of, 86
Moffett, John B., 151
Monroe, George H., 371–72, 433
Moore, Clifton H., 164, 230–31, 381, 437
Mostiller, Thomas, 347, 421
Moulton, Samuel W., 374, 434

Naples IL, 324
New Salem IL, 333
Newton, Joseph F., 377, 379, 380
Nicolay, John G., 321, 354, 370, 381, 405, 432; as secretary to Lincoln, 283; and train journey to Washington (1861), 309–14

"O, Why Should the Spirit of Mortal Be Proud" (Knox), 79
Osborne GA, 392, 394, 440
Ottawa IL, debate at, 232, 382
Owens, Mary, 56, 66, 68–69

Paddock, Stephen G., 370–71, 433
Parker, Theodore, 8–9
Parks, Samuel C., 128, 380
Pasfield, George, 371, 352, 35
patent infringement cases, 157–59, 187
Paterson, Isabel, xix
Patterson vs. Edwards, 170–74
Pease, E. B., 343
Peck, Ebenezer, 272, 319, 322, 378, 404
Peoria truce, 231
personal injury cases, 156–57

Personal Recollections of Abraham Lincoln (Rankin), 386, 391, 392, 393
Peterson, Merrill, 392
Piatt, Donn, 322, 405
Pickett, Thomas J., 260
Pierce, Edward L., 371–72, 433
Pitcher, John, 130
Powell, Beverly, 59, 348, 367, 431
Power, John C., 339, 362, 428
Prince, Ezra M., 350
Princeton IN, 365–66, 430

Radford, Reuben, 421
Radley, Hannah, 355, 424
Radley, Ichabod, 355, 424
Ralston, Mollie Herndon, 395
Rankin, Albert H., 441
Rankin, Amberry, 391
Rankin, Henry B., 298, 300, 386; business practices of, 391–92; illness of, 391; J. Connolly on, 347; letters by, 397, 442; parents of, 442; plagiarism by, 441; unreliability of, as a Lincoln informant, 391–97
Ray, Charles H., 378, 436
Remsburg, J. E., 432–33
Republican State Committee of Illinois, 378
Revere House, 361, 362
reviews of *The Real Lincoln*: in *The Bookman*, xxi; in *Boston Transcript*, xx–xxi; in *New York Call*, xx; in *New York Herald Tribune*, xix; in *New York Times*, xx; in *New York World*, xx; in *Review of Reviews*, xxi
Reynolds, J. W., 353
Richards, John T., 178, 385
Rickard, Sarah, 56, 66–68
Ridgely National Bank, 343, 368
Ridgely, N. H., & Co., 343, 368, 369
Ridgely, Nicholas, 426
Ridgely, William, 342, 343–44
Ridpath, John Clark, xxiii

Robertson, George, 331–33, 409–10
Robinson, Arnold, 412
Rock Island Bridge suit, 73, 177–87, 214
Rodman, Jesse, 16–18
Rodney, Anne, 371, 433
Rogers vs. Rogers, 148–49
Rowbotham, John H., 19–20
Ruckel, Jacob, 325, 326, 406
Rutherford, Hiram, 372–73, 374, 433
Rutledge, Ann, 66

Salzenstein, Charles, 392
Sargent, John Singer, 414
Sawyer, John, 424, 425
Scammon vs. Cline, 138
Schenck, Robert C., 322, 405
Scott, Winfield, 220, 305–6, 308, 323
Scranton, Charles, 372
Scripps, John L., 36–37
Seward, William Henry, 323, 384, 405–6,
    411
Sheridan, James B., 357, 426
Shields, James, 378, 436
slander cases, 160–67, 170–74
slaves, 195–98, 331–33. *See also* Bailey vs.
    Cromwell; Matson slave case
Smith, Ann Todd, 328
Smith, Caleb B., 294
Smith, Clark M., xxiii, 5, 292, 407, 408
Smith, George, 319, 404
Smith, Gerrit, 332
Smith, J. Taylor, 325, 406
Smith, Stephen, 407
Smith vs. Smith, 174–76
Smith, W. F. F., 373
Smoot, Coleman, 427
*The Southerner* (Dixon), 387
Sparrow, Elizabeth, 40, 44–45
Sparrow, Henry, 41–43
Sparrow, Thomas, 40, 44–45
Speed, Joshua, 37, 62, 68, 348
Spiritualism, 370
Sponsler, James W., 345, 420

Springfield IL: banks in, 343, 368; First
    Methodist Church in, 317; hotels in,
    344; Lincoln legends in, xxiv; Repub-
    lican rally in (1860), 321; social structure
    of, 66; square in, 333–34, 343–44, 412
Springfield Marine and Fire Insurance Co.,
    325, 345, 368
Springfield Marine Bank, 325
State Bank of Illinois, 368
Stephens, Silas, 429
St. Gaudens, Augustus, 384, 438
Stiles, Elias B., 359, 427
St. Nicholas Hotel, 344–45, 420
Stockton vs. Tolby, 156
Stockwell, Robert, 430–31
Stout, Ebenezer, 326, 407
Stuart, John Todd, 57, 131, 254–55, 258,
    326, 337; partnership with Lincoln, 135,
    139, 142, 155–56
Sumner, E. V., 220, 323, 405, 416
*Sunset Magazine*, 370
Supreme Court, 341–42
Sweet, E. D. L., 268, 269
Swett, Leonard, xxii, xxiv–xxv, xxix–xxx,
    76, 195, 418, 427; as gubernatorial candi-
    date, 359–60; and Lincoln, 192–93, 215,
    244; and W. H. Lamon, 376, 379–80,
    382

Tarbell, Ida M., 39, 391, 392
Teillard, Dorothy Lamon, 378, 380, 435
Thayer, Edward H., 348, 422
Thompson, Jacob C., 395, 441
Thornton, Anthony, 350, 434
Thornton, Hempstead, 196
Tilton, Lucien, 306, 323, 344, 405
Titsworth, A. D., 291
Todd, John, 369
Todd, Lyman Beecher, 375, 435
Todd, Robert S., 375, 435
Town, William, 365
Townsend, William H., xix, 395–96
Tracy, Gilbert A., 375–78, 435

Trailor murder case, 151
Treat, Samuel, 102–3, 372
Trumbull, Julia Jayne, 427, 436
Trumbull, Lyman, 281, 378, 397; biography of, by Horace White, 380, 383, 384, 385; election of, to U.S. Senate, 380; on Lincoln, xxix, 436; and S. Cameron, 383
Turnham, David, 23, 48, 130

Usher, John P., 126
Utley, William L., 330–33, 409

Van Bergen, Peter, 375, 434
Villard, Henry, 415
Vincennes IN, 327
Volk, Leonard W., xxix

Wallace, Frances Todd, 328, 375
Wallace, William S., 206, 309, 351, 423
Warren, W. B., 207–8
Washburne, Elihu B., 397
Watt, Jane M., 377, 436
Watt, John, 377, 436
Watterson, Henry, 33
Weber, Jessie Palmer, 394, 440
Weed, Thurlow, 384, 438
Weik, Jesse W.: appearance of, xxvi; biographical sketch of, xxii–xxvi; character and personality of, xxii–xxiii; death of, xxvi; freelance writing of, 401–2; habits of, xxvi; handwriting of, xxvi; on H. B. Rankin, 393; and Herndon, 4–7; interest of, in Lincoln, xxiii, 4; interviewing done by, 4, 60, 63, 83–85, 311–12, 401; law practice of, 400; lectures by, xxiv; political views of, xxii–xxiii, 400; reputation of, xxiv; research of, in Kentucky and Indiana, 30–32, 130–31
Weik, Mary Hays, xxv
Weldon, Lawrence, 162–64

Welles, Gideon, 384, 438
Wentworth, John, 379, 381, 437
White, Horace, xxix, 233, 376, 436; biography of Trumbull by, 380, 383, 384, 385; on Herndon, 1–2; letters by, 378–86; on Lincoln, 216, 227–28; on M. Delahay, 216; on S. A. Douglas, 232; on S. Cameron, 216
Whitney, Henry C., xxii, xxix, 211–12, 335, 380, 384; on Herndon, 2–3; and Lincoln, 51–53, 72–73, 76, 85–86, 161, 188–91, 194, 209, 211–12, 244, 257; reliability of, 193–94
Wiley, Eli, 328, 405
Willard Hotel, 340, 364
Williams, John, 283, 320, 325, 334, 345, 368, 369, 405
Wilmouth, Sim, 372
Wilson, Charles, L., 381, 437
Wilson, Douglas L., xxi
Wilson, Henry, 220, 227
Wilson, James Grant, 86–88
Wilson, James H., 386–87, 438
Wilson, John James Speed, 267–69, 307, 411
Wilson, Robert L., 112–13
Wilson, William, 372, 434
Wood, John, 323
Wood, Robert, 373
Wood, William, 373, 434
Woods, George, 325, 406
Wright, Erastus, 201, 361, 428
Wright, Lucy, 361

Yates, Richard, 338, 359–60, 386, 406, 412, 414

Zane, Charles S., 348–49, 422
Zane, John, 348, 422
Zumbrook, Louis, 387–88, 439–40